the grid

RED COMPENDIUM

First published 2018

ISBN 978 1 78506 695 5

Scripture Union, Trinity House, Opal Court, Opal Drive, Fox Milne, Milton Keynes, MK15 0DF, UK

Email: info@scriptureunion.org.uk

Website: www.scriptureunion.org.uk

British Library Cataloguing-in-Publication Data. A catalogue record of this book is available from the British Library.

Printed and bound in India by Nutech Print Services - India

Cover design: Kevin Wade

Internal design: Martin Lore and Sandra Taylor

Photography: Chris Brown

Please note that this content has been updated from previously published material.

Scripture Union is an international Christian charity working with churches in more than 130 countries.

Thank you for purchasing this book. Any profits from this book support SU in England and Wales to bring the good news of Jesus Christ to children, young people and families and to enable them to meet God through the Bible and prayer.

Find out more about our work and how you can get involved at:

www.scriptureunion.org.uk (England and Wales)

www.suscotland.org.uk (Scotland)

www.suni.co.uk (Northern Ireland)

www.scriptureunion.org (USA)

www.su.org.au (Australia)

CONTENTS

INTRODUCTION

Welcome to the *Grid Red Compendium*! We're so pleased you've chosen this book to help you in your work with 11- to 14-year-olds.

It is our prayer that the materials contained within these pages will equip and inspire you whilst engaging and empowering the young people you work with.

The material in this book has been compiled from the wealth of *Grid* content that Scripture Union has produced over the years – and with 52 sessions included, there should be plenty to choose from over the course of a year.

The *Grid Red Compendium* is part of the *Light* range of materials, which are designed to enable children, young people and adults to develop a personal relationship with Jesus, to understand the Bible and the Christian faith, and to live for God as light in a dark world.

- *Light* is about… discovering who God is, what he is like, what he does and how we can get involved in that. The Bible is 'light to live by', so it is the centre of every session for every age group in the Light range of resources. Everyone will be able to follow the story of salvation that runs through the Bible, with its focus clearly on Jesus.

- *Light* recognises that children and young people can know and respond to God and does not expect too little or too much from them.

- *Light* celebrates every step taken towards and with God, letting the Bible shape our thinking about human nature and relationships with children and young people, and the way in which we minister with and to them.

- *Light* values exploration and discovery, fun, feelings and creativity and uses these approaches to inspire children, young people and adults to meet God through the Bible.

We hope you enjoy this resource, and we pray that God will bless you and those you work with as you use it.

The Scripture Union Mission Innovation Team

HOW TO USE THIS BOOK...

This book provides 52 sessions of activities, and extra photocopiable resources, designed for your *Grid* group of young people aged 11 to 14. Choose sessions from this *Red Compendium* in any order to suit you and your group. You will also find that some sessions have further additional online resources which you will be able to download for free from the Scripture Union website, via the resource centre.

Leading up to Christmas time, you may wish to choose from the Christmas themed sessions (numbers 41 to 45). Around Easter time, you will find there are Easter themed sessions (numbers 46 to 52), to choose from. These 'seasonal' sessions are grouped together at the back of this book.

If you would like to work through a number of sessions on a similar theme with your Grid group, look out for the **More on this theme** boxes as you consider your session choice. Here you will find a list of other sessions on a related theme to the session you are looking at.

On page 7, you will find a helpful guide that explains **How to plan your session**... This section will help you to choose activities from within the sessions, including a selection of *Grid* activities to suit you and your group, enabling you to achieve the Learning aim for the session. Here you will also find a **Basic kit** list of essential items to keep handy for all your *Grid* group sessions.

Each session in this *Grid Red Compendium* is based on a Bible passage. You will find an **Index of Bible passages** on page 334 listed in the order they appear in the Bible.

The most important thing about this book is to enjoy using it to help you and your *Grid* group engage with the Bible and meet with Jesus, through a mixture of play, creativity, music, quiet reflection, noisy exuberance, and friendship!

HOW TO PLAN YOUR SESSION

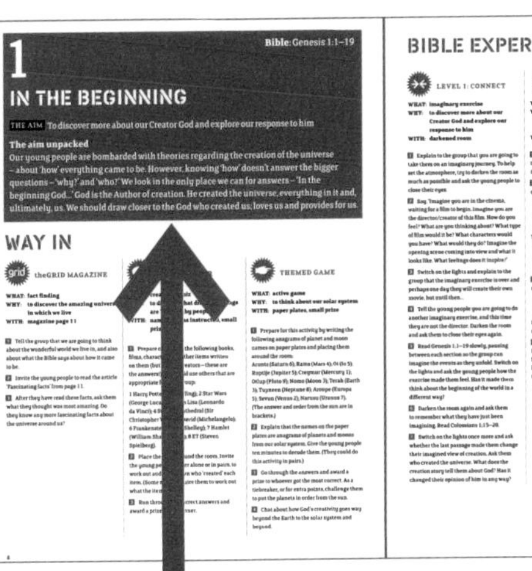
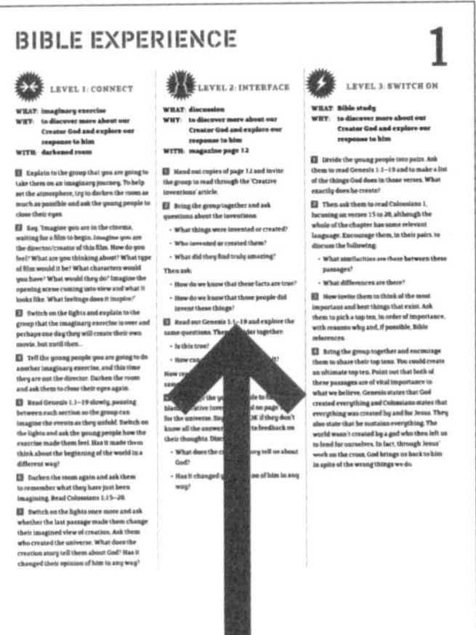
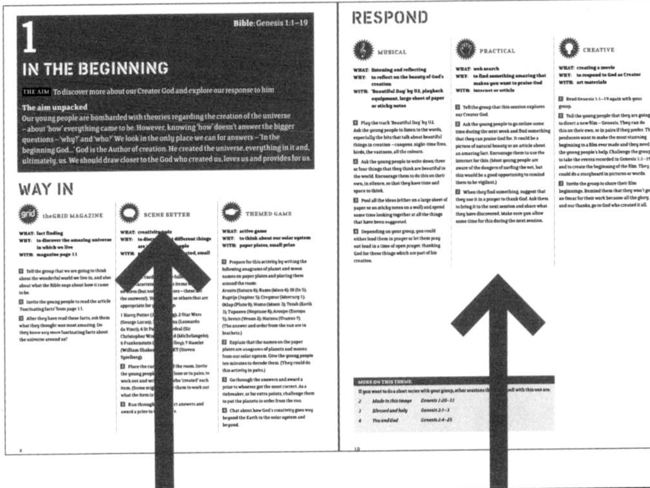

1

Read the Bible passage.

Think about your own group and situation: the individuals, the leaders, your equipment and facilities. Pray about your group and the individuals within it, and for God to guide you and help you as you prepare and lead the session.

Begin by reading the Bible passage. Then read **The aim** and **The aim unpacked** to find out how the Bible passage can relate to young people.

Sart choosing which activities you will do. The activities you use will be dependent on what kind of group you have. Different activities are tailored towards different groups, large or small, Sunday or mid-week, churched or non-churched.

2

Choose one of the Bible experience activities first. This is the heart of your session, as you help the young people explore the Bible and respond to God's message.

Level 1 Connect is the first level of Bible interaction, ideal for a group that is at the lower end of Bible literacy and interest.

Level 2 Interface is suitable for a group who are committed and want to learn more.

Level 3 Switch on is a more demanding, in-depth Bible study for committed young people who want to grow in their faith.

3

Choose one or more Way in activities to introduce the session's theme.

Scene setters introduce a link between the world of the young people and the aim of the session.

Themed games or activities act as an introduction to the session aim for larger or more 'open' groups and are suitable to use with non-churched young people.

grid One of these activities will usually use a magazine resource page.

4

Choose one or more Respond activities to help the young people relate what they have learned in the session to their lives, to help them live for God.

Musical uses music and sound as a response to God's Word.

Practical is an ongoing activity that the young people can take part in, reflecting the aim in their everyday lives.

Creative uses creative and imaginative skills to respond to God's Word.

Most sessions include **photocopiable resource pages** for you to copy and use with your group. All the resources are also available in a zip folder to download from **www.scriptureunion.org.uk**.

Basic kit

To run your session, you will need these items:
Bibles (*The Youth Bible*, New Century Version works best with *theGRID*), pencils, felt-tip pens, pencil sharpener, paper, glue sticks, sticky tape, scissors, sticky tack, sticky notes and erasers

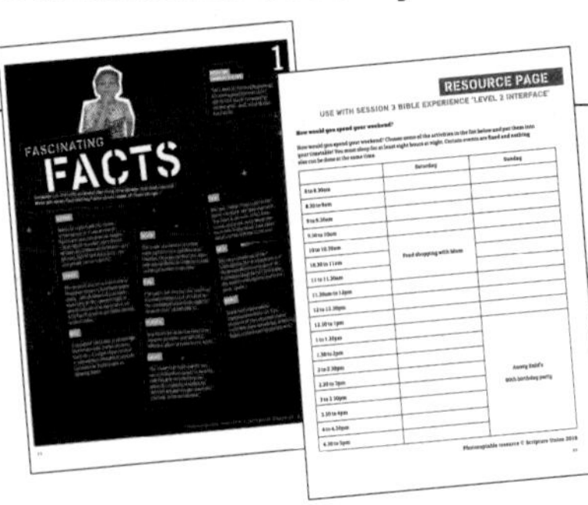

1

Bible: Genesis 1:1–19

IN THE BEGINNING

THE AIM: To discover more about our Creator God and explore our response to him

The aim unpacked

Our young people are bombarded with theories regarding the creation of the universe – about 'how' everything came to be. However, knowing 'how' doesn't answer the bigger questions – 'why?' and 'who?' We look in the only place we can for answers – 'In the beginning God...' God is the Author of creation. He created the universe, everything in it and, ultimately, us. We should draw closer to the God who created us, loves us and provides for us.

WAY IN

theGRID MAGAZINE

WHAT: fact finding
WHY: to discover the amazing universe in which we live
WITH: magazine page 11

1 Tell the group that we are going to think about the wonderful world we live in, and also about what the Bible says about how it came to be.

2 Invite the young people to read the article 'Fascinating facts' from page 11.

3 After they have read these facts, ask them what they thought was most amazing. Do they know any more fascinating facts about the universe around us?

SCENE SETTER

WHAT: creativity quiz
WHY: to discover that different things are 'created' by people
WITH: name cards as instructed, small prize

1 Prepare cards with the following books, films, characters and other items written on them (but not the creators – these are the answers!). You could use others that are appropriate for your group:

1 Harry Potter (JK Rowling); 2 *Star Wars* (George Lucas); 3 *Mona Lisa* (Leonardo da Vinci); 4 St Paul's Cathedral (Sir Christopher Wren); 5 *David* (Michelangelo); 6 *Frankenstein* (Mary Shelley); 7 *Hamlet* (William Shakespeare); 8 *ET* (Steven Spielberg).

2 Place the cards around the room. Invite the young people, either alone or in pairs, to work out and write down who 'created' each item. (Some might require them to work out what the item is first!)

3 Run through the correct answers and award a prize to the winner.

THEMED GAME

WHAT: active game
WHY: to think about our solar system
WITH: paper plates, small prize

1 Prepare for this activity by writing the following anagrams of planet and moon names on paper plates and placing them around the room:
Arunts (Saturn 6); Rams (Mars 4); Oi (Io 5); Ruptije (Jupiter 5); Creymur (Mercury 1); Otlup (Pluto 9); Nomo (Moon 3); Terah (Earth 3); Tupneen (Neptune 8); Aroupe (Europa 5); Sevun (Venus 2); Narusu (Uranus 7). (The answer and order from the sun are in brackets.)

2 Explain that the names on the paper plates are anagrams of planets and moons from our solar system. Give the young people ten minutes to decode them. (They could do this activity in pairs.)

3 Go through the answers and award a prize to whoever got the most correct. As a tiebreaker, or for extra points, challenge them to put the planets in order from the sun.

4 Chat about how God's creativity goes way beyond the Earth to the solar system and beyond.

BIBLE EXPERIENCE 1

LEVEL 1: CONNECT

WHAT: **imaginary exercise**
WHY: **to discover more about our Creator God and explore our response to him**
WITH: **darkened room**

1 Explain to the group that you are going to take them on an imaginary journey. To help set the atmosphere, try to darken the room as much as possible and ask the young people to close their eyes.

2 Say, 'Imagine you are in the cinema, waiting for a film to begin. Imagine you are the director/creator of this film. How do you feel? What are you thinking about? What type of film would it be? What characters would you have? What would they do? Imagine the opening scene coming into view and what it looks like. What feelings does it inspire?'

3 Switch on the lights and explain to the group that the imaginary exercise is over and perhaps one day they will create their own movie, but until then...

4 Tell the young people you are going to do another imaginary exercise, and this time they are not the director. Darken the room and ask them to close their eyes again.

5 Read Genesis 1:1–19 slowly, pausing between each section so the group can imagine the events as they unfold. Switch on the lights and ask the young people how the exercise made them feel. Has it made them think about the beginning of the world in a different way?

6 Darken the room again and ask them to remember what they have just been imagining. Read Colossians 1:15–20.

7 Switch on the lights once more and ask whether the last passage made them change their imagined view of creation. Ask them who created the universe. What does the creation story tell them about God? Has it changed their opinion of him in any way?

LEVEL 2: INTERFACE

WHAT: **discussion**
WHY: **to discover more about our Creator God and explore our response to him**
WITH: **magazine page 12**

1 Hand out copies of page 12 and invite the group to read through the 'Creative inventions' article.

2 Bring the group together and ask questions about the inventions:

- What things were invented or created?
- Who invented or created them?
- What did they find truly amazing?

Then ask:

- How do we know that these facts are true?
- How do we know that those people did invent these things?

3 Read out Genesis 1:1–19 and explore the same questions. Then consider together:

- Is this true?
- How can we prove it? Or disprove it?

Now read Colossians 1:15–20 and ask the same questions.

4 Challenge the young people to fill in the blank 'Creative invention' card on page 12 for the universe. Say that it's OK if they don't know all the answers, but invite feedback on their thoughts. Discuss:

- What does the creation story tell us about God?
- Has it changed your opinion of him in any way?

LEVEL 3: SWITCH ON

WHAT: **Bible study**
WHY: **to discover more about our Creator God and explore our response to him**

1 Divide the young people into pairs. Ask them to read Genesis 1:1–19 and to make a list of the things God does in those verses. What exactly does he create?

2 Then ask them to read Colossians 1, focusing on verses 15 to 20, although the whole of the chapter has some relevant language. Encourage them, in their pairs, to discuss the following:

- What similarities are there between these passages?
- What differences are there?

3 Now invite them to think of the most important and best things that exist. Ask them to pick a top ten, in order of importance, with reasons why and, if possible, Bible references.

4 Bring the group together and encourage them to share their top tens. You could create an ultimate top ten. Point out that both of these passages are of vital importance to what we believe. Genesis states that God created everything and Colossians states that everything was created by and for Jesus. They also state that he sustains everything. The world wasn't created by a god who then left us to fend for ourselves. In fact, through Jesus' work on the cross, God brings us back to him in spite of the wrong things we do.

RESPOND

MUSICAL

WHAT: listening and reflecting
WHY: to reflect on the beauty of God's creation
WITH: 'Beautiful Day' by U2, playback equipment, large sheet of paper or sticky notes

1 Play the track 'Beautiful Day' by U2. Ask the young people to listen to the words, especially the bits that talk about beautiful things in creation – canyons, night-time fires, birds, the vastness, all the colours.

2 Ask the young people to write down three or four things that they think are beautiful in the world. Encourage them to do this on their own, in silence, so that they have time and space to think.

3 Pool all the ideas (either on a large sheet of paper or on sticky notes on a wall) and spend some time looking together at all the things that have been suggested.

4 Depending on your group, you could either lead them in prayer or let them pray out loud in a time of open prayer, thanking God for these things which are part of his creation.

PRACTICAL

WHAT: web search
WHY: to find something amazing that makes you want to praise God
WITH: internet or article

1 Tell the group that this session explores our Creator God.

2 Ask the young people to go online some time during the next week and find something that they can praise God for. It could be a picture of natural beauty or an article about an amazing fact. Encourage them to use the internet for this. (Most young people are aware of the dangers of surfing the net, but this would be a good opportunity to remind them to be vigilant.)

3 When they find something, suggest that they use it in a prayer to thank God. Ask them to bring it to the next session and share what they have discovered. Make sure you allow some time for this during the next session.

CREATIVE

WHAT: creating a movie
WHY: to respond to God as Creator
WITH: art materials

1 Read Genesis 1:1–19 again with your group.

2 Tell the young people that they are going to direct a new film – *Genesis*. They can do this on their own, or in pairs if they prefer. The producers want to make the most stunning beginning to a film ever made and they need the young people's help. Challenge the group to take the events recorded in Genesis 1:1–19 and to create the beginning of the film. They could do a storyboard in pictures or words.

3 Invite the group to share their film beginnings. Remind them that they won't get an Oscar for their work because all the glory, and our thanks, go to God who created it all.

MORE ON THIS THEME:

If you want to do a short series with your group, other sessions that work well with this one are:

2	*Made in his image*	*Genesis 1:20–31*
3	*Blessed and holy*	*Genesis 2:1–3*
4	*You and God*	*Genesis 2:4–25*

1

Bible bit
Genesis 1:1–19

'Let's start at the very beginning; it's a very good place to start.' When God made the world he started with... well, what did he start with?

FASCINATING FACTS

Genesis 1:1–19 tells us about the very first things that God created. Here are some fascinating facts about some of those things...

WATER

Water is made from the atoms of two gases. It is two atoms of hydrogen and one atom of oxygen – H_2O. Water has only been found to exist in all three of its forms – gas (steam), liquid and solid (ice) – on one planet (so far!): Earth!

STARS

The nearest star to our own sun is Proxima Centauri, 4.22 light years away – which means if you were travelling at the speed of light, it would take you the equivalent of 4.22 Earth years to get there! So not so near then...

DAY

A standard Earth day is on average 86,400 seconds (24 hours) long. Each day is longer than the one it follows by 0.00000002 seconds because the Earth's spin is slowing down.

MOON

The moon is a natural satellite orbiting Earth in a synchronous rotation. This means that the same side always faces us – the dark side is always hidden from view.

SUN

The sun is our nearest star and has a surface temperature of 6,000 °C. Its core temperature is thought to be more than 15,000,000 °C.

PLANTS

Scientists estimate that there are between 220,000 and 420,000 different plant species in the world.

LIGHT

The speed that light travels in a vacuum (such as space) is exactly 299,792,458 m/s (metres per second), normally rounded to 300,000 kilometres per second or 186,000 miles per second.

SEA

The sea covers 70 per cent of the Earth's surface. We have explored less than 5 per cent of the deep ocean and know more about the dark side of the moon than about what's at the bottom of the sea.

SKY

The sky is made up of the troposphere, the stratosphere and the mesosphere and is about 90 kilometres high before you leave the Earth's atmosphere and enter outer space.

DARK

Black holes form when supermassive stars die. The pressure of the collapsed star is such that even something as fast as light can't escape the gravity well.

CREATIVE INVENTIONS

TV

What: TV
Who: John Logie Baird
When: 1929
Proof: The singer Gracie Fields was seen singing silently on the flickering TV screen, and then a few moments later her voice was heard through the same device.

TELEPHONE

What: Telephone
Who: Alexander Graham Bell
When: 1876
Proof: The most famous proof of the telephone, apart from the fact that many of us have one, is that in 1878 Bell demonstrated his invention to Queen Victoria. She was so impressed she asked him to fit them into the palace.

HOVERCRAFT

What: Hovercraft
Who: Christopher Cockerell
When: 1959
Proof: The hovercraft was seen floating on air by large numbers of the public in 1959. It was seen floating over concrete and then the sea.

COCA-COLA

What: Coca-Cola
Who: Dr John Pemberton
When: 1886
Proof: It was first sold at Jacob's Pharmacy in Atlanta. It cost five cents for a glass and was promoted as a 'brain tonic'.

THE UNIVERSE

WHAT: ______

WHO: ______

WHEN: ______

PROOF: ______

Bible: Genesis 1:20–31

2

MADE IN HIS IMAGE

THE AIM: To discover more about our Creator God and explore our response to him

The aim unpacked

Our young people are presented with evolution theories at school, and these are taught in a way that can seem contradictory to Christian beliefs. We should have a response. How do we deal with their questions and confusion? It is important that we address this issue openly, to avoid it becoming a stumbling block for some of our young people's developing faith.

WAY IN

theGRID MAGAZINE

WHAT: **filling in a family tree**
WHY: **to think about where we come from**
WITH: **magazine page 16**

1 Ask the young people to look at a copy of the family tree template from page 16 and, individually, to fill in as much as they can. Explain that it can be difficult to do this, as there are a lot of things we don't know. Emphasise that families come in all shapes and sizes. Be sensitive to any issues, such as divorce, stepfamilies, adoption or deaths in the family.

2 Divide the group into pairs and ask everyone to imagine what things might have been like for their ancestors. Throw in a couple of questions like:

- What might your relatives have been doing in 1912? What about in 1512?
- Could anyone in the room be a descendant of a king or queen? A Roman emperor?
- A biblical character? (Someone may say Noah or Adam and Eve. If they do, ask them what proof they have. Congratulate them if they think of using the Bible!)

3 Come back together and ask whether anyone knows of anyone in their family who has looked into their family tree. Ask why they think people want to know where they come from.

SCENE SETTER

WHAT: **haiku poem**
WHY: **to look imaginatively at God's creation**

1 Say that you are going to think about the world and respond in verse. Invite the group to think about the world in which they live, especially about animals and people. (These are referred to in the Bible passage, but don't tell the young people that yet.) Encourage them to include in their thoughts other images of the natural world.

2 Say that you want them to use their thoughts in a haiku poem. Explain that a haiku is a Japanese verse that has traditionally been associated with images of the natural world. The rules for writing a haiku are as follows: the whole verse should be 17 syllables long and should be in three lines. The first line should contain five syllables, the second seven syllables and the last five.

3 Give them some time to write their own haiku poems.

4 When they have finished, point out that they have been creative in describing the world around them and that today you will be looking at the creativity that went into creation itself.

5 You could keep the poems and use them as part of your worship later.

THEMED GAME

WHAT: **discussion and game**
WHY: **to wonder at the amazing human body**
WITH: **paper and pens**

1 Take a look together at the five amazing facts below about the human body. (You could enlarge them and put them up round the room.) Think about each one individually:

- The number of red blood cells in a microlitre (a millionth of a litre) of blood is up to 6 million.
- The largest organ in the human body is the skin.
- The body contains about 100,000 km of blood vessels.
- The average human has more than 100 billion nerve cells.
- The length of the intestine in our stomach is anywhere between 6 and 8.5 metres, depending on our age and size.

2 Ask the young people if they know of any other amazing things about the human body. (Be careful, depending on your group, to avoid less-than-wholesome discussion!)

3 Hand out paper and pens, and play a game of consequences – start by drawing the head of a person, fold over the paper and pass it to the next person, who draws a body, and so on. Enjoy looking at the finished creations, and reinforce the fact that we have a pretty amazing organism to live in!

BIBLE EXPERIENCE

LEVEL 1: CONNECT

WHAT: animal drawings
WHY: to discover more about our Creator God and explore our response to him

1 Give out felt-tip pens and paper and ask the young people each to draw their favourite animal. When everyone has finished their animal, compare the pictures and read Genesis 1:20–25. Chat for a while about why everyone chose that particular animal to draw – what about it do they like?

2 Then go on to chat about the differences between animals and people. Make a list together of some characteristics and then read Genesis 1:26–31. List some of the things that these verses say about humans. The list might include: created in God's image, male and female, in charge of everything on the Earth. In the opinion of the group, which is the most important thing on the list?

3 Ask the group why they think humans were the last thing God created. Why did God say that everything was very good? What does it mean to be made in God's image?

HELP FILE

- God is speaking as the Creator King, announcing his crowning work to the rest of the heavenly court (references to the heavenly court are found in the following verses: Genesis 3:22; 11:7; 1 Kings 22:19–23; Job 15:8; Isaiah 6:8; Jeremiah 23:18).
- There is no distinction between 'image' and 'likeness'. Both are used in the Old Testament and New Testament (see Genesis 5:1; 9:6; 1 Corinthians 11:7; James 3:9).
- Being made in God's image means every human being is worthy of respect and honour.
- Humanity is the climax of God's creative activity (see Psalm 8:5–8).

LEVEL 2: INTERFACE

WHAT: discussion
WHY: to discover more about our Creator God and explore our response to him
WITH: large sheets of paper

1 Say to the group, 'Ever wondered what happened to the dinosaurs? Why is Beyoncé so gorgeous and Aunty Beryl isn't?! Was Adam fit and Eve a babe? Actually, although these are light-hearted questions, they are also quite deep, if you think about them.'

2 Divide the young people into pairs and give each pair a large sheet of paper and some pens. Ask them to write down or draw anything that they would not have put into the world if they were God. These could be specific animals or types of people (for example, wasps), ideas or theories (for example, war) or human attributes (for example, greed). They should think about why, too.

3 Ask the pairs to present their lists to the rest of the group and to explain why they made these choices. If the young people are comfortable challenging each other, invite the other pairs to say whether they agree or disagree with what has been said.

4 Ask someone to read out Genesis 1:20–31.

5 Explain that God had to make choices about what went into creation. The Bible tells us about the creation of the universe, about God's role in it and about our place. Discuss what the creation account in Genesis tells us about the universe. You need to draw out that the event was planned and not a chance happening.

6 Ask them what they think is the significance of verse 26 for who we are and what we do. (See the 'Help file' for direction.)

LEVEL 3: SWITCH ON

WHAT: discussion of creation theories
WHY: to discover more about our Creator God and explore our response to him
WITH: magazine page 17

1 Before the session, you may wish to spend some time thinking through what you believe about creation. Make sure you know what your church believes too.

2 Invite the group to read the different creation theories that are on page 17.

3 In pairs, encourage the young people to discuss the theories and ask them if they have heard any other theories about where we come from.

4 Bring the group together and discuss the following questions about each of the theories:

- Do you think it is believable?
- What are the problems or difficulties with believing it?
- What is the starting point for each theory?
- Did the events of the theory happen by chance or by choice?
- Are humans a planned event, a mishap or a by-product?
- How does this compare with what the Bible says in Genesis 1:20–31?
- Does it agree or disagree with the Bible account?

5 If the questions haven't brought your group to this point yet, guide the discussion to say that the biblical account talks of God creating everything. It tells us that it wasn't an accident, but that everything was planned in detail – including us.

6 Now say what you believe and why. Use this time to chat with the group about what creation tells us about God. How does it help us understand God's character and nature?

RESPOND

MUSICAL

WHAT: **praising God for his creation**
WHY: **to acknowledge that God made each of us and to praise him for that**
WITH: **'Beautiful' by Christina Aguilera, playback equipment**

1 Play the track 'Beautiful' by Christina Aguilera. If possible, have the words available for the young people to read.

2 Remind the young people that they are beautiful. God thinks they are beautiful. He created them – every one a unique design. No one else is the same.

3 Read, or ask a good reader to read, Psalm 8:5. It says that God made us a little lower than the heavenly beings (or angels). Apart from these heavenly beings, God sees humans as more important than everything else he created.

4 Invite the young people to thank God, out loud, that he has made them and that they are 'very good'! Maybe you could shout it all together, or they could whisper it to the person next to them.

PRACTICAL

WHAT: **photo reminders**
WHY: **to remind the group that they are made by God**
WITH: **camera, photo printing equipment (optional)**

1 Read Genesis 1:26 and Psalm 8:5,6 to the young people.

2 Explain that 'made in God's image' means that each one of them is the climax of God's creative activity, and God has crowned them with glory and honour and made them rulers over the rest of his creation.

3 Use a camera to take a picture of each of the young people. (It is best to obtain permission from parents and guardians before doing this.) If you have printing equipment available, you could print the photos during the session. Write '[Name] is made in God's image' on each photo. (You may need to use a permanent marker or acetate pen.)

4 Encourage the young people to keep their photos. Remind them to thank God whenever they see them.

5 As they are made in God's image and are special, it means that everyone else is in that privileged position too. How will that change the way the young people relate to others?

CREATIVE

WHAT: **creative worship**
WHY: **to praise God for the whole of his creation**
WITH: **black, green and blue cloths, fairy lights, images of 'creation', chill-out music, tea lights, matches, laptop and projector**

1 Decorate the room creatively. Decorate one wall to represent space (use black cloths with white fairy lights to represent stars), one wall to represent the Earth (use the green and blue cloths) and another wall to represent the creatures God created (project images of animals and people on to the wall). Invite the young people to sit or lie on the floor and to think about God's creation as you play the chill-out music.

2 Read Genesis 1 and John 1:1–14 over the music. Play some suitable worship songs and invite the young people to join in with these. Suggest that they light the tea lights as the worship unfolds to symbolise the fact that darkness has not overcome the light (make sure the young people are careful when using the tea lights).

MORE ON THIS THEME:

If you want to do a short series with your group, other sessions that work well with this one are:

1	*In the beginning*	*Genesis 1:1–19*
3	*Blessed and holy*	*Genesis 2:1–3*
4	*You and God*	*Genesis 2:4–25*

Bible bit
Genesis 1:20–31

Have you seen the programme on TV called *Who Do You Think You Are?* It's where famous people find out about their ancestors and what happened to them. But who do you think you are? Who are your ancestors? Well, Genesis tells us that ultimately, we are made by God – made in his image. I wonder how they'd show that on *Who Do You Think You Are?*

FAMILY TREE

Many people are interested in finding out where they come from, and it's become a popular hobby. How far back into your family history can you go? Have a go at filling in the simple tree below to find out.

THE GREAT DEBATE

2

Below are several different theories about how the universe came into being. Take a look at them and look for similarities. Make some notes on your thoughts...

WHAT IS SIMILAR; WHAT IS DIFFERENT?

WHAT MAKES SENSE AND WHAT DOESN'T?

HOW DO YOU FEEL AFTER READING EACH OF THEM?

A CHRISTIAN ACCOUNT

Before anything there was God. God created everything that there is and ever was; nothing was created that was not created by God. God first created the universe and then created everything to exist within it. The pinnacle of creation was humanity, whom he made to be in his own image. God looked at everything he created and saw that it was good.

A BABYLONIAN CREATION

One Babylonian creation account is called the Enuma Elish, and a whole variety of gods are involved. Creation happened when the universe was formless and two gods created most things. A group of younger gods upset the older gods, who liked to rest, and they started to kill one another.

A god called Marduk was born. Through a lot of fighting, Marduk was proclaimed king of the gods. He decided to create humans and they were shaped out of the blood of one of the executed gods.

BALINESE CREATION

In Bali, one creation story goes something like this. At some point the world serpent, Antaboga, created the world turtle through meditation. On the back of the turtle are two coiled snakes. This forms the foundation of the world on which everything is placed.

ONE CHINESE CREATION

In one Chinese creation story the space of the universe was an egg. Phan Ku was inside the egg in a mass called 'nothing'. Phan Ku was the creator, the first being. He used a chisel to create the world – its rivers, valleys and mountains. Phan Ku separated 'yin' – the earth – from 'yang' – the sky. He put the sun in the day and the moon and stars at night. When Phan Ku died his fleas became humans.

A NON-GOD CREATION

The universe is here by accident, and may have been one of many universes that have existed. A collection of elements randomly contracted and then exploded. These elements by chance formed collections of stars and planets, formed by gravity. On Earth, and most probably on other planets too, random chemical processes formed first simple molecules, then proteins, then simple living cells. These cells evolved into complex creatures, including ape-descended humans, through genetic mutation.

READ GENESIS 1:20–31 AGAIN TO CHECK OUT THE BIBLICAL ACCOUNT. HOW DOES IT COMPARE TO THE OTHERS?

WHAT DO YOU BELIEVE?

3

Bible: Genesis 2:1–3

BLESSED AND HOLY

THE AIM: To discover more about our Creator God and explore our response to him

The aim unpacked

For many people, to rest on the seventh day and to keep it holy has become obsolete. So many things press in on our time that having an 'extra' day to do the shopping or to earn some extra cash is a bonus. But there are reasons why God commanded us to rest. We all need time to recover and recuperate from work and the trials of family life.

WAY IN

theGRID MAGAZINE

WHAT: discussion
WHY: to think about the value of rest
WITH: magazine page 21

1 Give out copies of page 21 and ask the group to look at 'Kick off your shoes'. Read it together and invite the young people to rate the various methods of relaxation on a scale of one to ten.

2 Go through the different ways of relaxing and then ask the young people to write their own favourite way of letting off steam in the space provided. Chat about all the different options and then ask, 'Why do we need to relax?'

SCENE SETTER

WHAT: 'restful' activity
WHY: to experience different people's ideas of rest
WITH: equipment for your chosen activities

1 Before the session, try to find out what one or two members of your group do to relax, and provide an opportunity for the whole group to do that in the session. It might be something easy to prepare for, such as reading, or something a little more difficult, such as dancing.

2 Provide two or three activities and give everyone the opportunity to have a go at each. When you have finished, discuss how relaxing everyone found the different activities. Make the point that not everyone finds the same things restful or relaxing – we are all different!

THEMED GAME

WHAT: board games
WHY: to think about taking time out
WITH: various games where you have to miss a go, such as Uno™ or Monopoly™

1 If you can, try to increase the likelihood of young people having to miss a go by including 'miss a go' cards from other games.

2 Show to the young people the games you have chosen and encourage them to play the game of their choice. Watch how they react when they have to miss a turn.

3 When the games have finished, or after a set period of time, chat together about what it was like to miss a turn. Elicit some emotions that the group felt, such as frustration or that it was unfair.

4 Encourage the young people to talk about times when it is good to take time out. Ask them how this differs from being forced to sit out.

BIBLE EXPERIENCE 3

LEVEL 1: CONNECT

WHAT: photostory
WHY: to discover more about our Creator God and explore our response to him
WITH: magazine page 22

1 Give out the copies of page 22 and invite the group to read the story together.

2 What are the young people's reactions to the story? Does anyone think any of the things Ron was doing were 'wrong' or 'bad' things to do? What do they think of Ron's weekend? Does it seem familiar?

3 Read Genesis 2:1–3 to the group. Recap together what has happened so far, filling in as many details as they can remember. Explain that, in the past, people have always observed a day of rest because of this passage (and others in the Bible). What does the group think of the concept of a day of rest?

4 Talk a little bit about how God made us and how we need to make sure we take time out from our busy lives to rest, as well as making time to spend with God.

LEVEL 2: INTERFACE

WHAT: weekend activity timetable
WHY: to discover more about our Creator God and explore our response to him
WITH: copy of pages 23 and 24 for each group of young people

1 Divide the young people into pairs or threes and give each group a copy of pages 23 and 24. Explain that the table represents their weekend. The things that are already in the table cannot be changed or moved. Each item on the list represents something that could be done this weekend. Challenge the young people to plan their weekend by writing the activities on to the timetable. It is impossible to fit all these things in, but you don't have to tell your group that!

2 After a while, get the group to feed back and explain the choices they have made and why. What are the consequences of each of these choices?

3 Read Genesis 2:1–3. Find out where, or if, the young people have set aside time during their weekend to rest or to set themselves apart to focus more on God. Ask the group the following questions:

- What are the possible consequences of not setting aside time to rest and to focus more on God?
- Do you think that how Christians spend their time (especially to do with the Sabbath) should be any different from everyone else? Why?

LEVEL 3: SWITCH ON

WHAT: discussion
WHY: to discover more about our Creator God and explore our response to him
WITH: large sheet of paper, marker pens

1 Read out (or ask a member of the group to read out) Genesis 2:1–3 and Exodus 20:8–11.

2 On a large sheet of paper write the word 'Sabbath'. Write down as many ideas or words that the young people can come up with to do with the word 'Sabbath'.

3 Turn the sheet of paper over and write the words 'Sacred space' on the back. Again, write down any ideas or words that come into their minds when they think of 'sacred space'.

4 Explain that, in some ways, the Sabbath is like making a sacred space for God and also for ourselves. The word 'Sabbath' means to set aside or to rest from what we are doing the rest of the time. It can be like creating a sacred space in our busy week where we can recharge our batteries – physically, emotionally and spiritually.

5 Ask the young people to discuss the following questions in pairs or threes:

- Have you experienced a time of 'sacred space' where you have met with God?
- How did you arrive at this place? For example, were you alone praying, were you listening to some worship music, were you in a church meeting?
- What kinds of things help you to set aside time for God and switch off from the week?
- What kinds of things make it hard to do this?

6 Come back together as a group and ask the following question:

- Imagine that sitting in this room there is someone who really wants to make sure they have a time of Sabbath each week – what one piece of advice would you give them?

7 Finish by encouraging the young people to set aside some space and time to chill out from their hectic lives and also to focus on God.

RESPOND

MUSICAL

WHAT: **listening to guided meditation**
WHY: **to respond to God's call to rest**
WITH: ***Tune In, Chill Out*** **book and CD (Christian Education), CD or MP3 of 'Be Still for the Presence of the Lord', playback equipment**

1 Encourage the young people to make themselves comfortable in a place where they won't be distracted by other people. Explain that you are going to listen to a track in which someone will describe a scene. Encourage them to close their eyes and imagine the scene as it is described.

2 Play track 4 from the *Tune In, Chill Out* CD. When it has finished, obtain feedback from the group:

- What did they think of the track they have just listened to?
- How did it make them feel?

3 You could have a sung worship response to this track. Sing, 'Be Still for the Presence of the Lord'. Continue to play the music while the young people consider their response.

PRACTICAL

WHAT: **making a commitment**
WHY: **to set aside time to spend with God**
WITH: **blank postcards**

1 Give each young person a postcard and a pen. Explain that you are going to ask them to make a commitment to set aside some time to have Sabbath this week.

2 Encourage each young person to write on their card a date and time in the coming week when they will spend time with God. Suggest that they write on their card how they are going to do this – for example, going for a walk, being somewhere safe, or being on their own.

3 Explain that, as a group, you are going to encourage each other to keep the commitment by reminding each other. Divide the group into pairs and invite them to swap contact details and when they should be reminded. Remember to be sensitive to any young people who, for whatever reasons, may not want to swap their details with someone else.

CREATIVE

WHAT: **clock face reminders**
WHY: **to remember why God created space to rest**
WITH: **card, scissors, marker pens**

1 Explain that you are going to create a reminder to set aside some time each week to rest and focus on God more closely.

2 Give out the card, scissors and marker pens and ask everyone to cut out a large circle. Then ask them to divide the circle roughly into seven (this doesn't have to be exact!) and to colour in one of the sections. You could encourage the young people to write or draw ways that they can enjoy their Sabbath time in this section too.

3 As you work, talk about why God created time to spend resting in him. If the young people have any response to this, they should write it in the rest of the circle. Alternatively, they could write out Genesis 2:1–3.

4 You could work together to make one large clock. This could be displayed in the room you use so that each week when the young people come in they will be reminded of what you have discovered today.

MORE ON THIS THEME:

If you want to do a short series with your group, other sessions that work well with this one are:

1	*In the beginning*	*Genesis 1:1–19*
2	*Made in his image*	*Genesis 1:20–31*
4	*You and God*	*Genesis 2:4–25*

3

KICK OFF YOUR SHOES

Bible bit
Genesis 2:1–3

Why did God take a day of rest? If he is all-powerful, surely he doesn't need a nice sit-down? Well, no, he doesn't, but we do, and it's a good principle to follow.

How often do you stop and relax?

How do you like to relax? Rate these suggestions on a scale of 1 (as relaxing as fingernails on a blackboard) to 10 (so laid back it's horizontal).

'Sitting around enjoying good food with good friends and settling down for an evening of great film watching.'

1 2 3 4 5 6 7 8 9 10

'Playing boxing on the Nintendo Wii – though my arms ache afterwards!'

1 2 3 4 5 6 7 8 9 10

'A good walk in the countryside. Getting close to the Creator through the creation.'

1 2 3 4 5 6 7 8 9 10

'Playing football helps me get rid of all my frustrations, and it's great if I manage to score a goal too!'

1 2 3 4 5 6 7 8 9 10

'Listening to music – and probably singing along too.'

1 2 3 4 5 6 7 8 9 10

'Sleeping!'

1 2 3 4 5 6 7 8 9 10

'Just sitting on the sofa and catching up on my thoughts or heading into town, grabbing a coffee and watching the world go by.'

1 2 3 4 5 6 7 8 9 10

'Reading a good book – you can escape into another world for an hour or so.'

1 2 3 4 5 6 7 8 9 10

What's your favourite way to relax? Write it here.

WHY DO WE NEED TO RELAX?

BUSY BUSY BUSY

Hey Ron! What are you up to at the weekend? Want to come round my house and hang out on Sunday?

I can't, mate, sorry. In the morning I'm going to church – I've got to help with the PA and then go to theGRID group, then give my mum a hand with the coffee afterwards. Then we're rehearsing for a sketch we're doing in next week's service.

Then, after lunch, I've got to do my maths homework. After that, I'm going to my gran's to mow her lawn and catalogue her huge collection of bus tickets – she's got some that date back to 1968!

After dinner, I'm going to church, where the youth group is leading the worship – I play the drums and the ukelele. Then we're heading off to the local homeless shelter to make soup and stew for the people who need it. And I've got to squeeze in my art homework too – a life-size picture of Cliff Richard!

What about Saturday?

No, I'm solving world hunger that day. See you later.

ARE YOUR WEEKENDS EVER THIS BUSY?
HOW DOES RON'S ATTITUDE COMPARE TO GENESIS 2:1–3?

USE WITH SESSION 3 BIBLE EXPERIENCE 'LEVEL 2 INTERFACE'

How would you spend your weekend?

How would you spend your weekend? Choose some of the activities in the list below and put them into your timetable! You must sleep for at least eight hours at night. Certain events are fixed and nothing else can be done at the same time.

	Saturday	Sunday
8 to 8.30am		
8.30 to 9am		
9 to 9.30am		
9.30 to 10am		
10 to 10.30am	Food shopping with Mum	
10.30 to 11am		
11 to 11.30am		
11.30am to 12pm		
12 to 12.30pm		
12.30 to 1pm		
1 to 1.30pm		Aunty Enid's 80th birthday party
1.30 to 2pm		
2 to 2.30pm		
2.30 to 3pm		
3 to 3.30pm		
3.30 to 4pm		
4 to 4.30pm		
4.30 to 5pm		

RESOURCE PAGE

USE WITH SESSION 3 BIBLE EXPERIENCE 'LEVEL 2 INTERFACE'

	Saturday	Sunday
5 to 5.30pm		
5.30 to 6pm		
6 to 6.30pm		
6.30 to 7pm		
8 to 8.30pm		
9 to 9.30pm		
9.30 to 10pm		
11 to 11.30pm		

Plan some of these activities into your weekend:

Cinema with friends (3 hrs 30 min total – afternoon or evening only)
Go to visit niece (1 hr 30)
Go to church (2 hrs 30 – Sunday morning only)
Play new video game (2–4 hrs)
Watch *The X Factor* (2 hrs 30 – Saturday night only)
Spend time with God and reading Bible (1 hr)
Go to McDonald's with mates (1 hr 30 – mealtimes only)
Go shopping with mates (4 hrs – morning or afternoon only)
Do history homework for school (2 hrs)
Take dog for long walk (1 hr)
Go to church youth group (2 hrs – Sunday evening only)
Watch DVD at friend's house (3 hrs)
Do Spanish coursework (2 hrs)
Tidy bedroom (1 hr)
Spend time on social media (1–3 hrs)

Bible: Genesis 2:4–25

4

YOU AND GOD

THE AIM: To discover more about our Creator God and explore our response to him

The aim unpacked

In this session, the focus is on how humans were created to be in relationship with each other and with God. Young people are often concerned about being accepted and liked by others, but this is not the same as being in relationship with others. The companionship between man and woman that God sets up in this passage is much more than that.

WAY IN

theGRID MAGAZINE

WHAT: true or false quiz
WHY: to introduce the idea of how amazing God's creation is
WITH: magazine page 28, prize

1 Hand out copies of page 28 and challenge the group to complete the 'Amazing animals' quiz. Emphasise that the answers must be exactly true to be classed as true.

2 Feed back the answers from page 333 and award a prize to the highest scorer.

SCENE SETTER

WHAT: game
WHY: to introduce the idea that we were not made to be alone
WITH: copies of page 30

1 This game should be handled sensitively, as it could provoke difficult emotions for some young people in your group. Divide the young people into groups, which should help anyone who often feels lonely not to feel too exposed. Hand out copies of page 30 and pens.

2 Give the groups a few minutes to rate the situations out of ten for how lonely or uncomfortable each one would make them feel. So 1 would be the worst or loneliest situation to be in and 10 would be the easiest.

3 After a few minutes, bring the group together for feedback. Did the groups get similar results? Has anyone ever been in a situation like one of these? How did they deal with it?

4 Conclude by saying that we often feel most at home when we are around other people, especially people who love us.

5 Make sure that you let the young people know who they can talk to about any issues raised in this activity. Be sure to follow your safeguarding policy.

THEMED GAME

WHAT: active game
WHY: to introduce the idea of things going together
WITH: large bag or covered box

1 Ask everyone to take off their shoes and put them into a large bag or box. Jumble them up.

2 Split the group into teams and line them up at the other end of the room to the shoes. Explain that each team sends one runner at a time, to, without looking, pick one shoe out of the bag and bring it back to their team.

3 The winning team is the first to collect enough matching pairs of shoes for half of their team.

BIBLE EXPERIENCE

LEVEL 1: CONNECT

WHAT: discussion
WHY: to discover more about our Creator God and explore our response to him
WITH: magazine page 29

1 Give out copies of page 29. Encourage the young people to look at the list of animals in 'Animal magic?' They should choose which, out of these animals, they find the most interesting, and why.

2 Ask the young people to feed back and discuss their choices.

3 Read Genesis 2:18–25. Ask the following questions:

- Why did God create all these things – including people (v 18)?
- Did God create all these things for himself or for the sake of others?
- What do you think this says about what God is like and what he wants for our lives?

4 Encourage the group to think back to their most interesting animal. Remind them that animals they think are dull may be very interesting to someone else! Also remind them that, although animals are great, human beings were made to be in relationship with God and with other people. Look again at verse 20. Adam didn't find among the animals a helper who was right for him.

LEVEL 2: INTERFACE

WHAT: reflection and/or discussion
WHY: to discover more about our Creator God and explore our response to him
WITH: gentle instrumental music (optional)

1 Play some quiet music and ask a volunteer to read Genesis 2:4–25. Ask the group to imagine the scene that the passage is describing.

2 On their own or in pairs, and with the music still playing, invite the young people to reflect on or discuss the following questions (read them out to the group, pausing between each question):

- What do you think the Bible means when it says we are made in God's image? (Refer back to Genesis 1:27.)
- How do you feel about yourself when you remember that you are made to be in relationship with God and with others?
- How might our attitudes to others change if we remember that they, too, are made in God's image, and made to be in relationship with him?

3 Read Psalm 8 over the music and ask the young people to listen to and reflect on the words. Then ask them to reflect on or discuss what being put in charge means to the way we should live.

4 Read Psalm 148 over the music and ask them to reflect on or discuss the following questions:

- How can the animals and the oceans praise God?
- Verse 13 says that God is more wonderful than anything that has been created. What should we do about that?

LEVEL 3: SWITCH ON

WHAT: film clip and discussion
WHY: to discover more about our Creator God and explore our response to him
WITH: DVD of *Castaway* (Dreamworks, 2000), playback equipment, page 31

1 Show the clip from *Castaway* where Tom Hanks turns the volleyball into a 'person' called Wilson by drawing a face on it and talking to it.

2 Ask the group the following questions:

- Why do you think Tom Hanks' character did this?
- How would you feel if you were on a desert island with no human contact at all – no sounds of a human voice, no iPod, no book to read, no mobile phone?
- What would you do?

3 Divide the young people into pairs and give each group a set of cards from page 31. Explain that you are going to read out a passage from the Bible. Whenever you mention a word that describes a picture on one of their cards, the teams must place that card in the middle of the room. Read out Genesis 2:18–25.

4 Ask the group, 'Why did God create the animals and eventually the woman (vs 20,22–25)?'

5 Finish by explaining that God created the creatures of the Earth and other people for us so that we could have companionship. That's why, if we were stuck alone on a desert island with no other humans at all, we would struggle – we were made to be with others. Also chat briefly about how we were made to be in a relationship with God. Ask, 'How do you think this is different from friendship with other people?'

RESPOND

4

MUSICAL

WHAT: singing or jamming
WHY: to experience being in a creative relationship with God and other people
WITH: selection of music for singing (choral or contemporary), musical instruments

1 If you're going to have a jamming session and know that some members of your group play instruments, ask them to bring their instruments along to the session.

2 Explain that you're going to do something musical all together, to praise God. If you are singing, give out the music and start to learn the song you have chosen. If you are jamming, start with a worship song you all know and then embellish it as you become more confident.

3 Spend time singing or jamming, reminding the group that this is praise, not performance. It doesn't matter what you sound like, as long as you are praising God sincerely.

4 Ask the young people what they think of how they all worked together. Encourage them to compare how four voices sound compared to one, a full band to one guitar, and so on.

PRACTICAL

WHAT: doing something to take care of the Earth
WHY: to encourage people to care for God's creation
WITH: large sheet of paper

1 Read out Genesis 2:15. Ask the young people, 'Why did God put the man in the garden?' Explain that if God wanted the man to take care of everything that had been created, he probably expects us to do the same.

2 On a large sheet of paper, write down some ways that the group could, this week, do something to care for the Earth and the people in it. This could be anything – for example, recycling waste, not leaving the computer or the TV on standby, doing a neighbourhood clear-up, doing acts of kindness for the community, or sponsoring an endangered animal.

3 Decide together as a group what you will do, and do it! Make sure you follow up on this so that the young people know they are accountable in some way – it's all too easy to say something in your session and then completely forget to do it!

CREATIVE

WHAT: reflecting and designing
WHY: to meditate creatively on the words of Psalm 8
WITH: art materials

1 Explain that psalms in the Bible are songs addressed to God. Psalm 8 is one of David's 'greatest hits'!

2 Invite the young people to read Psalm 8 on their own and to reflect on what it is about – praising God because of his creation.

3 With paper and pens, invite the young people to design a CD or vinyl cover for the imaginary album *David's Greatest Hits*, which features the hit 'Psalm 8'.

- What style of music would it be?
- What is it about?
- What packaging and marketing would be used?

4 Finish by reading Psalm 8 all together out loud.

MORE ON THIS THEME:

If you want to do a short series with your group, other sessions that work well with this one are:

1	*In the beginning*	*Genesis 1:1–19*
2	*Made in his image*	*Genesis 1:20–31*
3	*Blessed and holy*	*Genesis 2:1–3*

AMAZING ANIMALS

Can you work out which of these facts are true and which are false?

1 TRUE / FALSE — An ostrich's eye is bigger than its brain.

2 TRUE / FALSE — Polar bears have pink skin.

3 TRUE / FALSE — Penguins can't jump.

4 TRUE / FALSE — A crocodile cannot stick its tongue out.

5 TRUE / FALSE — Woodpeckers don't get headaches from all that pecking. Their skulls have air pockets to cushion the brain.

6 TRUE / FALSE — The praying mantis can turn its head 270 degrees.

7 TRUE / FALSE — A zebra is black with white stripes.

8 TRUE / FALSE — The giant squid has the largest eyes of any animal. They can be 39 cm across, which is 16 times wider than a human eye.

9 TRUE / FALSE — Orangutans and gorillas are the only animals besides humans to have fingerprints.

10 TRUE / FALSE — The longest recorded life span of a tapeworm is 35 years.

Bible bit
Genesis 2:4–25

Have you ever known what it's like to be lonely? Not just a time when all your mates are busy and you end up sitting flicking through all the channels on TV; I mean really lonely. Cats and dogs and other pets can help, but you can't have a conversation with them; you can't get to know them like you can another person. This is what Adam was experiencing here – we need to be in a relationship with other people and with God. There's no substitute for that.

4

ANIMAL MAGIC?

?

Which are your favourite animals? Which do you hate? Which are you scared of? Draw a heart over your favourite, and a cross through the one you hate.

?

Why do you think God created each one of these creatures?

?

What do you think this says about what God is like?

?

What do you think this says about what God wants for our lives?

?

Which one would be a good friend to you? Any of them?

If your favourite isn't there, draw it here.

RESOURCE PAGE

USE WITH SESSION 4 WAY IN 'SCENE SETTER'

All by myself!

Rate the following things out of ten, according to how lonely or isolated they would make you feel if you were in the situation.

1 = so uncomfortable you'd like to be transported to another universe right now!

10 = so easy you're as snug as a bug in a rug

1 It's your first day at a new school. You don't know anyone.

/10

2 You are sitting with a group of people who are going on and on about a band you've never even heard of.

/10

3 It's non-uniform day at school. All your so-called mates said they were going to wear all red. You turn up with red hair, red trousers, red top and red shoes. To your horror, no one else is wearing red.

/10

4 You are at a party and the friend you came with decides to spend most of their time chatting people up.

/10

5 You are in RE and a huge discussion kicks off about Christianity. The teacher picks you out and asks you, as the only person in the class who goes to church, what you think.

/10

6 You are desperate to see a new film that's on at the cinema but none of your mates will go with you. You decide to go on your own to see it.

/10

7 You go along to youth group as normal but none of your friends you normally hang around with are there.

/10

USE WITH SESSION 4 BIBLE EXPERIENCE 'LEVEL 3 SWITCH ON'

5

Bible: Genesis 18:1–15; 21:1–8

AT LONG LAST!

THE AIM: To discover that God is faithful to his promises

The aim unpacked

During the next three sessions we'll be discovering that, through the ups and downs of Abraham's family life, God remained faithful to his promises. In this session we'll discover that God is faithful and keeps his promises, as Sarah finally gives birth to a son. The Bible contains much evidence of God keeping his promises, and this should encourage us as we put our trust in God and eagerly wait for him to fulfil his remaining promises.

WAY IN

theGRID MAGAZINE

WHAT: sorting exercise
WHY: to think about the nature of promises
WITH: magazine page 35

1 Give everyone a copy of page 35. This contains a selection of promises that have been made by people – some famous, some biblical and some the young people probably hear – or make – frequently!

2 Ask the young people to score each promise out of ten, 0 being totally untrustworthy and 10 being completely trustworthy.

3 As a group, discuss the results. Conclude by making the point that the only true test of a promise is whether it actually comes true.

SCENE SETTER

WHAT: discussion
WHY: to think about the nature of promises

1 Ask the young people, 'What's the silliest/biggest/weirdest promise anyone ever made to you that actually came true?'

2 Encourage as many people as are willing to share their stories and allow time for other group members to ask questions so the stories can be explored. Try to do this in a light-hearted manner and have as much fun as possible.

3 Discuss which story is the best/funniest.

4 Make the point that hanging on to a promise can be really hard, and the more outrageous the promise is, the harder it is to believe it will happen.

THEMED GAME

WHAT: game
WHY: to pick up on the importance of laughter in the story that follows
WITH: chairs

1 This is an old game but it's very funny! Set out some chairs in a circle facing inwards. There needs to be one less chair than the number of young people in the group. Tell the group that the aim of the game is to make someone laugh.

2 Ask a volunteer to go first. They have to go up to a person in the circle and say, 'If you love me, honey, then smile.' That person must then reply, completely straight-faced, 'I do love you, but I just can't smile.'

3 If they don't laugh or smile, the volunteer must go up to someone else and say, 'If you love me, honey, then smile.' However, if they do laugh or smile, they swap places with the volunteer. The new volunteer then tries to make someone else in the group laugh, and so on.

4 Conclude by explaining that in today's story, Sarah found the news that she was to have a child so ridiculous that it made her laugh out loud.

BIBLE EXPERIENCE

LEVEL 1: CONNECT

WHAT: activity and discussion
WHY: to discover that God is faithful to his promises
WITH: copies of page 37, Bibles

1 Give everyone a copy of page 37 and ask them to spend a few minutes, individually, thinking about how easy or hard it would be to keep the promises.

2 Divide the young people into small groups and encourage them to chat about their results. Do most people agree with each other, or are there any significant differences between the results? Why might this be?

3 Gather the group together and challenge the young people to pick one of the promises that they could keep if they had to. Is there a promise that no one wants to keep?

4 God had promised to start a great nation through Abraham, to provide that nation with land and to give Abraham many descendants. You may like to read Genesis 12:1–9 to your group. Say that Abraham (Abram) and his wife, Sarah (Sarai), were already old at this point when they would have to move. Ask:

- How do you think they might have felt about God's promises?
- If you were in their situation, would you have been able to fully trust God?

5 Read Genesis 18:1–15 and ask:

- Would you have laughed if you were in Sarah's situation?

Now read Genesis 21:1–8 and chat together about what we can learn from this story. Ask:

- Do you believe that God is faithful to his promises?
- What things cause our faith to grow or shrink?

LEVEL 2: INTERFACE

WHAT: family trees
WHY: to discover that God is faithful to his promises
WITH: Bibles

1 Give everyone a sheet of paper and ask them to draw their family tree. Encourage them to go as far back as they can. Be aware that this might raise some painful emotions for some young people, particularly for any young people who have been adopted, or those with divorced parents or with close family members who have died, so handle this activity with care. Also ask whether anyone has a famous ancestor or is related (however distantly!) to someone famous.

2 Review the promises that God made to Abraham in Genesis 12:1–9.

3 Ask the young people whether they've ever laughed at something that turned out to be true and, if so, whether it left them feeling a little embarrassed. For example, their dad telling them he was in a rock band when he was younger or their mum telling them about the time she ran a marathon. Chat about why they might have initially laughed. Then read Genesis 18:1–15 and chat together about why Sarah laughed at the thought that she would have a child.

4 Now read Genesis 21:1–8 to show that God did keep his promise. Make the point that the history of God's people is traced back to this amazing story. The Jewish people have Abraham as the father of their nation.

5 If you have time, why not play the tedious link game. Say the names of two celebrities and challenge the group to link them together. Then explain that Matthew 1 provides us with a genealogy that links Jesus all the way back to Abraham. God really does keep his promises; therefore we can feel confident about some of the promises that have not yet been fulfilled (such as Jesus coming back again).

LEVEL 3: SWITCH ON

WHAT: Bible study
WHY: to discover that God is faithful to his promises
WITH: magazine page 36, Bibles, large sheets of paper

1 Divide the young people into small groups and invite them to talk about what makes a promise easy or difficult to believe.

2 Make sure everyone has a copy of page 36 and invite them to look at 'Hard to believe'. Challenge them to read through the verses in pairs or threes and to think up a newspaper headline that summarises each promise and, if possible, also indicates how Abraham may have felt about it. Invite all the groups to give a score between 1 and 10 to each headline, 1 being very hard to believe and 10 being easy to believe.

3 As a whole group, discuss why Abraham was (usually) prepared to trust God wholeheartedly. Go on to chat about what causes us to trust or doubt God.

4 Ask a few volunteers to read aloud Genesis 18:1–15. How do the young people think Abraham and Sarah would have felt? Find out whether anyone in the group has ever laughed at some unlikely news that they didn't believe, but later found out was true.

5 Conclude by reading Genesis 21:1–8 and allow a few moments of quiet to enable the young people to reflect on this astounding outcome. Encourage them to think about how these events may have affected Abraham and Sarah's relationship with God. Then chat about how stories like this influence what we think about God.

RESPOND

MUSICAL

WHAT: **song**
WHY: **to discover that God is faithful to his promises**
WITH: **music and lyrics for 'There is a Day' by Phatfish**

1 Either obtain a recording or ask some live musicians to play 'There Is a Day' by Phatfish. Use the song to focus the group's attention on Jesus' return – one of God's promises that has yet to be fulfilled.

2 Read 1 Thessalonians 5:1–11. Conclude by encouraging the young people to say a few short prayers thanking God for his faithfulness and asking him to help those who doubt.

PRACTICAL

WHAT: **interview**
WHY: **to discover that God is faithful to his promises**
WITH: **guest(s)**

1 Invite one or more guests to the session who would be willing to talk about God's faithfulness in their own lives and in the life of your church. They don't have to have an extremely dramatic story; it's important to know that God is faithful in the small things – the day-to-day realities of everyday life.

2 Invite your guest(s) to talk to the group about promises that have been fulfilled, and ones they are still waiting to be fulfilled. Ask them to share why they have faith in God.

CREATIVE

WHAT: **posters**
WHY: **to think about God's faithfulness**
WITH: **large sheets of paper, drawing materials**

1 In pairs, ask the young people to design a poster that communicates the ideas that 'good things come to those who wait' and 'God is faithful to his promises'. Encourage them to include an example on their posters, either from the story of Abraham or their own lives.

2 Once the posters are completed, ask everyone to show and explain their posters to the rest of the group.

3 Encourage a few people to thank God for his faithfulness and to pray that we would learn to be patient.

4 If possible, display the posters somewhere prominent.

MORE ON THIS THEME:

If you want to do a short series with your group, other sessions that work well with this one are:

6	*Are you sure, God?*	*Genesis 22*
7	*Matchmaking*	*Genesis 24*
8	*Family rivalries*	*Genesis 25:19–34; 27:1–45*

5

PROMISES, PROMISES

Bible bit
Genesis 18:1–15; 21:1–8

As *theGRID* picks up the story of Abraham and Sarah, we need to remember that they've been waiting many years for God to fulfil some of the promises he has made to them. They're both quite old, so it's hardly surprising that Sarah laughs at the thought of her giving birth to a son. However, God is faithful to his promises, and despite Abraham and Sarah's mistakes, she finally gives birth to a son.

Do you find it hard to trust God? If so, don't worry; most people doubt God at one time or another. But hopefully, as we explore Abraham's story, you'll be encouraged as we discover that God always keeps his promises.

Score each of these promises: '0' being totally untrustworthy, '10' being completely trustworthy.

I'LL **CALL YOU** BACK.

/10

I WILL NOT EAT CHOCOLATE DURING LENT.

/10

I WON'T BE LATE HOME TONIGHT.

/10

I WILL LOVE YOU UNTIL THE DAY I DIE.

/10

WE WILL WIN THE LEAGUE THIS YEAR.

/10

FROM 1 JANUARY **I WILL** GO TO THE GYM THREE TIMES A WEEK.

/10

THE LORD **WILL** RETURN LIKE A THIEF IN THE NIGHT.

/10

EVEN THOUGH YOUR WIFE IS OLD AND YOU HAVE NO CHILDREN **YOU WILL BE** THE FATHER OF MANY NATIONS

/10

HARD TO BELIEVE

Imagine you're a reporter for a newspaper and you've just found out about some of the promises God made to Abraham. Look up the following verses and, for each one, think of a snappy newspaper headline that summarises the promise and, if possible, also indicates how Abraham may have felt about it.

Genesis 12:2,3

....

1 2 3 4 5 6 7 8 9 10

Genesis 13:15,16

....

1 2 3 4 5 6 7 8 9 10

Genesis 15:4,5

....

1 2 3 4 5 6 7 8 9 10

Genesis 17:4–8

....

1 2 3 4 5 6 7 8 9 10

Genesis 17:15,16

....

1 2 3 4 5 6 7 8 9 10

Genesis 17:19–21

....

1 2 3 4 5 6 7 8 9 10

Now score each of the promises:
1 = very hard to believe
10 = easy to believe

WHY DO YOU THINK ABRAHAM WAS (USUALLY) PREPARED TO TRUST GOD?

WHAT CAUSES YOU TO DOUBT OR TRUST GOD?

RESOURCE PAGE

USE WITH SESSION 5 BIBLE EXPERIENCE 'LEVEL 1 CONNECT'

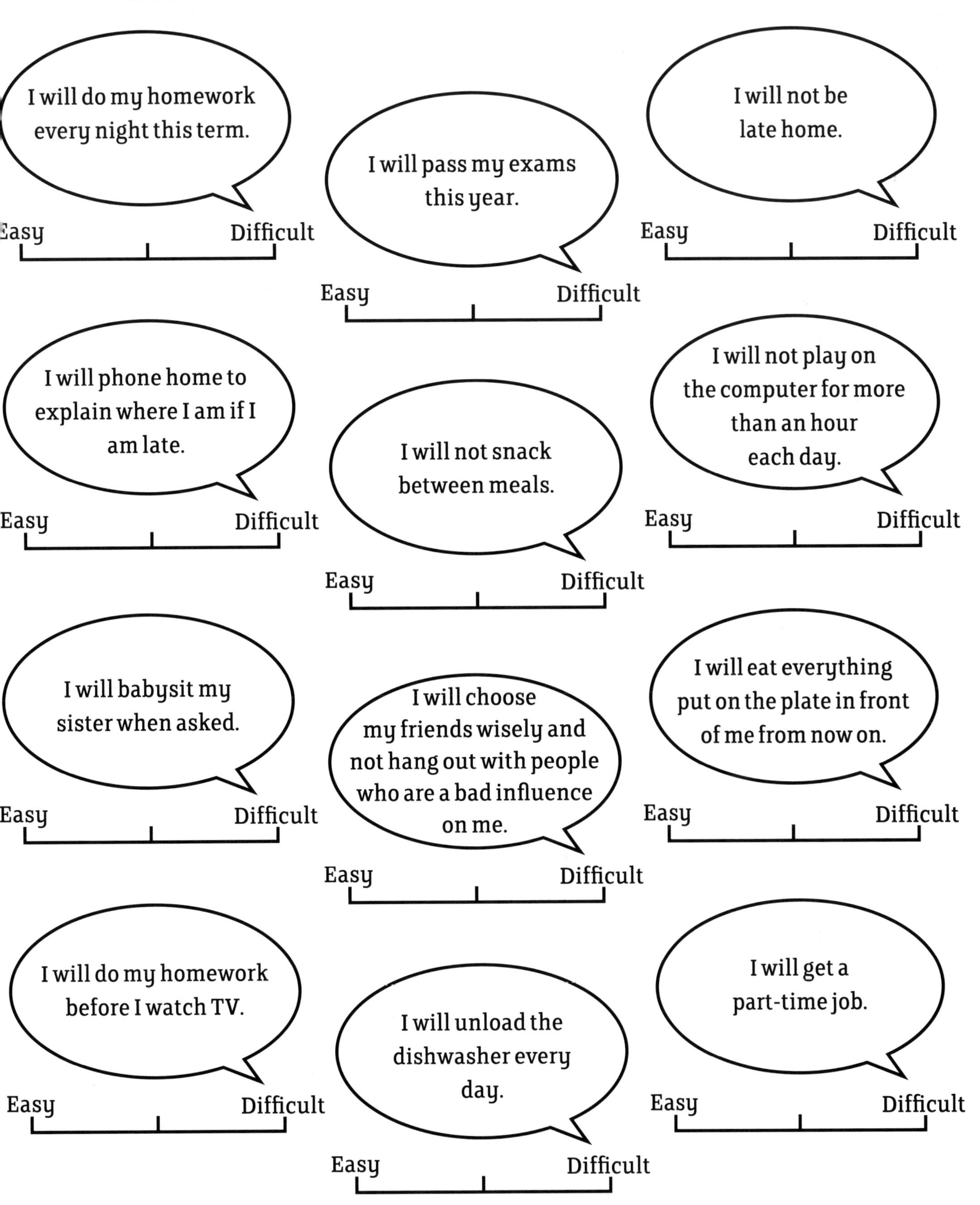

Bible: Genesis 22

ARE YOU SURE, GOD?

THE AIM: To discover that God wants us to trust his faithfulness

The aim unpacked

What are we to make of this story? What kind of God would ask someone to sacrifice their own son? To get to the heart of this story, we need to view the events through Abraham's eyes. If we do this, we'll not only be amazed at how much Abraham trusted God – we'll also discover a God who provides, is faithful and wants us to know that he is very different from all the other 'gods' that are around.

WAY IN

theGRID MAGAZINE

WHAT: **exercise**
WHY: **to think about sacrifice**
WITH: **magazine page 41, pens**

1 Make sure everyone has a copy of page 41. Ask them to consider the order in which they would be prepared to give these things up for ever!

2 Once they have done this, get them to chat about their results in small groups. Then, gather the groups together and see if there is any consensus about what would be the easiest or hardest to give up.

3 Briefly discuss how easy we would find it to trust God to help us cope if we gave up any of these things – perhaps just for Lent rather than for ever.

SCENE SETTER

WHAT: **craft**
WHY: **to link into the later teaching about mountain-top experiences**
WITH: **appropriate foodstuffs or papier-mâché equipment**

1 Explain to the group that much of this session's story takes place on a mountain. Therefore, we are going to make a mountain – well, a model of one! Get together some appropriate foodstuffs to make your mountain. For example, pizza dough, icing sugar, ice cream and melted chocolate (or some other appalling combination). Alternatively, you may like to get the group to make papier-mâché mountains.

2 While the mountains are being made, chat to the group about mountains. Why do many people find them so attractive? Why do people feel the need to climb them? What experiences do you have when it comes to climbing mountains? Why do many people feel so close to God when they are up a mountain?

THEMED GAME

WHAT: **drawing game**
WHY: **to link into changed perceptions and understandings**
WITH: **flip chart, marker pens**

1 Ask for a volunteer to start drawing a rough picture on a flip chart. Tell them not to make it obvious what they are drawing – if possible, brief them before the session that their picture should be open to interpretation so that people think it could be a number of different things!

2 After a few moments, stop the person drawing and ask a second person to come along and finish it off. Once the second person has finished the picture, ask the first person if it turned out the way they expected it to. Also ask the second person why they decided to finish the picture in the way they did.

3 Repeat this activity as time allows, so several people have a turn at drawing. Then introduce the session by explaining that the events we will be exploring probably surprised Abraham in many different ways and undoubtedly impacted how he saw God.

BIBLE EXPERIENCE

LEVEL 1: CONNECT

WHAT: activity
WHY: to discover that God wants us to trust his faithfulness
WITH: cards from page 43, signs, Bibles

1 Distribute the cards, ideally so each young person has one card. If your group is small, you'll have to give young people more than one card. Label the four corners of the room with the signs saying: 'God is like this'; 'God is a little like this/sometimes like this'; 'God is not like this at all'; 'Not sure'.

2 Get everyone to think about the 'quality' written on their card and then to go and stand in the corner they think is most appropriate. Now, find out which 'qualities' have ended up in which corner. Allow discussion about any areas of disagreement.

3 With the young people sitting in their separate corners, read, or paraphrase, Genesis 22:1–14. Then, ask if anyone feels their 'quality' is in the wrong corner. Provide the opportunity for the young people to move, if they want to. Get all the young people who are holding a quality of God that is seen clearly in this passage to stand up, however awkward that quality might be to understand fully.

4 Conclude by making the point that this story is set a long time ago in a culture where many people believed that the gods they worshipped required them to sacrifice children as a sign of commitment and to guarantee blessing. However, this story, along with the rest of the Bible, clearly tells us that Abraham's God, the God revealed to us in the Bible, does not want children to be sacrificed. The key to this passage is that Abraham continued to trust God in a very difficult situation and God provided. God always wants us to trust his faithfulness.

LEVEL 2: INTERFACE

WHAT: drama
WHY: to discover that God wants us to trust his faithfulness
WITH: Bibles, a large sheet of paper, marker pens

1 Divide the young people into small groups and give each group a large sheet of paper and a marker pen. Ask them to write down as many reasons as possible why life can sometimes be tough.

2 Then, still in their small groups, encourage everyone to share the toughest thing they've ever had to do (or the toughest experience they've ever been through). Ask them to tell the group about what helped in these situations and whether or not they felt that God was helping and supporting them. This discussion will require sensitivity – adapt it as you feel necessary for your group.

3 Gather the group together and ask a few volunteers to read Genesis 22 to the group. Then, in small groups, get the young people to prepare a news report covering this story. During the report get them to interview Abraham, Isaac and one of Abraham's servants and find out how they were feeling before, during and after this event.

4 Spend some time discussing how you think God might have felt before, during and after this event. Conclude by making the point that this story is set a long time ago in a culture where many people believed that the gods they worshipped required them to sacrifice children as a sign of commitment and to guarantee blessing. However, this story, along with the rest of the Bible, clearly tells us that Abraham's God, the God revealed to us in the Bible, does not want children to be sacrificed. The key to this passage is that Abraham continued to trust God in a very difficult situation and God provided. God always wants us to trust his faithfulness.

LEVEL 3: SWITCH ON

WHAT: Bible study
WHY: to discover that God wants us to trust his faithfulness
WITH: magazine page 42, pens, flip chart, marker pens, Bibles s

1 Ask a few volunteers to read Genesis 22. As the story is being read, get them to draw and annotate the 'feeling' graphs on page 42.

2 Get the young people to compare their graphs and discuss how they feel about this story. Then, get them to share all the questions they have about this passage. Write them on a flip chart.

3 Now get everyone to read the box on page 42. Explain to the group that we need to remember that this story is set in the Middle Bronze Age, 1600–1800 years before Jesus. Therefore, the cultural norms of Abraham's day were very different from ours. However, God is the same yesterday, today and for ever. So it's important that we do two things. One is to relate this story to all the stories in the Bible that communicate how God loves and protects his people. In doing so, we get a much bigger picture of God. Secondly, we must try to discover what Abraham would have learned about God from this incident.

4 Conclude by revisiting and discussing some of the questions you wrote on the flip chart earlier.

RESPOND

MUSICAL

WHAT: **Easter hymns**
WHY: **to praise God for his faithfulness**
WITH: **hymn words and music (live, CD or MP3)**

1 Make the link between this session's story and the sacrifice Jesus made for us on the cross. Then choose one or two 'classic Easter hymns' that speak of Jesus' sacrifice. Read some of the verses out to the group, perhaps over some instrumental music.

2 Share your own thoughts and feelings about the lyrics, and encourage the young people to do the same. Then either listen to, or sing, one or two of the hymns in their entirety.

3 There are lots of hymns you could choose; some possibilities are: 'Amazing Grace'; 'My Lord, What Love Is This?'; 'Thine Be the Glory'; 'When I Survey'.

PRACTICAL

WHAT: **exercise**
WHY: **to discover that God wants us to trust his faithfulness**
WITH: **a flip chart, marker pens, paper, pens**

1 Explain that God wants us to trust his faithfulness but he doesn't expect us to do so blindly. He provides us with lots of evidence to show that it's sensible to put our faith in him – the Bible is full of stories that illustrate that he is faithful. God has also given us brains, and he wants us to use them when it comes to making decisions and dealing with difficult situations. However, when we're thinking 'logically' we must not forget that God can do amazing and unexpected things. When faced with a difficult situation, it can be a good idea to make a pros and cons list. Just imagine what Abraham's list might have looked like!

2 In twos or threes, ask the young people to think of a decision they have to make, or will have to make in the near future. In their small groups, get them to make a pros and cons list.

3 Encourage them to look over their lists and think about God's place in it. Ask them to consider what their list says about their trust in God's faithfulness.

CREATIVE

WHAT: **drama**
WHY: **to discover that God wants us to trust his faithfulness**

1 Divide the young people into small groups and ask each group to create a short sketch, set today, that combines elements of this session's story and communicates how God wants us to trust in his faithfulness.

2 Give the young people an example before they get started, eg George believes God wants him to invite some of his friends to his church's youth group. He knows that doing so might mean he is teased for going to church, but he decides to trust in God's faithfulness and do it anyway.

3 Once all the groups have prepared their sketches, gather the young people together and watch them all.

4 Conclude by asking a few young people to say short prayers thanking God for his faithfulness.

MORE ON THIS THEME:

If you want to do a short series with your group, other sessions that work well with this one are:

5	*At long last!*	*Genesis 18:1–15; 21:1–8*
7	*Matchmaking*	*Genesis 24*
8	*Family rivalries*	*Genesis 25:19–34; 27:1–45*

6

Bible bit
Genesis 22

God asks Abraham to sacrifice his son Isaac, and Abraham is ready to go through with it. Then, God stops him at the last moment and provides a ram for him to sacrifice instead. Gulp! What are we to make of this story? What kind of God would ask someone to sacrifice their own son?

To get to the heart of this story we need to view the events through Abraham's eyes. If we do this we'll not only be amazed at how much Abraham trusted God – we'll also discover a God who provides, is faithful and wants us to know that he is very different from all the other 'gods' that are around.

Take a look at these items and consider the order in which you would be prepared to give these things up forever! Number the items '1' to '14': '1' being the item you would be most prepared to give up, '14' being the item you would be least prepared to give up.

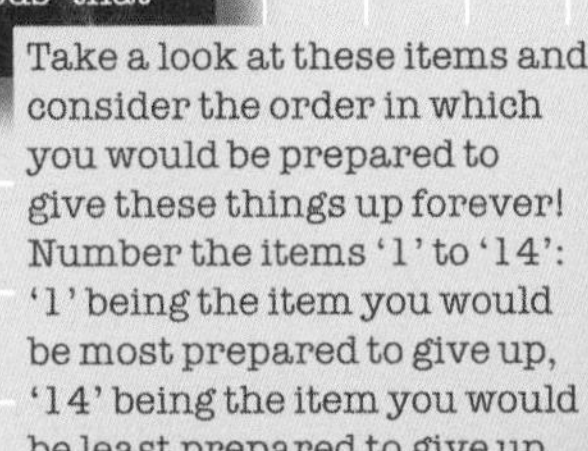

chewing gum

Give up

I feel

Great stories work on many different levels at the same time. Genesis 22 is a great story with many different levels. It's a story about obedience, God's provision and Abraham discovering that his God was very different from all the 'gods' that the people around him worshipped.

Abraham and his wife Sarah had held onto God's promise of a child for over a quarter of a century. However, the moment God asked him to sacrifice this child, he obeyed. He doesn't seem to try and put it off, he got up the next morning to go and do it.

So much of this story appalls us. It seems that this 'loving' God that we've learnt so much about is endorsing child cruelty – even to the extent of asking a child to be sacrificed as an act of worship to him. Surely this can't be right?

There's a lot to this story. Not only does it pay fantastic respect to Abraham's willingness to go the distance. Not only does it reveal to us a God who provides. There's more…

On this day, thousands of years ago, Abraham discovered that the God he worshipped – the God we worship today – was and is, very different from the other gods that the people around him, the Canaanites, worshipped.

You see, the Canaanites believed that their gods required the sacrifice of children. In Abraham's culture it was a common practice. Therefore, when God told Abraham to go and sacrifice Isaac, it wouldn't have come as a complete shock. Yes, he would have been extremely upset, and probably a little confused as to how this related to the promises he had received from God. But his willingness to go through with it shows us just how much he trusted God.

When Abraham went up the mountain he did so thinking that there were some similarities between his God and the Canaanite gods. However, by the time he had come down, he'd discovered that his God was very different.

As he went up the mountain he was probably thinking, 'This is what's always happened'. However, God provided him with a clear message while he was up the mountain, which said, 'I'm different, do things my way from now on'.

It can be hard to hear God's different voice in the noisy world in which we live. But never forget – our God is very different.

As you read Genesis 22, draw and annotate a graph that traces how you think Abraham and Isaac might have felt at various points during the story.

Abraham

feeling great

feeling terrible

Isaac

feeling great

feeling terrible

You

feeling great

feeling terrible

Think back over the past year, and mark on the times when you have felt particularly good or bad. What was going on to cause you to feel that way? What was your relationship with God like during those times?

USE WITH SESSION 6 BIBLE EXPERIENCE 'LEVEL 1 CONNECT'

Animal-hating	Child-hating	Sensible
Confusing	Faithful	Half-hearted
Greedy	Hopeful	Promise-maker
Liar	Murderer	Testing
Sympathetic	Over-the-top	Pathetic
Peaceful	Powerful	Promise-keeper
Violent	Weird	Wonderful

7

Bible: Genesis 24

MATCHMAKING

THE AIM: To discover that God continues to be faithful to his promises

The aim unpacked

God promised to make a great nation out of Abraham's descendants. Problem number one – Abraham didn't have a son. Eventually Isaac was born. Problem number two – Isaac didn't have a wife. In this session, we'll discover the amazing way in which Isaac met his wife, Rebekah. The cultural differences might be difficult to fully understand, but what shines through this story is the amazing ways in which God works and how he continues to be faithful to his promises.

WAY IN

theGRID MAGAZINE

WHAT: exercise
WHY: to introduce the idea of some events being amazing
WITH: magazine page 47, pens

1 Give everyone a copy of magazine page 47. Ask the young people, in pairs, to look at the list of headlines and order them from most amazing to least amazing.

2 Gather the group together and discuss where they agree and disagree. Then, get everyone to write a few newspaper headlines that capture amazing events in their own lives.

3 Then, once they have shared some of their headlines, as a whole group create a few newspaper headlines that recap Abraham's amazing life.

SCENE SETTER

WHAT: discussion
WHY: to think about dating and marriage
WITH: celebrity magazines

1 Divide the young people into small groups and give each group a selection of celebrity magazines.

2 Get each group to do some research on the 'big' celebrity relationships at the moment. What are they like? Is it possible to see through all the glitz and discover what the relationship is really like? Do you think they are happy?

3 Ask group members to talk to each other about what characteristics they would look for in their husband or wife. Also, ask people to share (if they would like to) how they imagine meeting their partner.

4 Explain to the group that choosing your husband or wife is one of the biggest decisions that most people make during their lives. Make sure you make the point that some people choose to stay single, and that's OK! Dating and marriage, especially the nature of the ceremony, vary hugely depending on your culture. In this session, we'll see just how different things were in Abraham's culture.

THEMED GAME

WHAT: mock game show
WHY: a fun way to introduce the idea that the story of Abraham is amazing
WITH: a game show host costume and a toy xylophone or keyboard

1 Before the session, get a leader (or yourself) to dress up as a game show host. Get a young person or other leader to play a short jingle on the xylophone or keyboard each time you say, 'Just amazing!'

2 Enter the room as the game show host. Say, 'Hello and welcome to *Just Amazing!* (jingle), the show where you, the audience, get to show us your amazing talents. Now, who's first on this week's *Just Amazing!* (jingle)?'

3 Encourage the young people to show off any amazing skills they have. For example, being highly flexible, having an amazing memory or being able to say the alphabet backwards. Each time someone shows off a skill say, 'Just amazing!' and play the jingle. It doesn't matter if the skill isn't that great.

4 Introduce the session by explaining that as you explore more of Abraham's story in this session, you'll continue to discover that God is 'Just amazing!'

BIBLE EXPERIENCE

LEVEL 1: CONNECT

WHAT: discussion
WHY: to discover that God continues to be faithful to his promises

1 Divide the young people into small groups and get each group to create a 'worst case scenario' for a blind date. Get them to either describe or act out their scenario to the rest of the group.

2 Then ask everyone in the group: 'If your friend was setting you up on a blind date, what three things would you definitely want to find out about your date beforehand?'

3 Summarise the story in Genesis 24 as follows: The events of Genesis 24 go beyond a blind date; this is an arranged marriage. Abraham asks his most senior servant to promise to get his son a wife from his own people, without taking Isaac back there. The servant is quite unafraid to tell God how he wants things done and he prays for a particular sign so he knows which girl is the right one. When a girl meets the criteria, he waves a bit of gold under her nose and she invites him to meet her family. It turns out that the woman the servant has found for Isaac is his cousin's daughter. The family agree that she should go and when she and Isaac meet it seems to be love at first sight.

4 Ask the young people to chat about these questions:

- What are the key differences between dating, engagement and marriage in our culture and Abraham's?
- How do you think the servant felt about being asked to do this?
- How do you think Isaac and Rebekah felt about all of this?
- What do we learn about God's faithfulness from these events?

5 Make the point that this was all part of God's plan for Abraham's descendants to become a nation. God remains faithful to his promises by providing a wife for Isaac. Ask the group to chat about why they think Abraham was so desperate for Isaac not to marry a Canaanite woman and why he didn't want Isaac to move away.

LEVEL 2: INTERFACE

WHAT: drama
WHY: to discover that God continues to be faithful to his promises
WITH: Bibles

1 Encourage the young people to spend a few minutes chatting about new relationship storylines that are appearing in their favourite TV soaps at the moment. Which ones do they think will last? Who would they love to see get together?

2 In small groups, get the young people to read through Genesis 24. Challenge them to create a modern-day version of the story as a soap opera would stage it.

3 Once the groups have acted out their soaps, ask them to discuss what we think we can learn from this story. Ask:

- What can we learn about God?
- How might we be able to relate this story to experiences we face in our lives?

Explain to the group that this story leaves us very little room to doubt that God was clearly guiding the servant's journey and bringing about his plans.

4 Conclude by discussing whether the young people believe God has a plan for their lives. Chat about how they think God reveals his plan to them and how they have experienced God's hand on their lives. Kick-start the discussion by providing examples from your own life.

LEVEL 3: SWITCH ON

WHAT: Bible study
WHY: to discover that God continues to be faithful to his promises
WITH: Bibles, copies of page 48

1 Give everyone a sheet of paper and ask them to divide it into three columns, titled, 'think', 'feel' and 'do'. Then allocate one of the following characters to each young person: Abraham, Abraham's servant, Isaac, Rebekah, Laban, Bethuel, Rebekah's mother and Rebekah's nurse.

2 As you read Genesis 24 to the group, get the young people to make notes about what they think their character would be thinking and feeling at various points of the story and what action they took.

3 Gather the group together and discuss each other's notes. Discuss what we can learn about what each character thought of God at the various points in the story.

4 Spend some time, in small groups, chatting about the key differences between dating, engagement and marriage in our culture and Abraham's. Ask your group if they have any friends who might have an arranged marriage and what they think about this.

5 Give everyone a copy of page 48 and work through the questions in twos or threes. Alternatively, divide the young people into four groups and allocate each group one of the sections of the story. Then, after they've had a few minutes to chat about their questions, ask everyone to feed back to the whole group.

6 Gather the young people together and chat through any questions they may have. Explain that this story shows us that God was very concerned about whom Isaac married. Ask the group to discuss whether they think God is interested in their relationships and why they think this. Encourage them to think about what they consider to be most important when developing boy/girlfriend relationships.

RESPOND

MUSICAL

WHAT: **song writing**
WHY: **to thank God for his faithfulness**
WITH: **paper, pens, instruments (optional)**

1 Get your young people to imagine they have been asked to write a song for Isaac and Rebekah's wedding ceremony. The song should tell a little bit of their story and praise God for his faithfulness.

2 Divide the group into twos and threes to write their songs. Depending on how musical the young people are, you could also provide a few instruments so they could compose a tune.

3 Once everyone has shared their creativity with the whole group, encourage a few people to praise God for his faithfulness.

PRACTICAL

WHAT: **encouragement**
WHY: **to encourage those who are struggling**

1 Ask everyone in the group to think of someone who is struggling to believe that God has a good plan for their lives.

2 Say a prayer on behalf of the group, leaving a time of silence for people to say their own prayer for the person they are thinking about.

3 Suggest that the young people encourage that person this week by contacting them. They could email, text or phone, visit them or make them a card.

CREATIVE

WHAT: **timeline**
WHY: **to remember God's amazing faithfulness over the years**
WITH: **a sheet of wallpaper, Post-it notes, pens**

1 Ask everyone to write down a few amazing things God has done in their lives onto Post-it notes (one thing per Post-it note). Get them to put an approximate date on each note.

2 Create a timeline (a sheet of wallpaper would be ideal) with a cross on the left-hand edge, 'present day' written three-quarters of the way along, and 'the future' written on the right-hand edge.

3 Make a note of some key events where God has shown his faithfulness and done amazing things. For example, mark on the timeline when your church began or ancestors became Christians. Then add all the Post-it notes to the timeline.

4 Now give everyone another Post-it and get them to write on it something they are concerned about in the future. Then, attach these to the right-hand side of the timeline.

5 Conclude by thanking God for the amazing way he works and for his faithfulness. Also, pray that we would have faith that he will help us in the future.

MORE ON THIS THEME:

If you want to do a short series with your group, other sessions that work well with this one are:

5	*At long last!*	*Genesis 18:1–15; 21:1–8*
6	*Are you sure, God?*	*Genesis 22*
8	*Family rivalries*	*Genesis 25:19–34; 27:1–45*

7

AMAZING HEADLINES

Number these headlines from 1 to 10: 1 being the most amazing, 10 being the least amazing.

Fiji win Rugby World Cup

Milton Keynes Dons 7 Manchester United 0

BOY FALLS FROM SEVENTEENTH FLOOR AND LIVES

Freak wrong number is long-lost sister

FOUR DAYS LOCKED IN CELLAR WITHOUT FOOD OR WATER AND LIVED

My heart stopped four times

Prime Minister says sorry for all the mistakes

GRAVE ROBBED; BODY MISSING

100–1 OUTSIDER WINS THE NATIONAL

Masterpiece worth millions found in loft

Bible bit
Genesis 24

God promised to make a great nation out of Abraham's descendants. Problem number one – Abraham didn't have a son. Eventually Isaac was born. Problem number two – Isaac didn't have a wife.

After learning from his previous mistakes, Abraham didn't want to rush things. He didn't want Isaac to marry just anyone – he wanted him to marry someone from his own people.

Lots of what happens in this passage might strike you as a little odd – this story is from a very different culture where things like dating, engagements and marriage were done very differently! However, don't let these differences prevent you from seeing the amazing ways in which God works and how he continues to be faithful to his promises.

You may live in a very different culture, but God still has a plan, he still works in amazing ways and he is still faithful to his promises.

RESOURCE PAGE

USE WITH SESSION 7 BIBLE EXPERIENCE 'LEVEL 3 SWITCH ON'

Matchmaking

Read Genesis 24:1–9
If you had been the servant, what would you have said to Abraham?

Why do you think Abraham was so keen for Isaac not to marry a Canaanite girl or to move away from the area?

Have you made any promises lately? If so, what can you learn from Abraham's servant?

Read Genesis 24:10–27
What can we learn about the servant's faith in God?

Presumably, the servant had learned everything he knew about God from Abraham. What can we learn about Abraham from this? In what ways should we be like Abraham?

Read Genesis 24:28–53
What can we learn about Rebekah's family from these verses?

How do you think you would have responded to Abraham's servant if you had been part of Rebekah's family?

Why do you think they responded like they did?

Read Genesis 24:54–67
What do we learn about God and his plans from this story?

Dating is usually done very differently these days. However, what key things can we learn from this story about relationships?

Bible: Genesis 25:19–34; 27:1–45

FAMILY RIVALRIES

THE AIM: To discover that God is faithful through imperfect people

The aim unpacked

The aim of this session is to encourage us all that God's promises can be fulfilled through imperfect people – which is a good job really, because there aren't too many perfect people around. Be sensitive as you lead this session. Some of the young people in your group may, for whatever reason, be struggling with family life at the moment.

WAY IN

theGRID MAGAZINE

WHAT: survey
WHY: to think about family relationships
WITH: magazine pages 52 and 53

1 Make sure everyone has a copy of the 'Family life survey' from pages 52 and 53. Give the young people plenty of time to complete the survey and add up their score.

2 Explain that the lower your score was, the more likely you are to be a peacemaker at home. The lowest scores were given for attempting to talk, negotiate and bring harmony rather than just opting to have a quiet life and hiding away from conflict.

3 Introduce the session by explaining that it's about two brothers – one who was 'Daddy's boy' and the other who was 'Mummy's boy'.

SCENE SETTER

WHAT: family misfortunes
WHY: to think about families
WITH: rubbish bin

1 Explain that this session is about a family with its share of problems.

2 Give out paper and pens. Invite the young people to write, 'I hate it when my...' and add the title of a family member (mum, dad, brother, sister) – not their name – and then complete the sentence. (Say that the papers will be anonymous, but some may be read out.) When they have finished, invite them to screw up the paper and throw it in the bin.

3 After a few minutes, read out a few of the sentences and see which ones other young people empathise with. Explain that families can be places of love but also of irritation. Today's session is about a major family falling out. Be sensitive to young people who may have difficult family situations.

4 At the end of the session you may want to destroy the papers in the bin and pray together that God would help the young people to be the family members he wants them to be.

5 Balance this exercise out by repeating it, but this time with the sentence, 'I love it when my...' This time, stick the pieces of paper on a wall.

THEMED GAME

WHAT: card game
WHY: to think about tricks and cheats
WITH: packs of cards

1 Explain to the group that you are going to play the card game Cheat. Divide the young people into groups of about four and give each group a deck of playing cards. They are to shuffle and deal the cards until there are none left.

2 The aim of the game is to be the first to get rid of all your cards. Everyone takes turns to play a single card or a set of cards of the same value (for example, three kings) onto the pile. As they place their cards they have to say what they are.

3 Players can lie about what they have played (for example, someone can say there are three kings when it's actually two aces hidden under one king). Other players can challenge them by saying, 'Cheat'. Then the cards that were just played have to be shown. If the person is lying, they have to pick up all the cards from the pile, but if they are telling the truth then the person who challenged has to pick up all the cards.

4 Explain to the group that this session is about someone who cheated his brother out of something very important.

BIBLE EXPERIENCE

LEVEL 1: CONNECT

WHAT: **the perfect crime**
WHY: **to discover that God is faithful through imperfect people**
WITH: **graph paper, cardboard, model cars, road maps, flip chart or whiteboard, marker pens, prize**

1 Explain to the group that it's unlikely that any other youth leader in the world will tell their group to do what you are about to! In small teams, challenge them to spend a few minutes devising a plan as to how they might go about stealing the Crown Jewels from the Tower of London! Using the equipment provided, they should prepare a presentation of their plan. You may like to start off by showing a TV or film clip of an elaborate robbery.

2 Invite each group to present their plan, then hold a secret ballot to vote for the best. However, when you award the winner's prize, don't go by the voting – make your own decision!

3 Ask a few volunteers to read aloud Genesis 25:19–34 and discuss how they feel about this trick. Now paraphrase Genesis 27:1–45. Again ask for the group's response. How do they think Isaac, Rebekah, Esau and Jacob would have felt as the story unfolded?

4 Explain that this story reveals that God is faithful through imperfect people. God's plan unfolded despite the fact that many of the people involved made mistakes and had serious character flaws. Chat together about how this makes the young people feel about themselves.

5 It's now time to own up to the trick you played earlier during the voting and announce the real winner. However, explain that there is not another prize. Discuss how this 'trick' makes the group feel and relate it to the story. Conclude by warning the group that if the Crown Jewels are stolen this week, you will report them to the police!

LEVEL 2: INTERFACE

WHAT: **story**
WHY: **to discover that God is faithful through imperfect people**
WITH: **Bibles, magazine page 54**

1 Invite some young people to read Genesis 25:19–34 aloud to the group. Ask the group members to share their reactions to this story: how does it make them feel?

2 Give out copies of page 54. Allocate parts and ask the actors to read it as dramatically as possible.

3 Again, before jumping in to explain everything, see how the young people react to the story. Give them space to talk about how the story makes them feel and how they think Isaac, Rebekah, Esau and Jacob may have felt as the story unfolded.

4 Discuss these questions:

- Do you think it's fair when cheats prosper?
- Do you think Jacob was actually a cheat? Why (not)?
- How does it make you feel knowing that God works through imperfect people?

5 Conclude by making the point that no one is perfect. Romans 3:23 tells us that 'all have sinned and are not good enough for God's glory'. But God, by his grace, makes it possible for us to have a relationship with him, and he chooses to work through us.

LEVEL 3: SWITCH ON

WHAT: **Bible study**
WHY: **to discover that God is faithful through imperfect people**
WITH: **Bibles**

1 Ask everyone to share with the group their favourite story. Then discuss these two questions:

- Why are stories told?
- How are stories told?

2 Ask a few volunteers to read Genesis 25:19–34 and then ask the same two questions.

3 Explain that many stories that are now part of our Bible were circulated orally for many years before they were written down. Stories such as this one would have been passed down from generation to generation so that children could learn about their history. This particular story explains the start of the ongoing rivalry between Israel (Jacob's people) and the Edomites (Esau's people).

4 Now ask some volunteers to read Genesis 27:1–45. Then ask, 'Why do you think this story was told?'

5 Discuss with the young people whether they think Jacob was a cheat, or whether he was just ensuring he got what he was entitled to (read Genesis 25:34). Explain that all the stories about how God built up the people of Israel into a great nation would have been very encouraging for the Jews to hear, as they clearly communicate God's faithfulness. Ask the young people to consider the lessons we can learn from the stories we've read today. Suggest, if necessary, that one of the things we can learn is that God is faithful through imperfect people.

6 Conclude by inviting group members to share stories from their own lives to encourage other people that God is faithful through imperfect people.

RESPOND

MUSICAL

WHAT: **song**
WHY: **to cry out to God about the unfairness in the world**
WITH: **guitar or some blues songs**

1 You may like to begin this activity by playing a couple of blues tracks (for example, something by Muddy Waters, John Lee Hooker or Eric Clapton) to give the feel of the style.

2 In advance, ask one of the leaders or young people to bring in a guitar and play a simple twelve-bar blues rhythm. Read the words of Psalm 22 and/or 137 over the rhythm. Explain that these 'lamenting psalms' are predecessors of today's blues music.

3 Encourage the young people to contribute their own verses to a blues song that laments how unfair the world can often seem, and to ask God to intervene.

PRACTICAL

WHAT: **praying**
WHY: **to pray for difficult situations**
WITH: **selection of recent local and national newspapers, your church's newsletter**

1 Lay out the main news pages from the papers and your church's newsletter face up on the floor.

2 Gather around the pages in small groups and share together the names of people and situations where bad things seem to be happening.

3 Encourage everyone to say short prayers asking God to help the people in these situations and to bring good things out of the bad events.

CREATIVE

WHAT: **posters**
WHY: **to encourage people that God can work through imperfect people**
WITH: **large sheets of paper, art materials**

1 If your young people know the Bible fairly well, ask them to make a list of some of the imperfect people who were used by God – for example, Moses was a murderer, David had an affair and Peter denied that he ever knew Jesus.

3 Divide the young people into twos and ask each pair to choose one of these characters. Then invite them to make posters with the materials provided. Explain that their posters will be displayed somewhere in the church and should encourage people that God works in and through imperfect people. Maybe something along the lines of 'God worked through X, so we're sure he can work through you!'

MORE ON THIS THEME:

If you want to do a short series with your group, other sessions that work well with this one are:

5	*At long last!*	*Genesis 18:1–15; 21:1–8*
6	*Are you sure, God?*	*Genesis 22*
7	*Matchmaking*	*Genesis 24*

FAMILY LIFE SURVEY

Read through the following scenarios. Which response best describes what you would think or do? Be honest!

1

Your little sister has been in your room and borrowed some of your clothes. Are you:

- A — Furious? You'll get her back.
- B — Annoyed? You'll be having a word.
- C — Irritated? You'll mention it to your parents.
- D — Fascinated? You'll see what she has chosen.

2

Your mum asks for help in the kitchen when you were about to phone your mate. Do you:

- A — Text them and say you'll call later?
- B — Call them but tell Mum you're 'just coming'?
- C — Go straight to the kitchen?
- D — Go and sulk in the toilet?

3

It's Saturday, but instead of being with your mates, you're in the car visiting horrid family members. On the journey, do you:

- A — Text your mates?
- B — Sulk moodily and ignore everyone?
- C — Have a catch-up chat with your family?
- D — Rant, moan and complain the whole way there?

6

Your dad's annoyed because you took too long to get ready and now you're both late. Do you:

- A — Chat cheerily as if nothing is wrong?
- B — Grovel and promise to try harder next time?
- C — Rant back at him for making you late the other day?
- D — Apologise and make him a card later?

7

You've been told to be home by 9pm which, in your opinion, is ridiculously early. Do you:

- A — See if there's any room for negotiation?
- B — Moan and stay out too late anyway?
- C — Make yourself a nuisance, hoping they'll buckle?
- D — Accept gracefully – it's nice they care about your safety?

8

Your birthday present is not what you wanted. Do you:

- A — Make yourself feel better by secretly trashing it?
- B — Ask if they still have the receipt?
- C — Moan at them for picking a stupid present?
- D — Thank them and try to keep quiet?

8

4

Your dad has made dinner tonight. He's not very good at cooking but tries to help. Do you:

- A Vomit on the table in protest?
- B Thank him and offer to help next time?
- C Eat it grudgingly?
- D Say that you'd rather have takeaways?

5

One of your DVDs is missing from its case. Do you:

- A Accuse everyone in the house in turn?
- B Go straight to whoever is usually at fault?
- C Ask at the next mealtime if anyone has seen it?
- D Ignore it and expect it will turn up?

9

You're on a family holiday but no one wants to do anything except read and sunbathe. Do you:

- A Organise a game of beach cricket?
- B Nag and moan until someone plays with you?
- C Go and make friends with people further along the beach?
- D Subtly bury your dad, his wallet and the hotel keys in the sand?

10

It's Christmas Day afternoon! Are you:

- A Moaning because it's all so boring these days?
- B Too stuffed to move?
- C Putting up with pointless chat from elderly relatives?
- D Offering to help with whatever's next?

Score yourself, depending on what answer you have ticked for each scenario, as follows:

1. a=4, b=3, c=2, d=1
2. a=2, b=3, c=1, d=4
3. a=2, b=3, c=1, d=4
4. a=4, b=1, c=2, d=3
5. a=3, b=4, c=1, d=2
6. a=3, b=2, c=4, d=1
7. a=2, b=4, c=3, d=1
8. a=2, b=3, c=4, d=1
9. a=1, b=3, c=2, d=4
10. a=4, b=3, c=2, d=1

Score 30–39
You expect family life to revolve around you and are always wanting people to entertain you. If a decision doesn't go your way, you're likely to kick off.

Score 20–29
You can be quite patient and gentle – but you have your limits. Often, if there's conflict, you run away and hide from it rather than dealing with it.

Score 10–19
You are a fantastic son or daughter and your brothers and/or sisters just love having you around! Are you sure you're not an angel?

FAMILY RIVALRIES

Cast: Isaac, Esau, Jacob and Rebekah
Set: Isaac is in bed. He calls for Esau.
Feel: A bit *EastEnders*

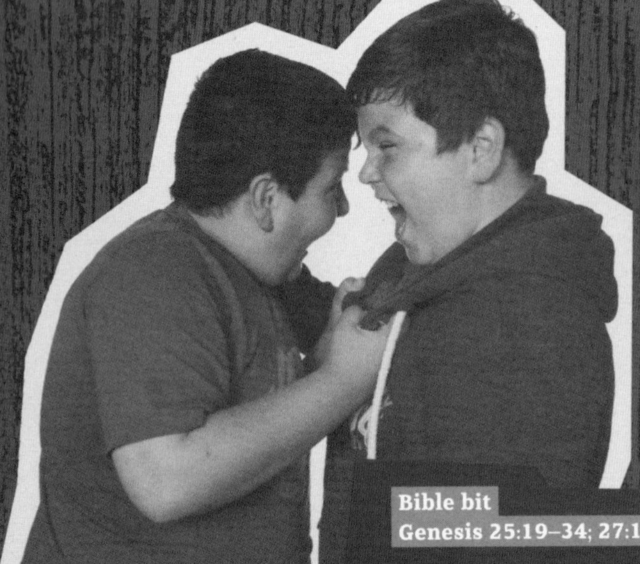

Isaac: Esau!
Esau: Yes, Dad?
Isaac: I feel so old now. You are a good hunter. Go and catch some dinner and then we will eat together. I fear it may be my last.
Rebekah: *(Whispering.)* Jacob!
Jacob: Yes, Mum?
Rebekah: Go and get a couple of goats from the field. While Esau is out catching something I'll make a meal and you can pretend to be your brother. Then Dad will give you the blessing.
Jacob: Like, duh, Mum. Esau's the hairiest man I know. Even our blind dad will know the difference.
Rebekah: Trust me. I'll sort it. Put your brother's clothes on.
Jacob: What?
Rebekah: Do it. And put these goat skins over your arms and round your neck.
Jacob: *(Approaching Isaac.)* Hey, Dad. I got your lunch.
Isaac: Good boy. How come you were so quick?
Jacob: God helped me.
Isaac: And what happened to your voice? You sound like your brother. Are you pulling my leg? Come here.
Jacob: *(Trying to speak differently.)* No, Dad. It's me, Esau. Feel my skin.
Isaac: *(Rubbing his son's neck and arms.)* Funny. You sounded just like your brother for a bit. He's a bit of a twister if you ask me, but *(inhaling deeply)* there's no mistaking the smell of you. I bless you.
Jacob: *(Running out to his mum.)* Yeah, fooled him. The silly old man. He can die now.
Rebekah: Calm down. He may be old but I love that man.
Jacob: Sorry, Mum.
Esau: Hey, everyone. I'm back. Let's get cooking! *(Silence.)* OK, ignore me if you want but I'm gonna make Dad's dinner. *(Approaching Isaac.)* Hey, Dad. Brought you some wild meat stew.
Isaac: What's this? Are you having a laugh?
Esau: No, Dad. It's me, Esau. Eat up your favourite food.
Isaac: Then I'm sorry but your conniving, cheating brother has had the blessing. I know it's tough but it's gone now. He's got it.
Esau: Bless me too, Dad! Please?
Isaac: Can't, son. You know the rules. We need rules. One blessing, once. Jacob's gone and nicked it.
Esau: Where is he? I'll kill him!
Rebekah: *(To Jacob.)* I think you'd better leave town for a bit...

Bible bit
Genesis 25:19–34; 27:1–45

This story isn't necessarily clear cut. Was Jacob wrong to trick Isaac the way he did? After all, Esau did just give away his rights as the firstborn son to Jacob in return for some food. Perhaps Jacob realised the significance of God's promises whereas Esau didn't? Who did deserve Isaac's blessing?

However you answer those questions, it would appear that Isaac's family was a little dysfunctional! Through this story we can be encouraged as we discover that God works through imperfect people – which is a good job really, because there aren't too many perfect people around.

Bible: Exodus 16:1 – 17:7

THE WILDERNESS YEARS

THE AIM: To live each day relying on God

The aim unpacked

With this session, we pick up the story of Moses after he led the Israelites out of Egypt and look at the need to rely on God. Relying on God was something the Israelites had to do as they travelled through the desert. However, it did not mean that they always felt close to God or actually did rely on him. The same is true for us today.

WAY IN

theGRID MAGAZINE

WHAT: **case studies**
WHY: **to introduce some areas of need for 11–14s**
WITH: **magazine page 59, flip chart or whiteboard**

1 Hand out copies of page 59. Challenge everyone to suggest answers to the problem-page letters in 'You know what you need?' You could work on the replies together by reading them out and then asking for suggestions.

2 Alternatively, ask the group to work on answers individually or in pairs and then feed back their ideas.

3 Ask, 'How do these needs compare with those of people who don't have enough food, clean water or somewhere to live?' (The immediate reaction might be that these needs are much more important, but help them to see that a whole range of personal needs can be very painful to the individuals concerned.)

4 Ask the group to imagine the letters are from Christians. Would they change their answers in the light of the Israelites' experience in the desert? Use this to explore what it means to rely on God in the kinds of 'desert' situations that young people face today.

SCENE SETTER

WHAT: **grumbling competition**
WHY: **to think about our reactions to needs**
WITH: **prize**

1 Invite the young people to be competitors in *The Whingiest Link*. (Anne Robinson impressions are optional!) You provide a topic that they must all complain about. Go round in a circle with each person saying one whingy thing; anyone who hesitates or is not sufficiently whingy is eliminated. Continue with a different topic until only one person is left. You could include:

- the price of music downloads
- the school toilets
- the taste of Marmite or Vegemite
- this room
- people who grumble all the time
- unfair group leaders

2 Award the prize to the person who was eliminated first.

3 Ask the young people what they grumble about most. Which of those things are important issues and which are just things that annoy us? When people have genuine, big needs they may grumble, but in what other ways might they (and we) react?

THEMED GAME

WHAT: **target game and quiz**
WHY: **to find out about desert conditions**
WITH: **plastic bottles with tops, page 60, soft ball, two identical larger containers**

1 To prepare, copy and cut up page 60 and stick each statement to the bottom of a plastic bottle. Put some water in each bottle (varying amounts) and put the tops on. Stand the bottles at one end of the room with spaces between them.

2 Explain that you are in the desert and the aim of the game is to find water. Play in two teams. The teams take turns to try to knock over one of the bottles with the ball. If they succeed, they must read out the tip stuck to the bottom of the bottle. Their team must agree whether it is genuine or fake. If the team is correct, tip the water from the bottle into that team's container. Continue until all the bottles have been knocked over. The team with the most water wins. Choose any additional rules you may need (such as they should throw only from behind a line, or they must roll the ball along the floor).

3 Finish with a comment about how difficult it is to survive in the desert. It's a massive challenge for anyone who is not used to it.

Answers: 1 T; 2 F; 3 F; 4 F; 5 T; 6 T; 7 F; 8 T; 9 T; 10 F

BIBLE EXPERIENCE

LEVEL 1: CONNECT

WHAT: **drama and personal story**
WHY: **to live each day relying on God**
WITH: **pages 61 and 62, Bibles, guest (optional)**

1 Perform the sketch from pages 61 and 62, or arrange in advance for two of your young people to perform it. It can be read, but will be better if it is learned and acted out.

2 Ask the group to suggest what they would like to say to Zak in this situation. Encourage varied answers without saying that they are 'right' or 'wrong'. Ask what they would like to say to Bek.

3 Explain that although the sketch relates to events in the Bible thousands of years ago, the big question it raises is still an issue now: 'Can we trust God when things get tough?' Talk about a relevant experience in your own life. Don't make it all sound too easy – just be straightforward and honest about a real Christian life. Alternatively, interview a guest with a relevant life story.

4 Read Exodus 17:1–7 to the group to see what happened to the real people in Zak and Bek's situation.

LEVEL 2: INTERFACE

WHAT: **reacting to events**
WHY: **to live each day relying on God**
WITH: **Bibles, soft ball**

1 Ask each group member to write down privately what they might say in each of the following situations – just one phrase or sentence:

- Your group leader has taken you camping two days' walk from the nearest house. You ran out of food 12 hours ago.
- A school friend gives you some strange-looking new food to try.
- A teacher gives you instructions that don't make sense.
- Your group leader tells you to memorise a verse from the Bible about God's love.

2 Recap the story so far – the Israelites have been set free from Egypt, after crying out to God for help.

3 Now ask the young people to imagine they are the Israelites in the desert. Either read or ask a young person to read the following verses of Exodus 16:1 – 17:7. After each section, throw a soft ball at random from person to person. Ask each one to say something that they might have said as an Israelite at that point in the story, using ideas from what they wrote for the situations in point 1. After everyone has contributed, or when ideas are exhausted, read the next verses:

- Exodus 16:1,2 (grumbling)
- Exodus 16:3,9–15a (reaction to manna)
- Exodus 16:15b–19 (reactions to Moses' instructions)
- Exodus 16:20–24,31,32 (reactions to keeping some manna)
- Exodus 17:3–7 (reactions to having no water)

4 Chat about the following questions:

- Was it reasonable for the Israelites to grumble when they were without food and water?
- How do you react when things are tough for you? Does it make you feel less confident about God?
- What can we do to rely on God every day?

LEVEL 3: SWITCH ON

WHAT: **applied Bible study**
WHY: **to live each day relying on God**
WITH: **Bibles, magazine page 58**

1 Read Exodus 16:1–3 together, and recap together the story so far in Exodus. Discuss:

- How well did the Israelites rely on God when things got tough?
- Was that reasonable?
- Would we have reacted in the same way?
- Why should we rely on God?

2 Give out copies of page 58. Ask the young people, in pairs, to decide which statements are 'good' reasons, and which are 'bad' reasons for relying on God. They should discuss why the reasons are good or bad, and then compare their answers with the rest of the group. Afterwards, encourage them to read Exodus 16:4–18.

3 Discuss, 'What reasons did the Israelites have for trusting God after this?' Ask the young people to look out for any of the 'good' reasons: for instance, 'God had cared for them', 'God was always with them (v 10)', 'God showed them who he is (v 12)'. Draw out that some of the 'bad' reasons for trusting God may crumble when things get tough. Look at Exodus 17:1–7 to see what happened soon after.

4 Ask, 'How can we rely on God?' Ask each person to look at the different ways of relying on God, and encourage them to choose one that they would like to work on. Share ideas and tips for actually doing them. Agree on any that you can put into practice as a group and plan how you are going to do that.

RESPOND

MUSICAL

WHAT: **declaration of trust**
WHY: **to affirm that we rely on God**
WITH: **selection of backing music reflecting different moods, playback equipment, words of the declaration of trust (see below) displayed, flip chart or whiteboard**

1 Ask the young people to suggest one thing that they all need to remember from today's session, such as, 'to rely on God' or, 'God is always with us'. This needs to be in their own words, not yours. Turn their ideas into a declaration beginning 'We...' or 'God...' For instance, 'We will rely on God', or 'God will always be with us'. You could run two or three statements together. Display the declaration on a flip chart, screen or whiteboard.

2 Use the declaration as a collective response of trust in God. It will be even more effective if the young people take turns to say the introductory three-word phrases:

- Wherever we go, we... (or God...)
- Whoever we meet, ...
- However we live, ...
- Whenever we fail, ...
- Whatever life brings, ...

3 Say your declaration of trust in God over different background music that reflects different moods, such as peaceful, stormy, confident or mysterious. (The easiest sort of music to use is instrumental, but what about trying it over some contemporary 'angry' forms of music? Find 'radio-friendly' versions of songs that speak about life's problems. You could ask your young people for suggestions.) Ask the group to comment on which works best. Point out that whatever our mood and circumstances, we can rely on God.

PRACTICAL

WHAT: **making time for God**
WHY: **to make time for personal prayer and reflection in our daily lives**
WITH: **paper, pens**

1 Show the group a large envelope in which you have collected a few items to reflect your week: for example, a ticket, a TV magazine clipping of something you watched, an item picked up while walking, a receipt.

2 Give each group member a similar empty envelope. Ask them to take it away and use it to collect items from their lives between now and the next session. They can include anything at all. Suggest that, as they do this, they remember that God is with them in that part of their lives and that they talk to him about it (for example, an item from school – talk to him about school). Invite them to bring the filled envelopes back next time. With a younger group, you could give a more structured list of about ten items to find, such as a sheet of paper, something plastic, something orange, something from someone who lives with you, something from school, a food wrapper.

3 At the next session, look together at what they have collected. Use this to get to know each other better and to emphasise that God is with us in every part of our lives – so we can rely on him in every part too.

4 Close by praying for the group, asking God to be with them through everything they do and to give them the strength to rely on him.

CREATIVE

WHAT: **making a manna jar**
WHY: **to remember what God has done for us**
WITH: **large jar or other container, assorted craft materials (such as glue, coloured paper, stickers, glitter glue, paint)**

1 Talk about the manna jar in Exodus 16:32–34. This was one person's supply of manna for one day, kept in a special jar so no one would ever forget what God had done for them in the desert.

2 Work together to create a 'manna jar' for your group. Explain that, inside it, you will keep reminders of what God has done for you. Anyone in the group can suggest things to put inside. You can add to it in future sessions – for example, reminders of answered prayers (such as a hospital name bracelet when someone recovers from illness) or items linked to Bible passages you look at (such as a cross).

3 Invite the young people to decorate the container: they need to 'own' the project. After decorating it, invite ideas of what to put inside and find or make these. With a larger group, some can do the decorating while others work on items to go inside.

4 Place the collected items around the jar in the centre of the group. Spend time thanking God for all he has done for us – in difficult and good times. Do this in silence or with background music, or pray openly, depending on your group.

5 Don't forget to add items in future sessions – your own ideas and the young people's. From time to time, take them all out and chat about them, to help you all remember what God has done and to pray.

MORE ON THIS THEME:

If you want to do a short series with your group, other sessions that work well with this one are:

10	*The top ten dos and don'ts*	*Exodus 19:16 – 20:17*
11	*Face to face*	*Exodus 33:7–23; 34:1–9,29–35*
12	*Multidimensional worship*	*Exodus 35:20 – 36:7; 39:32 – 40:38*

WHY SHOULD WE RELY ON GOD?

The Israelites' grumbling in Exodus 16:1–3 shows that they weren't always great at relying on God, but would we have been any better? And why should we rely on God anyway?

Put a tick by the 'good' reasons, and a cross by the 'bad' reasons.

- ☐ Because God knows us completely and loves us.
- ☐ Because of who God is.
- ☐ Because God will give me all I want.
- ☐ Because God has cared for me in the past.
- ☐ Because he has told us to.
- ☐ Because things are going well for me.
- ☐ Because God likes good people like me.
- ☐ Because God is always with us.
- ☐ Because my friends in the group do.

God soon provided the Israelites with a very good reason for trusting him. Check out Exodus 16:4–18 to find out what it was.

HOW CAN WE RELY ON GOD?

There are many different ways that we can rely on God. Tick one of these that you want to work on over the next few weeks.

- ☐ Make choices in the way we think God wants.
- ☐ Find things to thank God for in any situation.
- ☐ Pray anywhere, any time.
- ☐ Look to other Christians for help.
- ☐ Remember that God is with us.

9

YOU KNOW WHAT YOU NEED?

Dear *theGRID*,

My problem is that everyone thinks I'm useless. My mates make fun of me because they're all better at stuff than I am. My dad always moans at me at home. And the teachers always point out the mistakes in my work and never say anything good. I'm sick of it all.

Downhearted of Dudley

Dear Downhearted,

I think that...

I just want to ask you...

You could try...

Dear *theGRID*,

I have been ill, on and off, for the last five years. In the bad patches, I find it very hard to keep going. Sometimes I just want to give up. It looks as if my illness may carry on for years to come. How can I face the future?

Perplexed of Perth

Dear Perplexed,

I think that...

I just want to ask you...

You could try...

RESOURCE PAGE

USE WITH SESSION 9 WAY IN 'THEMED GAME'

1 Plan your route between watering places carefully.

2 Find cistern beetles, which have special water pouches, and squeeze them.

3 Drink the water supplies you are carrying as soon as possible. Your body is a better way of transporting water.

4 Go to the top of a hill and catch water from passing clouds.

5 Turn over half-buried stones just before sunrise. Dew will form on the cool underside.

6 Look out for bees. They fly in a straight line to and from water, up to 1 km away.

7 Collect your spit and save it to drink again later.

8 Look out for pigeons and doves – they can only exist near fresh water.

9 Use dirty water to soak your clothes, so you lose less water by sweating.

10 Follow the penguins.

USE WITH SESSION 9 BIBLE EXPERIENCE 'LEVEL 1 CONNECT'

Dying for a drink

Characters: Zak (male) and Bek (female)

Scene: The beginning of Exodus 17 (go and read it!). The Israelites are in the desert and running out of water. Zak and Bek have come out early in the morning to try to collect dew. Zak sits down, depressed. Bek is busy looking for suitable big, flat stones and heaving them over.

Zak: This desert is a total nightmare. Burning hot in the day and here we are in the middle of the night and it's freezing.

Bek: It isn't the middle of the night, Zak, it's nearly sunrise. And if you helped with the work, you wouldn't be so cold.

Zak: How can I help when I'm so thirsty?

Bek: Look, here's a good big, flat rock. Now, one, two, three, urghhh!

(She manages to roll the rock over and immediately crouches, nose to its upturned side.)

Nice and cool; now wait for the dew to form.

Zak: Anything happening, Bek?

Bek: Sssh!

Zak: Well?

Bek: I think it's just starting.

(Zak leaps up, rushes over and starts licking the stone.)

Bek: Hey! You've wrecked it.

Zak: There wasn't anything there anyway.

(He flops down again.)

Bek: Oh, I'm so thirsty. I can't go on much longer. Why is this happening to us?

Zak: Moses. That's why.

USE WITH SESSION 9 BIBLE EXPERIENCE 'LEVEL 1 CONNECT'

Bek: But hasn't God looked after us so far?

Zak: What? As soon as we got into this desert we ran out of water and then we could only find that really disgusting stuff.

Bek: But Moses made it good and clean.

(She starts again looking for suitable stones and flipping them over as the dialogue continues.)

Zak: I haven't trusted this whole plan from the start. We shouldn't have left Egypt in the first place.

Bek: And God has given us food to eat – manna on the ground that we collect every day.

Zak: Well, that's dodgy too, isn't it? First we run out of bread completely. Then we find this weird stuff to eat that goes off if you keep it. If some god is doing this, why can't he just give us a good supply of decent bread that will keep?

Bek: But God must be doing it. Hasn't he shown himself to us in a shining cloud? He set us free from Egypt and he's with us in the desert. He must be.

Zak: So why doesn't he give us some water then?

Bek: I don't know. I don't know. I don't know.

(She collapses.)

Zak: I'm going to find Moses. He brought us out here to murder us. Well, perhaps I'll just organise for him to be the first to die.

(Exits, helping Bek to walk.)

Bible: Exodus 19:16 – 20:17

THE TOP TEN DOS AND DON'TS

THE AIM: To examine how to do God's will

The aim unpacked

In this session, we'll be thinking about God's commandments – his rules – and we'll also consider the bigger picture whereby we are called to follow Jesus. Throughout the session, we need to point out that salvation doesn't come by keeping the Ten Commandments. The emphasis needs to be on 'doing God's will' by having faith in Jesus and allowing the Holy Spirit to change us in the way God wants him to.

WAY IN

theGRID MAGAZINE

WHAT: **alien advice**
WHY: **to introduce the idea that advice is given to benefit the person on the receiving end**
WITH: **magazine page 68**

1 Ask the young people to imagine that they have been asked to give advice about life on Earth to an alien who has just arrived from the planet Zork. Distribute copies of page 68 and ask the young people to complete the 'Alien helpline' quiz.

2 Bring the group together and share the results. Is anyone on their way to the planet Zork?

3 Draw out the idea that if we want what's best for someone – their safety, happiness and well-being – we'll give them good rules to live by; not rules that stop them doing everything, but rules that give them the best chance of the very best life.

SCENE SETTER

WHAT: **origami**
WHY: **to illustrate the idea of doing something the best way**
WITH: **origami paper, scrap paper, instructions for a simple origami model**

1 Practise the origami model in advance. If you can't get origami paper, use squares of quality coloured or white paper.

2 Say that you're going to demonstrate how to make a fantastic origami model. Look at the instructions in a dismissive way; sneer disdainfully and say you can do it fine without those, thank you very much. Demonstrate, folding the paper in a completely slipshod way, using scrap paper, and not creasing it properly. The finished model should look a total wreck.

3 With a worried air, say that it should have turned out better than that. Ask why on earth it didn't. (Because you didn't follow the instructions properly.) It was easy, fast and cheap, but it wasn't the best. Throw it away.

4 Now invite everyone to have a go at making the model properly, using the origami paper and following the instructions.

5 Say that today you'll be thinking about the best way to live.

THEMED GAME

WHAT: **game without rules**
WHY: **to show that rules can be for our good**
WITH: **large safe space, soft ball, two goals**

1 It's best not to try this with a very physical group, as someone may get hurt, but if you think it will be safe, this idea makes for a powerful illustration. Say that the aim of the game is to score as many goals as you can. Shout, 'Go!'

2 It probably won't be long before the players are demanding rules or instructions, or claiming that someone is cheating. Say it's impossible to cheat – there are no rules. You have no instructions – just play.

3 After they have had a go, and before open warfare breaks out, stop the game and ask what went wrong. With no rules to play by, there is no game; the smaller, weaker players miss out. It's boring for all except the few who can get hold of the ball, and it can be dangerous. Ask for some suggestions of rules, then play again, following the rules suggested.

BIBLE EXPERIENCE

LEVEL 1: CONNECT

WHAT: sorting
WHY: to examine how to do God's will
WITH: copies of cards from page 69, flip chart or whiteboard, Bibles

1 Divide the group into teams of between two and five. Give each team a set of the commandment cards from page 69. Say you are looking for the top five commandments.

2 Give the teams two minutes to read and sort out the top five commandments for each of the following categories:

- The top five commandments I should live by to make the world a better place.
- The top five commandments other people should live by to make the world a better place.
- The top five commandments everyone in the world throughout history should live by to make the world a better place.
- The top five commandments that show us the best way to live.

3 On a flip chart, keep score for each commandment, giving a point every time it features in a top five. Don't worry if the ridiculous ones score high – this is to be expected.

4 Declare which commandments are the top five overall. If it hasn't arisen already, point out that some people think God gave his Ten Commandments to make life miserable and restricted. Explain, however, that God was really trying to show his people the best way to live – just like the best way to use a new gadget is to follow the maker's instructions so you get to know all its cool features and don't break it. God shows us how to love him and other people. He also gave good advice for all people everywhere, throughout history.

5 Still in their groups, challenge the young people to list the Ten Commandments that God gave to Moses. Remind them that God wants to show us the best way to live – not the easiest way.

6 Check their lists against Exodus 20:1–17 by reading it to the group.

LEVEL 2: INTERFACE

WHAT: debate
WHY: to examine how to do God's will
WITH: a copy of page 69 or each commandment written on a strip of paper, hat (or box or bag), dice

1 Divide the group into pairs. If you have fewer than 20 in your group, decide whether each pair will debate more than one commandment or whether you will not cover them all. Cut out the individual commandments from page 69 and place them in a hat, box or bag.

2 Each pair draws a commandment out of the 'hat'. One of them rolls the dice. If they get an even number, they have one minute to convince everyone that the commandment shows us the best way to live. If they get an odd number, they have to convince everyone (in one minute) that the commandment is irrelevant, out of date, unnecessary or a waste of time. The other member of the pair will take the opposite view.

3 Give everyone some preparation time. They can help each other if they wish.

4 Run each debate, allowing comments from the 'floor' after each speaker. Alternate which side of the debate goes first each time. After each pair has spoken and comments have been taken, vote on whether the commandment goes or stays.

5 See what you're left with at the end and repeat any really good points that were made, especially any which demonstrate that the Ten Commandments are God's way of showing us the best way to live – how best to love God and the people around us. If we ignore any of them, either we or other people may get hurt. It may be worth reminding the group that we are only one generation of people living in relatively few years of world history. The Ten Commandments had to be relevant to people over thousands of years in very varied geographical and social settings. Explain that we can find the Ten Commandments in Exodus 20:1–17.

LEVEL 3: SWITCH ON

WHAT: role play
WHY: to examine how to do God's will
WITH: magazine pages 66 and 67, Bibles

1 Say that God gave Moses the Ten Commandments to help his people to live their lives in the best possible way. They show how we can love God and love other people. Invite the group to read Exodus 20:1–17 quietly, asking God to speak through his Word to them as they read. Then ask, 'Are the Ten Commandments still relevant today?'

2 Distribute copies of pages 67 and 68 and invite the young people to read through the 'Sticky situations'. Encourage them to work in pairs to choose one situation and to act it out, giving it a believable ending of their own. (It doesn't necessarily have to be the 'right' ending!)

3 As you watch each scene, ask the rest of the group:

- How are these people going against what God says in one or more of the commandments?
- Who gets hurt?
- How could they have realistically behaved differently in a way that would keep God's laws?

If someone has a suggestion, let them act out the ending of the scene with their 'better' reaction. Ask: Do you all believe it could work out like that? If not, keep trying until, as a group, you find a way that most people can believe.

4 With an older group, you could explore a more complex situation where it seems that keeping one commandment would mean breaking another – for example, if a parent tells a child to lie for them. You could invite the young people to suggest others.

RESPOND

MUSICAL

WHAT: **music-based discussion and prayer**
WHY: **to see how attitudes can be influenced by music**
WITH: **current musical hits, several pieces of playback equipment, 'Wisdom' by Iona (from *Journey into the Morn*) or other meditative music**

1 Say that the musical culture we live in sends out many messages that may not help us to stick to God's best way to live. Say that you have put out a number of music players to listen to in the next five minutes. Ask the young people to go round and listen to what's playing on them and to decide whether each song helps them to live by one or more of the Ten Commandments or whether it encourages them to go against the Ten Commandments. (Alternatively, depending on the available space, keep the group together and play the tracks one after another.) Encourage them to make a note of particular words from any of the songs to back up their opinions. (Try to make sure you have 'radio-friendly' versions of the songs.)

2 After about five minutes, bring them all back together and ask them to feed back what they have found out.

3 Ask everyone to sit in their own space with a pen and paper. Play 'Wisdom' by Iona (or another strong, meditative track). The young people should use the time to think prayerfully through what they have learned in this session and to ask God to speak to them about any areas in their lives where they need to live more closely by the Ten Commandments. They could write down anything to help them remember their reflections.

PRACTICAL

WHAT: **active response**
WHY: **to help the young people make a positive personal response to the Ten Commandments**
WITH: **copies of page 69 or the commandments written out individually, copies of page 70, quiet music, playback equipment**

1 Sit together in a circle. Give out the stone tablet outlines from page 70 and put the jumbled-up slips of paper with the commandments on them, from page 69, in the centre of the circle. Give out glue sticks.

2 Say that God always gives us a choice in the way we live. We can choose to live his way or not. While he would love for us to choose the best way to live, he doesn't force us. It's our decision. This is an opportunity for us to make an honest response to God and to commit ourselves to doing his will.

3 Say that, just as the stone tablets were blank before God gave them to Moses, so these paper versions are blank. Ask the group to look through the cut-up commandments on the slips of paper and to decide for themselves which ones they want to really try to keep this week. They can glue these to their stone tablet as a sign of their commitment to God's way of living. Alternatively, if they prefer, they can write the commandments on the tablets.

4 Play some quiet music to create a prayerful atmosphere as they do this.

5 Encourage them to take their 'tablets' home as a visual reminder of their promise to God to do his will.

CREATIVE

WHAT: **clay craft**
WHY: **to remind the young people of one commandment**
WITH: **Bibles or copies of page 69, air-drying clay, cocktail sticks, leather cord or similar**

1 Ask everyone to choose one commandment that they will really make an effort to keep in the coming weeks in order to do God's will.

2 Give a small piece of air-drying clay to each person and ask them to make a disc out of it. They should then make a small hole in it, large enough for the cord to go through, and use a cocktail stick to etch the number of the commandment they want to work at. On the other side, encourage them to scratch a cross as a reminder that Jesus' death turned the commandments into promises. Explain that through the power of the Holy Spirit and through faith in Jesus we can do God's will. Give them some time to add any extra decoration they would like to their discs. Remind the young people that the original commandments were written on tablets of stone as a sign of how long-lasting they are.

3 When the discs are dry, each young person should thread the leather cord through the hole and wear it as a necklace, bracelet or zip-pull, as a visual and physical reminder.

MORE ON THIS THEME:

If you want to do a short series with your group, other sessions that work well with this one are:

9	*The wilderness years*	*Exodus 16:1 – 17:7*
11	*Face to face*	*Exodus 33:7–23; 34:1–9,29–35*
12	*Multidimensional worship*	*Exodus 35:20 – 36:7; 39:32 – 40:38*

STICKY SITUATIONS

Bible bit
Exodus 20:1–17

It's tempting when we read passages like these to think, 'What a lot of rules; how can anyone keep those? God is such a spoilsport.' However, the Ten Commandments were never intended to be a mere set of rules or ethics. Rather, they were principles and instructions by which the people could respond to the majesty of God, as described in Exodus 19:16–20. The Israelites were to be single - minded in their devotion to the One who had delivered them from Egypt.

Today, as we try to follow these principles and do God's will, it's good to remember that we are not alone in our efforts. We have faith in Jesus and can ask the Holy Spirit to help us.

Look at these sticky situations. Think about how each one might end and write it in the box for each situation.

1

You're at the bus stop. Your mate tells you to say you're underage and get on the bus for a child's fare. It saves 50p!

2

You borrow your sister's skirt to wear to a party (she was out, or you would have asked her permission, honest) and it gets torn. You put it back in her room and hope she doesn't notice. She does and comes into your room. She's not a happy bunny!

NS
10
3
You need new trainers for school. You're shopping with your mum. You know you need designer trainers like everyone else. But she's found a nice pair of supermarket brand for £5.99.
5
The window is definitely broken. Mrs Walter wants to know whether it was you or Dazza – the only people nearby at the time. If you admit it was you, it'll be all your allowance for the next ten years to pay for it. But Dazza gets loads of pocket money. And you don't like him anyway.
4
Joe's your best mate. He's going out with the gorgeous Julie. Julie's friend Jenna says Julie fancies you, not Joe. There's Julie on her own – now's your chance to ask her out.
6
Your best mate could get you a job in the local shop but you'd have to work at the time your theGRID group meets. He thinks it would be a great idea – it pays really well.

ALIEN HELPLINE

Imagine you've been asked to give advice to an alien who has just arrived from the planet Zork. How would you answer these questions?

1

How should I greet the humans I meet?

a) You should smile (turn up the corners of your mouth) and say, 'Hello!'
b) You should never greet anyone. They could be dangerous. Run away, screaming loudly, if they approach you.
c) Punch them in the face and shout, 'Yo, Stinkbag! Was your gran a gorilla?'

2

What should I do to cross a road?

a) Look in both directions and, if no traffic is coming, cross quickly and carefully.
b) Don't ever cross roads. It's far too dangerous. Walk round them. It might be a few hundred miles to the far end, but it's safer.
c) Close your eyes and crawl slowly into the middle of the road.

3

What should I eat?

a) Try a small portion of fruit, vegetables or dairy product and see if they suit you.
b) Don't eat anything – it could be poisonous or explosive.
c) Eat anything that has a skull and crossbones on it.

4

How should I behave at the gatherings called 'football matches'?

a) Watch what everyone else does and enjoy yourself.
b) Never go to a football match – they're really violent.
c) Wear different colours from everyone else and go round telling them to keep the noise down as they're giving you a headache.

5

How should I behave in town centres?

a) Walk around, browsing in the shops, and enjoy yourself.
b) Town centres are full of vicious criminals with deadly weapons. Stay at home.
c) Run around smashing shop windows, shouting, 'Oggy, oggy, oggy!'

6

How should I ride my bicycle?

a) Take your cycling proficiency test and enjoy riding safely.
b) A bicycle? A bicycle? Are you mad? You could fall off! Get injured! Get oil on your trousers! Sell it immediately!
c) Take it straight to the nearest motorway and ride very slowly down the fast lane, waving to the traffic that hoots at you.

7

You have something called the internet. What is it?

a) It's a great way to collect information and to have fun. To avoid dangerous sites, buy a web-screening program.
b) It's full of terrible websites with appalling pictures that will ruin your life for ever. Don't go near it.
c) Type in anything you want and believe everything it tells you on every site you visit. Buy anything that pops up and give out your credit card number to everyone who asks for it.

8

I have seen many fast food outlets. What are they?

a) They can be good once in a while.
b) Fat! Sugar! Ecologically unsound! Teenagers! Germs! Run away!
c) Never eat anywhere else – you need at least five meals from them each day, plus snacks, and make sure you drop the wrappings on the pavement outside.

HOW DID YOU SCORE?

Mostly A:
Please will you come back to my planet for a visit? You're such a kind, thoughtful, generous and responsible human.

Mostly B:
Please come to my planet and I'll give you a padded underground bunker where you can hide for 300 light years.

Mostly C:
Please come to my planet and I'll introduce you to the Voracious Man - eating Six-headed Squid of Zork. It's probably safer than the advice you've given me.

USE WITH SESSION 10 BIBLE EXPERIENCE 'LEVEL 1 CONNECT', 'LEVEL 2 INTERFACE', RESPOND 'PRACTICAL' AND 'CREATIVE'

1 You must not have any other gods.	2 You must wash your hands before eating.
3 You must not squeeze your pimples, or anyone else's.	4 You must not make any idols or worship them.
5 You must not use the name of the Lord your God thoughtlessly.	6 You must be kind to animals, especially your ox and donkey.
7 You must not play ball games on the grass.	8 Remember to keep the Sabbath day holy.
9 Honour your father and mother.	10 Be nice to your brothers and sisters.
11 You must not do anything enjoyable, as it is probably sinful.	12 You must not murder anyone.
13 You must not be guilty of adultery.	14 You must not watch Cert 18 films when you are only 13.
15 You must not offend your neighbour.	16 You must not steal.
17 You must not tell lies about your neighbour.	18 You must eat five portions of fruit and vegetables every day.
19 You must not want to take your neighbour's property.	20 You must put down the toilet lid before leaving the bathroom.

USE WITH SESSION 10 RESPOND 'PRACTICAL'

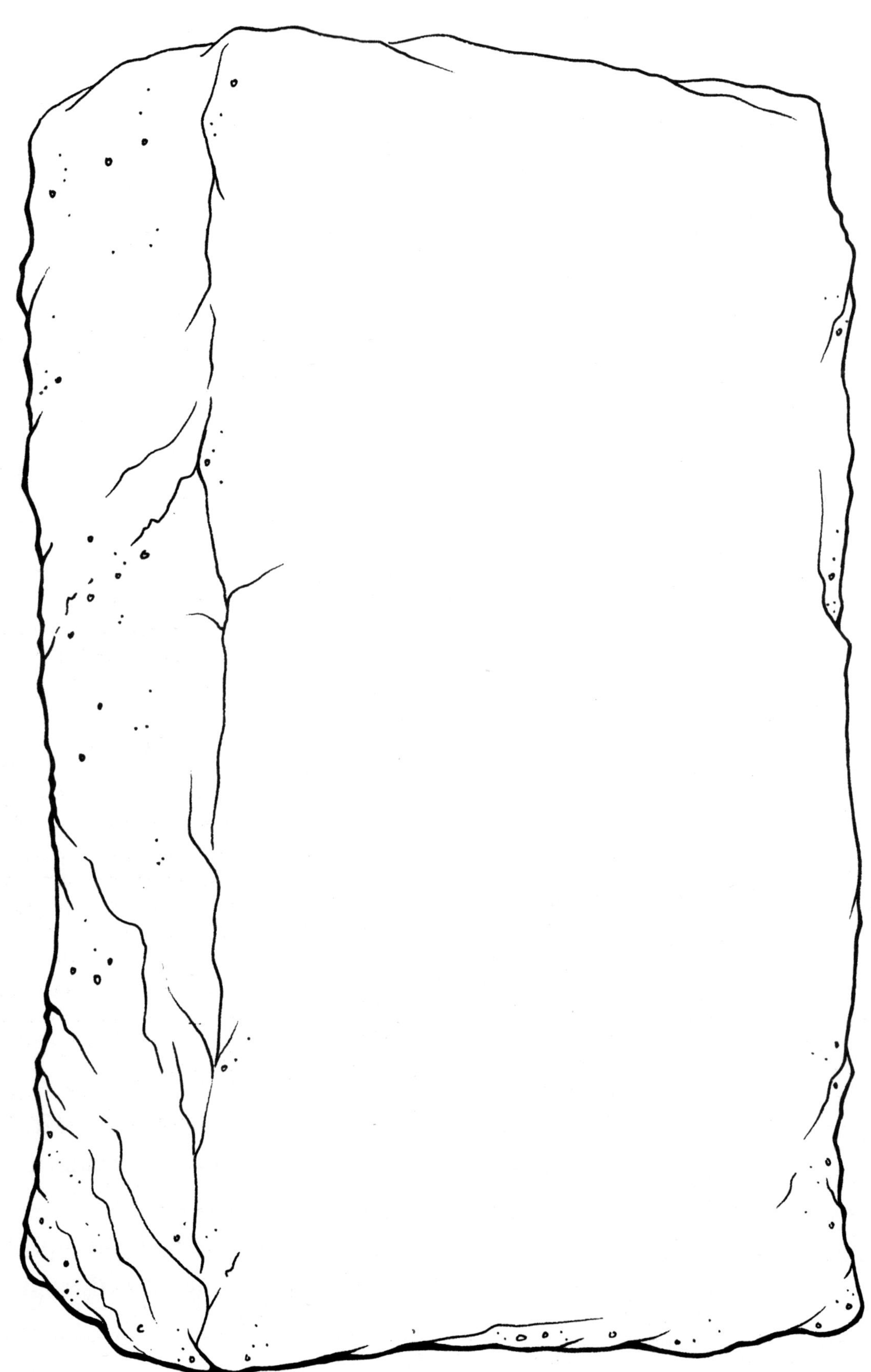

Bible: Exodus 33:7–23; 34:1–9,29–35

11

FACE TO FACE

THE AIM: To experience a close relationship with God

The aim unpacked

Anyone who follows God has a relationship with him. Often we can reduce that relationship to a cerebral or reasoned relationship. However, relationships work on a variety of levels. Our young people live in a world where experience is of the utmost importance. If we want them to have a deep relationship with God, we need to let them explore what being close to God is like.

WAY IN

theGRID MAGAZINE

WHAT: reading and discussion
WHY: to see who we would most like to meet face to face
WITH: magazine page 74

1 Distribute copies of page 74 to the young people and invite them to read the article 'Face to face'.

2 Encourage them to get into small groups to discuss the questions at the bottom of the article. Come together again and invite feedback.

3 Ask the young people to share with everyone who they would most like to meet. Encourage them to say why they would like to meet that person. Leaders could also say who they would most like to meet. (The person need not be living!)

4 Conclude by saying that Rachel and Emma's experience of meeting their pop idol was not as they had expected. They would have learned from their experience of coming 'face to face' with their idol that he was not all that he was cracked up to be! Say that this is the way we learn about relationships – by experiencing the reality of what someone else is really like.

SCENE SETTER

WHAT: personal reflection
WHY: to look at close relationships

1 Give out paper and pens. Ask the young people to find a space on their own to reflect on the people they are closest to. It could be family, friends or others. Invite them to draw themselves (or to write their name) in the middle of the sheet of paper and then to add people around them either close to the centre or further away, according to the closeness of the relationship. Ask them to jot down who the people are and something about their relationship with each one.

2 After a few minutes, encourage them to get into pairs and share with someone else what they have written and why they feel close to these people (at least as much as they are comfortable about sharing). Leaders could also share (young people often find it helpful to hear what the leaders have to say, and it can encourage them to share too). Be sensitive here to any young people who may feel that they do not have any close relationships.

THEMED GAME

WHAT: game
WHY: to show that knowing someone takes all our senses
WITH: blindfold, prizes

1 Ask the young people to spread out around the room. Blindfold one young person. Encourage the rest of the group to change places and then stay where they are.

2 Call out the name of a group member. The blindfolded person has to find that person by touching only the heads of the young people. Encourage the rest of the group to try not to giggle and give the game away!

3 When the blindfolded person is sure they have found the person, they should take off the blindfold. If they are correct, give them a prize; if they are wrong, ask for another volunteer. Play as many times as you wish, with different volunteers being blindfolded.

4 Explain that, to know who someone is, we need to use as many of our senses as possible, not just touch.

BIBLE EXPERIENCE

LEVEL 1: CONNECT

WHAT: memory quiz
WHY: to know what a close relationship with God is
WITH: Bibles, page 75, small prize (optional)

1 Run the following quiz, with your group working in small teams or as individuals. Award a prize, if you wish. Make sure each group or person has a pen and paper to write their answers.

2 Use the questions from page 75. Before each set of questions, ask a young person or another leader to read the Bible passage aloud. Explain that everyone needs to pay attention because the answers are all in the Bible passages. Then each team or individual is to silently write down their answers.

3 Gather everyone together again and read out the answers while each team or individual keeps their own score. Award a small prize to whoever has the most correct answers. If you have a tie, use the tiebreak question to decide a winner.

4 If you have time, read the three Bible passages again: Exodus 33:7–23; 34:1–9,29–35. The young people could do some of the reading, if possible from *The Dramatised Bible* or a contemporary language version such as *The Message* or *The Word on the Street*. Encourage feedback, discussion or questions about things they didn't understand. If you don't know the answers yourself, tell them you'll find out and report back next session (and then remember to do it!).

5 Explain to the group that we can all have a close relationship with God, like Moses did, because of Jesus – all we need to do is spend time with him.

LEVEL 2: INTERFACE

WHAT: in-depth Bible study
WHY: to know what a close relationship with God is
WITH: Bibles

1 Read out the following quote to the young people: 'Moses needed to know that God was with him – and so do we.'

2 Divide your young people into three groups and give each group a Bible, a pen and some paper. (Alternatively, stay as one group and work through all the Bible passages together.) Ask Group 1 to read Exodus 33:7–23; Group 2, Exodus 34:1–9; and Group 3, Exodus 34:29–35.

3 After each group has read their Bible passage, invite them to write down any ideas that come from it that illustrate what it means to have a close relationship with God. For example:

- Exodus 33:7–23: The Lord spoke to Moses and assured him that he would go with him.
- Exodus 34:1–9: Verses 6 and 7 in particular are full of ideas.
- Exodus 34:29–35: Moses' 'shining' face is a visible sign of his relationship with God.

4 Come back together and ask each group to read their Bible verses and share what they have found out. Discuss as a group any particular things they found interesting or hard to understand.

5 Conclude by saying that, if we want to experience this close relationship with God, we must first have faith in Jesus and then, like Moses, be obedient, willing, faithful and courageous. We, too, will then have the promise that is written in 1 Corinthians 13:12 (CEV): 'Now all we can see of God is like a cloudy picture in a mirror. Later we will see him face to face. We don't know everything, but then we will, just as God completely understands us.'

LEVEL 3: SWITCH ON

WHAT: TV interview-style activity
WHY: to know what a close relationship with God is
WITH: pages 76 and 77, video camera and TV or computer with speakers (optional)

1 In advance of the session, invite four group members to prepare and perform the 'So who is this God then?' sketch from pages 76 and 77. This drama could be pre-recorded and played back to the group as a video interview to make it look like an interview on a TV programme.

2 Alternatively, distribute copies of pages 76 and 77 and invite the group to read the drama. They could do this on their own, in pairs or in small groups.

3 Conclude by coming together and explaining that the sketch is based on events that can be found in the Bible in Exodus 33:7–23 and Exodus 34:1–9,29–35. Moses had a close relationship with God because he looked for it. We can have a close relationship with God as well. When we have a relationship with God, it changes us, as it changed Moses (although we may not get the 'tan'); others will be able to see that we have something special.

RESPOND

MUSICAL

WHAT: comparing words from love songs
WHY: to experience an intimate relationship with God
WITH: examples of secular and Christian songs expressing love, playback equipment

1 Before this week's session, ask the other leaders and the young people to bring their favourite love song. This can be any style of music, but needs to contain words expressing love for another person.

2 Play the love songs they have chosen. Ask the young people to listen to what the lyrics are saying and what emotions the singer is expressing (presumably love for another person, possibly wanting to be in the person's presence, wanting to share their whole life with that person).

3 Now play a worship song that expresses our desire to be in the presence of God.

4 Compare the two songs: what do they have in common? Possible answers could include:

- They are both about the desire to be in the presence of the person they love.
- They desire to have a relationship with that person.
- They want to express their love by acts of commitment.

5 Finish by listening to the worship song again, encouraging the young people to reflect on and respond to the lyrics. Alternatively, sing a worship song about having an intimate relationship with God. Some songs that could be used are:

- 'To Be in Your Presence (This is my desire)' by Noel Richards
- 'What a Friend I've Found' by Martin Smith
- 'I Sing a Simple Song' by Craig Musseau

PRACTICAL

WHAT: journal keeping
WHY: to experience a close relationship with God
WITH: notebooks for journals, sticky labels

1 Explain to the young people the idea of keeping a journal – to jot down any thoughts, ideas, Bible verses and so on that they may wish to remember.

2 Give each young person a notebook, a pen and a sticky label. Invite them to stick the label on the front of their book and write their name on it. Suggest that they personalise them at home.

3 Ask them to write today's date on the first page of their book. Then encourage them to find a space on their own to reflect on today's session. Invite them to write down any thoughts they have about this session's Bible passage: has anything spoken to them, challenged them, inspired them? Do they feel that they already have a close relationship with God? If not, do they want one?

4 Then ask them to write one sentence about how they could start or maintain a close relationship with God – for example, by expressing their commitment to him (again) through prayer, or by going to a Bible study or youth group.

5 Encourage the young people to take their journals home with them and to use them to continue writing about their spiritual journey. This is a good exercise, as it's often only when we look back that we realise how much God has been doing!

5 This activity could be linked with the Respond 'Creative' activity.

CREATIVE

WHAT: reflection, writing and drawing
WHY: to experience a close relationship with God

1 Offer the young people the opportunity to make their own response to this session's teaching by writing their own poem, rap or piece of prose. If they prefer, they could draw something to illustrate how they feel. If you did the *Respond* 'Practical' activity, suggest that they do this in their journals.

2 Come back together as a group and ask for volunteers to share what they have written or drawn.

3 Another option here would be to invite any young people who like dance and movement to choreograph some movements to a worship song they like on this session's theme – the movements should represent a response to God's call for us to have a close relationship with him through faith in Jesus.

MORE ON THIS THEME:

If you want to do a short series with your group, other sessions that work well with this one are:

9	*The wilderness years*	*Exodus 16:1 – 17:7*
10	*The top ten dos and don'ts*	*Exodus 19:16 – 20:17*
12	*Multidimensional worship*	*Exodus 35:20 – 36:7; 39:32 – 40:3*

FACE TO FACE

Bible bit
Exodus 33:7–23; 34:1–9,29–35

Moses had an amazing and unique relationship with God. God spoke to him as a man speaks with his friend. Because of this, Moses was able to ask God to renew his covenant with the Israelites. Moses was hungry for God; he wanted to go deeper and to see his glory. God could only grant his request in part. Verse 20 states that no one can see God's face and live, because his holiness would be too overwhelming for them to bear. So how come it suggests otherwise in verse 11? Probably because Moses was inside the tent and God was outside so the tent curtain acted as a shield between them. When Moses did finally experience God's glory, it had an amazing effect: his face shone as it reflected something of God.

How hungry are you for God? Do you want him to transform you so much that others start to see the effect in your life?

Rachel had waited for nine months to see her pop idol in concert and, to top it all, she was actually going to meet him in person! Already she was panicking about what she would say to him. Rachel tried on all her clothes – what should she wear?

Her dad called out, 'Rachel, the taxi's here! Time to go!' As Rachel and her best friend, Emma, sat in the taxi on the way to the concert, they talked non-stop about their pop idol. They talked about how wonderful he was, how amazing his singing was, his great dress sense and what a cool life he led mixing with the rich and famous! How they envied him!

The concert was brilliant, and now the long-awaited moment had come – time to meet their idol backstage, face to face.

In his dressing room the atmosphere was tense. Their pop prince arrived, demanded food and drink and specific clothes to put on; he ordered people around and looked very moody. He barely noticed Rachel and Emma; he just said hi and reluctantly gave them his autograph. He then made it very plain that it was time for them to leave!

HOW DO YOU THINK RACHEL AND EMMA FELT?

WHO WOULD YOU MOST LIKE TO MEET?

A POP STAR, SPORTS STAR, FAMOUS AUTHOR, ARTIST OR MUSICIAN?

A POLITICIAN, WORLD LEADER, MEMBER OF ROYALTY, FAMOUS HISTORICAL PERSON OR WILLIAM SHAKESPEARE?

SOMEONE ELSE?

USE WITH SESSION 11 BIBLE EXPERIENCE 'LEVEL 1 CONNECT'

Quiz

Read Exodus 33:7–23.

1 Why would the people go to the 'Meeting Tent'?
To ask God something.

2 How did God speak to Moses?
Just like a friend – face to face.

3 What would happen if anyone were to see the full glory of God?
They would die.

Read Exodus 34:1–9,29–35.

4 What passed in front of Moses?
The Lord.

5 The Lord is a God who ... Name two of the things God does.
God will show mercy, be kind, doesn't get angry quickly, shows love, shows faithfulness, is kind to thousands of people, will punish the guilty but forgives sin and evil.

6 What had happened to Moses' face?
It was shining because he had talked with God.

Tiebreak question

In two or three sentences, explain what your quiz answers might mean for us, if we have an intimate relationship with God, like Moses did.
An example: We can all ask God questions, and he will talk to us like a friend, but we can't yet see the full glory of God. The Lord will be where we are and he will forgive us because of his love. And with our sins forgiven, we can shine like Moses.

RESOURCE PAGE

USE WITH SESSION 11 BIBLE EXPERIENCE 'LEVEL 3 SWITCH ON'

So who is this God then?

'Our Father in heaven, may your name always be kept holy. May your kingdom come and what you want be done, here on earth as it is in heaven. Give us the food we need for each day. Forgive us for our sins, just as we have forgiven those who sinned against us. And do not cause us to be tempted, but save us from the Evil One.' (Matthew 6:9b–13)

Scene: TV chat show

Characters:
TV presenter
The Very Reverend Doctor Sebastian Cook, theology lecturer
Miriam Oborama, Pentecostal Christian
David Philps, sixth-form student

TV Presenter: Good evening. The big question today is, 'So who is this God then?' I'd like to welcome the Very Reverend Doctor Sebastian Cook, who teaches theology at the University of Braincoombe. *(Dr Cook nods slowly.)* Also Miriam Oborama, representing the Full Gospel Church in Brixheep. *(She nods emphatically with a huge smile.)* And finally, David Philps, a sixth-form student from Somerset. *(He nods.)*

First to you, Doctor Cook: Who is this God then?

Dr Cook: Well, according to those who believe in him, God is the Supreme Being, the Maker of all things. He is not a human like us, but I suppose, in language we can understand, he is a supernatural being. Because he isn't with us in a physical sense, we have to believe in him by faith.

David Philps: But how can you believe in something that isn't there?

Dr Cook: I didn't say he isn't there – I said he isn't with us in a physical sense.

TV Presenter: So we can never see or feel or know this God?

Miriam: Well, brother, with God anything is possible! Remember, he is the Supreme Being. Praise the Lord!

Dr Cook: Here, let me show you an example from the Bible. Moses, the guy who led the Israelites out of slavery in Egypt, knew there was a God. In fact, God often spoke to him.

USE WITH SESSION 11 BIBLE EXPERIENCE 'LEVEL 3 SWITCH ON'

Miriam: Hallelujah! Moses was always talking to God. He knew God was there and so he spoke to him, and because Moses spoke to him, God answered. That is faith!

TV Presenter: Erm... yes, Miriam. Please go on, Doctor Cook.

Dr Cook: Well, Miriam is right. Moses did go out and seek God. In fact, he asked if he could actually see him.

David Philps: But you said you can't see God because he isn't like us.

TV Presenter: Yes, what do you say to that?

Dr Cook: Well, in the Bible it says that Moses asked to see God's glory. It's all there in Exodus 33:18–23. But God's reply was that no one can see him and live.

Miriam: That's my amazing God!

Dr Cook: But God understood that Moses wanted to see him. So he allowed his glory to pass in front of Moses, but he covered Moses with his hand until he had passed, so Moses was able to see the back of God.

David Philps: So we can see God?

Miriam: If you look for God, and seek him, he will reveal himself to you.

Dr Cook: It may not be in the dramatic way that Moses saw God. And in fact, after Moses had just seen the back of him, Moses' face shone like the sun – a bit like one of those fake tans.

Miriam: Yes, once we have met God we are all different – he changes us for the better, praise him. But as you can see, we are still ourselves with our own differences and styles!

TV Presenter: Yes, you two are certainly different, but you both believe in God. David, what do you think?

David Philps: Well, it certainly seems that they have a faith and they believe that God exists. I suppose the only way to know for sure is to look for God and see if he responds.

Dr Cook and Miriam *(together)*: Oh, he will. Praise the Lord!

TV Presenter: Well, it's been an inspiring discussion. Thanks to you all. *(Looks at all of his guests.)* And next week we will continue this theme as we look at, 'Why did Jesus have to die?'

12

Bible: Exodus 35:20 – 36:7; 39:32 – 40:38

MULTIDIMENSIONAL WORSHIP

THE AIM: To explore new dimensions of worship

The aim unpacked

The Holy Tent, and everything related to it, was to give a visual representation to the Israelites that God was with them. It was a foretaste of what true worship is. For us, it shows that worship is related to the whole of our lives, as Paul later points out in Romans 12:1, and is not just the singing of a few songs.

WAY IN

theGRID MAGAZINE

WHAT: **discussion**
WHY: **to begin to think about what worship is**
WITH: **magazine page 82**

1 Make sure everyone has a copy of page 82 and ask them to look at the article on worship. Give the young people five minutes or so to go through the list individually, adding their comments, or discussing it in pairs.

2 Bring the group together and ask them to share which items on the list they have ticked and why. As you go through them, you may want to add that David danced nearly naked as he praised God when the Ark of the Covenant was brought to Jerusalem; and that Hosea the prophet married an unfaithful woman because God told him to. Does that change what they have ticked?

3 Ask the young people to share what they have written in answer to the question, 'What do you think worship is?' Do they agree with everything that has been written? Is there anything they would add to the list?

4 Explain that in this session they'll be looking at expanding on what is understood as 'worship'.

SCENE SETTER

WHAT: **people bingo**
WHY: **to begin to think about what skills and abilities we have**
WITH: **copies of page 83, small prize (optional)**

1 Give a copy of page 83 to each person. Explain that on the resource page is a list of achievements. The object of this activity is, for each achievement listed, they must find a member of the group who has done that activity. When they have found them, they need to get them to sign their name over that activity. The aim is to see how many of the activities they can get signed by other members of the group. If they fill their card and get all the activities signed, they should shout, 'Bingo!'

2 Give the group several minutes, depending on how large the group is. You can either finish when someone shouts 'Bingo!', or bring them all back together and see who has the most activities signed. You could offer a prize if you've done this as a competition.

3 Explain that we have all achieved things. What we can achieve is often linked to our skills and abilities. We all have them, although some may be more developed than others. In this session, they'll be looking at how people can use their skills and abilities for God.

THEMED GAME

WHAT: **multi-skilled relay race**
WHY: **to begin to think about our skills and abilities**
WITH: **large safe space, various props (optional)**

1 In advance, plan and prepare your relay race, with a variety of different legs. These could be simple, like skipping or walking heel to toe backwards, or silly like ballet dancing or pretending to be a certain animal. Alternatively, they could use props, such as dressing up, running and then taking the costume off again, or hopping using crutches. You need to have enough legs for each member of the team to do at least one.

2 Divide the young people into teams based on the number of legs, resources and group members. Say that they are going to have a relay race but each 'leg' is different. Explain what each one is and then ask the teams to decide which member will run which leg, based on who they think will be best at it. Each person should do at least one leg.

3 Run the race. If time allows, run it again allowing the teams to change who runs which leg if they think the team's skills could be better used.

4 If appropriate, explain that today they'll be looking at people who used their skills and abilities to help others to worship God.

BIBLE EXPERIENCE 12

LEVEL 1: CONNECT

WHAT: visual reading
WHY: to explore new dimensions of worship
WITH: magazine page 81, Bibles

1 Give out pens and paper. Ask for some confident volunteers to read Exodus 35:20 – 36:7. Invite the rest of the group to doodle while they read, imagining what all the things in the passage looked like.

2 Give everyone a copy of page 81 and ask them to look at 'Really wild worship'. Here they'll find an image of the Holy Tent, which the gifts and the skills of Bezalel and Oholiab were used to create.

3 Explain to the group that the Israelites had been rescued from Egypt by God and now they were starting to work out how they could worship him. The Holy Tent was part of this.

4 Invite the group to look at the image of the Holy Tent while someone reads Exodus 39:32 – 40:38. It is a long reading but don't hurry it. You want the group to visualise what they are listening to with the image. If appropriate, encourage them to point out or draw on the image each of the specific things mentioned in the passage.

5 Following on, point out that the reading culminated with God allowing his presence to be in the Tent. God was now living with his people. Their worship was not just singing and praying; it also involved their location and God with them at that specific place. With the Holy Spirit, we too have God living with us. God's presence, his Spirit, is with us each and every day, everywhere we go.

LEVEL 2: INTERFACE

WHAT: discussion
WHY: to explore new dimensions of worship
WITH: Bibles

1 Divide the young people into threes and ask each small group to spend a minute or two thinking about the things they are good at. What skills and abilities do they have? It doesn't matter how good they are at them; they don't have to be major skills. If they are having difficulty, the others in the group could suggest what skills they have.

2 Bring the whole group back together and share what they have discussed, emphasising that we all have abilities – from reading and writing to being a maths genius or a star sportsperson. The question is, 'What do we do with what we have?'

3 Read Exodus 35:20 – 36:7 together, either by asking a few volunteers or by going round the group reading a verse each.

4 Back in their threes, ask the young people to look at what has happened in the passage, especially at what Bezalel, Oholiab and the other people did. Invite them to make a list of all the different things that people did or gave for the Holy Tent. Point out that they were all taking part but doing different things – they were using their gifts and abilities and supporting the work through their gifts. The skills, abilities and 'stuff' that they had were being used, but used for what?

5 Back as a whole group, read Exodus 39:32 – 40:38 together. Refer to 'The aim unpacked' to help, and explain that the Holy Tent represented God being with the Israelites. Their worship wasn't just about making a sacrifice or doing the right thing. God wanted to involve the whole community – all their gifts, skills and abilities.

LEVEL 3: SWITCH ON

WHAT: Bible study
WHY: to explore new dimensions of worship
WITH: Bibles, Bible dictionaries and commentaries (optional)

1 Look at the following four passages from the Bible and then discuss the questions together. Alternatively, divide the young people into four groups and give each group a passage to look at, and then come back together to share and feed back to everyone else. If possible, have Bible dictionaries or commentaries available for the young people to refer to.

- Exodus 35:20 – 36:7; 39:32 – 40:38: What spiritual gifts were on display? What was the result of the building of the Holy Tent?
- 2 Chronicles 3,4: Does anything strike you as amazing about the Temple? Why do you think the details are so important?
- Matthew 27:45–56: What did the ripping of the curtain in the Temple represent? If the Temple is not our focus for worship, what is?
- Romans 12:1,2: What does this mean for our understanding of worship? How can we live our lives as worship? What does this mean?

2 There are no right or wrong answers to these questions. However, you should try to guide the group to an understanding that God is with us, through his Holy Spirit, just as he was with the Israelites in their Holy Tent. This has been made possible by Jesus' death on the cross, which brings us into a full relationship with God. We therefore live a life of worship in response to God being with us. Everything we do – all our skills and abilities – can be used to worship God, because our whole lives are to be an expression of worship to him.

3 Finish with a time of silent prayer and encourage each of the group members to ask God for more of his presence in their lives.

RESPOND

MUSICAL

WHAT: singing
WHY: to remind us that worship can be sung too
WITH: appropriate worship music, playback equipment or musical accompaniment

1 Remind the group that the Holy Tent was a focus of worship for the Israelites, just as our churches, or the places where we meet, are often the focus for us. Although we should live our whole lives as worship, there is still room for what many of us perceive to be 'traditional' worship.

2 Invite the young people to choose some of their favourite worship songs and either listen to them reflectively or sing them together. Encourage them to choose songs that encourage a change in their lives in response to God's presence, such as:

- 'Purify My Heart' by Brian Doerkson
- 'Lord, You Have My Heart' by Martin Smith

Invite them to consider how the words that they sing or hear can be translated into action for the rest of their lives.

3 Close in prayer, asking God to be with us all the time in everything we do, so that our lives would become an example to all of multidimensional worship.

PRACTICAL

WHAT: Bible reading
WHY: to see the detail that worship of the Almighty can entail
WITH: Bibles

1 Remind the group that today's Bible passage was quite long, just like the preparations for the Holy Tent were, but eventually all the preparations led to God's presence being with the Israelites.

2 Explain that one way we can bring more of God's presence into our lives is to get into the Bible a little more. As such, and related to today's Bible passage, we are going to make a commitment to try to read a chapter of the Bible each day throughout the coming week. The chapters are Exodus 35, 36, 37, 38, 39 and 40. These chapters give the full details of the Holy Tent that were summarised in today's readings.

3 Ask the young people to write the chapters on a bookmark-sized piece of paper and take them home. They can read one chapter each day this week, ticking them off as they go.

4 As they read their Bibles at home, encourage them to pray, asking God to help them worship him in every detail of their lives – however small and insignificant – and to live a life of multidimensional worship.

CREATIVE

WHAT: Holy Tent card
WHY: to remind us that worship is multidimensional
WITH: small pieces of card, art materials, magazine page 81 or other image of the Holy Tent

1 Remind the young people that the Holy Tent was the focus for the Israelites' worship while they were in the desert, and it also symbolised that God was with them. Today we don't need the Holy Tent because God is with us through his Holy Spirit. However, it is still good to remind ourselves now and again!

2 Give everyone a credit card-sized piece of card and ask them to draw a representation of the Holy Tent. They can refer to the image on page 81 if you have it, or to a study Bible or Bible dictionary. As they create their image, encourage them to pray silently and invite God to be present in their lives.

3 Once they have done this, they can turn the card over and write the words of Romans 12:1 on the back as an encouragement for them to stay focused on God and to live every part of their lives as an act of multidimensional worship.

4 Encourage the young people to take the cards away with them and keep them somewhere that they will be seen often, eg in a wallet or purse.

MORE ON THIS THEME:

If you want to do a short series with your group, other sessions that work well with this one are:

9	*The wilderness years*	*Exodus 16:1 – 17:7*
10	*The top ten dos and don'ts*	*Exodus 19:16 – 20:17*
11	*Face to face*	*Exodus 33:7–23; 34:1–9,29–35*

Bible bit
Exodus 35:20 – 36:7; 39:32 – 40:38

The verses above describe how the Israelites created the Holy Tent, also known as the 'Tabernacle'. This tent was the focus of their worship while they were in the wilderness. What's amazing is that the whole community was involved in the making of the Holy Tent and it was created using their skills. Ultimately, the Holy Tent led to God's presence being with the people. Their whole lives were shaped by God being with them. God can be with us today, too. How hungry are you for God? Do you want him to transform you so much that others start to see the effect in your life?

WHAT'S WORSHIP?

Look at the list below and put a tick in the boxes against the ones you think are valid forms of worship.

- ☐ GOING TO WORK
- ☐ MAKING A CUP OF TEA
- ☐ DANCING (NEARLY) NAKED
- ☐ SINGING SONGS IN CHURCH
- ☐ SINGING HYMNS IN CHURCH
- ☐ SINGING SONGS AT HOME
- ☐ PRAYING
- ☐ WALKING THE DOG
- ☐ FEEDING THE HOMELESS
- ☐ WAVING BANNERS
- ☐ PAINTING
- ☐ BEING QUIET

WHAT DO YOU THINK WORSHIP IS?

RESOURCE PAGE

USE WITH SESSION 12 WAY IN 'SCENE SETTER'

Sign your name if you have...

Run a mile	Played an instrument	Read your Bible this week	Made someone smile this week
Played for the school team	Got an A grade	Got a C grade	Told a joke
Created a drawing	Played an online game	Written an email to someone	Written a letter to someone
Gone swimming	Written a story	Read a book	Listened to someone tell you a problem

13

Bible: 1 Samuel 16:1–13; Psalm 23

ABOUT A BOY

THE AIM: To see how God provides for his people

The aim unpacked

This is the first session of four that look at the early years of David's life. Through what happens to David we see that God works through his people to provide for his people. God doesn't do this. Through Samuel he chose David, who was young and weak on the outside but had a God-focused heart.

WAY IN

theGRID MAGAZINE

WHAT: **discussion**
WHY: **to begin to think about leadership**
WITH: **magazine page 87, flip chart or whiteboard**

1 Distribute copies of page 87. Encourage your young people to fill in the survey.

2 Invite them to feed back their results to the whole group. Turn their results into rough pie diagrams on the flip chart or whiteboard. So, for instance, 65% of your young people may want a leader who is under 30, 25% may want someone who is over 30 and 10% may want a teenager; or maybe 50% want someone who is 180 cm tall and male, 35% want someone 165 cm tall and female and... you get the idea.

3 After having a laugh at the results, suggest that in the Bible the only important quality required of a leader is that they are chosen by God.

SCENE SETTER

WHAT: **craft**
WHY: **to think what it would be like if we provided for ourselves**
WITH: **old magazines and newspapers, glue, large sheets of paper**

1 Explain that in this session you're going to focus on God's choice of a leader and king.

2 Working in groups, invite the young people to cut bits of people out of magazines and assemble their perfect leader. Give different groups different themes to work on, such as:

- the best-looking leader
- the wisest leader
- the coolest leader

3 Ask the groups to glue the body parts on the large sheets of paper to construct their leaders and to label each part with the names of the people they took them from. For example:

- the looks of Kate Moss
- the listening ears of an agony aunt
- suits by Armani

4 Invite each group to show to everyone the leader they have made and then summarise what key qualities you think they were looking for.

THEMED GAME

WHAT: **dressing-up relay**
WHY: **to think about judging by appearances**
WITH: **dressing-up clothes, large dice for each team**

1 Put a pile of dressing-up clothes at the end of your area, divided into six piles: tops; bottoms; shoes; hats; accessories; coats and jackets. Number the piles '1' to '6'.

2 Divide the group into small teams. On the command 'Go!' each player in turn runs to the end of the room and throws a dice. They take one item of clothing from the appropriate pile according to the number on the dice, put it on and return to their team.

3 The game continues until a player throws the number of a pile that is empty. This player returns to their team and is required to wear all of their team's dressing-up clothes at once. When they are fully dressed, they win.

4 Parade the winner. Ask what everyone would make of this person as a leader if we had to judge by appearances.

BIBLE EXPERIENCE

LEVEL 1: CONNECT

WHAT: game
WHY: to see how God provides for his people
WITH: tray with basic grocery provisions (including olive oil), Bible, picture of the Prime Minister, bottle of water, small box labelled 'medicine', image of a house, text book, flip chart or whiteboard (optional)

1 Say that God provides for his people. Discuss the difference between wants and needs. (Make two lists on a flip chart if necessary.)

2 Show the items on the tray and say that these represent the basic necessities for life – food, water, shelter, health, education, leadership, God. Explain that in one minute you will remove one item. The young people will have to work out what you have removed. Hide the tray, remove an item, show the tray again and challenge everyone to guess what was removed.

3 Repeat until only one item, the picture of the Prime Minister, is left. (Gradually decrease the viewing time, to five seconds for the last two objects.) Discuss whether this would be everyone's choice if they could only choose one of the essential items.

4 Read or paraphrase the story of David's election as leader and king in 1 Samuel 16:1–13, or act it out by having seven volunteers stand in line (with 'David' hiding behind them) and rejecting them one by one until only 'David' is left.

5 Demonstrate anointing by marking the forehead of 'David' with the olive oil.

6 Discuss why leaders are important: What would life be like with no leaders? Would it work, or would some people assume or be given leadership responsibility without any official title?

7 Finally, take a vote:

- Is leadership a natural talent, a developed skill, or both?
- Which does God seem to use the most?

LEVEL 2: INTERFACE

WHAT: drama with Bible study
WHY: to see how God provides for his people
WITH: copies of page 89, Bibles, flip chart or whiteboard

1 Discuss how the group would go about finding a new leader for a country. Say that if the person had to be God's choice, how would they check? Refer to the 'Scene setter' activity, if you did it.

2 Explain that one of the big themes of the Bible is that God provides for his people. In 1 Samuel 16, God provided a new leader when the old one was rejected.

3 Give out copies of page 89 and invite everyone to look at the 'Leader idol' sketch. Allocate the roles and read it through together. If your group enjoys drama, you could consider preparing a performance for your church service or another meeting. Alternatively you may like to role play a version of 'Leader idol' to choose a leader for your group.

4 Now distribute Bibles and read 1 Samuel 16:1–13 together. Briefly demonstrate that the 'Leader idol' sketch is based on what happened in the Bible. You may want to flesh out the role of Samuel (the prophet) a little and say why God was dissatisfied with Saul, Israel's first king.

5 Make a list together on the flip chart or whiteboard of the sorts of hopes and aspirations people have when a new leader is installed. Now do the same for the hopes the people had for King (in waiting) David. Keep this sheet for future sessions so you can add to it. Over these four sessions we shall focus on David's life before he actually became the monarch, while Saul was still king.

LEVEL 3: SWITCH ON

WHAT: Bible study
WHY: to see how God provides for his people
WITH: Bibles, magazine page 88, copies of page 90

1 Get everyone into pairs or threes and give out Bibles. Invite one person in each pair or three to read aloud 1 Samuel 16:1–13 and another to read Psalm 23.

2 Ask the young people to discuss these questions and then feed back as a whole group:

- What do shepherds do?
- What is the life of a shepherd like today?
- What would it have been like 1,000 years BC?
- If a leader had been a shepherd first, what sort of a leader do you think they might become?

3 Distribute copies of page 88 and read the two versions of Psalm 23. One is positive; the other is negative.

4 Invite the pairs or threes to write a version of Psalm 23 that fits with their world but still keeps the same structure and key points. Distribute a copy of page 90 to each pair or three. It sets out a simple structure to the psalm that will help them write their own version. Example first lines might be, 'The Lord is my social worker...'; 'The Lord is my maths teacher...'; 'The Lord is my team captain...'; 'The Lord is my mother...'

5 Allow 15 to 20 minutes for this, then come back together to listen to the results. Discuss any interesting observations that arise. Say that, just as shepherds provide for all the needs of their sheep (it is not in their financial interest for any harm to come to them), so God provides for us. He may prod and poke us occasionally, as a shepherd prods and pokes a sheep that is heading for danger, but he has our safety at heart.

RESPOND

MUSICAL

WHAT: **singing**
WHY: **to use Psalm 23 in worship**
WITH: **music on CD or MP3 and playback equipment, or musical accompaniment**

1 There have been many versions of Psalm 23 set to music, including Crimond (the tune used at funerals), 'The King of Love My shepherd Is', 'Brother James' Air', 'The Lord's My Shepherd (Trust in you alone)'. Sing or play a verse of each and ask the young people to share which one they prefer and why.

2 If your group doesn't want to sing, you could encourage them to participate by reading the psalm together slowly, pausing between verses, over quiet instrumental music.

PRACTICAL

WHAT: **letter writing**
WHY: **to encourage leaders**
WITH: **computer with internet access and email account (optional), flip chart or whiteboard**

1 Think together of some things your local leaders (church, council or school) are doing well. Invite the young people to write to them or email them to encourage and thank them, and to ask if there are any ways the group can help them or if there is anything they would like the group to pray for. They will probably be quite surprised at this and may even want to visit you to talk about it.

2 Pray for your leaders together – as many as the group can think of. Make a list of their names on the flip chart or whiteboard and then read the list out slowly, encouraging prayer for each person during a brief pause between the names.

CREATIVE

WHAT: **journal**
WHY: **to remember what we asked God for**
WITH: **hardback notebook**

1 Challenge the young people to keep a note of the things they pray for as they ask God to meet their needs, session by session.

2 Alongside this, have a 'journal table' during your session and appoint someone to be the journalist. This person should record what happens in the session in some way – perhaps a story, a factual account, minutes, notes, a poem or a picture. As it builds up it will provide an interesting record of your sessions and the things you pray for together.

3 This provides an opportunity for the more creative, introverted young people to be involved in the session. Some will appreciate this, but make sure a different person does it every time.

MORE ON THIS THEME:

If you want to do a short series with your group, other sessions that work well with this one are:

14	*Hunky gory*	*1 Samuel 17:1 – 18:5*
15	*He's just a jealous guy*	*1 Samuel 19:1–17*
16	*I'm not the bad guy*	*1 Samuel 24*

13

Bible bit
1 Samuel 16:1–13; Psalm 23

God is on the lookout for a new king. The current one, Saul, is going downhill quick, losing it in a big way. So who does God choose – the biggest, strongest, most handsome guy on the planet? Er, nope – he chooses a little shepherd lad, who likes to write music; a bit of an emo if ever I heard of one. Why? Well, because God is looking for more than what is on the outside; he knows what is in our hearts. Take a look at Psalm 23 to see what was in David's heart – a total reliance on God.

IDEAL LEADER

Answer each question with what you think is important for a leader to have or be. If you think something doesn't matter, leave it blank.

IN ORDER TO RUN THIS COUNTRY PROPERLY A LEADER NEEDS TO BE:

HEIGHT...	
GENDER...	
HAIR COLOUR (OR ANY RESTRICTIONS)...	
AGE...	
WEIGHT...	
ETHNIC ORIGIN...	
REGIONAL ACCENT...	
EDUCATIONAL ACHIEVEMENTS (MINIMUM)...	
UNIVERSITY ATTENDED...	
FOOTBALL TEAM SUPPORTED...	

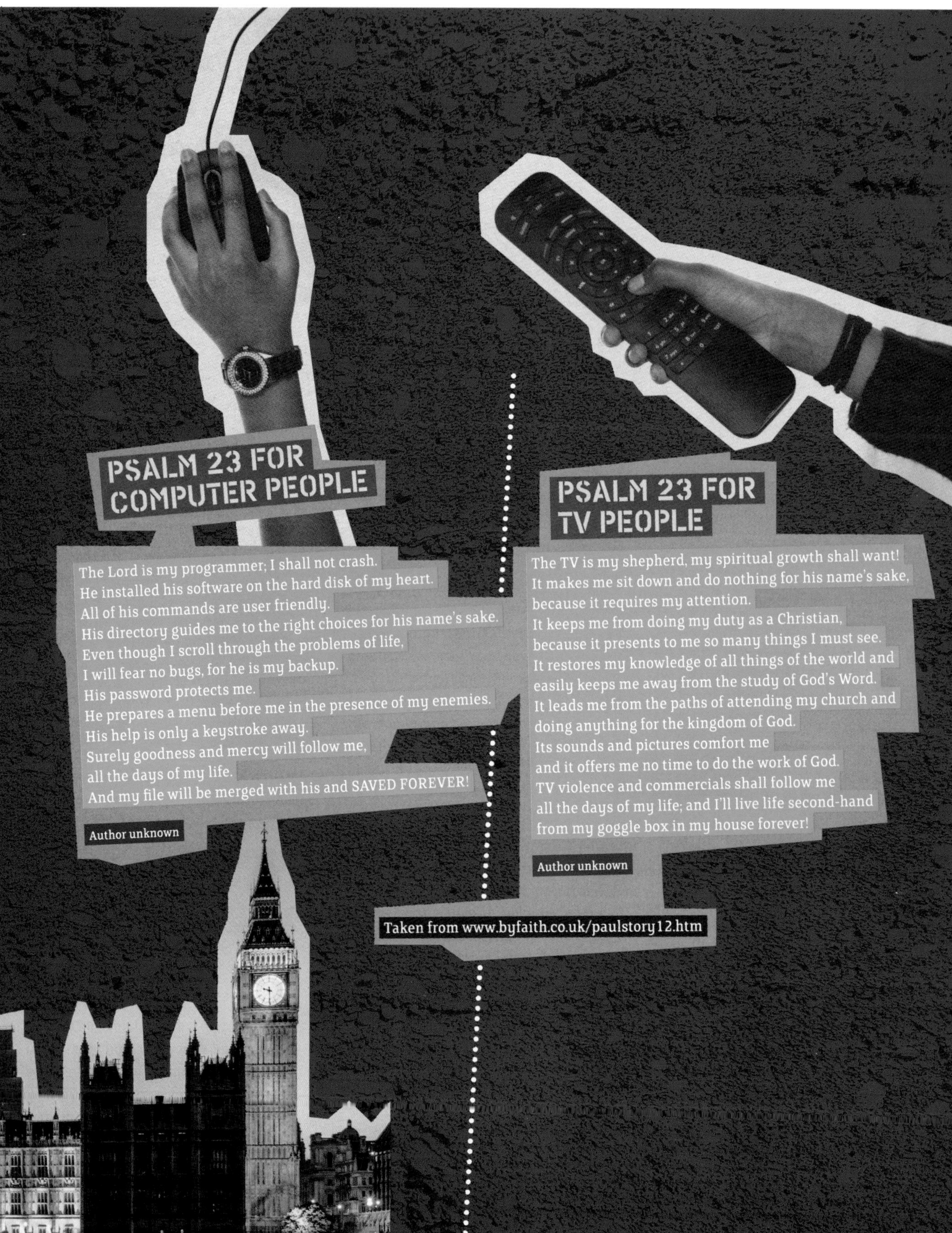

PSALM 23 FOR COMPUTER PEOPLE

The Lord is my programmer; I shall not crash.
He installed his software on the hard disk of my heart.
All of his commands are user friendly.
His directory guides me to the right choices for his name's sake.
Even though I scroll through the problems of life,
I will fear no bugs, for he is my backup.
His password protects me.
He prepares a menu before me in the presence of my enemies.
His help is only a keystroke away.
Surely goodness and mercy will follow me,
all the days of my life.
And my file will be merged with his and SAVED FOREVER!

Author unknown

PSALM 23 FOR TV PEOPLE

The TV is my shepherd, my spiritual growth shall want!
It makes me sit down and do nothing for his name's sake,
because it requires my attention.
It keeps me from doing my duty as a Christian,
because it presents to me so many things I must see.
It restores my knowledge of all things of the world and
easily keeps me away from the study of God's Word.
It leads me from the paths of attending my church and
doing anything for the kingdom of God.
Its sounds and pictures comfort me
and it offers me no time to do the work of God.
TV violence and commercials shall follow me
all the days of my life; and I'll live life second-hand
from my goggle box in my house forever!

Author unknown

Taken from www.byfaith.co.uk/paulstory12.htm

USE WITH SESSION 13 BIBLE EXPERIENCE 'LEVEL 2 INTERFACE'

Leader idol

Narrator: Today is the final round of *Leader Idol*, a competition to choose a new leader to replace King Saul. We go over to our outside broadcast unit in Bethlehem.

Outside broadcast: Well, here we are. You join us just as the going is getting really exciting. The sons of Jesse have all got through to the last round and everyone is keen to see who will be the first to audition. And it's Eliab. He's tall. He's dark. He's handsome. He's the oldest. Surely he will give a good account of himself, having got this far. We know he was popular in the earlier rounds. Let's see if we can hear the judges.

Samuel: No. We're not going for looks or height here. We're going for talent, pure and simple. Next.

Outside broadcast: Well, we always thought Samuel would be a hard one to please. But has he spotted who he wants? He has a bit of a reputation as a prophet. And here comes Abinadab. Have to say, his name may count against him. People want leaders with names they can pronounce.

Samuel: No, we don't want Abida... Adin... Abanda... him.

Outside broadcast: Thought that might be the case. Next up – Shammah.

Samuel: Next!

Outside broadcast: Another surprise. Nethanel is next.

Samuel: No.

Outside broadcast: Raddai.

Samuel: Oh, purlease!

Outside broadcast: Ozem.

Samuel: Waste of my time. Get rid of him. And that other one. (*Shouting to offstage*) Jesse! You got any more sons? I'm sure it's one of yours we need.

Outside broadcast: Well, what a turn-up! All Jesse's seven sons have been rejected, and the judges are asking if he has any more. And what's this? Apparently there is one more, but he's so young he hasn't been entered. He's coming down from the hillside. And here he is. A bit red-faced but indeed young, fit, and handsome too.

Samuel: Ladies and gentlemen – your new king!

Outside broadcast: And on that bombshell we hand you back to the studio.

Narrator: So there we have it, ladies and gentlemen. David, son of Jesse, will be the new leader of Israel. Just got to wait for the present one to die first. Goodnight!

RESOURCE PAGE

USE WITH SESSION 13 BIBLE EXPERIENCE 'LEVEL 3 SWITCH ON'

Psalm 23

The Lord, my shepherd (v 1):

Section 1

- Is ahead, leading
- Taking me to green pastures (v 2)
- Taking me to calm waters (v 2)
- Restoring strength (v 3)
- On the right paths (v 3)

Section 2

- Is alongside guiding
- Armed to protect (v 4)

Section 3

- Is a shepherd and a friend
- We eat with him (v 5)
- We live in his house (v 6)

Bible: 1 Samuel 17:1 – 18:5

14

HUNKY GORY

THE AIM: To develop our potential as God's people

The aim unpacked

This is the second of four sessions looking at the early years of David's life. We witness David developing his potential by putting his trust in God and overcoming the mighty hunk in a gory and, to be honest, quite horrific manner. This isn't a nice story about overcoming bullies by being cleverer and psychologically bigger than them. This is all about relying on God and reaching our potential through his grace.

WAY IN

theGRID MAGAZINE

WHAT: **monologue and discussion**
WHY: **to think about victories against the odds**
WITH: **magazine page 94, drama props (optional)**

1 Give out copies of page 94 and invite everyone to look at the football radio commentary. You might like to get a good reader to read it as a monologue, sitting on a chair with a microphone.

2 Ask the group, 'Why are events such as this referred to as "giant-killings"?' Can the young people think of real examples (not just from the world of football) where the little person overcame the large? How about:

- in other sports?
- victories in law courts?
- in school rule changes?

SCENE SETTER

WHAT: **game**
WHY: **to think about targets**
WITH: **waste bins, items to throw such as ping-pong balls, paper darts, pine cones**

1 Play a selection of target games while sitting around a central target, taking turns. A good way to do this is to sit in a circle with a container such as a waste-paper bin or bucket in the centre. Alternatively, you could set up targets to knock down, such as skittles, water bottles or tin-can pyramids. Make sure you keep score.

2 Say that this session will be about hitting a particular target right between the eyes. A lot of target work is about practice. Find out how many of the young people think they started improving at hitting the target after they'd had a few turns.

THEMED GAME

WHAT: **game**
WHY: **fun with targets**
WITH: **two baseball caps covered in double-sided sticky tape, selection of light objects such as polystyrene cups, ping-pong balls or rolled-up paper**

1 Divide the young people into two teams and ask a volunteer from each team to wear the cap.

2 Get the teams to sit alongside each other with the cap-wearers about five metres away.

3 Emphasise safety in this next activity, and make sure the items you have chosen to throw will not cause injury. Let the young people know that they will only be allowed to take part if they are sensible!

4 Challenge the young people to take it in turns to throw the objects with the aim of getting them to stick to their teammate's cap. The teammate is not allowed to move their bottom from the floor but they may move their head once a throw has been made.

BIBLE EXPERIENCE

LEVEL 1: CONNECT

WHAT: **story with illustration and discussion**
WHY: **to develop our potential as God's people**
WITH: **pages 95 and 96, tape measure**

1 This session's Bible passage (1 Samuel 17: 1 – 18:5) is a captivating story. Read aloud the paraphrase from pages 95 and 96.

2 Use volunteers, and if necessary a tape measure, to demonstrate the comparative heights of the two men (Goliath was about three metres tall). For safety's sake, get them to do this lying on the floor.

3 Discuss what enabled David to reach his full potential as a giant-killer. In smaller groups if necessary, encourage everyone to discuss these questions:

- In what areas of your life do you feel you have potential but are unable to achieve it? What's stopping you?
- What practical steps could be taken to overcome these obstacles?
- What is the potential of God's people? What could they become and do? What's stopping them?
- What practical steps could be taken to overcome these obstacles?

4 End with this quote. Evangelist J John says David could have had one of two possible attitudes when he faced the giant Goliath: 'He's so big; I'd better run away', or 'He's so big; how can I miss?'

LEVEL 2: INTERFACE

WHAT: **Bible study**
WHY: **to develop our potential as God's people**
WITH: **Bibles, copies of page 97**

1 Give out Bibles and, in pairs or threes, ask the young people to read 1 Samuel 17:1 – 18:5.

2 Distribute copies of page 97 and challenge each pair or three to search the Bible verses to fill in part 1.

3 After a few minutes invite everyone to feed back their answers. Make sure they have covered these points:

- David's problem – his country was at war and he had an opportunity to help
- David's resources – speed, strength, sling training
- David's skills – fighting skills learned through shepherding
- David's attitude – God wants this so God will give him success
- David's result – victory, success, promotion, goodwill

4 Now ask the young people to think individually about a difficulty or opportunity in their own lives. Ask them to fill in part 2 of the resource sheet.

5 After a while, encourage them to find a partner they trust and to pray for each other.

6 Conclude by encouraging everyone to use their:

- courage: David's decision to do what God had called and equipped him to do was a pointer to Jesus who had a similarly difficult decision to make – the cross or a quiet life?
- single-mindedness: despite Goliath's taunts, David was not put off (vs 42–44). Will we be put off doing what God wants if people taunt?
- application: David's priority had been sheep. David had been anointed king some time earlier but had to wait until the right time. God has tasks for us all and the right time for us to do them.

LEVEL 3: SWITCH ON

WHAT: **Bible story and discussion**
WHY: **to develop our potential as God's people**
WITH: **pages 95 and 96, DVD of *Raiders of the Lost Ark*, playback equipment (optional)**

1 Remind everyone of the scene in *Raiders of the Lost Ark* where Indiana Jones is confronted by a number of sword-bearing warriors. He defeats them all using his strength and his whip. A final warrior arrives – bigger and more evil-looking than the others, juggling his huge sword in a show of speed and skill. Can Indy match him? We never find out, for he draws his pistol and shoots the man dead. Indy beat the warrior in the same way David beat Goliath – superior weapons technology.

2 Read 1 Samuel 17:1 – 18:5, or use the paraphrase on pages 95 and 96.

3 Explain that David was confident with slings. His skill at wrestling bears and lions was well known, but that gave no certainty of victory. World-class goalkeepers miss penalties, and well-tried recipes turn out wrong. The knowledge that everything will probably be OK is not certainty of success. David's stone might miss. Goliath might have the first blow. David's courage lay in his unswerving faith that God would help him.

4 Ask the young people to share how they might feel in the same situation.

5 In silence, encourage everyone to think about and write down their own personal 'Goliaths'. Now ask them to write the resources they have at their disposal to overcome each problem. Then, if the problem still seems huge, encourage them to think about ways the problem could be broken into smaller parts. Is there something practical they can do now?

6 Emphasise that we only develop our potential when we overcome new problems or stretch ourselves in new situations. On such occasions, God's people learn to rely on God for help. David tackled a new situation using his skills and resources, and with the knowledge that he was on God's side.

RESPOND

14

MUSICAL

WHAT: **song or chant**
WHY: **to worship God for David's triumph**
WITH: **music and instruments (for the song)**

1 For younger groups, the song 'Our God is a great big God' with actions might work well.

2 For others, practise this hand-clap beat in a 4/4 time: clap, clap, pause, clap, pause, pause, pause, pause. Start quietly, reach a crescendo and then get quieter again. Over this add various chants such as:

- Our God (pause) reigns'
- We have vic-tory'
- 'Da-vid was king'

PRACTICAL

WHAT: **problem solving**
WHY: **to use young people's wisdom and potential**

1 Challenge the group members to use their creative thinking skills on some of the problems that are facing the church or youth group.

2 In small groups, encourage them to break the problems down into small parts and then to list the church's skills, resources and opportunities. Come up with solutions together, especially ones where the young people might be able to help!

3 Present any new thinking to the church leaders, or try to implement some of the ideas in the youth group.

CREATIVE

WHAT: **illustration**
WHY: **to remind everyone of their potential in God**
WITH: **masking tape**

1 Use masking tape to mark out the shape of the body of a 3-metre giant, somewhere where it will be seen by many people for a few days. Make sure you have permission to do this in whichever location you choose.

2 Add the slogan (in masking tape) – 'God's people: slaying giants for 3,000 years. Join us.'

MORE ON THIS THEME:

If you want to do a short series with your group, other sessions that work well with this one are:

13	*About a boy*	*1 Samuel 16:1–13; Psalm 23*
15	*He's just a jealous guy*	*1 Samuel 19:1–17*
16	*I'm not the bad guy*	*1 Samuel 24*

HUNKY GORY

Bible bit
1 Samuel 17:1 – 18:5

OK, unless you have been in a permanent state of sleep your whole life, you'll know a little bit about David killing the giant Goliath – a story about the little guy defeating the big bully. Hurrah for the little guy; bullies don't prosper, they'll get their comeuppance!!!!

NO! This isn't about that at all. Read it through. This is about relying on God. With God on our side we don't need anything else, and anything is possible. We can reach our true potential. Go on – take a look at the story.

Radio commentary

You join us in the 85th minute of the FA Cup Third Round tie between AFC **Little Chipping on-the-Wold Rovers** and **Chelsea**. Chelsea, **Premiership champions, European favourites** and assembled at a cost of many millions of pounds – players earning tens of thousands of pounds a week. Little Chipping are a **bunch of part-timers** who earn their living delivering mail, cleaning windows and settling insurance claims, among other things.

Of course, Chelsea didn't join the FA Cup until this round, the **Third Round proper**, so this is their first FA Cup tie. Little Chipping have played a preliminary round, four qualifying rounds, one of which needed a replay, and of course the first and second round matches against Tranmere Rovers and Torquay United, both of which went to replays, extra time and penalties.

And now their defence has **held firm** for most of this match. After some pre-match taunting about how Chelsea were going to break the FA Cup scoring record, could the biggest crowd this small club has ever seen be about to have the thrill, and the financial reward, of a replay? **They have five minutes to hold out.** Dave Little, their goalkeeper, at only 167 cm – the **smallest keeper** in this year's competition – has stopped everything coming his way with a **sensational performance**.

And what's this? Chelsea's attack has broken down on the edge of the Little Chipping area and striker Kenny Saul has broken away. He's fast. All the Chelsea players are the wrong end of the pitch. **He's through.** They won't catch him. He takes the ball on. He rounds the goalkeeper who brings him down. **Penalty!**

And look who's going to take it. It's **Dave Little**. He's scored in previous penalty shoot-outs. He seems **nerveless**. He removes his goalie gloves and cap. He calmly steps up. He normally blasts them. The referee whistles and Little hits it straight down the middle. Petr Cech, lucky to still be on the pitch, dives out of the way. **It's there!** It would have hit Cech right between the eyes if he'd stayed still. **Little Chipping have scored and there won't be time to kick off again. Chelsea are out. What a giant-killing!**

USE WITH SESSION 14 BIBLE EXPERIENCE 'LEVEL 1 CONNECT' AND 'LEVEL 3 SWITCH ON'

David and Goliath

It was a standoff – the Israelite army on one hill, the Philistines on the other. They faced each other. They taunted each other. Neither side wanted to attack because, in warfare, defending higher ground gives you an advantage. So across the valley they traded insults.

'You cowards.'

'You wimps.'

'Come and have a go if you think you're hard enough.'

'We'll fold you in half.'

The Philistines had a big bloke. Seriously big and then bigger still. His armour alone was heavy enough to kill an ordinary Israelite soldier. He was so big he couldn't lift a shield big enough to protect himself as well as all his weapons, so a bloke went in front of him carrying it. Tough job.

The big bloke suggested, tauntingly of course, that they forget the 'army versus army' thing and do the 'one man versus one man' thing. Winner takes all. This would save a lot of bloodshed but had one small drawback: whoever stepped forward from the Israelite army was very likely to get folded in half and half again and end up becoming fertiliser for Philistine crops. So no great rush to volunteer then.

The Israelite king even offered incentives such as tax breaks, treasure and one of his daughters, but still no one took their chance. Maybe his daughters weren't that pretty. Who knows?

For 40 days the big Philistine issued his challenge. Once in the morning and once in the evening without a day off, so you have to admire his stamina. His name was Goliath, which isn't Hebrew for 'big, ugly, taunty bloke'.

David had some brothers in the Israelite army and, since he'd heard they weren't actually fighting at the time but only involved in a slanging match, he went to see if his brothers were OK. He took them some cheese as a gift, so let's hope it wasn't a long journey.

When he got there, he happened to hear the big, ugly, taunty bloke do his big, ugly, taunty thing. David made a few enquiries about why Goliath hadn't had his head cut off yet and his brothers got a bit naffed off at this, suggesting that leaving the sheep by themselves wasn't the smartest thing David had ever done, but thanks for the cheese. They thought

USE WITH SESSION 14 BIBLE EXPERIENCE 'LEVEL 1 CONNECT' AND 'LEVEL 3 SWITCH ON'

he'd come to watch the battle, which was a big spectator sport in those days as it took place in a small area rather than everywhere, and you could usually find a safe place to watch.

So David proposed showing them he was serious by offering to go and fight Goliath. Everyone told him he would be folded in like about nine or something because they weren't that good at maths, and David said, 'Whatever,' but he was used to killing lions and bears and, anyway, God had told him to do it – which sounds a bit intimidating. They said, 'OK,' while sniggering into their hands a bit and checking their maths.

So Saul, the king, had David dressed in armour, and when David got up nothing happened because it was a bit heavier than cheese.

David took the armour off, checked his arms and legs still worked, and went to get some stones for his sling. He hadn't told anyone he was going to win by superior weapons technology, mainly because they didn't understand the words 'superior', 'weapons' or 'technology'.

David moved towards Goliath who set out, quite clearly, his new fertiliser recipe that involved quite a lot of David. David liked this idea and shouted his own fertiliser recipe back. It was an improved recipe because it had better ingredients. OK. More ingredients.

Goliath ran at David who ran at Goliath who ran at David who ran at Goliath who... well, you get the picture. Then Goliath stopped because a stone in the forehead tends to do that to a man. He had a surprised look on his face and a not-working look on the rest of him. David cut Goliath's head off with his own sword since he didn't seem to be needing it any more.

The rest of the Philistines ran away to become part of the much-improved fertiliser recipe at Gath, which isn't Philistine for 'growbag'.

David kept Goliath's head for himself, which was a bit morbid.

And King Saul said to David, 'Whose son are you?' And David said, 'Jesse's,' which was the truth although not the sort of thing it was wise to say to a king without explanation.

And then it all got dreadfully complicated. David became popular, the king's son Jonathan became his best mate and gave him pressies, and Saul gave him a promotion. But Saul also began to get just the teeniest bit jealous.

USE WITH SESSION 14 BIBLE EXPERIENCE 'LEVEL 2 INTERFACE'

Part 1	Part 2
• David's problem	• My problem
• David's resources	• My resources
• David's skills	• My skills
• David's attitude	• My attitude
• David's result	• My result?

15

Bible: 1 Samuel 19:1–17

HE'S JUST A JEALOUS GUY

THE AIM: To see how God protects his people

The aim unpacked

This is the third of four sessions looking at the early years of David's life. David has become pretty popular since his victory over Goliath. But King Saul is jealous and, like many people who become jealous, he lashes out. But God is looking after David. Remember God has chosen David to be king – it is his plan. God protects his plan even through tough and difficult times.

WAY IN

theGRID MAGAZINE

WHAT: **quiz**
WHY: **to begin to think about protection**
WITH: **CD or MP3 of 'Protection' by Massive Attack, playback equipment, magazine page 101**

1 Play the track if you have it. You can download it from several sources. It includes the line, 'I stand in front of you; I'll take the force of the blow.'

2 Distribute copies of page 101. Invite everyone to work on the activity entitled 'Safe not sorry', matching the protective equipment to the right pursuits.

3 Introduce the session as being about the way God protects his people. If you think your group might already have some ideas about this, ask them to work out creatively which piece of protective equipment in the activity is most like the way God protects, and why.

SCENE SETTER

WHAT: **interview or demonstration**
WHY: **to introduce the idea of protection**
WITH: **protective equipment for a sport or pastime**

1 If you can, invite a guest to demonstrate some protective equipment. A good person to invite might be:

- a cricket batsman
- a hockey goalkeeper
- a beekeeper
- a builder or welder
- a member of a battle re-enactment society

2 Interview the person about the different functions of all the protective equipment they wear. Ask them what it would be like to do their activity without the protective gear. If you are unable to invite someone, get hold of some protective equipment and demonstrate it with another leader.

3 Say that this session is about the way God protects his people.

THEMED GAME

WHAT: **penalty shoot-out**
WHY: **to think about protection**
WITH: **football, goal, dice**

1 Hold a penalty shoot-out competition. Ask for a volunteer or leader to be the goalkeeper. If your group members all enjoy football, run a conventional penalty shoot-out competition.

2 If you need to make it more interesting, or to help some who might otherwise not enjoy it, add these handicaps:

- Shoot with the 'wrong' foot
- Shoot with no run-up
- Shoot with a blindfold on
- Throw a dice to allocate a particular part of the goal they must aim for to score: 1 = bottom left; 2 = top left; 3 = bottom centre; 4 = top centre; 5 = bottom right; 6 = top right

BIBLE EXPERIENCE

LEVEL 1: CONNECT

WHAT: **story**
WHY: **to see how God protects his people to see how God protects his people**
WITH: **magazine page 102, bed (of sorts!), bedclothes, pillows, wig**

1 Prepare a leader (or a responsible young person) in advance to be in on this activity. You will need a wig that matches your hair colour and style. Set up a makeshift 'bed' in the space where you meet.

2 Ask the prepared leader or young person to leave the room for some reason. Then demonstrate to the rest of the group how to fool someone that you are in bed, using two pillows and the wig.

3 Ask if anyone has ever used this deception. Find out why (if they will say). Then hide behind the 'bed'.

4 When the leader or young person comes back in, they should go over to the bed and give the 'occupant' a severe beating. They could say something like, 'Aha! [Your name] is lazing in bed when they should be working. I'm going to really wake them up today to teach them a lesson.' After a few moments, come out from your hiding place, interrupt them and ask what they are doing. Ham up the mistake.

5 Distribute copies of page 102 and ask everyone to turn to 'Royal soap: Episode 1'. Read aloud the paraphrase of 1 Samuel 19 while everyone else follows.

6 Ask if anyone has ever felt supernatural protection. What happened?

7 Explain that the Bible is full of accounts of God's people overcoming amazing odds to succeed. Taken individually, these stories might seem like coincidences, but put together they lead to the unshakeable conclusion that God will equip and protect those he calls for special work.

8 Ask the young people if they know that protection, and listen to their stories. Find out if they would like to ask God for that protection.

LEVEL 2: INTERFACE

WHAT: **art and craft**
WHY: **to see how God protects his people**
WITH: **magazine page 102, Bibles, drawing materials**

1 Summarise the story of young David so far (you could use 'Royal soap: Episode 1' from page 102). Now read 1 Samuel 19:1–17 together from a modern Bible translation such as *The Message* or the Youth Bible.

2 Tell the group that they have been commissioned to make a commemorative plaque in honour of David's life so far, with the theme 'God protects'. If they want a Latin motto for this, it would be *Deus protegit*.

3 Show them the examples of heraldic shields on pages 101 and 102 and suggest that they use some of the ideas to create a shield of their own. Divide them into pairs or threes to do this. They might want to refer back to the Bible passages they've looked at so far. They could perhaps include musicianship, bravery, shepherding, escape, and anything else they have learned about David experiencing God's calling, equipping and protection.

4 When they have finished, invite them to show and talk about the results, explaining each part of their designs.

5 Ask what they would put on their own shield if they were devising one and whether they would be happy with the same motto.

LEVEL 3: SWITCH ON

WHAT: **Bible study**
WHY: **to see how God protects his people**
WITH: **Bibles**

1 Distribute Bibles. Allocate each of the young people a character to follow in the Bible verses:

- David
- Saul
- Jonathan
- Michal
- A random soldier
- A random servant

2 Now invite them to read 1 Samuel 19:1–17 in pairs or threes.

3 Ask the young people to share how they think their character felt at the beginning and end of the story. Did their character experience God's help, protection or equipping?

4 Think about and discuss how many different ways God seemed to offer protection (such as escape, cover-up, warning).

5 See what conclusion the young people draw from this. Explain that one of the Bible's summaries of David is found in Acts 7:46, where it says that he 'pleased God'. God protected David because David was on God's side. Being on God's side is a place of the greatest safety.

6 If your group members enjoy role play, choose a volunteer for each character. Interview them about their part in the story and ask them what they feel about the role of God – David's God.

RESPOND

MUSICAL

WHAT: **song**
WHY: **to thank God for his protection**
WITH: **CD or MP3 of 'Protection' by Massive Attack, playback equipment**

1 Play the Massive Attack song, 'Protection'. (If you used it in the *Way in* activity, play it again!) As it plays, invite everyone to reflect on God's protection. Make the point that God stands in front of us taking the force of many blows. He has already given us the resources to cope with whatever might come our way.

2 Over the instrumental parts of the song, invite group members to pray aloud if they want to.

3 If you're unable to get hold of the song, simply display the words, 'I stand in front of you; I'll take the force of the blow'. Use them as a focus of thanksgiving while playing other instrumental music in the background.

PRACTICAL

WHAT: **discussion**
WHY: **to offer God's protection to others**

1 Encourage the young people to discuss whether there are any people at school who could do with some practical protection. Do they know of anyone who is being bullied, for instance? What sorts of things happen in their school from which people may need protection? Discourage them from sharing names or giving specific information which may lead to gossip.

2 Challenge the group to share God's protection with the people they have just thought of. Invite them to make a list of practical steps they could take to help, such as walking with them to the bus stop, phoning them in the evening or inviting them to something fun, such as this group.

3 Pray for those people and situations together and encourage the young people to commit themselves to asking God to help them share his protection with others.

CREATIVE

WHAT: **craft**
WHY: **to be reminded of God's protection daily**
WITH: **magazine page 102, drawing materials**

1 This activity builds on *Bible experience* 'Level 2 Interface'.

2 Invite the young people to think about things that protect them in their day-to-day lives.

3 Distribute copies of page 102 and invite the young people to look at the template for a heraldic shield. Ask them to copy the outline onto a piece of paper and then to divide it into four sections.

4 In each section of the shield they should draw a design or write some words that explain how they feel protected, under the headings:

- physical (such as with shelter)
- mental (such as by learning)
- spiritual (such as through prayer)
- emotional (such as through friends)

5 Finally, ask them to come up with a motto for the protection they enjoy. The motto should express their appreciation of God's protection in their lives. Look at the results together and encourage the young people to put their shield somewhere prominent at home where it will remind them daily to thank God.

MORE ON THIS THEME:

If you want to do a short series with your group, other sessions that work well with this one are:

13	*About a boy*	*1 Samuel 16:1–13; Psalm 23*
14	*Hunky gory*	*1 Samuel 17:1 – 18:5*
16	*I'm not the bad guy*	*1 Samuel 24*

Bible bit
1 Samuel 19:1–17

I often listen to the radio, and when something I don't like comes on I turn it off. Saul has a bit of a different approach to musical criticism. Saul is really losing it now; he is saying one thing and doing another, and David's life is in danger. But God is working behind the scenes. He has people helping him and keeping God's future king safe.

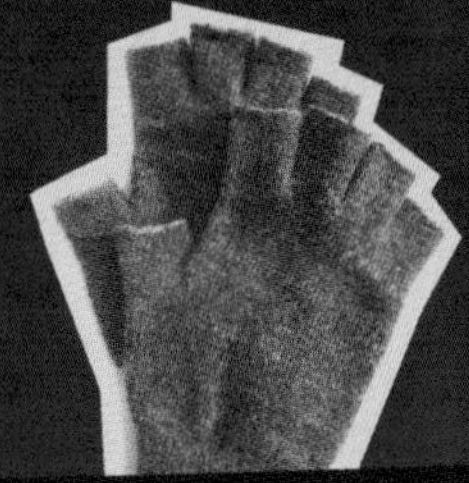

SAFE NOT SORRY

Oops! Everyone has forgotten a crucial piece of protective equipment. Match up the stuff with the person who might need it most. Some of the gear could fit more than one pursuit. You should be able to do the match-up by a process of elimination once you have allocated the unique stuff to the right owner.

Clue: chefs don't need to rope up.

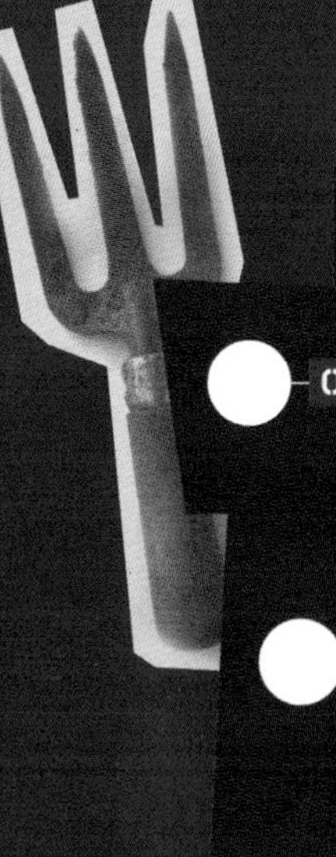

1 OPENING BATSMAN	A OVEN GLOVES
2 SCAFFOLDER	B CRASH HELMET
3 FOOTBALLER	C SHIN PADS
4 CLIMBER	D FACE MASK
5 MEDIEVAL SOLDIER	E ROPE
6 CHEF	F GLOVES
7 SURGEON	G SHIELD
8 WELDER	H PROTECTIVE GLASSES
9 MOTORCYCLIST	I HARD HAT
10 GARDENER	J PADS

ROYAL SOAP: EPISODE 1

The story so far: King Saul is going a bit doolally and his servants find a young man, David, who plays him music to calm him down. When a tricky opponent turns up on the battlefield, the same man turns out to be a bit of a giant-killer, although the king has forgotten his name. On top of all his abilities the man is also good-looking.

David, the good-looking, giant-killing musician, becomes best friends with the king's son Jonathan and gets promoted in the army because of his ability. The king becomes jealous of the popularity of this rising star and tries to manipulate him by giving him one of his daughters, cheaply, in marriage. She is called Michal, but she isn't a bloke. Then the king plots to kill the man, who is now his son-in-law.

In this chapter, the king's son 'has a word' with his dad who agrees to try not to kill the man, but then the king loses it and throws a spear at him while he is playing soothing music. The man escapes to his own house but the king sends men to kill him there. Back at his house the man escapes again, this time out of a window while his wife (the king's daughter – do keep up!) fools everyone with the old 'goat's hair and statue under the bedclothes' trick.

SHIELDS OF PROTECTION

DESIGN A SHIELD FOR DAVID

This could include musicianship; bravery; shepherding; escape; anything else you have learned about David experiencing God's calling, equipping and protection.

Bible: 1 Samuel 24

16

I'M NOT THE BAD GUY

THE AIM: To learn to live with mercy in an unmerciful world

The aim unpacked

This is the final session of four looking at David's early years. Despite all that had happened to David, he didn't take revenge and kill Saul. So often we are expected to act in a certain way. But David didn't do what was expected, or what he could have done to make things easier for himself. In our own lives this is easier said than done, but with God's help we can overcome, just as David did.

WAY IN

theGRID MAGAZINE

WHAT: **illustration and discussion**
WHY: **to think about what mercy is**
WITH: **magazine page 106, dictionary, flip chart or whiteboard (optional)**

1 Distribute copies of page 106 and invite everyone to look at 'Have mercy'. It's a story about mercy. Either ask a good reader to read it aloud or give everyone a short time to read and digest it.

2 Discuss what the story tells us about mercy.

3 Share (perhaps display on a flip chart or whiteboard) a dictionary definition of mercy: 'Abstention from infliction of suffering or punishment; disposition towards forgiveness'. Discuss any of the long words, or look them up, until you have a definition that everyone understands.

SCENE SETTER

WHAT: **merciful words**
WHY: **to begin to think about mercy**
WITH: **flip chart or whiteboard, sticky tack, dictionary, page 107**

1 Copy the word cards from page 107 and cut them out. Shuffle them and deal them out among the young people and any other leaders.

2 Divide a sheet of flip chart paper or a whiteboard down the centre. Head one half 'Merciful' and the other 'Unmerciful'.

3 Invite everyone to take a piece of sticky tack and stick their word(s) on whichever side they think is appropriate. The nearer the centre they place the word, the more ambiguous in meaning it might be. Some words could straddle the line if they wish.

4 Discuss any areas of disagreement. Use the dictionary as the final arbiter of truth and justice.

THEMED GAME

WHAT: **gunge quiz**
WHY: **to think about risk versus mercy**
WITH: **pots of gunge, cover-up clothes, washing facilities, towels, general knowledge questions**

1 Warn the young people in advance to bring a change of clothes. Alternatively, have some cover-up clothes ready for them to slip on over their normal gear. You will also need some gunge – either food-based (rice pudding or custard) or something like Gelli Baff.

2 Pair everyone off with someone with whom they get on well. Any couples, housemates or family members among the leaders should play together.

3 Choose three pairs at random. One person sits on a chair and the other stands. Let them decide which way around.

4 Give the standing person this dilemma – they can either be gunged or attempt to answer a general knowledge question. If they answer it correctly, no one will be gunged; if they get it wrong, their partner will be gunged.

5 Afterwards, or later in the session, interview the innocent partners about how it felt to be helpless and reliant on someone else's mercy.

BIBLE EXPERIENCE

LEVEL 1: CONNECT

WHAT: **Bible story telling**
WHY: **to learn to live with mercy in an unmerciful world**
WITH: **Bible**

1 Paraphrase the first part of the story of David and Saul in the cave – 1 Samuel 24:1–4. Emphasise:

- Saul wanted to kill David and had tried to do so on several occasions.
- Saul didn't know that David was in the cave when he went in there (for a wee).
- This meant that David had the opportunity to surprise Saul and could easily have got rid of him. Then David would have become king.

2 Discuss all together or in pairs:

- What would you have done?
- What do you think happened next?

3 Continue to summarise the story, from verses 5 to 8. Emphasise:

- David chose not to kill Saul but to leave to God the timing of his succession.
- He cut off a bit of Saul's – wait for it – robe, to show that he could have killed him but instead had mercy.

4 Discuss again: How do you think Saul would have felt about this?

5 Continue the story, from verses 9 to 22. Saul realised that David had shown him mercy and that this was God's leading. He then accepted that David would one day succeed him as king.

6 End by explaining that mercy often feels less right than revenge, but its lasting consequences are superior. Suggest that the young people think about this next time they want to pay back a wrong with another wrong.

LEVEL 2: INTERFACE

WHAT: **quiz and discussion**
WHY: **to learn to live with mercy in an unmerciful world**
WITH: **magazine page 106, page 108, Bible**

1 Give out Bibles or copies of page 106. Get everyone to read either 1 Samuel 24 in their Bible or the paraphrase 'Royal soap: Episode 2'.

2 Ask whether anyone can think of a leader who has been assassinated.

3 Explain that in national life down the ages, murder has often been practised as a way of making progress. Violence has often been used as a way to solve problems. In fact, the opposite is true. Saying, 'You are wrong but we will go along with you because you are our leader', will stand you in better stead when you expect others to do the same with your preferred leaders later. However angry protesters are, however unreasonable they think the authorities are being, the person who throws the first stone sets back the momentum of the protest. It will only lead to violence and to what 1 Samuel 25:31 beautifully describes as '... the staggering burden of needless bloodshed ...' (NIV). David resisted revenge.

4 Hand out copies of the 'How merciful are you?' quiz from page 108. Give the young people a few minutes to complete it and work out their score. Help any who are having difficulty with the scoring.

5 Invite any who wish to share their results to do so, but don't press anyone. Some may have been shocked by their score and want to keep it to themselves. Pray (quietly) that this is a life-changing moment for them.

6 Give thanks, briefly, for the grace of God – grace meaning 'undeserved mercy and love', or God's Riches At Christ's Expense.

LEVEL 3: SWITCH ON

WHAT: **Bible study**
WHY: **to learn to live with mercy in an unmerciful world**
WITH: **Bibles**

1 Divide the young people into two groups. Ask one group to read 1 Samuel 24 and the other to read 1 Samuel 26.

2 Ask the groups to summarise their chapter for each other.

3 Ask if they would have been able to resist taking revenge. Explain that it can sometimes be very hard for a leader to hear the word of God clearly. Talk about these five reasons why David might have killed Saul:

- The opportunity happened twice. First the cave, now the camp. How tempting for David to think, *It must be the Lord's will.*
- The advice of his friends was to do it. How tempting for David to think, *It must be the Lord's will.*
- The need for Saul to go was clear. He was going mad. How tempting for David to think, *It must be the Lord's will.*
- The call on David as the future king was clear. How tempting for him to think, *It must be the Lord's will.*
- Revenge: Saul had been wrongly trying to kill David for weeks. Revenge would be sweet and would end this unreasonable chase. How tempting for David to think, *It must be the Lord's will.*

Yet David heard a different voice – perhaps a more distant, quieter voice. 1 Samuel 3:1 suggests that normality for the community of Samuel was that God didn't speak to the people.

4 Invite someone to read Luke 22:39–46. In Gethsemane, another great leader listened hard to God and concluded that it was necessary to go to his death in order to have mercy on the world, rather than to carry on preaching and healing.

5 Discuss areas where the young people find it hard to hear God's voice, or to exercise mercy. Pray for each other.

RESPOND

MUSICAL

WHAT: **music**
WHY: **to demonstrate that God's mercy is endless**
WITH: **two appropriate pieces of music, one with a long ending and one with a tuneful melody (perhaps a worship song), playback equipment**

1 Play a track that has a very long ending – the sort of rock song where everyone makes a lot of noise until the drummer says stop would be appropriate.

2 Explain that God's love and mercy really do go on for ever. They're not like a song that doesn't seem to know how and when to stop, but rather a tune that God consistently plays. It is his melody.

3 Play your second piece of music as you encourage the young people to think and pray about this.

PRACTICAL

WHAT: **research**
WHY: **to see who is helping the world become a more merciful place**
WITH: **computer with internet access**

1 Together, research the work of organisations such as:

- Amnesty International – www.amnesty.org.uk
- Mercy Ships – www.mercyships.org.uk
- Mercy Corps – www.mercycorps.org.uk

These organisations are all involved with demonstrating God's mercy to those in need. If you don't have internet access during the session, you could research the organisations in advance and print off some information for the young people to look at.

2 Find an organisation or project to support financially or with interest and prayer. The Amnesty site includes a section that youth groups can get involved with.

CREATIVE

WHAT: **prayer**
WHY: **to pray for those needing God's mercy today**
WITH: **old local newspapers**

1 It's easy to think of mercy as something that is needed by those who live in far-off places. Use the local papers to identify people and places locally where mercy and grace would help.

2 Do the newspapers suggest your locality has a merciful nature? Were there any stories highlighting mercy rather than its lack?

3 Now lay some of the key stories on the floor and pray about them, perhaps moving around the room and praying in groups huddled around the various stories.

MORE ON THIS THEME:

If you want to do a short series with your group, other sessions that work well with this one are:

13	*About a boy*	*1 Samuel 16:1–13; Psalm 23*
14	*Hunky gory*	*1 Samuel 17:1 – 18:5*
15	*He's just a jealous guy*	*1 Samuel 19:1–17*

ROYAL SOAP: EPISODE 2

David escaped from King Saul's evil clutches and went to war for a bit of a break. The king had given his daughter to David as his wife, but he took her back and gave her to another guy. Meanwhile, David had found another couple of wives anyway – you could do that in those days.

Catching up with David, King Saul made several more attempts to kill him, but David had surrounded himself with holy people, and everyone who tried to kill him became so overcome with holiness they couldn't do it. Even the king himself became holy, for a bit.

Back at the palace, the king expected David to show up for a special feast but he skived off. The king's son Jonathan, David's best mate, covered for him so the king tried to kill him too. Nutter!

Our hero, David, found himself on the run, escaping from the king four more times, each with a little story attached:

In a holy place he was so hungry he ate consecrated communion bread, which annoyed some people.

In the presence of another king – a man so scary David had to pretend to be mad to get away – David was sent away with the response, 'I have enough mad people in my kingdom; who needs more?'

In a cave, David became the leader of a band of 400 people, all either distressed, in debt or discontented. Normal, then.

In a forest, the desert and the hills, he continued to evade capture. David found King Saul in a cave having a pee (check the Bible, that's what it says). He could have killed him but instead he cut off a bit of the king's garment and withdrew. He was such a reasonable guy, he even got a bit of a guilty conscience about this. Later he produced it (the cloth, not the conscience) as evidence of his mercy.

Saul's flaw was that he turned away from the Lord. Nothing else he did wrong was therefore relevant.

David's flaw was that he sinned from time to time while following the Lord. Everything he did wrong was forgivable.

Listen for the voice of the Lord. If it's different from the way your leaders are behaving, be prepared to speak out – you may be the prophet. But be prepared to be ignored, too; that's often what happens to prophets. Frustrating, isn't it?

HAVE MERCY

A woman was about to see her son executed for several crimes. Desperate, she approached the king who had ordered the death penalty. 'Have mercy on my son,' she pleaded. 'Please have mercy.'

'Madam,' said the king, 'your son is a criminal and has committed serious crimes. He does not deserve mercy.' Turning to the executioner he said, 'Proceed.'

'Of course he doesn't deserve it,' said the woman, bravely continuing. 'If he deserved it then it would be pardon, not mercy.'

It is said that the king was so impressed with this answer that he cancelled the execution.

RESOURCE PAGE

USE WITH SESSION 16 WAY IN 'SCENE SETTER'

Absolution	Accepting	Acquittal	Alarm	Amnesty	Anxiety	Appreciation
Attention	Benevolence	Care	Clemency	Coldness	Compassion	Concern
Consideration	Cruelty	Distress	Dread	Empathy	Exoneration	Fear
Forgiveness	Fright	Grief	Harshness	Horror	Iciness	Kindness
Leniency	Meanness	Misery	Moderation	Niceness	Pain	Pardon
Pity	Punishment	Release	Reprisal	Retribution	Revenge	Sorrow
Sympathy	Terror	Thoughtfulness	Understanding	Vengeance	Warmth	Worry

RESOURCE PAGE

USE WITH SESSION 16 BIBLE EXPERIENCE 'LEVEL 2 INTERFACE'

How merciful are you?

1 A fly is annoying you while you work at home. Do you...

a) splatter it with a newspaper?

b) crush it with your bare hands?

c) ignore it and hope it leaves or dies?

d) open the window so it can fly out?

2 Your normally reliable friend owes you some money. She has promised to give it back today, but has forgotten to bring it to school. Do you...

a) beat her with sticks?

b) beat her with words?

c) go round to her house after school and get it?

d) let her off until tomorrow?

3 In a movie the hero has caught a villain. It is the last scene. Do you hope...

a) they make friends?

b) the villain gets a beating?

c) the villain gets taken to the nearest police station?

d) the hero gets a beating?

4 A friend who talks too much has phoned. Do you...

a) hang up?

b) find something else to do while you are listening?

c) listen irritatedly?

d) listen with attention?

USE WITH SESSION 16 BIBLE EXPERIENCE 'LEVEL 2 INTERFACE'

5 Your friend gives you back a book they borrowed. The cover is battered and coffee-stained. It looks as if they dropped it in the bath too. Do you...

a) say, 'Thank you'?

b) say, 'Thank you' but look cross?

c) beat them with sticks?

d) demand compensation?

6 In a burger bar the service is slower than usual and the counter staff are obviously stressed. Do you...

a) leave and go somewhere else?

b) add to their stress by complaining about the service?

c) try to be extra-friendly and polite?

d) order as usual but ask to have a word with the manager afterwards?

7 Your brother or sister has borrowed your favourite T-shirt without asking. Do you...

a) do nothing?

b) borrow something of theirs without asking?

c) ask for it back, accepting that this is what your brother or sister is on the earth for?

d) trash something of theirs?

8 Your friend is always late and today is no different. Do you...

a) accept this without any grace whatsoever?

b) accept this graciously?

c) give them an earful of abuse as usual – isn't that the point of having friends?

d) have a friendly chat about why this is?

USE WITH SESSION 16 BIBLE EXPERIENCE 'LEVEL 2 INTERFACE'

9 Your friend pulls out of a long-planned party because they have to look after a sick relative. Do you...

a) ask why someone else can't do it?

b) totally understand?

c) phone the sick relative to check if it's the truth?

d) go berserk?

10 How forgiving do you think you are?

a) Forgiving? What's that then?

b) Not enough – I get annoyed with myself when I'm mean

c) A bit, but people annoy me from time to time

d) Totally – I'm not perfect either!

Scores:

1 a) 2; b) 1; c) 3; d) 4

2 a) 1; b) 2; c) 3; d) 4

3 a) 4; b) 2; c) 3; d) 1

4 a) 1; b) 2; c) 3; d) 4

5 a) 4; b) 3; c) 1; d) 2

6 a) 2; b) 1; c) 4; d) 3

7 a) 4; b) 2; c) 3; d) 1

8 a) 2; b) 4; c) 1; d) 3

9 a) 3; b) 4; c) 2; d) 1

10 a) 1; b) 3; c) 2; d) 4

Explanation:

10–20 You think revenge is a dish best served cold. You are icy. Consider a career as a professional assassin.

21–30 On balance, you are balanced. You show some forbearance and forgiveness but can get irritated by your freinds and family.

31–40 You are very patient and almost saintly. Don't let people walk all over you. Be willing to complain or stand up for yourself from time to time.

Bible: 1 Kings 17

17

EXTREME PROPHECY

THE AIM: To see God at work through his prophet

The aim unpacked

In this session we examine God's power and justice as it's seen in the life of Elijah. We hear of an extreme case of God providing for Elijah and his landlady. The Bible is full of seemingly amazing stories and events. These may seem far away from the everyday lives of the young people. However, God is still the same and is able to show his power and justice through us today if we follow him.

WAY IN

theGRID MAGAZINE

WHAT: **quiz**
WHY: **to think about the character of a prophet**
WITH: **magazine page 114, flip chart or whiteboard, marker pen**

1 Hand out copies of magazine page 114.

2 Ask the young people to identify the qualities they would expect to find in an Old Testament prophet. (They could work in pairs if they wish.)

3 Invite feedback, then work out the top and bottom three qualities. Display these on the flip chart or whiteboard.

4 Refer to your results later in this session and in the next three sessions to work out how accurate your conclusions were.

SCENE SETTER

WHAT: **art**
WHY: **to display some of the images that will come up in the passage**
WITH: **painting and collage materials, large sheets of paper to hang on the walls (such as lining paper)**

1 Encourage the young people to create some scenery together that you can use as a backdrop for the next few sessions. Give them a list of things that will appear in the Bible passages over the next few sessions:

- ravens (large crow-like birds)
- loaf of bread
- child
- earthquake
- fire
- bulls
- chariot
- crown
- bunches of grapes

2 Invite the young people to create small and large images of these things and place them on the larger sheets of paper. These will work as visual reminders of the events of the sessions.

3 Decorate the walls of the meeting room with the collages. Use them as visual aids.

THEMED GAME

WHAT: **food charades**
WHY: **to think about being hungry**
WITH: **list of different types of food, prize (optional)**

1 Before the session, make a list of lots of different types of food, eg eggs, mashed potato, spaghetti, chocolate cake.

2 Divide the young people into at least two teams and choose one member of each team to be the mimer. Give each mimer a list of food items and challenge them to mime each item to their team without using any words. Challenge the teams to guess as many as they can in a set amount of time. You could award a prize of some sweets to the winning team.

3 Ask the young people if they feel hungry now, after thinking about all that food! Ask them, 'What is the hungriest you can ever remember being?'

4 Drop in at the end of this that water is an even more important necessity for survival than food. If appropriate, say that this session you'll be thinking about someone who needed to be kept fed.

BIBLE EXPERIENCE

LEVEL 1: CONNECT

WHAT: guessing game
WHY: to see God at work through his prophet
WITH: flip chart or whiteboard, marker pen

1 Not all the young people at this interest level will believe there is a God who cares for them. In order to connect with them, ask:

- What sort of things would you expect a powerful God, who cares for you individually, to do?

Make a list of the answers on the flip chart or whiteboard.

2 Explain that you are going to read a passage from the Bible and that you will be leaving gaps at the end of each part and asking them, 'What would you have done?'

3 Read or paraphrase the story of Elijah from 1 Kings 17, starting with verses 1–4. Ask, 'What would you have done if you'd been Elijah?'

- Take responses, then read verses 5–9. Again ask, 'What would you have done if you'd been Elijah?'
- Take responses, then read verses 10–14. Ask, 'What would you have done if you'd been the widow?'
- Take responses, then read verses 15–18. Again ask, 'What would you have done if you'd been Elijah?'
- Take responses, then read verses 19–23. Ask, 'What would you have said if you'd been that widow?'
- Take responses, then read verse 24. Ask, 'Would you have been convinced that this was a man of God? Why, or why not?'

4 End by explaining that this is the story of a great man who, the Bible tells us, trusted a powerful God to care for him.

LEVEL 2: INTERFACE

WHAT: Bible study
WHY: to see God at work through his prophet
WITH: magazine page 115

1 Ask the young people to imagine they are teachers. Read the letter on page 115. How would they respond to this letter?

2 Read or paraphrase 1 Kings 17. Ask the group to imagine they are King Ahab.

- How do they respond to this story?
- Is it as unbelievable as the letter from Robbie?

3 List some of the things that happen in the passage that they think are unbelievable.

LEVEL 3: SWITCH ON

WHAT: Bible study
WHY: to see God at work through his prophet
WITH: Bibles, laptop with internet access or book of names (optional), flip chart or whiteboard, marker pen

1 Find out before the session what your name means.

2 Tell the young people what your name means. Ask them if they know what theirs means. If possible, look some up.

3 Challenge the young people to think of someone called Elijah. How about Elijah Wood (the actor)? Can anyone guess what the name might mean? The meaning is 'Yah is El', or 'Yahweh is God' or 'The Lord is my God'.

4 Ask the young people to read 1 Kings 17 in pairs and to make a note of any instances where there is evidence that Elijah is a man of God.

5 Share the results and write them on a flip chart or whiteboard. Begin to build up a word picture of a person of God.

6 Explain that Elijah has burst onto the scene without any biography or announcement. He is just 'there' suddenly in 1 Kings 17. Over a few short chapters of 1 Kings, the account is told of a man of God so exciting that when Jesus came, people wondered if he might be Elijah returned (Mark 6:15; 8:28).

RESPOND

17

MUSICAL

WHAT: **singing**
WHY: **to focus on God's work throughout history**
WITH: **words and music for 'These Are the Days of Elijah' by Robin Mark, playback equipment**

1 These Are the Days of Elijah' is a good, up-tempo song which your group might enjoy singing. It reminds us of God's provision down the ages, through the prophets, priests and kings of the Old Testament and latterly through Jesus.

2 If your group does not like singing, display the lyrics and invite some volunteers to read them over some instrumental music.

3 Close with a prayer, asking God to work through each member of the group to show his power and justice to the world.

PRACTICAL

WHAT: **feed the hungry**
WHY: **to continue the prophet's work by helping to overcome food shortages**
WITH: **internet access (optional)**

1 One of the many reasons Jesus was associated with Elijah was that they both did food miracles. We cannot make everlasting bread in the way Elijah or later Jesus did, but we can help to feed others. Invite the young people to think of some ways – for example, giving to famine relief charities, collecting food for homeless projects or local foodbanks.

2 Encourage the young people to decide on one thing they can do to help and to commit to doing it. If your church collects food for those who are less well off, encourage the young people to take part in this. (This will also involve them more in the activities of the wider church.) Think about other ways they can integrate this into their daily lives, such as using the 'Everyclick' search facility (www.everyclick.com/) to raise money for charity.

3 We have learned through this session that famine is always with us, but it is not God's desire that people should go hungry. Pray that God might use what the young people give for his glory.

CREATIVE

WHAT: **drawing a 'prophet'**
WHY: **to reinforce the observations we have made about Elijah**
WITH: **large sheet of paper (or length of wallpaper), marker pens**

1 Review with the young people the qualities of a prophet that they looked at in the *Way in* 'Quiz' activity (if you did this). Invite them to assess how accurate they were according to the passage.

2 Invite the young people to make a human outline on the paper by drawing around a young person.

3 Ask them to write the heading, 'Today's holy people need to...' above the outline and then write as many phrases or qualities as they can around it, inspired by the passage.

4 End with a prayer that we might allow God to work through us and be prepared to look out for God at work through others.

MORE ON THIS THEME:

If you want to do a short series with your group, other sessions that work well with this one are:

18	*Great Baals of fire*	*1 Kings 18*
19	*I'm not the one and only*	*1 Kings 19*
20	*Not beyond justice*	*1 Kings 21:1–19; 22:29–40*

Bible bit
1 Kings 17

Wow. One chapter and we have life, death, drought, no food, some food, miracles and a prophet. But for Elijah the prophet, that is pretty much all in a day's work. Israel was going through a very hard time. Their current king, Ahab, was a really nasty guy – and I mean nasty! God showed his power and his desire for justice through Elijah so don't expect things to be boring!

CHARACTER OF A PROPHET

A prophet walks through the door and into the room. (No, it's not the start of a really bad joke!) What would you expect the prophet to be like? Below are some words to describe a person's character. Decide which ones you think might describe a prophet, or come up with some of your own.

As you read more of Elijah's story, return to this page and see how your guesswork matched up with what the prophet Elijah was really like.

- [ ] ____________
- [ ] FRIGHTENED
- [ ] DEMANDING
- [ ] ____________
- [ ] REASSURING
- [ ] ____________
- [ ] AGGRESSIVE
- [ ] TIRED
- [ ] ____________
- [ ] ____________
- [ ] PRAYERFUL
- [ ] ____________
- [ ] SARCASTIC
- [ ] VIOLENT
- [ ] HOLY
- [ ] HUNGRY
- [ ] ____________
- [ ] POWERFUL
- [ ] DEPRESSED
- [ ] ____________
- [ ] OBEDIENT
- [ ] CONFIDENT
- [ ] ____________

Weather
1 Kings 17
Exceptionally dry for many years

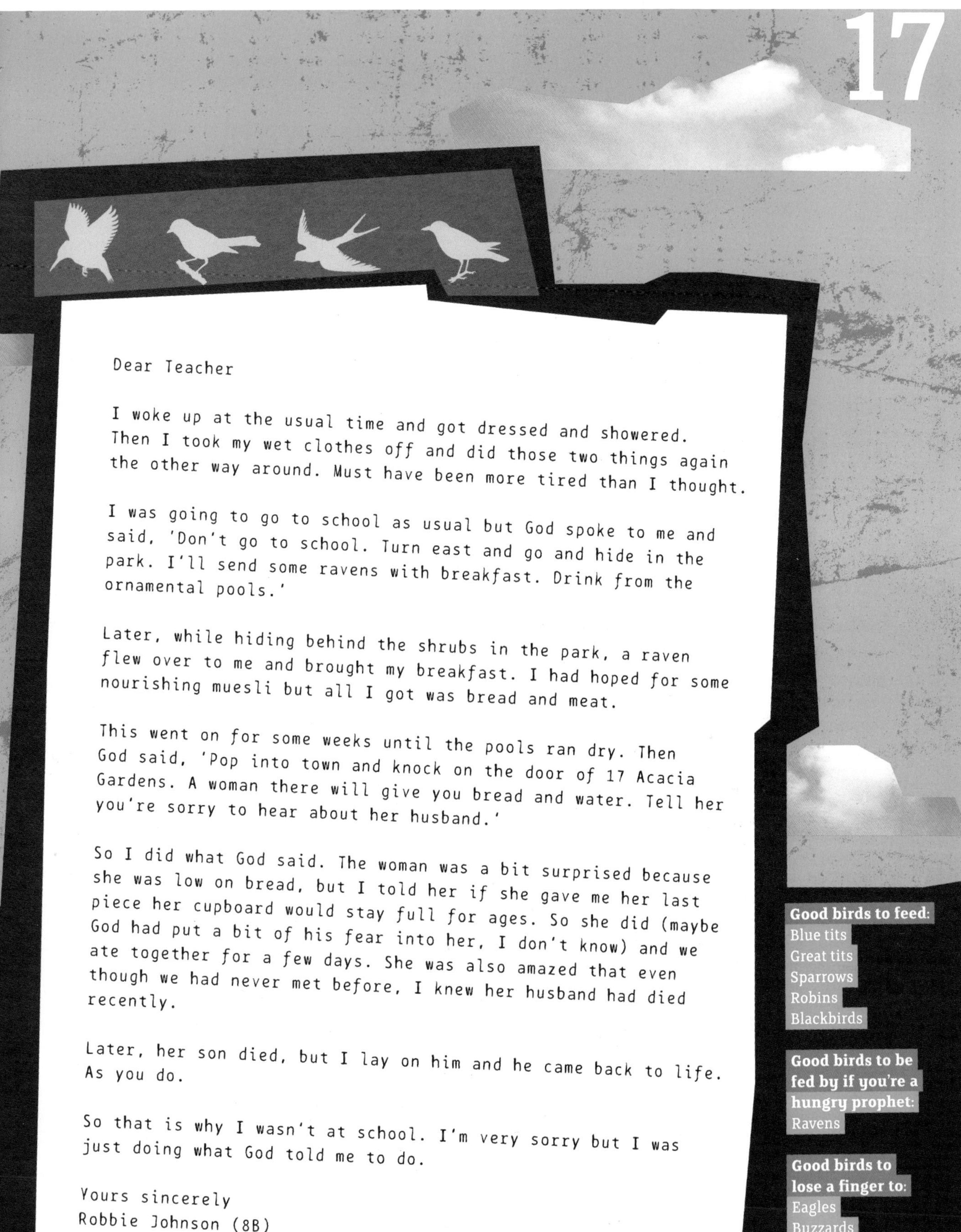

Dear Teacher

I woke up at the usual time and got dressed and showered. Then I took my wet clothes off and did those two things again the other way around. Must have been more tired than I thought.

I was going to go to school as usual but God spoke to me and said, 'Don't go to school. Turn east and go and hide in the park. I'll send some ravens with breakfast. Drink from the ornamental pools.'

Later, while hiding behind the shrubs in the park, a raven flew over to me and brought my breakfast. I had hoped for some nourishing muesli but all I got was bread and meat.

This went on for some weeks until the pools ran dry. Then God said, 'Pop into town and knock on the door of 17 Acacia Gardens. A woman there will give you bread and water. Tell her you're sorry to hear about her husband.'

So I did what God said. The woman was a bit surprised because she was low on bread, but I told her if she gave me her last piece her cupboard would stay full for ages. So she did (maybe God had put a bit of his fear into her, I don't know) and we ate together for a few days. She was also amazed that even though we had never met before, I knew her husband had died recently.

Later, her son died, but I lay on him and he came back to life. As you do.

So that is why I wasn't at school. I'm very sorry but I was just doing what God told me to do.

Yours sincerely
Robbie Johnson (8B)

Good birds to feed:
Blue tits
Great tits
Sparrows
Robins
Blackbirds

Good birds to be fed by if you're a hungry prophet:
Ravens

Good birds to lose a finger to:
Eagles
Buzzards

18

Bible: 1 Kings 18

GREAT BAALS OF FIRE

THE AIM: To consider that God is the only God

The aim unpacked

In this session, Elijah goes up against the prophets of Baal and we see God's power at work through his prophet. Our young people often face situations where they have to stand up for God against the majority. These situations may not be as dramatic as Elijah's experience, but they will take lots of courage. Encourage the young people to keep God at the centre of their lives.

WAY IN

theGRID MAGAZINE

WHAT: quiz
WHY: to introduce the pyrotechnics of the passage to follow
WITH: magazine page 119

1 Give out copies of page 119 and ask the young people to find the article about safety instructions.

2 Invite them to get into pairs to work out where they might see those instructions and also some places where the warnings might be amusing – for example, on the door of the room where you hold your youth meeting, 'May contain nuts'.

3 Explain that the Bible story we're going to read would probably fall foul of several safety regulations, even before we get to the merciless slaughter.

4 If you did the 'Character of a prophet' exercise last session you may want to refer to it now to refresh everyone's memory. (Alternatively, do it now as another scene setter activity.)

SCENE SETTER

WHAT: game
WHY: to think about making tasks difficult

1 Divide the young people into two teams. Each team takes it in turns to name a task the other team has to do (in their imaginations). The other team has to send the task back to the first team but make it slightly more difficult. For example:

- Team 1: Go to the shops and buy some pop.
- Team 2: Hop to the shops and buy some pop.
- Team 1: Hop to the shops and buy a case of pop.
- Team 2: Hop to the shops, buy a case of pop and carry it back one-handed.

You get the idea. The more you do it, the more ridiculous it will become.

2 Explain that this session will include a ridiculous escalation of a challenge. Look out for it.

INTERNET GAME

WHAT: to think about improving through experience
WITH: computer or tablet with internet access

1 Go to www.albinoblacksheep.com/games/invisiblemouse. In this simple game your mouse 'disappears' and you have to guide it over a short course which starts simply and becomes treacherous.

2 See who can achieve the most levels. If you aren't very good, a gloating caption will tell you that 'You suck' – sorry.

3 Explain that this game becomes more difficult as it progresses through the levels. To complete it you need to improve and overcome the obstacles. In this session we will see someone else who overcomes obstacles, but not through his own skill.

BIBLE EXPERIENCE 18

LEVEL 1: CONNECT

WHAT: **drama**
WHY: **to consider that God is the only God**
WITH: **Bibles, or printouts of the passage**

1 Read 1 Kings 18:16–40. If it is read well, this is a strong enough story to hold the attention of most groups. For a very unchurched group it may help if you don't announce that it is from the Bible until after you've read it.

2 Invite the young people to ask questions to ensure that they have understood the key point of the story – the power of the true God compared to the lack of power of non-gods.

3 Now divide the young people into smaller groups of three or four, if necessary. Invite them to turn the story into a drama. They could bring the story up to date by using contemporary characters if they wish.

4 After giving them some preparation time, watch the dramas and allow everyone to comment on each sketch.

5 Discuss with the young people whether they think there is a God and what power he has. Lead on to these questions:

- Do they experience that power at work in their lives? How?
- If they don't, and they would like to, what do they think they should do about it?

6 Allow appropriate time for follow-up, one to one, for anyone who is especially interested.

LEVEL 2: INTERFACE

WHAT: **Bible study with illustrations**
WHY: **to consider that God is the only God**
WITH: **pack of cards, magazine page 120**

1 If you can, do a simple card trick or other magic trick to introduce this activity.

2 Give out copies of page 120 and read together the story of the magician's volunteer.

3 Find out if anyone has ever been in the audience when a magician asked for a volunteer to help with a trick. Has anyone actually been a volunteer? What do they think happened next in the story?

4 Read the passage from 1 Kings 18. Explain that, although it looks and sounds like a piece of magic, it was only too real. As the slaughter of the false prophets afterwards demonstrated, these people died for their magic – or lack of it. It also showed that God was the only God around who was able to do this sort of thing.

5 Discuss with the group:

- Why did Elijah encourage the false prophets?
- Why did he go to so much trouble to make God's job harder?
- What do the group think the Lord's 'power' (v 46) means today?

LEVEL 3: SWITCH ON

WHAT: **Bible study**
WHY: **to consider that God is the only God**
WITH: **Bibles**

1 There is a certain pantomime quality to the way the story is told in 1 Kings 18. Read the passage together and encourage the young people to either boo or cheer as each character is mentioned. Stop for each new character and ask the young people their reasons for either booing or cheering. The correct responses should be:

- The Lord: cheer at God's name, the Creator (Genesis 1:1)
- Elijah: cheer at God's prophet, a man of God (1 Kings 17:24)
- Ahab: boo a bad king (1 Kings 16:30)
- Obadiah: cheer a devout believer (1 Kings 18:3b)
- Jezebel: boo a bad queen who killed the Lord's prophets (1 Kings 18:4)
- Baal: boo a false god (1 Kings 16:31)
- Asherah: boo a false god (1 Kings 16:33)

They are all introduced in the first half of the story so you should be able to read the second half interrupted only by boos and cheers in the correct places.

2 Discuss these questions, either as a large group or in pairs (if you discuss them in pairs you will need to feed back to the group as a whole to finish):

- Why was it seen as so important to be harsh on followers of foreign gods?
- What might be the lesson for us today about our belief in God?
- We no longer kill false prophets, but do we do enough to emphasise the true God? What more could we do?

RESPOND

MUSICAL

WHAT: **song**
WHY: **to think about God's holiness**
WITH: **CD or MP3 of 'Can You Heal Us (Holy Man)' by Paul Weller (from the album *Wild Wood*), playback equipment, song lyrics**

1 Play the song 'Can You Heal Us (Holy Man)'. If possible, display or have copies of the lyrics available for people to read.

2 Briefly discuss the lyrics. Some may find them taunting; others may consider them to be holy.

3 Alternatively, or as well, you could use the following songs to sing about and praise the power of God:

- 'There Is Power in the Name of Jesus' by Noel Richards
- 'Show Your Power (He is the Lord)' by Kevin Prosch
- 'Send the Fire' by William Booth/Lex Loizides

PRACTICAL

WHAT: **prayer**
WHY: **to pray about serving God**
WITH: **watering can, pile of twigs, plastic sheeting**

1 Using the twigs and wood on the plastic sheeting, make an altar for burning a sacrifice, as Elijah did in the reading today. (Don't burn it unless you can build it outside and in safe conditions. And don't use the plastic sheet if you're burning it!)

2 Ask the young people to stand around the 'altar' and pray quietly to God. This first time they should pray that God's power will be at work in their home. They might want to pray about a specific situation that they are facing.

3 After a short time of silent prayer, sprinkle some water onto the altar to remind the group that when the water was put onto Elijah's altar it didn't stop God being able to show his power. Likewise, God can use his power for the prayers just prayed.

4 Repeat the prayer and water cycle twice more, once asking for God's power to be at work when they are at school and once for God's power to be at work when they are out with their friends.

5 You could give each young person a twig as a reminder that they have God's power with them.

CREATIVE

WHAT: **question**
WHY: **to think about serving God**
WITH: **copies of page 121, quiet devotional music, playback equipment**

1 Give out copies of page 121, 'How can God use me?'

2 Play some quiet devotional music and invite the young people, on their own, to think of answers to the questions and write them down.

3 Encourage them to share their answers and pray for each other in small groups as appropriate.

MORE ON THIS THEME:

If you want to do a short series with your group, other sessions that work well with this one are:

17	*Extreme prophecy*	*1 Kings 17*
19	*I'm not the one and only*	*1 Kings 19*
20	*Not beyond justice*	*1 Kings 21:1–19; 22:29–40*

18

SAFETY INSTRUCTIONS

The world is becoming full of safety instructions. We cannot be trusted to open a plastic bottle of milk without first being made aware of the danger that it may contain milk. Really?

Here are some safety instructions. Where would you expect to see them?

ALWAYS DILUTE	DO NOT TRY TO CONNECT TO MAINS WITHOUT READING INSTRUCTIONS THOROUGHLY	STORE IN A COOL, DRY PLACE AWAY FROM STRONG LIGHT AND ODOURS	MAY CAUSE DROWSINESS
BEST BEFORE 2012	DO NOT ADD WATER OR EXPOSE TO HEAT	DO NOT USE IF WEARING LOOSE CLOTHING	DO NOT OVER-TIGHTEN
KEEP AWAY FROM NAKED FLAME	ALWAYS WEAR THE PROTECTIVE EQUIPMENT PROVIDED	DO NOT SWIM WHEN THE RED FLAG IS RAISED	MAY CAUSE DEATH
ALWAYS KEEP THE SAFETY CATCH ON WHEN NOT IN USE	DO NOT USE IF YOU ARE TAKING ANY OTHER MEDICATION – IF IN DOUBT, TALK TO YOUR DOCTOR	MAY CONTAIN NUTS	MAY DETERIORATE IF LEFT EXPOSED TO AIR FOR LONG PERIODS
KEEP AWAY FROM THE EDGE OF THE PLATFORM	DEEP WATER	ONLY USE AS PART OF A CALORIE-CONTROLLED DIET	THIS VEHICLE MAY TURN RIGHT WITHOUT INDICATING

Bible bit
1 Kings 18

Do you ever find it hard to speak up for God? Perhaps to suggest your friends stop doing something because it upsets you and may upset God too. How many times during the day do you have to speak up for your Lord? If you are anything like me, it won't be many, if at all. Here, though, we see exactly how it should be done. Elijah knows his God and knows the power that God has and so he stands up. He does more than that though – he taunts those who don't believe in God – he laughs at them and then lets God show that he is the One.

Weather
1 Kings 18
Isolated fiery downpour followed by widespread heavy showers

THE MAGICIAN'S VOLUNTEER

We were three rows from the front of the stage as the magician called for a volunteer to help with the next trick. The volunteer needed to have a watch. 'Me, me!' I shouted, forcing my hand as high in the air as I could. I was there for a birthday treat and one of my presents had been a cool new watch.

Amazingly, the magician pointed straight at me. His glamorous assistant came down and took me by the hand to lead me back to the stage. Close up she wasn't quite as 'glamorous' as I'd expected. She had lots of make-up on – I mean lots.

The trick involved a piece of cloth and my new watch. And a hammer. Oh dear.

I handed over my watch and, er, watched as the watch was wrapped in the cloth. I was asked to feel the watch through the cloth to check it was still there. It was.

The magician placed the cloth on a table and hit it with the hammer several times. Nothing could have survived. Nothing mechanical anyway.

He invited me to feel the cloth, carefully. I felt. My worst fears were realised as I felt bits of broken casing and sharp edges through the cloth.

The magician apologised and sent me back to my seat. He said he'd try and think of some way to make it up to me. Before I could make any suggestions he said I should check I hadn't imagined the whole thing and left the watch in my pocket. I thought he was being silly, but...

Have you ever been to a show like this?
What do you think happened next?
How does this story compare to what happened in 1 Kings 18?
How does the magician compare to the prophets of Baal?
How does he compare to Elijah?

How can God use me:

at school?

at home or hanging out with friends?

at the shops?

when I rest?

19

Bible: 1 Kings 19

I'M NOT THE ONE AND ONLY

THE AIM: To be confident that we are not alone in fighting for God's justice

The aim unpacked

We are bombarded through the media, friends and even church with the message that Christianity is on the decline and that no one believes in God any more. Despite that message, Christianity is still the biggest religion on the planet. Elijah felt like he was the only one fighting for God. Although he stood alone on Mount Carmel, he wasn't alone in the big scheme of things, as God was about to reveal.

WAY IN

theGRID MAGAZINE

WHAT: icebreaker
WHY: to think about how difficult an activity is to do
WITH: magazine page 125, flip chart or whiteboard, marker pen

1 Before the session, look at the list of unlikely events on page 125. Make preparations for one or two of them to actually happen in your session. Giving everyone free sweets is the easiest to do.

2 In the session, give out copies of page 125 and challenge the young people to put the events in order of unlikelihood.

3 Share results and agree on an order together – if you can.

4 Say that today's session is about a very unlikely event. Carry out the unlikely event you have prepared now.

SCENE SETTER

WHAT: box-stacking
WHY: to practise cooperation
WITH: lots and lots of boxes (shoeboxes are ideal but any will work)

1 Gather lots of boxes for this activity. Shoeboxes work best (you may be able to get some from a shoe shop or purchase some cheaply); otherwise regular packing or cereal boxes will do.

2 Divide the young people into two teams. Challenge each team to build an arch with the boxes which the whole team can walk under.

3 Watch the teams and note who cooperates and who wants to take over.

4 If you have time, you could try other challenges like:

- to build a shelter which the whole group can fit into
- to build a structure to take the weight of a member of the group (safety warning – this shouldn't be very high off the ground)
- to build the tallest, free-standing tower

5 Say that in this activity the young people had to work together to achieve a successful outcome. In the Bible passage we'll explore today, Elijah discovered that he wasn't alone in working for God.

THEMED GAME

WHAT: non-competitive games
WHY: to encourage cooperation

1 Divide the group into two teams and get them to line up opposite each other. Give the first person in each group a balloon.

2 Get the young people into pairs and ask each pair to find a space to do the following challenges:

- Sit back to back with elbows interlinked. Each partner pushes with their feet until they are standing up.
- Sit facing each other, feet touching, holding hands. They must stand up.
- Stand facing each other, holding each other's left legs off the ground. They must sit down.
- Lie on their backs with their feet touching. They must cycle their legs together.

2 Say that in this activity the young people had to work together to achieve a successful outcome. In the Bible passage we'll explore today, Elijah discovered that he wasn't alone in fighting for God.

3 If you did the 'Character of a prophet' previously, you may want to refer to it now to refresh everyone's memory.

BIBLE EXPERIENCE

19

LEVEL 1: CONNECT

WHAT: **Bible study with activities**
WHY: **to be confident that we are not alone in fighting for God's justice**
WITH: **Bibles, ball of wool, chair**

1 Ask the young people to share examples of occasions when they ran away. Who were they running from? How did they feel? (Be sensitive to the possibility that some members of the group may have needed to run away, perhaps from a bully or even from home.) Ask what might have helped them to stay rather than run.

2 Read 1 Kings 19:1–18. Discuss:

- What was Elijah scared of?
- How did he recuperate? When God asked Elijah what he was doing, he gave the same answer twice (vs 10,14). What did he say?

3 Tie someone to a chair with a single strand of thin wool. Let them break out. Now tie them to the chair by wrapping the wool round them many times and challenge them to break out. Ask the volunteer to tell you how much harder it is to break out. Make the point that we may feel inadequate on our own but together we are stronger.

4 Read 1 Kings 19:19–21. Ask the group how many people Elijah was told were on his side in the previous section (7,000). How many more does he get? (One – Elisha.) Explain that it is great to have a personal assistant, but it is even better if that person is an apprentice – someone learning the job with a view to taking over. The church has worked like this for almost 2,000 years – passing on the good news to the next generation.

LEVEL 2: INTERFACE

WHAT: **Bible study**
WHY: **to be confident that we are not alone in fighting for God's justice**
WITH: **magazine page 126, Bibles**

1 Give out copies of page 126. Invite the young people to discuss their ideal 'Dream team' with a partner.

2 Bring the group together to compare the results and discuss any similarities or disagreements.

3 Read 1 Kings 19 to the young people. Discuss:

- What help did Elijah have at the start?
- What help could Elijah have done with?
- What help did God give him?

4 Elijah was tired and depressed so God gave him a team of 7,000 (1 Kings 19:18) and a personal assistant who would eventually succeed him. Ask:

- What sort of support and encouragement do we have as Christians?
- What else would we like?

LEVEL 3: SWITCH ON

WHAT: **Bible study**
WHY: **to be confident that we are not alone in fighting for God's justice**
WITH: **Bibles**

1 Explain that Elijah, victor over hundreds of false prophets, now runs away from one woman. God's victory is soon forgotten. Ask the young people, 'What has God done for you that you easily forget?' Allow them to share their stories. (Be prepared to lead this discussion and go first.)

2 Invite everyone to find James 5:17, 18 and ask someone to read it out. Remind them that Elijah was 'a human being just like us'. He ran away from a bad experience. Depression is a common human problem which even Elijah suffered from.

3 Now read 1 Kings 19. Identify together the things which kept Elijah going. (If necessary, direct them to specific verses to cover the points below.)

- He kept talking to God (v 4)
- He kept dealing with his physical needs (vs 5–8)
- He removed himself from the problem (vs 4,8)
- He began to understand the nature of special events – God is not always in the earthquake and fire; sometimes he is a still small voice (vs 11, 12)
- He got help – 7,000 day-to-day helpers (v 18) and one special one – Elisha (v 21)

4 The time on Mount Carmel was so exhilarating that it easily led to a 'downer'. Ask the young people to share any stories of how they have felt when they returned home from Christian holidays, camps or house parties.

5 Recap the things that kept Elijah going: prayer, physical needs being met, holiday or rest, special events and routine, help. Invite the young people to identify their own needs. Ask, 'Are you missing one of the five things?' Pray together, asking God to meet their needs.

RESPOND

MUSICAL

WHAT: **chorus**
WHY: **to build a beautiful piece of harmony**
WITH: **words to the hymn 'Dear Lord and Father of Mankind'**

1 Most groups can make music even without instruments! Ask the most musical person in the group to pitch a note.

2 Invite everyone to hum, whistle, 'do-wop' or 'la la' that note. Add a rhythm, with clicks, stamps, claps or even beatboxing.

3 Practise, with the music getting louder and softer. Take the volume right down and ask a good reader to read out the words of the hymn 'Dear Lord and Father of Mankind'.

4 Explain that the 'still, small voice of calm' image is taken from 1 Kings 19.

4 Close with prayer, asking God to speak to each member of the group through his still, small voice of calm.

PRACTICAL

WHAT: **prayer**
WHY: **to support each other in prayer**
WITH: **hat**

1 Ask everyone to write their name on a piece of paper and throw it into the hat. Mix them up and invite everyone to take one out. If anyone has their own name they should swap it.

2 Ask everyone to find the person on their piece of paper. Invite them to find out two things that person would like prayer for. Encourage the leaders to join in so that the young people pray for leaders and vice versa. (You could do this every session and give some time to catch up with the prayer person from the session before.)

3 Pray for each other in silence to end the activity, and remind everyone to continue to pray throughout the week.

CREATIVE

WHAT: **sky gazing**
WHY: **to remember God's presence with us for all time**
WITH: **permission (if necessary) to go outside your meeting area with the young people**

1 Take the group outside, somewhere safe. Invite them to lie face up on the ground and to look at the sky (whatever the weather or time of day).

2 Point out that Elijah lived in the ninth century BC, nearly 3,000 years ago, yet when he looked at the sky he saw the same as we see now. God is in control of this planet and always has been. Remind the group that there are Christians all around the world who are looking at the same sky.

3 Encourage the young people to pray in silence or aloud, thanking God that he is with them, always has been and always will be with them, and that there are many other Christians all around the world, worshipping God and following him.

MORE ON THIS THEME:

If you want to do a short series with your group, other sessions that work well with this one are:

17	*Extreme prophecy*	*1 Kings 17*
18	*Great Baals of fire*	*1 Kings 18*
20	*Not beyond justice*	*1 Kings 21:1–19; 22:29–40*

19

Bible bit
1 Kings 19

Elijah has stood up for God, shown that Baal is a complete waste of time and killed all of Baal's prophets. And for these good deeds he's told he's going to be killed. Like all sane people, he decides to run for it, because he is scared. Elijah feels as if he is the only one around being used by God, but he is wrong – very wrong – as God reveals himself and his people.

LIKELY OR UNLIKELY

Here is a list of things that are unlikely to happen any time soon. All you have to do is put them in order of unlikeliness, with 1 as the most unlikely thing to happen, and 10 as the least unlikely. You never know, you might be surprised!

A You will see someone get covered in jelly today. ☐

B Someone you know can recite 1 Kings 19 – off by heart. ☐

C You will be given some free sweets. ☐

D Tranmere Rovers will be promoted next season. ☐

E Take That will merge with One Direction this year and become a supergroup. ☐

F An astronaut will reach Mars next year. ☐

G The compulsory national minimum pocket money will be £10 a week. ☐

H There will be a power cut while you read this. ☐

I In a shuffled pack of cards all the aces end up next to each other. ☐

J One of your family will have their head shaved today. ☐

666

Weather
1 Kings 19
Heavy winds, earthquakes and fire

DREAM TEAM

Sometimes we all need a little help from our friends. Elijah did! So God gave him a team of 7,000 helpers and a personal apprentice called Elisha, who would carry on his work when he couldn't any more.

You have been given the following jobs. You can ask anyone in the world, dead or alive, real or fictional, to help you with your tasks. Who would you get on your dream team?

1. Your English homework.
2. Wash up the family's dishes, or stack the dishwasher.
3. Go into town and buy three suitcases.
4. A paper round.
5. Take a training session for the school hockey team.
6. Prepare a meal for six.
7. Landscape your neighbour's garden.
8. Be Prime Minister for a day.
9. Organise a street party for a special occasion.
10. Run the morning service at your local church.

DREAM FESTIVAL

Who would be in the line-up if you could invite bands or artists to your very own music festival?

Teamwork motto

'None of us is as smart as all of us.'

Bible: 1 Kings 21:1–19; 22:29–40

NOT BEYOND JUSTICE

THE AIM: To be encouraged that no one is beyond God's justice

The aim unpacked
In this session we look at two kings. The first is Ahab, who shows his injustice by the way he deals with his subjects. The second is God, who shows his justice by the way he deals with his people. It is easy for our young people to think that there is nothing they can do to change the world. While this is true in some circumstances, we should remember that nothing is beyond God.

WAY IN

theGRID MAGAZINE

WHAT: **exercise**
WHY: **to think about justice**
WITH: **magazine page 130**

1 Ask the young people if they have ever heard anyone say, 'The punishment should fit the crime.' Give out copies of page 130.

2 Say that some of the punishments are quite minor; others more serious. The aim is for the young people to think of an offence that might have been committed to warrant each of these punishments.

3 Ask the young people to work in pairs or threes to come up with answers and then have fun sharing them.

SCENE SETTER

WHAT: **grape tasting**
WHY: **to think about grapes**
WITH: **grapes, blindfolds, rosette**

1 Before the session, purchase a selection of grapes – green, black and red. For a more varied challenge introduce pitted cherries and olives too. (Be aware of food intolerances.)

2 Hold a blindfolded tasting contest to see who can identify the correct colour or type of fruit from its taste alone. If your young people are unfamiliar with these fruits, give them the opportunity to taste the fruit with their eyes open before starting the challenge.

3 Award a rosette to the champion taster. Explain that wine is made from grapes, and in this session you will be hearing about a vineyard, where grapes are grown. (Cherry and olive stone spitting championships are great fun too!)

THEMED GAME

WHAT: **chariot races**
WHY: **to have fun with the Bible scene**
WITH: **chairs or bollards**

1 Play this game outdoors or in a large hall. Mark out a course with bollards or chairs. Be aware of health and safety considerations.

2 Put the young people into teams of four. The two tallest young people in each team must face each other and hold each other's wrists, crossing their arms over for extra strength. The third (and smallest) person should sit on this 'seat'. The fourth team member stands behind them, holding the seated person at the waist.

3 The 'chariots' then race around a course. If at any point the chariot comes apart it must stop and rebuild before continuing. Interfering with the other chariots is, of course, to be discouraged.

BIBLE EXPERIENCE

LEVEL 1: CONNECT

WHAT: **quiz and discussion**
WHY: **to be encouraged that no one is beyond God's justice**
WITH: **magazine page 131, page 132**

1 Say that it is clear from the Bible that Ahab was the worst king ever to have ruled Israel (1 Kings 16:30–33; 18:18; 21:25,26). In 1 and 2 Kings, individual mistakes can sometimes be forgiven, but what matters most to the writers of the books is whether the kings followed the Lord or not.

2 Give out copies of page 131 and ask the young people to fill in the 'Worst ever' chart. If time is limited, choose one or two of the sections only, or three from each.

3 Read aloud, or ask two young people to read, the summaries of the two passages from page 132.

4 Discuss these questions with the young people:

- Do you think God is a God of judgement? Why? How does this make you feel?
- Do you expect to be judged one day? Why? How do you feel about this?
- Have the events in the New Testament changed this? If so, how? (You may have to prompt them to think about how the events of Easter enabled God's justice to be satisfied.)

LEVEL 2: INTERFACE

WHAT: **Bible study**
WHY: **to be encouraged that no one is beyond God's justice**
WITH: **Bibles, flip chart or whiteboard, marker pen**

1 Ask some volunteers to read these verses to give a glimpse into the character of King Ahab:

- 1 Kings 16:30–33 (the worst king ever)
- 1 Kings 18:18 (abandoned the Lord)
- 1 Kings 20:43 (sullen and angry when he didn't get his way)
- 1 Kings 21:25,26 (behaved in the vilest manner)

2 Divide everyone into small groups and ask them to chat about what they would like more than anything else in all the world. Challenge them to come up with a plan to get the thing they want, by whatever means. Invite them to share their plans.

3 Read 1 Kings 21:1–19. Discuss these questions with the young people:

- What did Ahab want?
- Why couldn't he have it?
- What did he do?
- What was the verdict on him?

4 Talk about justice. Do the young people think it exists in the world? If someone commits a crime, they can expect to be arrested, tried in court and given a sentence which fits the crime. At home we can expect punishment if we do wrong. The Bible teaches us that there is justice about the whole of life too.

LEVEL 3: SWITCH ON

WHAT: **Bible study**
WHY: **to be encouraged that no one is beyond God's justice**
WITH: **Bibles**

1 Read together 1 Kings 21:1–16.

2 Discuss with the young people their feelings about the behaviour of the various characters: King Ahab, Queen Jezebel and Naboth. Ask:

- Which of the characters do they identify with?
- Who was in the right?
- Who was in the wrong?
- Were all the characters treated fairly?
- What do they think should happen next?

3 Now read 1 Kings 21:17–19. Discuss these questions:

- Is this how you hoped the situation would be resolved?
- If you were Elijah, would you have taken the prophecy to the king? Why or why not?

4 Now read 1 Kings 22:29–36. Discuss with the young people their feelings about the behaviour of the various characters: King Ahab, King Jehoshaphat, a soldier from Israel, a soldier from Aram, the king of Aram. Ask the same questions as before.

4 Now read 1 Kings 22:37–40. Discuss this question:

- Is this how they hoped the situation would be resolved? Why or why not?

Lead into a more general discussion about God's judgement and how this relates to a phrase often heard – 'Life's not fair.'

RESPOND

MUSICAL

WHAT: music
WHY: to pray about the feelings raised by this Bible series
WITH: CD or MP3 of music from *The Planets* by Holst, playback equipment, dimmed lighting

1 Some of the events in the Bible passages for this session and in this series have been violent and cruel. Give the young people time and space to think and pray through their reaction to them while listening to a powerful piece of classical music.

2 Invite everyone to find some space and to make themselves comfortable. Dim the lights or use a couple of table lamps instead.

3 Play the first movement of Holst's *The Planets* suite – 'Mars, the Bringer of War'.

4 Finish by explaining that the culture was very different at the time of Elijah, but God is still a just God.

PRACTICAL

WHAT: prayer
WHY: to respond to God's judgement with prayer for people
WITH: newspapers

1 Spread out on the floor the news pages of some local and national newspapers. Invite the young people to wander around and find a story about a situation where it seems as if there is no justice.

2 Invite everyone to pray, either aloud or in silence, for the situations they have looked at in the newspapers. Remember to pray for God's will to be done, and for the accusers and the accused, the victims and the perpetrators.

CREATIVE

WHAT: art
WHY: to build up a picture of Elijah
WITH: large sheet of paper, marker pens

1 Draw an outline of Elijah, as large as possible. There are some simple line drawings in the Good News version of the Bible which may guide you.

2 Recap together the previous few sessions about Elijah and decorate the drawing of him with the key points from the prophet's life.

3 Thank God for the life of his prophet Elijah and ask God to let your group be a light for God's justice in the world today.

4 Display the result, perhaps where other members of the church can see it so they can see what you have been doing.

MORE ON THIS THEME:

If you want to do a short series with your group, other sessions that work well with this one are:

17	*Extreme prophecy*	*1 Kings 17*
18	*Great Baals of fire*	*1 Kings 18*
19	*I'm not the one and only*	*1 Kings 19*

CRIME AND PUNISHMENT

What offences might have been committed to deserve these punishments?

Bible bit
1 Kings 21:1–19; 22:29–40

Now here is a very nasty man. Ahab is not good at all. We've heard a little about him in the previous pages of *theGRID* but now we see exactly what he gets up to. And he is the king, which means he can do what he wants and get away with it... or can he?

Well, read on to find out, but as you'll see, God's justice eventually catches up with everyone – even kings.

Weather
1 Kings 21,22
Pools of blood

FIVE YEARS IN PRISON.

SPEND SATURDAY AFTERNOONS CLEANING THE STREETS.

LIFE IMPRISONMENT.

GROUNDED FOR A WEEK.

WRITE, 'I MUST NOT ...' ONE HUNDRED TIMES.

ONE HUNDRED HOURS' COMMUNITY SERVICE REMOVING GRAFFITI.

AFTER-SCHOOL DETENTION.

A FINE OF £60 AND THREE POINTS ON YOUR DRIVING LICENCE.

GO TO YOUR ROOM AND THINK ABOUT WHAT YOU HAVE DONE.

NO POCKET MONEY THIS WEEK.

20

WORST EVER

Who do you think is (or was) the worst ever:

SPORTSPERSON?

COOK?

RADIO DJ?

MUSICIAN?

COMEDIAN?

TV PERSONALITY?

WORLD LEADER?

ARTIST?

SINGER?

WRITER?

And in your area what is the worst:

SHOP?

CAFÉ?

BUILDING?

OTHER LANDMARK?

STREET?

JOB?

LOCAL TV PROGRAMME?

LOCAL RADIO SHOW?

ROAD JUNCTION?

SCHOOL?

And in your own home, what is the worst:

PIECE OF MUSIC?

BOOK?

MEAL?

POSTER?

ROOM?

CHAIR?

THING YOU HAVE TO DO TO HELP?

HABIT?

RULE?

ORNAMENT?

RESOURCE PAGE

USE WITH SESSION 20 BIBLE EXPERIENCE 'LEVEL 1 CONNECT'

The crime: a summary of 1 Kings 21:1–19

King Ahab wanted a vineyard near to the palace but the owner wouldn't sell it to him. Ahab's wife, Jezebel, arranged for false accusations to be made against the vineyard owner who was consequently stoned to death by a mob. Then Ahab took the vineyard. Elijah the prophet was sent to the king to speak out God's judgement. God said that Ahab would die a bloody death, just as the vineyard owner had.

The punishment: a summary of 1 Kings 22:29–40

King Ahab went into battle in disguise. Even though the enemy didn't recognise him, a random arrow hit him between the pieces of his armour and he was wounded badly. He stayed propped up in his chariot all day, bleeding to death. Eventually he died, just as Elijah the prophet had said he would.

Bible: Psalm 19

21

THE WONDERS OF GOD

THE AIM: To remember that God is our Creator

The aim unpacked

Everywhere we look we are surrounded by God's creation, whether that is in the blue (or grey) sky that surrounds us, the trees and flowers, or in the people we find around us. We too easily forget that we were made in the image and likeness of God. We destroy things, individually and collectively, but we are also creative. Because God is our Creator, we are precious, as is all of his creation.

WAY IN

theGRID MAGAZINE

WHAT: **creation and humankind**
WHY: **to think about what it means to be created by God**
WITH: **magazine page 137**

1 Hand out copies of page 137 and ask the young people to read through 'God our Creator'.

2 In pairs or small groups, invite them to talk through what they have read. Ask them to discuss the following questions:

- Does what they have read here match with what they thought or had heard about God as Creator?
- Why do you think it is important that we acknowledge we are created by God?

3 Explain that when we recognise that God is our Creator we view the world in a different way. We see that it is a gift and we realise that our role in relation to the world and each other is quite specific. When we ignore our role as stewards of God's creation, we can forget that we were created in the image and likeness of God.

SCENE SETTER

WHAT: **Banksy artwork**
WHY: **to explore the idea that we are all creative**
WITH: **magazine page 136**

1 Ask the young people to look briefly at the example of Banksy's artwork on page 136. Say that Banksy is an artist who uses his creativity to share some very powerful messages.

2 Ask the young people to come up with suggestions of the different ways people are creative. As they come up with different ideas, make a list of their suggestions.

3 Split the young people into two or three smaller groups and explain that you would like them to create a short drama about creativity. Allocate an equal number of the ideas from your list to each group. Explain that they must include each of these ideas in their drama and form a coherent storyline!

4 Give the groups time to prepare their sketches and then ask each group to perform their sketch to everyone else.

5 Explain that in our world there are all sorts of ways of being creative. Christians believe that this is because we are made in the image and likeness of a Creator God.

THEMED GAME

WHAT: **drawing game**
WHY: **to think about how we can all be creative**

1 Form a circle and then give each person a sheet of paper and a pen.

2 Ask them to begin to draw an object at the top of the sheet of paper. Explain that they should just draw one element of the picture and then fold the paper over so that just the edge of their picture is visible.

3 Now ask them to hand their sheet of paper to the person on their left. That person should then add something to the picture, fold it over and pass it on. Keep going around the circle until everyone has added something (or you run out of space!).

4 When the pictures return to their starting point, ask the young people to open them out and look at the pictures that have been created. Ask the following questions:

- Did what you received at the end of the activity match what you imagined would be drawn at the start?
- Can you see how different people have been creative within the task?
- Does this change your view of creativity?
- Can being creative happen as part of a team or is it better on an individual level?

BIBLE EXPERIENCE

LEVEL 1: CONNECT

WHAT: **Pictionary**
WHY: **to think about creativity**
WITH: **magazine page 137 (optional)**

1 Ask the young people to get into teams of at least four and play a quick game of Pictionary using words from Psalm 19 (eg sun, bridegroom, athlete, gold, honey).

2 Ask the young people what they think it means to be creative. Would they include playing Pictionary as something creative?

3 Give everyone a Bible or a copy of Psalm 19 from magazine page 137 and read it together slowly.

4 Ask the young people to reflect on the images and claims attributed to God that are in the psalm.

5 Invite the young people to think about the various ways that they are creative and to consider how this could be a reflection of God's creativity within them.

LEVEL 2: INTERFACE

WHAT: **Interface**
WHY: **Bible study**
WITH: **to uncover some of the deeper meaning in Psalm 19**

1 Give everyone a Bible and invite the group to read together Psalm 19 from a traditional translation.

2 Now read Psalm 19 from *The Message* paraphrase.

3 Invite the young people to think about the following questions:

- This psalm is full of imagery. Which images stand out to you?
- What do you think verse 10 is suggesting about God's Word?
- Have you ever heard the phrase 'the fear of the Lord'? What do you think it means?
- Do you think it is important to please God, if he is our Creator?

4 As a group, think of ways that the young people as individuals or a group might be able to recognise God as their Creator in their daily life. These might be in the home, at school, or in the community.

LEVEL 3: SWITCH ON

WHAT: **creation and creativity**
WHY: **to understand more deeply that God is our Creator**
WITH: **gold-coloured sheets of paper**

1 Hand out Bibles to the young people and read Psalm 19 together. Then discuss the following questions as a whole group:

- How does believing God is your Creator change your understanding of creativity?
- Do you ever think of God as creative? What kinds of things come to mind when you think of creation?
- What can we know about God from reading this psalm? What knowledge do we uncover about him?
- How do you respond to the fact that God created the heavens and the earth? Are there things that help you believe this or make you disbelieve this?

2 Ask the young people: What is the most beautiful and breathtaking view of nature you have ever experienced?

3 Split the young people into small groups and give each group a sheet of gold-coloured paper. Ask them to write onto it words which represent the way the 'world' perceives gold, eg precious, special, rare, expensive etc.

4 Then, still in small groups, ask the young people to discuss the following two questions:

- What do you think the psalmist might be referring to in verse 7 when he states 'The law of the Lord is perfect...'?
- When the psalmist refers to God's laws as being 'more precious than gold', what do you think he is stressing about the value of God's Word?

5 Invite some feedback from the small groups and then suggest that they tear up their piece of gold paper into small pieces. Then ask the group to pick up one of the Bibles they read from earlier and insert the gold pieces of paper randomly inside the Bible. Remind the young people that God's Word is far more precious than gold, and we should think of it as being worth so much more than any of the words written on the paper.

RESPOND 21

MUSICAL

WHAT: **meditation**
WHY: **to help the young people think about how awesome it is to be created by God**
WITH: **music for 'The Heavens are Telling' by Haydn**

1 Invite the young people to share any thoughts they may have on where they see the creativity of God in the things that surround them.

2 Play 'The heavens are telling' by Haydn.

3 Ask the young people to get into small groups and talk about what God might be saying to them through the song that might challenge or affirm what they already think.

4 Encourage the young people to pray about these things in their small groups.

PRACTICAL

WHAT: **creative camera activity**
WHY: **to see the creativity of God in the world around us**
WITH: **digital cameras or phones, laptop or screen to display photographs**

1 Invite the young people to get into pairs or threes.

2 Give each group of young people a camera and invite them to go out into the surrounding area (with an adult leader if appropriate) and to take photographs of the things they see around them that express creativity to them.

3 Bring all the groups back together and invite them to share the photographs they have taken with one another and to explain briefly why they think the photographs they have taken show creativity. Invite the young people to offer positive and constructive thoughts on what they have produced. Are there any things they would add/remove from the contributions of other groups?

4 Close by praying for the young people as they seek to remember that they are surrounded by signs of God's creation.

CREATIVE

WHAT: **play dough prayers**
WHY: **to help young people think about being creative**
WITH: **play dough, reflective worship music, playback equipment**

1 Invite the young people to gather in a circle.

2 Start the worship music and explain that if we believe that God is creative and that we are creative too, then there is no reason why we shouldn't take this creativity into our prayer life. Invite the young people to select some play dough and use it to shape a prayer to God.

3 When everyone who wishes to has created something, pause the worship music and ask any young people who are prepared to do so, to share with others what they have created.

4 Conclude by praying for the young people and asking God to help us remember that he is our Creator and we are creative because he is.

MORE ON THIS THEME:

If you want to do a short series with your group, other sessions that work well with this one are:

22	*God wins*	*Psalm 20*
23	*God is near*	*Psalm 22:1–5*
24	*God is good*	*Psalm 23*
25	*Light the way*	*Psalm 119:9–16,105*

Bible bit
Psalm 19

We are surrounded by reminders of the creativity of God. From the view of the moon in the sky at night to the leaves on the trees, everywhere we look we are surrounded by God's creation. We can even see God's creativity in the people around us, or even in ourselves if we look carefully enough. With all the other messages we receive from our world, it is easy to forget that we are created in the image and likeness of God. We destroy things, including ourselves through war, but we are creative. Some of us are artistic, some talented at sport; others are talented with words or in music. We are all creative. Sometimes we think we are far from creative but when we do this we are not viewing ourselves as God does.

BANKSY ARTWORK

Do you see the work of Banksy as creative?
Are there any insights we can find into the creativity of God in the work of Banksy?
Does this make you see creativity differently?

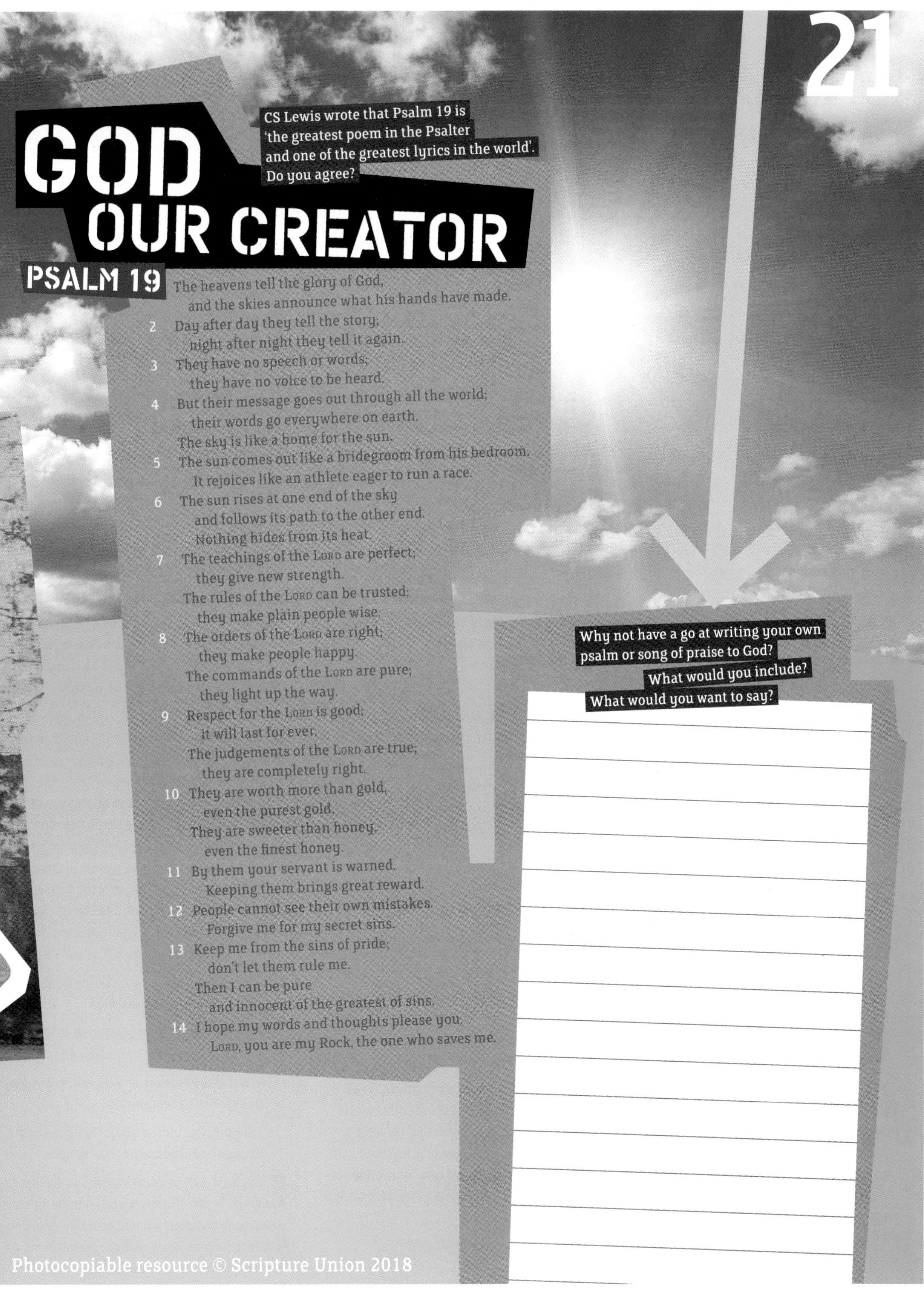

21

GOD OUR CREATOR

CS Lewis wrote that Psalm 19 is 'the greatest poem in the Psalter and one of the greatest lyrics in the world'. Do you agree?

PSALM 19

The heavens tell the glory of God,
and the skies announce what his hands have made.
2 Day after day they tell the story;
night after night they tell it again.
3 They have no speech or words;
they have no voice to be heard.
4 But their message goes out through all the world;
their words go everywhere on earth.
The sky is like a home for the sun.
5 The sun comes out like a bridegroom from his bedroom.
It rejoices like an athlete eager to run a race.
6 The sun rises at one end of the sky
and follows its path to the other end.
Nothing hides from its heat.
7 The teachings of the Lord are perfect;
they give new strength.
The rules of the Lord can be trusted;
they make plain people wise.
8 The orders of the Lord are right;
they make people happy.
The commands of the Lord are pure;
they light up the way.
9 Respect for the Lord is good;
it will last for ever.
The judgements of the Lord are true;
they are completely right.
10 They are worth more than gold,
even the purest gold.
They are sweeter than honey,
even the finest honey.
11 By them your servant is warned.
Keeping them brings great reward.
12 People cannot see their own mistakes.
Forgive me for my secret sins.
13 Keep me from the sins of pride;
don't let them rule me.
Then I can be pure
and innocent of the greatest of sins.
14 I hope my words and thoughts please you.
Lord, you are my Rock, the one who saves me.

Why not have a go at writing your own psalm or song of praise to God?
What would you include?
What would you want to say?

22

Bible: Psalm 20

GOD WINS

THE AIM: To remember to ask God for help

The aim unpacked

God wants to answer our calls to him and he can help us. God has given us free will though, so while he is able to help and is in fact best placed to help us, he only helps us when we ask him to. This session aims to challenge us to not simply wait until we are desperate to seek God's help, but to remember to ask God to help us regularly.

WAY IN

theGRID MAGAZINE

WHAT: discussion
WHY: to think about what it means to offer help
WITH: magazine page 141

1 Hand out copies of page 141 and ask the young people to read the article 'Help!'.

2 In pairs or small groups, invite them to talk through what they have read and answer these questions:

- What does it mean to help someone?
- Are there times when you have had to choose between helping yourself and helping someone else? How have you made this choice?
- Is it possible to help people and completely disregard our own needs?
- Why do you think we see helping people as such a good thing to do?
- What difference do you think it might make to know that God longs to help you?

3 Explain that when we recognise that God longs to help us, we see the world differently. It can make those things that seem so apparently impossible possible, giving us confidence to face each day. It can also encourage us not to feel isolated or alone. We always have God with us, prepared to help if we are prepared to ask for his help.

SCENE SETTER

WHAT: story of help
WHY: to explore the idea that anyone can offer help
WITH: magazine page 141

1 Ask the young people to look briefly at the story of a young person helping others on page 141.

2 Say that people of all ages can help. Ask: Can you think of people you know who help others, either on their own or with a group of others?

3 Ask the young people to come up with suggestions of the different ways we can help others.

4 Ask: How do you identify the places where you are going to help? What is the role of God when we offer help? Should we be stepping back and inviting God to do more without us? How do you think God's help and our help relate to one another?

5 Explain that in our world there are all sorts of ways of helping others. Christians believe that we can call on God for help whenever we need to and psalms like Psalm 20 encourage us that we can do this. We can even call on God to help us as we help others.

THEMED GAME

WHAT: obstacle course
WHY: to enable us to work together and grow in our trust in each other
WITH: a large space, various items to form obstacles, blindfolds

1 Divide the group into teams and explain that in their teams they are going to tackle an obstacle course. The person undertaking the obstacle course will also be blindfolded, meaning they will need to listen to their team members as they verbally guide them along the course safely. It is a test of trust and listening. The winning team is the one whose members complete the course safely and in the shortest time. Be sure to risk assess this activity prior to the session.

2 When the game is over, ask the young people the following questions:

- How did it feel to put your trust in your team when you were blindfolded?
- What skills did you need in order to guide your friends successfully?
- Was simply guiding your friends verbally enough or did you want to help them more?

3 Explain to the group that while this was a fun game, it also illustrates how challenging it can be to put your trust in other people. God wants to help us as we seek to navigate every obstacle that we encounter in life.

BIBLE EXPERIENCE

LEVEL 1: CONNECT

WHAT: **trust game**
WHY: **to think about how we can help one another**
WITH: **copies of Psalm 20**

1 Explain to the young people that we are going to be thinking about asking for help and trust today.

2 Ask them to get into threes. Explain that you are going to ask them to play a game of trust and vulnerability. One young person needs to stand with their eyes closed and then, on the count of three, fall backwards into the arms of their waiting friends who will catch them. Make sure you supervise this activity carefully to avoid any injuries!

3 Make sure everyone has had a go at falling and catching, if they want to.

4 Ask the young people to reflect on this experience:

- What was it like to be the person placing your trust in your friends to catch you?
- What was it like to be tasked with catching a friend?
- What did it feel like as you leant back?
- Was it easy to trust your friends? What things were you concerned about?

5 Share Psalm 20 with the group and invite them to read it. Ask the following questions:

- What does the psalm tell us about God's character and nature?
- Is there anything in the psalm that you find unusual or surprising or that you do not understand?
- Why do you think the psalm finishes so strongly?

6 Explain to the group that we are going to be thinking about remembering to ask God for help.

LEVEL 2: INTERFACE

WHAT: **Bible study**
WHY: **to explore Psalm 20**
WITH: **page 142**

1 Give everyone a Bible and invite the group to read together Psalm 20.

2 Ask: What do you think we learn from this psalm about God's help?

3 Hand out copies of page 142 and ask the young people to answer the questions either individually or in pairs.

4 Bring the group back together and invite feedback on the questions. Then ask the following:

- How do you think God might help us today?
- Do you think it is important that God wants to help us?
- What do we need to do in order to receive God's help?

5 As you close, encourage the group to think about the fact that we need to ask God for help and what this might mean for our approach to problems and challenges.

LEVEL 3: SWITCH ON

WHAT: **Bible study**
WHY: **to understand more deeply that we can take our concerns to God**

1 Ask the young people to get into pairs or small groups.

2 In these pairs or small groups invite them to share something they need help from God with.

3 Encourage the young people to listen to each other's needs and then to pray for one another.

4 Continuing in pairs or small groups ask the young people to discuss the following questions:

- What makes you trust someone? What are their characteristics or skills?
- Do you feel that you trust God? How would you say you know this?

5 Call the group back together and ask for feedback from their discussions if appropriate. Explain that Psalm 20 shows us that we can take all of our concerns and deepest thoughts to God. This psalm reveals a level of trust in God that has developed over time and is a result of the writer's experience of God at work in his life. The question that seems to be reinforced throughout the psalm is: who do you trust?

6 Be aware that the topic of trust can be difficult for some young people. Try and recognise any members of your group who might be finding it difficult and draw alongside them, offering to talk and pray with them if appropriate.

RESPOND

MUSICAL

WHAT: **reflection**
WHY: **to think about how it is important that people help one another**
WITH: **music video for Birdy's 'People Help the People', playback equipment**

1 Invite the young people to share any thoughts they may have on helping people and why this is important.

2 Play 'People Help the People' by Birdy.

3 Ask the young people to get into small groups and think about what God might be saying to them through the song that might challenge or affirm what they already think.

4 Encourage the young people to pray about these things in their small groups.

PRACTICAL

WHAT: **research**
WHY: **to discover local organisations which help people**
WITH: **laptops or tablets to be used by the group**

1 Invite the young people to get into pairs or threes.

2 Give each group of young people access to a laptop or tablet. Invite them to research local charities and organisations which are working with groups or individuals in need of help.

3 Bring all the groups back together and invite them to share the information they have found through their research. Invite the young people to reflect on the various organisations that they have identified and to see if there are any that have particular resonance with them.

4 As a group, discuss the varying needs of the different organisations and charities you've considered and reflect on whether there are ways that you can help them.

5 Close by praying for the organisations you've identified and ask God to bring his help to them.

CREATIVE

WHAT: **prayer collage**
WHY: **to think about what it means to ask God to help**
WITH: **newspapers and magazines, reflective worship music, playback equipment**

1 Invite the young people to gather in a circle.

2 Start the worship music and explain that while God wants to help us, we need to learn to ask him for help. Invite the young people to use the newspapers and magazines to identify situations and places across the world that are in need of God's help. Using the words and images the young people identify, draw together a collage and then using a marker pen write the word 'Ask' across the top of the images.

3 Encourage the young people to split into pairs and to pray specifically that God might help these situations and give them courage to ask for help in the areas that they need assistance.

4 Conclude by praying for the young people and asking God to help us all.

MORE ON THIS THEME:

If you want to do a short series with your group, other sessions that work well with this one are:

21	*The wonders of God*	*Psalm 19*
23	*God is near*	*Psalm 22:1–5*
24	*God is good*	*Psalm 23*
25	*Light the way*	*Psalm 119:9–16,105*

HELP!

What does it mean to offer help?
What does it mean to ask for help?

Helping people is something that many of us do often without realising. Whether it is directly helping with a chore around the house, or simply sitting and listening to your grandma reminisce, many of us are involved in 'helping' activities regularly. We often offer help.

Asking for help is a different thing altogether. For many of us, there is little worse than asking for help from our friends, never mind from God. But God is willing and eager to help his people. Throughout history God has helped and responded to his people.

How difficult do you find it to ask for help?
Is it easier to ask God for help than it is to ask your friends for help?
Why do you think God is so eager to help his people?

HELPFUL HANNAH

I help my parents out at home by doing chores and jobs around the house. When mum asks me to do a job, I can sometimes feel quite reluctant, but I always remind myself that I'm doing something to help. And if no one does the dishwasher, how will the plates get clean for meal times?

I also help at school as part of the school council and I always look out for people who are upset. If you start by doing one thing to help, then it spreads to the next and the next and the next. If you help others at school, maybe you could become popular for being helpful instead of being popular for your looks or something else like that!

I help out at church as well, by volunteering on the media team. This is where you set up the laptop and then project the lyrics for each hymn or worship song that we sing at church onto the screen. We have a rota for this job so when it's my turn to do it, sometimes I can feel a bit reluctant. But like I do with my chores at home, I remind myself that I'm doing it for a purpose and then I find it's actually quite fun!

Hannah, age 11

RESOURCE PAGE

USE WITH SESSION 22 BIBLE EXPERIENCE 'LEVEL 2 INTERFACE'

1 How many different types of people can you think of who help others as part of their job? List them here.

2 How many different types of people can you think of who are in need of help?

3 What does Psalm 20 show us about God's willingness to help?

4 How can we know that God will help us?

5 What does the psalm say we should trust in? (Psalm 20:7)

6 The psalm ends very positively. Why do you think it does so?

7 Do you think this psalm has any relevance to how God might help us today?

Bible: Psalm 22:1–5

23

GOD IS NEAR

THE AIM: To remember that God can be trusted even when times are hard

The aim unpacked

Many people mistakenly believe that a relationship with Jesus means that they will be protected from difficult and painful experiences. But there are always times when God feels far away, and this experience is even familiar to Jesus. While on the cross, Jesus quotes these words from Psalm 22. God understands and his promises can be trusted.

WAY IN

theGRID MAGAZINE

WHAT: **discussion**
WHY: **to think about what it means to trust God when times are hard**
WITH: **magazine page 146**

1 Hand out copies of magazine page 146 and ask the young people to read through the article 'My God, my God, why have you forsaken me?'

2 In pairs or small groups, invite them to talk through what they have read and to consider the following questions:

- What characteristics of God seem important to you?
- Have you ever experienced a difficult time in your life? Did your relationship with God change as a result of this?
- Why do you think that there are times when God seems absent?

3 Explain that we all have times when we feel that we have lost God in the darkness of our situation or circumstances. What this psalm shows us is that it is perfectly acceptable to be honest with God about this and to express this however we wish. What the psalm also shows us is that rather than basing our faith and belief in God on our emotional response to a situation, we should cling tightly to the experience and knowledge of God that reminds us he is worthy of our trust.

SCENE SETTER

WHAT: **trusting God**
WHY: **to explore the idea of trusting God**

1 Say that trusting God at those times where he seems absent or life is tough is a challenge. It can feel like there are a lot of tough times in life, from the stress and pressure of exams and coursework to the frustration of family. The question that we so often find ourselves returning to is: where is God?

2 Invite the young people to work in pairs or small groups to suggest some things that they find difficult or that make them feel afraid.

3 Ask the young people to continue working in their pairs or small groups to think about who they want to be with them when they feel afraid or alone.

4 Finally ask the young people to think about what it might look like to trust God even when you can't see him.

5 Explain that God is always there with us but we need to be regularly reminded of this because when things become difficult it is easy to forget.

THEMED GAME

WHAT: **guided drawing**
WHY: **to enable us to work together and grow in our trust in each other**
WITH: **blindfolds**

1 Divide the young people into pairs.

2 Ask one young person to be the 'artist' and the other to be the 'instructor'. The artist should then be blindfolded and given a pen and piece of paper.

3 Draw a simple shape, eg a house, a cat, a car, on a piece of paper and hold it up so that all 'instructors' can see.

4 They must then instruct the artist to draw the image without saying what it is. For example, if you have drawn a house, they may only use phrases such as 'Draw a vertical straight line. Now draw a square' etc.

5 Give the groups a sensible amount of time to complete their drawings, then remove blindfolds and compare the artists' images to your original image. How well did everyone do?

6 Explain that a life following Jesus is sometimes similar to this. There are times when we sense that we have a little help from God, moments when we sense we have a lot of help from God and times when any help from God seems absent. It is at these times that we need to remember that God is there alongside us, guiding, leading and listening.

BIBLE EXPERIENCE

LEVEL 1: CONNECT

WHAT: questionnaire
WHY: to think about how we decide who we are going to trust
WITH: magazine page 147

1 Explain to the young people that we are going to be thinking about who we trust and why we make those decisions.

2 Give out copies of the questionnaire from page 147 and ask the young people to complete this, considering why they are making the choices that they are.

3 Invite the young people to form pairs or threes and ask them to compare their answers to the questions. Are they the same or are there differences? Where there are differences, why do they think they have different responses?

4 Now invite the pairs or threes to join together to form small groups. Ask the young people to share and compare their answers in these groups. Where are the similarities and differences?

5 Bring the whole group back together and explain that when we decide who we are going to trust we consider a range of different information. For some individuals, for example a police officer, their role and uniform draws people to trust them. For others, it is our experience of them, their reliability, a proven track record. In fact, in our culture today our experience of something is given importance in terms of our decision making. There are many reasons why we trust people.

6 Read Psalm 22:1–5 together and discuss these questions:

- What emotions do you think are in the heart of the writer?
- Why do you think the writer has chosen to begin this psalm by asking questions of God? What does this suggest to you about how we should relate to God?
- The psalm ends with a strong declaration of faith based on the activities of God in the past. What does this show us about how we should approach our problems?
- How do we continue on the journey with God?

LEVEL 2: INTERFACE

WHAT: discussion
WHY: to see that God can be trusted even when times are hard
WITH: flip chart, marker pens

1 Prepare three sheets of flip chart paper with the following headings: 'Yes, God can be trusted when times are hard because...', 'No, God cannot be trusted when times are hard because...', 'Parking space'.

2 Explain that the theme of this session is 'God can be trusted even when times are hard.' Ask the young people: In your experience, can God be trusted? Invite the young people to write down on the sheets of paper all the evidence they can think of to show that God either can or cannot be trusted. If they have a question or comment that doesn't fit either heading, then write it on the 'parking space' sheet.

3 Read together Psalm 22:1–5 and ask:

- What seems to be going on here? Where is God?
- Do you think the writer believes God can be trusted even when times are tough?
- Why do you think the writer uses such raw language in the opening verses?

4 Now look at the sheets of paper. Explain that there may well be times and moments when it appears that God is no longer there and in our humanity we don't understand where God has gone or what he is doing. What might it mean to trust God even when times are hard?

5 Look at the questions on your 'parking space' sheet and discuss any remaining issues, emphasising that this is difficult and Christians often disagree about the answers.

6 Give each young person a sheet of paper and ask them to write down one key question that they still have on the subject. Encourage them to take this away and to pray about it through the week. Try and revisit these at your next session.

LEVEL 3: SWITCH ON

WHAT: Bible study
WHY: to understand more deeply that God can be trusted even when times are hard

1 Read Psalm 22:1–5 together as a group and check that the group understand all the words that are used.

2 Ask the young people to share their immediate responses.

3 Ask the following questions for reflection:

- Do you find it easy to be honest with God?
- How do you feel when God seems not to answer?
- Have you ever been in a situation where you are so worried about something that you are unable to sleep? What did you do?
- Do you think that God can be trusted? Why or why not?

3 Explain that Christians believe that based on who God is – our experience and our knowledge of him – he is trustworthy and is with his people even when times are hard. When times are hard it can be more difficult to see the work of God in our lives, or to recognise that God has a role in our lives at all. It is at these times that we can cry out to God and ask him to help us, just as we see in Psalm 22.

RESPOND

23

MUSICAL

WHAT: **reflection**
WHY: **to use music and the story behind it to show that God can be trusted even when we can't see him**
WITH: **music video for 'You Never Let Go' by Matt and Beth Redman, the story of writing the song from page 148, playback equipment**

1 Play 'You Never Let Go' by Matt and Beth Redman.

2 Share the story of the writing of the song with the young people and ask them if this changes the way that they engage with it. Does knowing it came from a place of darkness and uncertainty change its meaning?

3 Listen to the song again and ask the young people if there are elements of the music or lyrics that stand out to them now they know how it was created?

4 Encourage the young people to pray about these things in their small groups and then come back together and summarise the thoughts and reflections.

PRACTICAL

WHAT: **prayer**
WHY: **to ask God to help us to trust him**

1 Invite the young people to get into pairs or threes for a time of prayer.

2 Encourage them to share with one another an example of a time when God has proven trustworthy from either their own experience or from what they know about God in the Bible.

3 When they have shared, remind them that in the Gospels Jesus tells us that if we ask then God will hear and will give us what we ask for. So it seems appropriate to ask God for his help to trust him. God knows what we need and he will meet us in that place. Invite them to share one prayer need with each other and then to spend some time praying for one another.

4 When the young people have prayed with one another, encourage them to continue asking God to help them to trust him on into the week. Try and make time the next time you meet to find out how this has gone for the young people.

CREATIVE

WHAT: **trust list**
WHY: **to build up some knowledge and information about God that will sustain us when he feels distant**
WITH: **craft materials**

1 Make sure there is enough equipment for each young person present to create a book. Give them card, paper, scissors and other materials as you wish.

2 Explain that one of the things that can sustain us and help us feel that God is near when times are hard is to record and create a record of the things God has done in our lives, or the truths we know about his nature.

3 In this activity the young people are going to create a personalised booklet that they can use to keep a record of their journey with God. Encourage them to make the booklet as personal to them as they like. If there is time, encourage the young people to begin to fill the pages with examples of things God has done, and truths about his nature.

4 Conclude by praying for the young people, for their engagement with the booklets and asking God to help us all to trust him.

MORE ON THIS THEME:

If you want to do a short series with your group, other sessions that work well with this one are:

21	*The wonders of God*	*Psalm 19*
22	*God wins*	*Psalm 20*
24	*God is good*	*Psalm 23*
25	*Light the way*	*Psalm 119:9–16,105*

MY GOD, MY GOD, WHY HAVE YOU FORSAKEN ME?

Bible bit
Psalm 22:1–5

'Nobody said it was easy' is sung by Chris Martin of Coldplay in their popular song 'The Scientist'. This is a statement that could be written about our journey as disciples of Christ. Many people believe that a relationship with Jesus means that they will be protected from difficult and painful experiences. This is simply not the case. What we do have is someone who can be trusted even when times are hard.

This is all easy to say, but much more challenging to live out in reality.

Our world is broken. There is war, famine, terrorism, disaster across the world. There are relationship breakdowns, sickness, death and pain for us all personally. Our families, our friends, and we ourselves struggle and suffer and the question 'Where are you, God?' may have been in our mind. Psalm 22 shows us that we can take this question to God, in its raw state, and give it to God. It is natural to wonder if God can be trusted when times are hard. What do you think?

Use this space to write your own psalm to God about how hard it can be to trust him.

Have you ever felt abandoned by someone? Have you ever felt abandoned by God?

There are times in all our lives when we feel like we are on our own. When these times arise there are all sorts of things that help us to feel a bit better about things. These may be memories of how things can be, people who make us feel better, or simply some time alone. Since many of us have experienced this in our earthly lives it is difficult for us to understand that God can be different, that he never abandons us, even when we feel like he has, and that he is faithful and dependable always.

How difficult do you find it to believe that God can be trusted?

Who do you like to be around when you're feeling low? What things make you feel better or adjust your perspective?

How can you help yourself to remember that God is faithful and dependable?

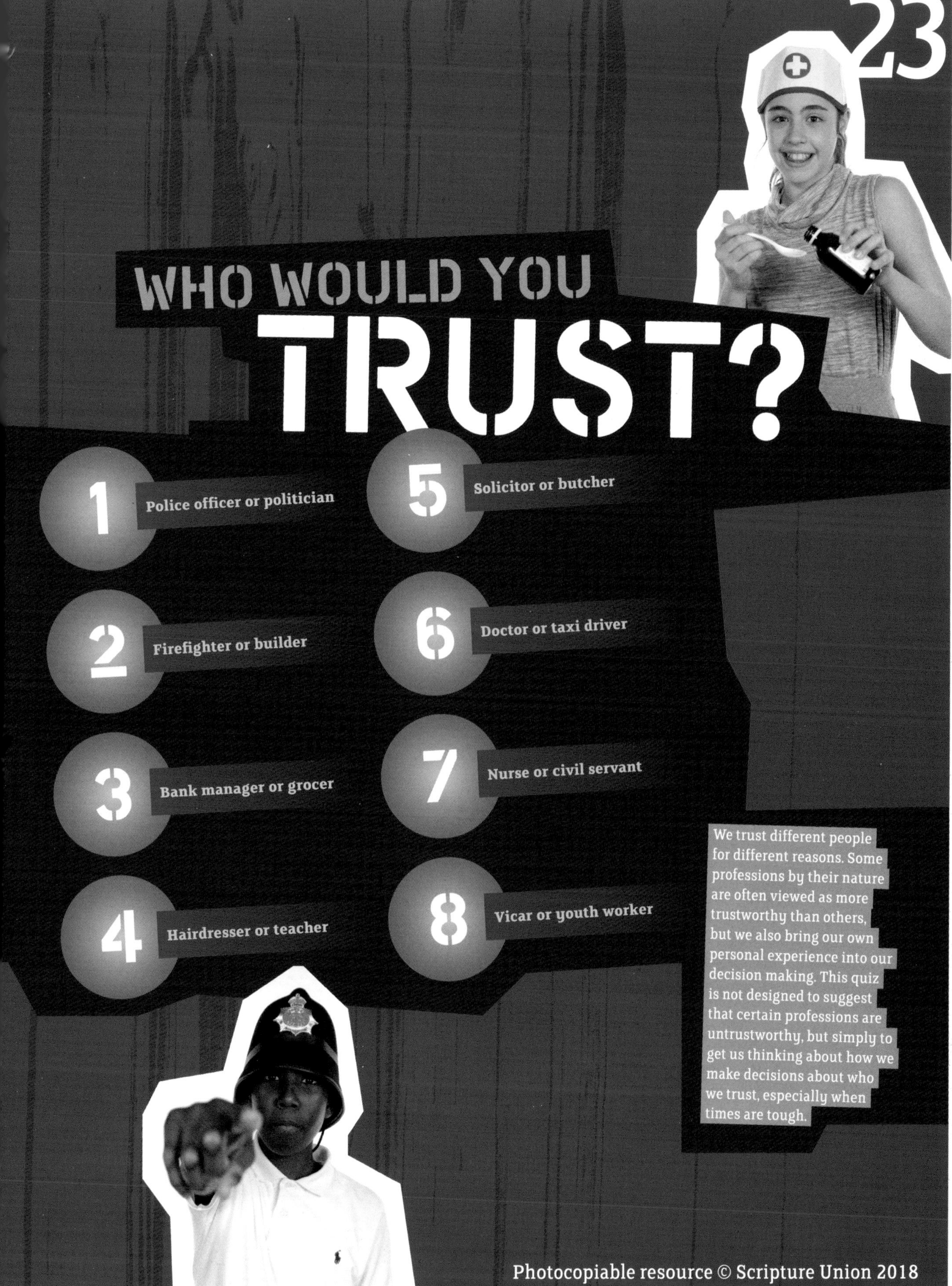
23
WHO WOULD YOU
TRUST?
1 Police officer or politician
2 Firefighter or builder
3 Bank manager or grocer
4 Hairdresser or teacher
5 Solicitor or butcher
6 Doctor or taxi driver
7 Nurse or civil servant
8 Vicar or youth worker
We trust different people for different reasons. Some professions by their nature are often viewed as more trustworthy than others, but we also bring our own personal experience into our decision making. This quiz is not designed to suggest that certain professions are untrustworthy, but simply to get us thinking about how we make decisions about who we trust, especially when times are tough.
Photocopiable resource © Scripture Union 2018

RESOURCE PAGE

USE WITH SESSION 23 RESPOND 'MUSICAL'

'As Christians, we can't escape from pain in this world, whether that's going through hard seasons personally or watching our loved ones do the same. But here's our distinctive: Even in the darkest and most disturbing moments, as real and as painful as they might be, we stand on an even greater reality. It's the truth of God who never lets go and never loses control. The One who never changes, is always good and merciful, always strong and mighty to save. Standing on the unshakeable truth of our God, we can make it through the storms of life. More than that, we find that we have a song in our hearts. For even in the toughest times, we look at Jesus and find plenty of reasons to continue singing out His praise and calling on His name. When we lift up the name of Jesus in worship, it overflows into evangelism ... A while back, my wife Beth and I were in a really painful situation. She had just had another miscarriage, and it happened to be the week of the London bombings. So out of us flowed "You Never Let Go," a little song of faith and trust.'

Matt Redman

Interviewed by Christa Banister for crosswalk.com

© Christianity Today International, 2007

Bible: Psalm 23

GOD IS GOOD

THE AIM: To think about all that God provides for us

The aim unpacked

Psalm 23 is one of the most well-known of all the psalms. We are all looking for guidance and help – a shepherd if you like – and God wants to provide for us. Psalm 23 speaks of God meeting our every need, wherever we are, whatever we are going through, and reminds us that not only does God provide good things, but he provides these in abundance.

WAY IN

theGRID MAGAZINE

WHAT: **challenge**
WHY: **to think about the things God provides for us**
WITH: **magazine page 153**

1 Hand out copies of page 153 and ask the young people to read through the shepherd facts.

2 Say that just as a shepherd cares for and provides for their sheep, so God provides for us. In pairs or small groups invite them to take it in turns to suggest things that God provides. The first person suggests something that they feel God provides for his people and the second person follows until they have (hopefully!) created a long list.

3 After a few minutes draw the group back together and ask if there is anything that they want to share with the whole group, perhaps something that they think other groups may not have considered.

4 Explain that the psalm we are considering together is all about God's provision for his people and his goodness in what he provides.

SCENE SETTER

WHAT: **clay modelling**
WHY: **to think about what it means to provide for others**
WITH: **clay**

1 Give a lump of modelling clay to everyone and invite them to make a simple model of something that they believe God has provided for them. They can choose to make anything but remind them that this is not a test of artistic ability and that it is simply about thinking about what it means to provide for others.

2 Give a second lump of modelling clay to everyone and say that having identified something that they believe God has made for them, they now need to choose something that another member of the group has created and make something that would work alongside what they have created. For example, if someone has made a house, you might want to make a garden, or something inside the house.

3 Display the models on a tray and invite the young people to share what they have each created and where they see God providing this for them or others. Explain that in the psalm we are reminded of God's good provision for us and we have not only considered that in this activity but we have also provided for others ourselves. God wants us to use our gifts and abilities to help others.

THEMED GAME

WHAT: **follow the leader!**
WHY: **to enable us to imagine ourselves as sheep and God as our Shepherd**
WITH: **a large space**

1 Explain that you are going to play a simple game of 'follow the leader'.

2 Invite one young person to leave the room and in their absence identify one person to be the leader.

3 Ask the young person to return to the room and to try and work out who the leader is.

4 The whole group needs to follow the leader in everything they do. As soon as the person identifies the leader the game is over. You can play this repeatedly as time allows.

5 Explain that Psalm 23 is all about God providing for us as our Shepherd. Sheep respond to the things that their shepherd does in the same way that we were responding to the leader in the game.

BIBLE EXPERIENCE

LEVEL 1: CONNECT

WHAT: imagination station
WHY: to become aware of the good promises of God in Psalm 23
WITH: magazine page 152

1 Encourage the young people to make themselves comfortable to listen to the Bible verses by sitting or lying down. As they do so, invite them to imagine that they are part of a group listening to a teacher speak about God's goodness. Play some reflective music and read Psalm 23 slowly and clearly while the young people try and imagine this as a reality in their life.

2 Ask the group how they found trying to imagine this. Were there images that were easier to imagine than others? What was easiest to connect with? What was most difficult? What did they think about different parts of the psalm? Were there any that they felt particularly drawn to?

3 Invite the young people to read the words about the promises of God and complete the questionnaire on page 152. Then ask the following questions:

- What do you think God provides for his people? What does the psalm suggest?
- What do you think the 'very dark valley' might refer to?
- What do we learn about God from verse 5 where it says 'you fill my cup to overflowing'?
- Can you think of any other times in the Bible where a cup is important?

4 Conclude by praying for the group and inviting God to help them see his goodness in the coming week.

LEVEL 2: INTERFACE

WHAT: Bible study
WHY: to see that God is good and wants to provide for his people
WITH: Bibles, a copy of Psalm 23 from *The Message*, page 154

1 Read Psalm 23 together from a traditional translation.

2 Then read Psalm 23 together from *The Message*.

3 Ask the young people to consider the following questions:

- Were you familiar with this psalm before today?
- Which bits of the psalm really stand out to you, and why?

4 Then, split the young people into small groups and give each group a Bible and the questions from page 154. Depending upon the size and ability of your group you may want to allocate just one or two of the questions to each small group as opposed to asking them to discuss every one.

5 Explain that Psalm 23 uses the image of sheep and shepherds because the writer, King David, was a shepherd and so he was relating his relationship and understanding of God to something that was extremely familiar to him. The goodness of God is expressed throughout the psalm and the provision of God is also key.

LEVEL 3: SWITCH ON

WHAT: Bible study
WHY: to understand that God is our Provider
WITH: Bibles

1 Ask everyone to read Psalm 23 on their own and then ask:

- Why do you think David wrote this psalm?
- What do you think the overall message of this psalm is?

2 Explain that this is a psalm that emphasises the goodness and the provision of God. It is a psalm that is familiar to many and is often used at funerals and as a comfort for those who are ill. But it has images that are useful to people at all stages of faith.

3 Ask the young people to find a space in your meeting room where they can be alone and reflect on the following questions:

- How does this psalm make you feel?
- Does the psalm show you anything new about God, or confirm anything you already believed?

4 After a time, call the group back together and give opportunity for feedback if appropriate. Then ask the young people to split into pairs and discuss the following questions:

- What do you think it means when it uses the phrase 'he lets me rest'?
- Can you think of any ways that God refreshes you? Where do you find relaxation and refreshment?
- Do you have any examples of how God has guided you?

5 Finally, ask the young people to consider which elements of the psalm are particularly significant for them and to share these in their pairs.

RESPOND

MUSICAL

WHAT: reflection
WHY: to consider God's provision
WITH: two versions of 'The Lord Is My Shepherd' with different musical arrangements, playback equipment

1 Explain that, like many psalms, Psalm 23 has been set to a wide range of music and that you are going to play just a couple now for them to listen to and reflect on.

2 Play the first version and ask God to speak to you all through it before asking the following questions:

- Which elements of the psalm were particularly brought to life in this version?
- Are there any elements that you feel were missing or lacking in emphasis?

3 Now play the second version and ask the questions again.

4 Close the section with a prayer inviting God to continue to speak to the young people through the music and psalm outside of the meeting and asking him to help you all remain mindful of his provision.

PRACTICAL

WHAT: thankfulness booklet
WHY: to act as a reminder of God's good provision for us
WITH: paper, pens, card

1 Make sure there is enough equipment for each young person to create a booklet. Give them card, paper, scissors and other materials as you wish.

2 Explain that one of our responses to God's provision might be thankfulness and adopting a posture of gratitude. God provides for us. We can create a record of the things God has provided for us in a book of thankfulness.

3 In this activity the young people are going to create a personalised booklet that they can use to keep a record of their journey with God. Encourage them to make the booklet as personal to them as they like. If there is time, encourage the young people to begin to fill the pages with examples of their thankfulness.

4 Conclude by challenging the young people to find three things that they can be thankful for each day this week and to come back to your next meeting ready to share them!

CREATIVE

WHAT: Psalm 23 map
WHY: to explore the different elements of the psalm
WITH: page 155

1 In advance prepare a large picture of the different areas mentioned in the psalm. Perhaps include a sheep pen, hills, table, valley etc. This doesn't have to be a stunning masterpiece but at least be visual enough for the young people to identify the different elements of the psalm.

2 Give each young person a sheep from page 155 to cut out and personalise so that they can identify it (if they want it to remain anonymous then suggest they don't do anything that would make it identifiable to others).

3 Invite the young people to think about where in the picture they would see themselves at this time and to place their sheep in that space.

4 When everyone has done this, say a prayer for each person there, asking God to meet them where they are and to assure them of his generous and good provision.

MORE ON THIS THEME:

If you want to do a short series with your group, other sessions that work well with this one are:

21	*The wonders of God*	*Psalm 19*
22	*God wins*	*Psalm 20*
23	*God is near*	*Psalm 22:1–5*
25	*Light the way*	*Psalm 119:9–16,105*

Bible bit
Psalm 23

Psalm 23 is one of the most well-known of all the psalms. It speaks of all the things that God gives us and how generous and good he is to us. The vibrant and powerful images that fill the verses connect with our human lives in a very deep way. The image of a shepherd looking after his sheep, while having less relevance in our culture today, speaks clearly about a love and care that is shown in action. We are all looking for guidance and help – a shepherd if you like – and God wants to provide for us.

Psalm 23 speaks of God meeting our every need, wherever we are, whatever we are going through, and reminds us that not only does God provide good things, but he provides much more than we could ever ask or imagine.

SHEPHERD FACTS

DID YOU KNOW?

In Old Testament times, shepherds cared for their sheep night and day. They led them to grassy areas to graze and took them to clean, calm water to drink.

In the hot summer, shepherds moved their flocks to cooler pastures on higher ground. For days on end, shepherds worked and slept outdoors.

Sheep had complete trust in their shepherd and followed the shepherd's voice even when walking through dangerous places.

Shepherds anointed their sheep with oil (especially on their heads) to protect them from flies, gnats, mosquitoes, and other insects.

At night, shepherds guarded the sheepfold or sheltered the flock in a cave. If the howl of a hyena scared the sheep in the darkness, the shepherd's voice would calm them.

Each evening, shepherds counted the sheep and checked their health. The shepherd would call and the flock would follow him to the pasture.

Shepherds used a heavy wooden rod as a weapon against wild animals that would harm the sheep. The rod was also used to discipline the sheep.

The shepherd's staff was a long stick, often with a crook or hook on one end. Shepherds leaned on the staff when climbing and also used it to guide the sheep and to rescue them when they got stuck.

Jesus is our Shepherd. Just as shepherds care for their sheep night and day, he cares for us; he takes care of us and protects us. We can trust God even when we are in difficult situations and we can go to God when we are stressed or concerned. God looks after us and protects us. He rescues us when we get stuck.

24
THE PROMISES OF GOD
What does God promise us? Answer true or false.
1 Eternal life
TRUE FALSE
2 An easy life
TRUE FALSE
3 Forgiveness of sin
TRUE FALSE
4 He is in charge
TRUE FALSE
5 Rest
TRUE FALSE
6 Popularity
TRUE FALSE
7 Lots of money
TRUE FALSE
8 Challenges
TRUE FALSE
9 Guidance
TRUE FALSE
10 He is with us
TRUE FALSE
11 A lot of friends
TRUE FALSE
12 We will get our own way
TRUE FALSE
There are many promises that God makes to his followers – several that are mentioned in Psalm 23. But God also tells us that while he is faithful to his promises and provides for us generously, this doesn't mean we won't face challenges in life. We will experience life in this world in all of its fullness, and God will be with us through it all.
Photocopiable resource © Scripture Union 2018

RESOURCE PAGE

USE WITH SESSION 24 BIBLE EXPERIENCE 'LEVEL 2 INTERFACE'

1 What do you think it means when it says he 'lets me rest in green pastures' (v 2)? If rest is an important part of God's goodness to us, where do we find this rest?

2 How do you think God guides us along 'paths that are right' (v 3)?

3 When you hear the phrase 'a very dark valley' (v 4), what do you think of?

4 How do you think a relationship with God helps us to 'not be afraid' (v 4)?

5 What does verse 5 suggest about the generosity and goodness of God?

6 If 'goodness and love' (v 6) follow us all the days of our lives, what do you think this might mean about the way we should live our lives?

USE WITH SESSION 24 RESPOND 'CREATIVE'

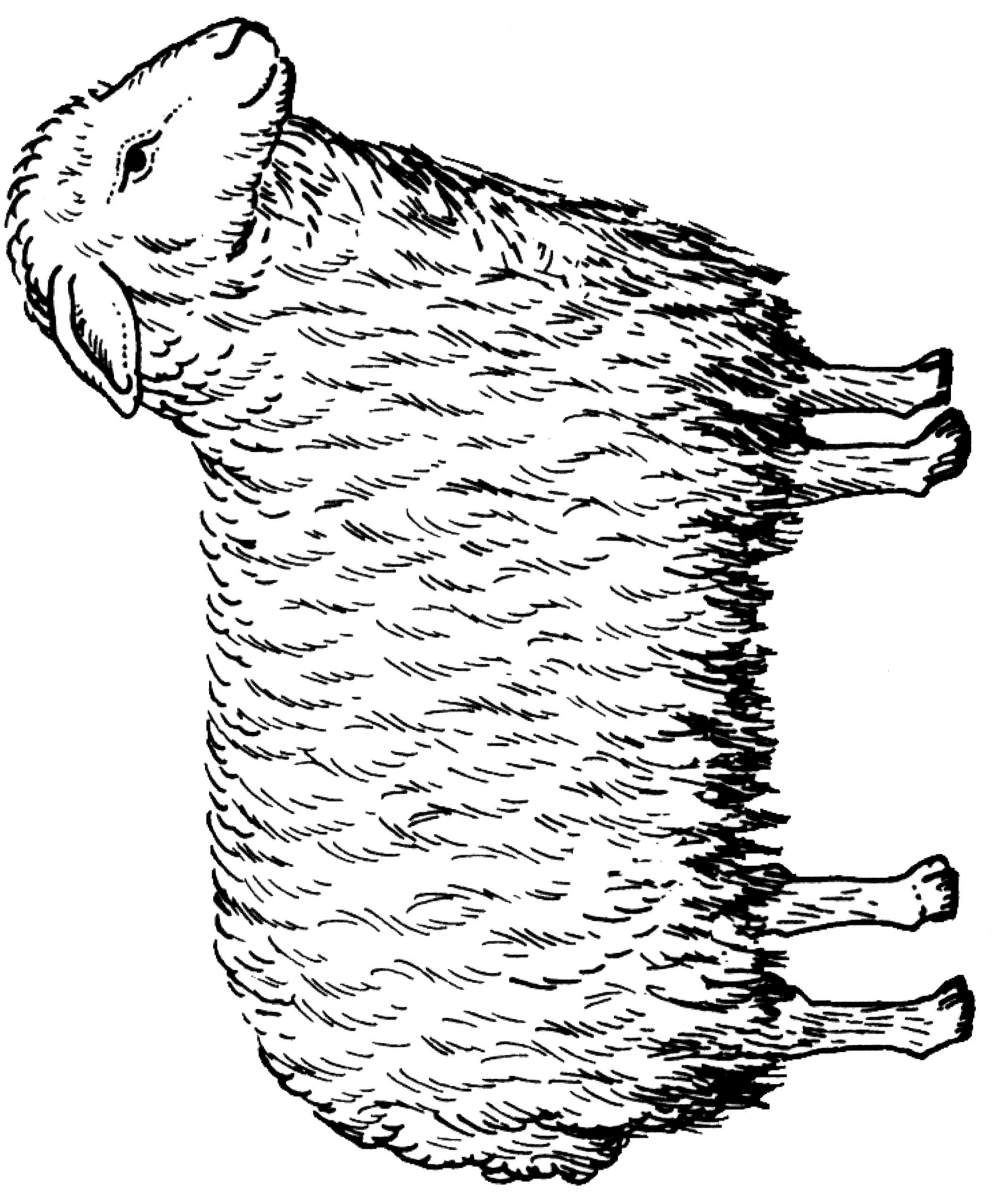

25

Bible: Psalm 119:9–16, 105

LIGHT THE WAY

THE AIM: To find out what it means to live in God's light

The aim unpacked

The psalmist in today's passage is quite adamant that the way to live in God's light is to stay close to God's Word. But that phrase is a little ambiguous. We obviously mean the Bible, don't we? Perhaps, but not everything in the Bible is a direct quotation from God. The Gospels describe the message of Jesus Christ, and John even calls Jesus 'the Word'. So perhaps there is some wonderful imagery going on here. The Word is more than just words.

WAY IN

theGRID MAGAZINE

WHAT: pairing-up activity
WHY: to introduce the theme of one thing needing another to work properly
WITH: magazine page 159

1 Hand out copies of page 159 and ask the group to see if they can match the items with the person or people who need them.

2 Once they've done this, go through the answers together. There is one item for each character, so everything should be linked up!

3 Explain that each item shown helps one of the people to do their job, to fulfil their role or to make them who they are. Ask the group if they can think of any other similar items and characters.

4 Explain that in this session they'll be looking at what we need and how it can help us to live our lives in God's light.

SCENE SETTER

WHAT: finding a place on a map
WHY: to introduce the theme of being guided
WITH: detailed maps

1 Before the session, get hold of some detailed maps, preferably of an area other than where you live. You will need to locate an obscure place on the map and then find a starting point somewhere else on the map. Then create a route and a guide for the group to follow to find the destination. Try to make it so that the group has to follow the directions exactly to find the location. If you can provide multiple maps and guides, the activity will work better.

2 Divide the young people into teams so that each group has a map and guide. Then challenge them to find the destination using the guide you have given them. You could have a race, but be careful not to offer a prize unless all the locations are equally difficult to find, or unless you give each team the same map and guide.

3 If appropriate, go on to explain that in today's session they'll be looking at how we need God's guidance in our lives and how we can live by God's light.

THEMED GAME

WHAT: blindfolded drawing
WHY: to introduce the theme of needing guidance
WITH: blindfolds

1 Hand out some pens and paper to the group and ask them to draw any animal. Once they've done this, invite them to show their picture to the rest of the group.

2 Now give everyone a blindfold and ask them to put them on so that they can't see anything.

3 Once this is done, ask them to turn their sheet of paper over and draw a different animal. Invite them to take the blindfolds off and, again, to share what they have drawn. The results should be a little more humorous than before.

4 You can repeat this as many times as you have time for, with different subjects. Afterwards, explain that they'll be seeing that it isn't just when drawing pictures that we need to be able to see what we're doing. We need to shed some light on the whole of our lives.

BIBLE EXPERIENCE

LEVEL 1: CONNECT

WHAT: **discussion and study**
WHY: **to find out what it means to live in God's light**
WITH: **magazine page 160**

1 Ask the young people to think in small groups for a few minutes about the question, 'What is the Bible?' Obtain feedback. If it hasn't come up, mention that many people think that the Bible just tells people what not to do.

2 Ask the group to look at the activity called 'Rules and regulations' on page 160. Use the questions at the bottom of the page to prompt further discussion.

3 Ask, 'So does the Bible just tell us what we shouldn't do?' Point out that the verse from Micah is like a 'Golden Rule', taking all the 'Do not...' rules and turning them into positive things we should do instead.

4 Invite a volunteer to read Psalm 119:9–6,105. Ask, 'How can someone sound so happy about being told what to do?' Explain that the psalmist had realised that God's rules brought him guidance and freedom. God gives rules because he has our well-being in mind.

5 Encourage the young people to look again at the 'Do not...' rules and discuss in pairs why each one is good for us. Perhaps they could reword them into positive 'Golden Rules'.

6 Ask, 'What effect does Jesus' death and resurrection have on all this?' Point out that the Bible is not just a set of rules and regulations but a collection of writings showing how God has interacted with his people throughout history. God has been guiding his people, but they haven't always used the light he has given. Today, Jesus' death and resurrection have brought us into God's presence and, through the Holy Spirit, we can have God's light living within us.

7 Ask someone to read Jeremiah 31:31–34 and finish by thanking God for his light in our lives.

LEVEL 2: INTERFACE

WHAT: **meditation**
WHY: **to find out what it means to live in God's light**
WITH: **page 161, ambient music**

1 Explain to the young people that we often hear that we should follow God, live God's way and ask God for guidance. But these things are often easier said than lived out. One reason for this is that we often turn to the Bible for specific answers because we think of it as a resource book for Christian living, then sometimes we become frustrated if it doesn't seem to have something that comments on our particular modern situation. We need to remember that primarily the Bible is a collection of writings that describe God's walk with his people, how he guided them and how he lit their path. Reading with this in mind, we can still find guidance from God, but in a different way.

2 Put on some ambient music and invite the group to listen to a meditation. Read the meditation from page 161, making sure you pause when prompted. Depending on your group, encourage them to listen and think silently, or you could give out pens and paper (or a copy of the resource page) for the young people to jot down their thoughts.

3 Leave some time at the end for the young people to reflect on the meditation.

4 Finish by explaining that after what Jesus did to bring us into a relationship with God, the Holy Spirit can live within us, guiding us and changing the rules and regulations into promises, and enabling us to live according to God's plan for us. For example, 'Do not lie,' becomes, 'I don't want to lie.'

LEVEL 3: SWITCH ON

WHAT: **rewriting the psalm**
WHY: **to find out what it means to live in God's light**
WITH: **Bibles**

1 It may be helpful to use some of the questions and thoughts from 'Level 1 Connect' as discussion starters. Point out that the Bible is not just a set of rules and regulations but a collection of writings that show how God has interacted with his people throughout history. God has been guiding his people, but they haven't always used the light he has given. Discuss some of the different ways God is described as communicating with his people in the Bible.

2 Now ask someone to read Jeremiah 31:31–34 and say that the time Jeremiah is speaking about is here and now. Jesus has sent the Holy Spirit to guide us and to be with us. God's light can be in our hearts, leading us from within. Because of that light, we are no longer bound by the rules in the Bible that tell us not to do things. With a restored relationship with God, and the Holy Spirit in our hearts guiding us, 'Do not lie,' becomes, 'I don't want to lie.'

3 Invite the young people to read Psalm 119 in pairs, focusing on verses 9–16 and 105, but they can read more if they want to (and if they have time). Ask them to discuss why they think the psalmist was filled with joy by God's law. After a few minutes, encourage them to feed back to the rest of the group.

4 Give everyone some paper and ask them to rewrite Psalm 119:9–16,105 in their own words. They should try to make it as personal as possible. If anyone wants to share what they have written at the end, encourage them to do so, but allow privacy as well, where needed.

RESPOND

MUSICAL

WHAT: **singing**
WHY: **to thank God that we can live in his light**
WITH: **words and music for 'Jesus, Jesus, Holy and Anointed One' by John Barnett, playback equipment or musical accompaniment**

1 Remind the group that to live by God's light we need to stay close to God and keep him close to us. This has been achieved by Christ's actions on the cross, his resurrection and the gift of the Holy Spirit.

2 Sing or listen together to the song, 'Jesus, Jesus, Holy and Anointed One', focusing on the words and worshipping the God who lights our path.

3 If you have time, encourage the young people to come up with their own words of praise to fit with the music – either from the Bible passage or from their own imaginations. Sing the song again with the new lyrics.

4 Finish with a time of open prayer, allowing the group to ask God to light their lives fully, to guide them and to help them live life to the full.

PRACTICAL

WHAT: **Bible reading encouragement**
WHY: **to see that by reading the Bible we can live in God's light**
WITH: **selection of Bible-reading guides**

1 Before this session, get hold of some Bible-reading guides to give to each young person in your group.

2 Remind the young people that the psalmist was pretty much overjoyed at spending time with his version of the Bible. Ask the young people how they feel about reading the Bible – they don't have to feel guilty if their reaction is not quite the same!

3 Explain that one of the problems with the Bible is that we can find it hard to understand. The most recent parts of it were written almost 2,000 years ago, so it isn't always easy. Perhaps you could discuss as a group some of the things that the young people find hard or confusing. But say that, as Paul says in 2 Timothy 3:16, it is vital for us to read the Bible because, by doing so, we develop our relationship with God.

4 Explain that there are many guides available to help us read the Bible. Give out a selection and encourage the young people to try to make a time each day when they can read the Bible and spend some time with God.

5 Finish with a time of prayer, thanking God that we can live in his light and learn more about him through reading our Bibles.

CREATIVE

WHAT: **Bible heart**
WHY: **to have a visual reminder of God's Word written on our hearts**
WITH: **Bibles, card**

1 If you looked at Jeremiah 31:31–34 in the *Bible experience* section, remind the young people about what they read. If not, ask a volunteer to read the passage aloud and then explain that Jeremiah was talking about a time when God's teachings would be written on people's hearts. This is now a reality as the Holy Spirit lives within us, guiding us and helping us to live in God's light.

2 Give everyone a piece of card and ask them to draw two heart shapes the same size and to cut them out. Either use coloured card or ask the young people to colour in the hearts before they cut them out.

3 Now invite the young people to think of their all-time favourite Bible verse. Encourage them to share what it is, if they would like. Have some suggestions ready in case anyone gets stuck.

4 Ask the group to copy the verse onto a new piece of paper, then fold it up and place it between the two heart shapes. Glue the two shapes together so that each person has their very own piece of God's Word written inside their hearts.

5 Say that the young people should keep the hearts safe and use them as an encouragement to follow God through what is written in the Bible.

6 Close with a time of silent prayer, encouraging the young people to ask God to place his Holy Spirit in their hearts.

MORE ON THIS THEME:

If you want to do a short series with your group, other sessions that work well with this one are:

21	*The wonders of God*	*Psalm 19*
22	*God wins*	*Psalm 20*
23	*God is near*	*Psalm 22:1–5*
24	*God is good*	*Psalm 23*

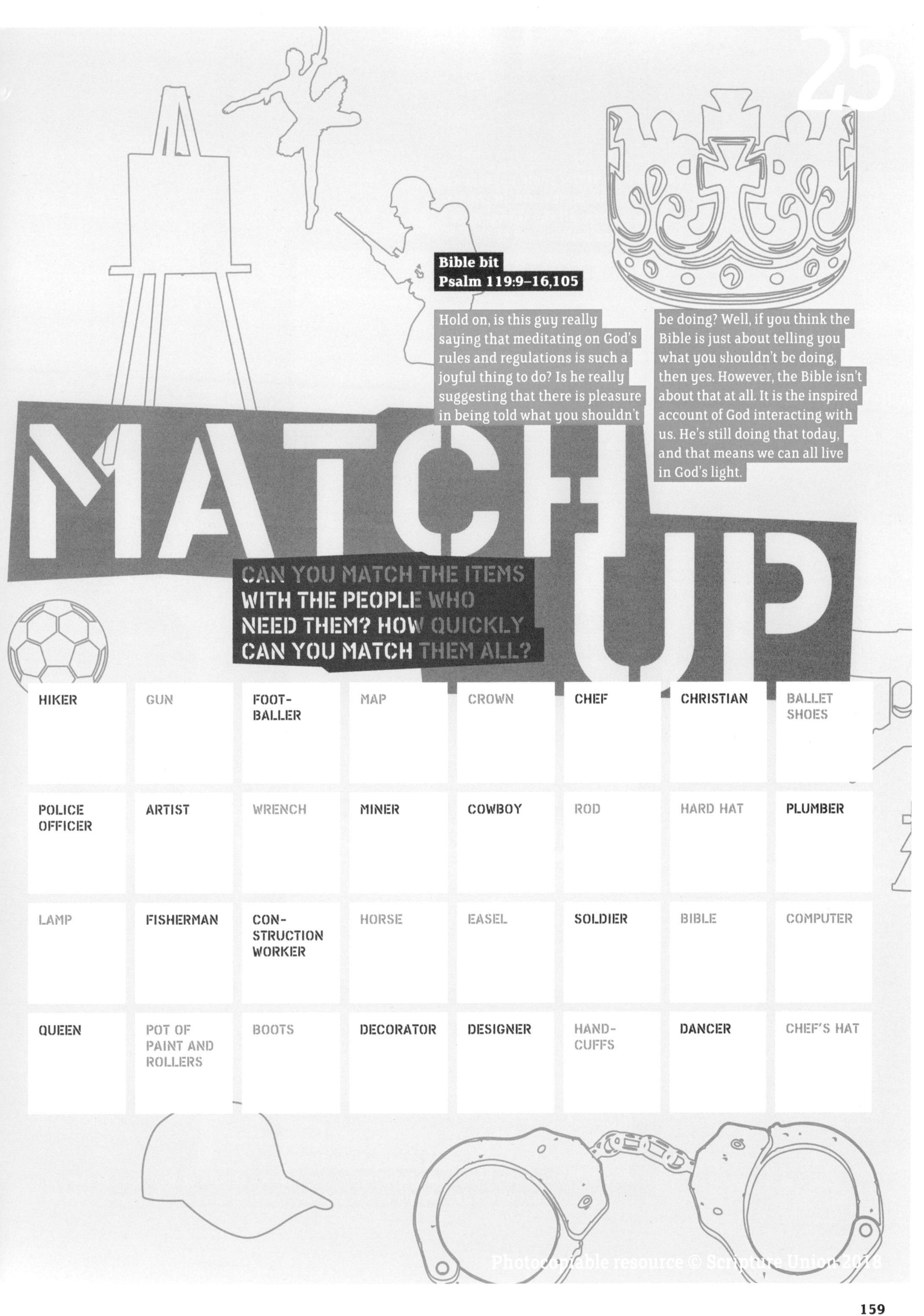

Bible bit
Psalm 119:9–16,105

Hold on, is this guy really saying that meditating on God's rules and regulations is such a joyful thing to do? Is he really suggesting that there is pleasure in being told what you shouldn't be doing? Well, if you think the Bible is just about telling you what you shouldn't be doing, then yes. However, the Bible isn't about that at all. It is the inspired account of God interacting with us. He's still doing that today, and that means we can all live in God's light.

MATCH UP

CAN YOU MATCH THE ITEMS WITH THE PEOPLE WHO NEED THEM? HOW QUICKLY CAN YOU MATCH THEM ALL?

HIKER	GUN	FOOT-BALLER	MAP	CROWN	CHEF	CHRISTIAN	BALLET SHOES
POLICE OFFICER	ARTIST	WRENCH	MINER	COWBOY	ROD	HARD HAT	PLUMBER
LAMP	FISHERMAN	CON-STRUCTION WORKER	HORSE	EASEL	SOLDIER	BIBLE	COMPUTER
QUEEN	POT OF PAINT AND ROLLERS	BOOTS	DECORATOR	DESIGNER	HAND-CUFFS	DANCER	CHEF'S HAT

RULES AND REGULATIONS?

Take a look at the Bible passages written in the boxes and, in the space provided, write all the things that each passage tells us not to do.

COLOSSIANS 3:8,9

MATTHEW 5:21–48

ROMANS 14:13

EXODUS 20:1–17

WHAT ABOUT MICAH 6:8?

So is the Bible just about telling us what we should or shouldn't be doing? What effect does Jesus' death and resurrection have on all this?

USE WITH SESSION 25 BIBLE EXPERIENCE 'LEVEL 2 INTERFACE'

Meditation on Psalm 119:9–16,105 (New Century Version)

9 How can a young person live a pure life?
By obeying your word.
Think about your own life. How pure is the journey you are on? How often do you turn to God's Word for guidance? (pause)

10 With all my heart I try to obey you.
Don't let me break your commands.
Is this your prayer? How often do you call out to the Lord for help? Can you commit more to following God? (pause)

11 I have taken your words to heart
so I would not sin against you.
Is your walk with God just on a [Sunday or whenever your group meets] or do you stroll all week long with God in your heart? (pause)

12 Lord, you should be praised.
Teach me your demands.
Is our attitude one of listening and learning when we read the Bible? Do we naturally link praise with being told what to do? (pause)

13 My lips will tell about
all the laws you have spoken.
If we see the Bible as just being about rules and regulations we're not likely to be telling others. But a God living in us, guiding us, is something else. (pause)

14 I enjoy living by your rules
as people enjoy great riches.
This is where we were designed to be; this is how we can feel about living in God's light. (pause)

15 I think about your orders
and study your ways.
We need to understand; we need to know. Not everything is straightforward and easy to understand. (pause)

16 I enjoy obeying your demands,
and I will not forget your word.
How much of the Bible can you remember? And how often do we pick the Bible up and smile as we read it – surrounded by God's love? (pause)

105 Your word is like a lamp for my feet
and a light for my path.
If we want to know where we are going and how we should live, we need our path to be illuminated. The light is from God and it shines from the Bible.

26

Bible: Isaiah 6

HIGH AND LIFTED UP

THE AIM: To be aware of the awesomeness of God and to serve him

The aim unpacked

As followers of Christ, we have the calling to go and share the good news with others. However, as we look at the example of Isaiah, we see that his mission was preceded by an intense, awe-filled meeting with God. Although we may not all have such a vivid encounter with God, we can still have feelings of awe and wonder for our Creator.

WAY IN

theGRID MAGAZINE

WHAT: **discussion**
WHY: **to see that places and people can induce feelings of awe**
WITH: **magazine pages 165 and 166, celebrity magazines**

1 In advance, get hold of some celebrity magazines (such as *OK!*), making sure they are age appropriate.

2 Distribute copies of pages 165 and 166 and invite everyone to look at the 'Awesome buildings'. Ask them to think about how impressive the buildings are. How would they feel if they were to play at the Millennium Stadium or the Melbourne Cricket Ground? What would they think if they were going to get married in St Paul's Cathedral or visit the Taj Mahal? Or if they were about to go on stage at Wembley or the Sydney Opera House?

3 Flick through the celebrity magazines and look at the people in them. Which ones would the young people be excited to meet? Would they get tongue-tied if they ever got the chance to speak to them? Are any of them truly awe-inspiring or glorious?

SCENE SETTER

WHAT: **top ten**
WHY: **to think about what we find amazing**
WITH: **flip chart or whiteboard, marker pens, magazine page 166 (optional)**

1 Divide the group into pairs. Encourage them to discuss the most amazing special effects they have ever seen in films or in adverts on TV. There are some examples on page 166 that might help get them started.

2 Once they have done this, bring the group back together and create a list of the most amazing ones on the flip chart or whiteboard.

3 Discuss what it is that make the effects 'special'. Why is it that certain things are amazing but others are not?

4 From your list of amazing effects, create a super top ten list by inviting the young people to vote whether they think each effect on the list is amazing or not while you write up the scores. Make a list of the top ten from their most popular votes.

5 Explain that during this session you'll be looking at an amazing, awe-inspiring event that happened to a guy called Isaiah many years ago.

THEMED GAME

WHAT: **consequences game**
WHY: **to consider why we think some people are great and others are not**

1 Play a version of the game Consequences, using the following guidelines (and discouraging any offensive answers!):

- [name of celebrity you admire]
- met... [name of celebrity you don't admire]
- The first celebrity said, 'I'm great because...'
- 'and you're talentless because...'
- The second celebrity said, 'Well, I think...'

2 After you have played the game, ask the young people what makes them admire some celebrities and not others.

3 If appropriate, explain that when we admire certain celebrities, we can easily live in awe of them and think they're something special. However, they are just people – like all of us. Later we'll be looking at something that really is special and very awe-inspiring.

BIBLE EXPERIENCE

LEVEL 1: CONNECT

WHAT: reconstruction of Isaiah's vision
WHY: to be aware of the awesomeness of God and to serve him
WITH: copies of Isaiah 6, pens or highlighters, multisensory materials to reconstruct the vision (such as a large chair, lengths of fabric, incense, music, lights)

1 Give out a copy of the Bible verses to each young person. Ask them to read the verses and highlight all the different senses that Isaiah used to take in the vision of God.

2 Challenge the group to think about how they might try to reconstruct the things they have marked in the Bible verses. Show them the materials you have brought along and work together to create your own 'throne room' using the Bible passage as a reference. Try to create a space where the young people can use all their senses and spend time reflecting on their response. If you can, why not use dry ice to add to the effect?

3 Sitting together in or around your 'installation', discuss what the young people's reactions might have been if they had encountered this vision themselves. How did Isaiah react? Point out that Isaiah didn't know what God wanted him to do, but he responded positively anyway. Would the young people have done this or would they have wanted to know what God had in mind first? Does this experience of God encourage them more or less to go and tell others about him?

4 Give the young people the opportunity to reflect on what they have got out of these Bible verses and on what God might be saying to them.

LEVEL 2: INTERFACE

WHAT: discussion
WHY: to be aware of the awesomeness of God and to serve him
WITH: flip chart or whiteboard, marker pens, page 168

1 Give a copy of page 168 to each young person. Read Isaiah 6 together in sections (verses 1–5; 6,7; 8–13). After each section, invite the young people to discuss their reaction to what is happening, using the questions on the resource page as a prompt. You could either discuss these all together, or divide into smaller groups and then feed back. In the more open-ended questions, allow the young people to express their opinions and give them time to come to their own conclusions. Their reactions might differ completely from your expectations. Write their thoughts on a flip chart or whiteboard.

2 When you have talked about the Bible verses and have written down the young people's thoughts, compare this passage with the story of Paul meeting Jesus on the road to Damascus in Acts 9:

- What are the similarities and differences between the two stories?
- Why does God reveal himself to us in different ways? Encourage the young people to think about other revelations of God they have read about (eg Exodus 3).
- Does this change any of the thoughts that were written down when thinking about Isaiah 6? (They might like to reflect on what Paul went through as stated in 2 Corinthians 11:23b–27 and compare it to what God had in store for Isaiah.)

3 Finally, discuss with the young people what they might face if they follow God's call. Point out that we won't know everything we will have to face, just as Isaiah and Paul didn't know. Be encouraging, though, and remind the young people that they can speak of God's glorious love because they have experienced it themselves! Be available to pray with anyone who doesn't feel they have experienced God's love for themselves.

LEVEL 3: SWITCH ON

WHAT: imagination station
WHY: to be aware of the awesomeness of God and to serve him
WITH: contemplative music, playback equipment, magazine page 167

1 Encourage the young people to make themselves comfortable to listen to the Bible verses, sitting or lying down. As they do so, challenge them to imagine what Isaiah saw when God appeared to him in the Temple. Play the music and read out Isaiah 6:1–7 slowly and clearly while the group members close their eyes and try to imagine what Isaiah saw.

2 Ask the group how they found trying to imagine the scene. What was easiest to picture? What did they find most difficult? What did they think about the different parts of the vision? Invite questions and look together at page 167, which illustrates and explains some of the symbolism behind the vision.

3 Ask the young people what they think their reaction would be if they were to see this vision, as they think about what some of it means. Would they believe their eyes? How would you feel if you were to see such a thing?

4 Read Isaiah 6:8–13 to the group. What do the young people think of Isaiah's reaction?

RESPOND

MUSICAL

WHAT: **considering a song and writing another**
WHY: **to think musically about God's calling**
WITH: **words and music to an appropriate worship song, playback equipment or musical accompaniment, Bibles**

1 Sing together or listen to a worship song which speaks of God's glory, his presence and our response to it. Some suggestions include:

- 'Welcomed In to the Courts of the King (Facedown)' by Matt Redman
- 'Here I Am, Standing Amazed (Glorious majesty)' by Andy Bromley, Gary Sadler and John Hartley
- 'Holy, Holy' by Brenton Brown

2 Invite the group to look at the words of the song you've just sung or listened to and think about what these words are saying to them. Discuss what they think about the words – do they express their own feelings? If not, why not?

3 Explain that the vision Isaiah saw was a truly glorious one. The vision was also a call to be sent on a mission from God. Our experience of God's glory should prompt a response.

4 Encourage the young people to think about words that express their feelings towards God's glory and their response to it. Ask them to write their own song or poem, using the words the creatures used to praise God in Isaiah 6:3 – 'Holy, holy, holy is the Lord All-powerful. His glory fills the whole earth.' How would they continue? Would they continue to praise God in this way? Would they go on to ask God to be with them while they serve him?

5 If the young people wish to, encourage them to read out their songs or poems as an act of worship.

PRACTICAL

WHAT: **commissioning and prayer**
WHY: **to repent before setting out to answer God's call**
WITH: **bowl of water, towels, contemplative music, playback equipment**

1 Read Isaiah 6:6,7 again. What does the group think the purpose of the coal was? Explain that lips are symbolic of a person's whole body and life – everything they have said and done – and that the creature was purifying Isaiah before God so he could go and speak God's word.

2 Remind the young people that this process of purification is no longer necessary because Jesus has paid the price – we can be made pure through his dying for us on the cross. Tell the group that we still have to say sorry for the things we have done wrong, and this is what you are going to do now. To symbolise purity, you are not going to use hot coals, but water.

3 Play some background music quietly and encourage the young people to spend some time thinking about what they might want to say sorry to God for. Invite them to come forward when they are ready and to wash their hands in the water to symbolise that they have been forgiven.

4 After they have washed their hands, encourage everyone to think quietly about what God might be calling them to do. They should then pray about these things silently, asking God for help to do his will.

5 You may wish to pray together about things the young people might be going through at home or school because they are already following God's call. Make sure you are both authentic and encouraging in your prayers.

CREATIVE

WHAT: **craft**
WHY: **to create a reminder of God's glory and his call to us**
WITH: **art materials, page 169**

1 Give the young people a copy of the throne template from page 169, along with some paper and the art materials. Encourage them to create a glorious throne by drawing round the template and decorating the throne. In the middle of the throne, they should write God's words from Isaiah 6:8: 'Whom can I send? Who will go for us?'

2 As they are doing this, chat with the group and try to discover their reaction to the Bible verses. Are they ready to accept God's call? Or are they still exploring the idea of a glorious God?

3 When they have finished, encourage the young people to take their thrones home. They could use them as a focus to help them pray about their response to God's glory and to what he might be calling them to do.

26

Bible bit
Isaiah 6

'Awesome' can be a bit of an over used word these days, but back in the Old Testament it really meant something. Isaiah was about to be called to an important mission when he experienced this intense, awe-filled meeting with God. While we might not have such vivid encounters as he did, we can still feel a sense of awe and wonder for our Creator. When we see the amazing things he can do, then, just like Isaiah, it becomes our mission to go and tell others about him too!

AWESOME BUILDINGS

HOW WOULD YOU FEEL IF...

YOU HAD THE CHANCE TO PLAY IN THE MILLENNIUM STADIUM?

YOU WERE GOING TO GET MARRIED IN ST PAUL'S CATHEDRAL?

YOU WERE INVITED TO STAY OVER AT THE TAJ MAHAL?

YOU WERE ABOUT TO SING ON STAGE IN THE SYDNEY OPERA HOUSE?

SPECIAL FX

Isaiah had a totally awe-inspiring vision in Isaiah 6. Today we are bombarded by amazing special effects on the TV, films and other media! Here are some of our favourites – what are yours?

- Smaug the dragon and his hoard of gold in *The Hobbit: The Desolation of Smaug*.
- Iron Man walking into and out of his suit in the *Avengers* and *Iron Man* films.
- Dr Ryan Stone spinning out of control in space in *Gravity*.
- Ethan Hunt climbing the skyscraper in *Mission Impossible: Ghost Protocol*.
- Rey and Finn escaping Jakku in the Millennium Falcon in *Star Wars VII: The Force Awakens*.

ISAIAH'S VISION

26

1 **THE TEMPLE**
Where God lived on earth in the time before Jesus came. Jesus was God on earth, God made human. We now also have the Holy Spirit who is with us all the time.

2 **FLYING CREATURES**
Their name literally means 'burning ones'. Fire was a symbol of God's holiness. They are above God, because that was the traditional position of a servant – they are God's servants.

3 **WINGS**
The flying creatures covered their eyes because even they couldn't look on God – he is too holy. They left their ears uncovered so they could hear and obey God.

4 **THE THRONE**
A symbol of being a king.

5 **THE ROBE**
A symbol of where God meets the earth in the Temple.

6 **SHAKING**
This is often the reaction to the presence of God. In Psalm 18:7, the whole earth shakes in God's presence!

RESOURCE PAGE

USE WITH SESSION 26 BIBLE EXPERIENCE 'LEVEL 2 INTERFACE'

Isaiah 6

Verses 1–5:

- How would you describe God appearing to Isaiah?

- What was Isaiah's reaction? What do you think about it?

- How do you think you would have reacted?

Verses 6 and 7:

- What was the significance of the hot coal? (Page 167 has some information on the symbolism in Isaiah's vision.)

Verses 8–13:

- What was Isaiah's reaction to God's call? What do you think of it?

- How would you describe what God asked Isaiah to do?

- Why do you think God's description seemed so bleak?

USE WITH SESSION 26 RESPOND 'CREATIVE'

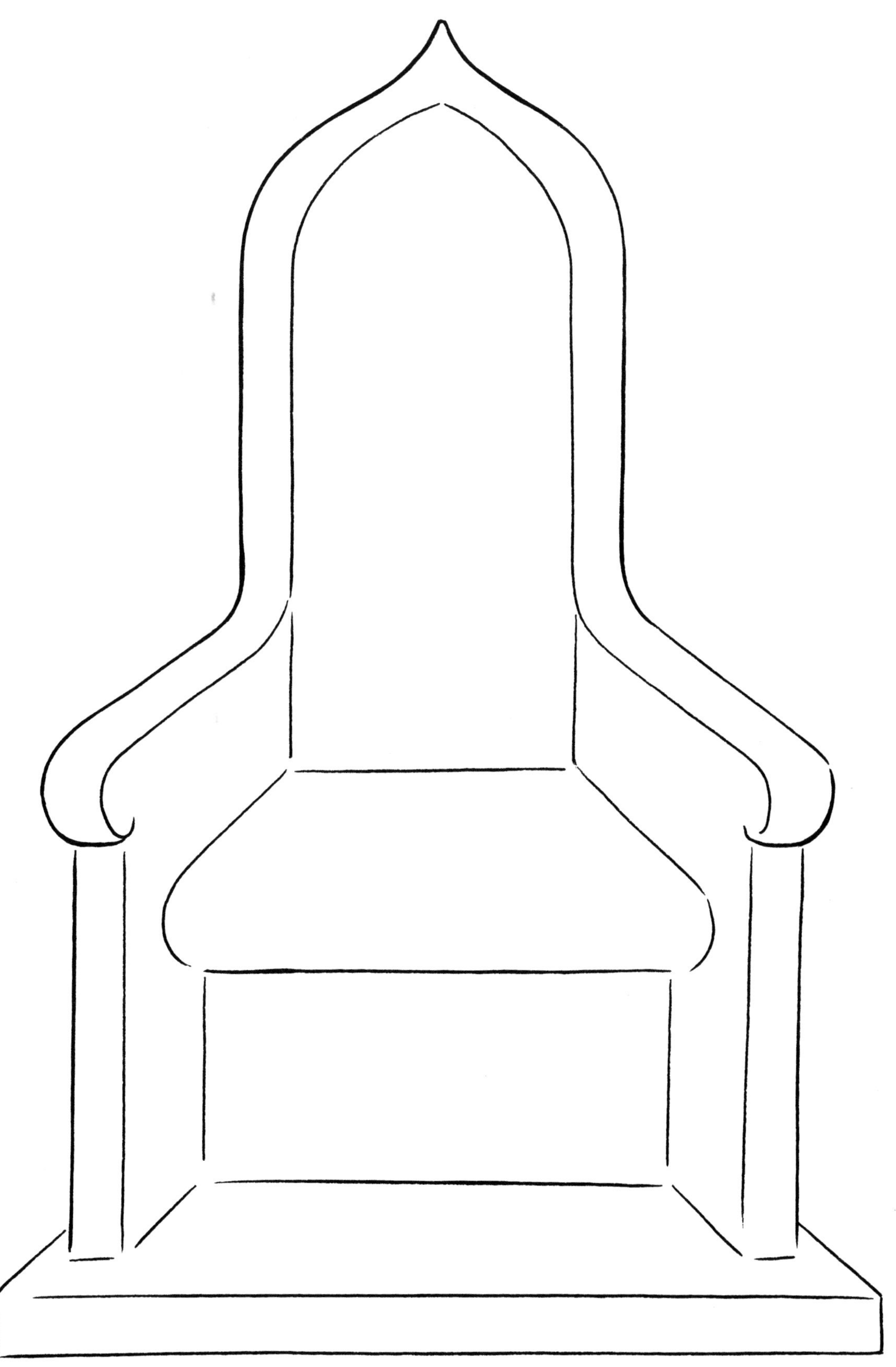

27 UNCLEAN!

Bible: Matthew 8:1

THE AIM: To discover more about our powerful God and explore our response to him

The aim unpacked

As our young people grow up, they begin to understand their own developing identity. An integral part of their development is acceptance by society and by their peers. There are many reasons why young people may feel left out – perhaps because of the way they look act. Jesus overcame society's barriers in order to bring healing – this was one aspect of the 'good news' to the sick man.

WAY IN

theGRID MAGAZINE

WHAT: **reading and discussion**
WHY: **to look at things that we find horrible and unacceptable**
WITH: **magazine page 173**

1 Ask your group members to look at the article entitled 'Gross' on page 173.

2 Invite them to feed back to the whole group about which things they find horrible and try to stay clear of.

3 Use the following questions to discuss further:

- What is it that makes something unacceptable to us?
- Is it based on what we see?
- Is it based on what could happen or what will happen? What are the unwritten rules that our society sticks to: for example, are we all supposed to be afraid of spiders? Why or how might these come about?

4 Chat about whether the young people avoid certain things because of how they feel, or because of how they are 'supposed to feel'.

SCENE SETTER

WHAT: **board game**
WHY: **a fun way of dealing with things that we'd rather not deal with**
WITH: **Operation board game**

1 Set up Operation and play it together. Chat about how difficult it is to get some of the bones out of the man!

2 When you have finished and congratulated the winner, chat about any broken bones or illnesses the young people have had. What did those illnesses feel like? Why did they feel that way?

3 Explain that serious physical illness is something that society often tries to keep at arm's length. It is not just our society that does this, as we'll see later

THEMED GAME

WHAT: **ball tag**
WHY: **to try to be the last one out – one who is left out**
WITH: **large room, soft ball**

1 Play a game of ball tag.

2 Choose one person to start off. They t the ball at one of the other young people them. Once others have been tagged they allowed to pick up the ball and tag others

3 The winner is the last one not to be ta by the ball. Congratulate the winner.

4 The winner has become the winner b being different – not tagged – in this gam real life, being different can cause proble

BIBLE EXPERIENCE

LEVEL 1: CONNECT

WHAT: discussion about rights
WHY: to discover more about our powerful God and explore our response to him
WITH: national newspapers or access to news websites

1 Ask the group to think about what rights they have, perhaps as a citizen of their country, as a human being, or as a member of their school or a club. Ask them to get into pairs and to come up with lists.

2 Look at the newspapers or news websites together and see if you can find any stories about people who have limited rights, or who feel their rights are being infringed. Discuss as a group how the young people would feel if any of the rights on their lists were to be taken away from them.

3 Read Matthew 8:1–4 together.

4 Explain that, at the time of Jesus, people with leprosy or other skin diseases had few rights. This was because of the rigorous laws that had been created to keep them out of society in order to stop the diseases from spreading. Sufferers were seen as unclean outcasts. Can the young people think of any modern equivalents of this kind of prejudice?

5 Ask the young people to suggest some actions that might have helped these people but that would have been contrary to acceptable behaviour at the time. Be sure to point out that Jesus did more than just 'help' the man with the skin disease – he healed him.

LEVEL 2: INTERFACE

WHAT: reflection
WHY: to discover more about our powerful God and explore our response to him
WITH: magazine page 174, page 175

1 Ask the young people to read the article 'Alone and afraid' copied from page 174, on their own. Give them time to reflect but don't invite any questions or feedback at this point.

2 Invite the group to relax and listen to the meditation from page 175, which is the same story from a different point of view.

3 Ask a volunteer to read Matthew 8:1–4 to the group.

4 Invite the group to give feedback, comment or ask questions. Discuss:

- What is your impression of Jesus?
- What do you make of his power?

LEVEL 3: SWITCH ON

WHAT: Bible study
WHY: to discover more about our powerful God and explore our response to him
WITH: commentaries, study Bibles, information on skin diseases from www.leprosy.org

1 Invite the young people to read Matthew 8:1–4 on their own and then, in pairs, to discuss the following questions:

- What had Jesus been doing on the mountain?
- Why did Jesus tell the man to go and show himself to the priest? (Other passages which may help here are Leviticus 13:1–23; 22:4–7 and Numbers 5:2–4.)

2 If there is time, invite the young people to search the Bible for other stories involving skin diseases: the story of Naaman in 2 Kings 5, for example. What themes are similar to today's main story?

3 Jesus told the man to go and see the priest. The priest would have given the man the all clear and allowed him to return to a 'normal' life. Ask the young people to discuss the following questions in their pairs:

- How did Jesus show his power in this story?
- What things can stop people living normal lives today?
- How can the church help these people?
- What difference might Jesus' power make to these people?

4 Encourage the young people to feed back their answers and opinions.

RESPOND

MUSICAL

WHAT: song and prayer
WHAT: to ask God to bring us closer to him
WITH: words and music of 'Angel in Disguise' by Delirious?, playback equipment

1 Ask the group to recap on what Jesus did in the story. Emphasise to the young people that Jesus used his power to break down physical and social barriers.

2 Explain that we can do things that make us feel like outcasts from God. Perhaps we are struggling with something that makes us feel far away from God.

2 Use the song 'Angel in Disguise' together as a way of talking to God, by either singing along or by reading the words as it is played.

PRACTICAL

WHAT: discussion and prayer
WHY: to ask Jesus to use his power to break through barriers

1 Ask the group to suggest any areas in today's society where people are excluded through no fault of their own. Are people left out because they have a particular illness or disability? Or is it because they have particular hobbies which aren't popular or cool? Have a time of prayer, asking Jesus to show his power in those situations and to break down barriers.

2 Suggest that the young people examine what they can do to break down barriers. It might be to make the group more accessible to others or to befriend people who are left out. Pray again, this time asking Jesus to work through the young people as they seek to follow his example.

3 Be sensitive to any young people in your group who may feel excluded themselves, either within the group, or in another situation. Depending on your group, you may like to invite them to talk about how they have felt, and what they would find helpful; alternatively, ensure they are given space to join in at their own level.

CREATIVE

WHAT: time of thanks
WHY: to thank Jesus for his awesome healing power
WITH: balloons, marker pens

1 Give out the balloons and ask the young people to blow them up.

2 When everyone has an inflated balloon, ask them to write on their balloon something that they have been impressed with about Jesus' power. It could be something that they have heard today, or something they have already discovered about Jesus' power and lordship.

3 When everyone has written something, talk as a group about what they have written.

4 Encourage everyone to throw their balloon into the air and to shout out what they have written. Then they should tap the balloons gently around the room and, every time they hit a balloon, they should shout, 'Thanks for...' and then whatever is written on that balloon.

MORE ON THIS THEME:

If you want to do a short series with your group, other sessions that work well with this one are:

28	*Sick!*	*Matthew 8:5–13*
29	*In danger!*	*Matthew 8:23–27*
30	*Hungry!*	*Matthew 15:29–39*

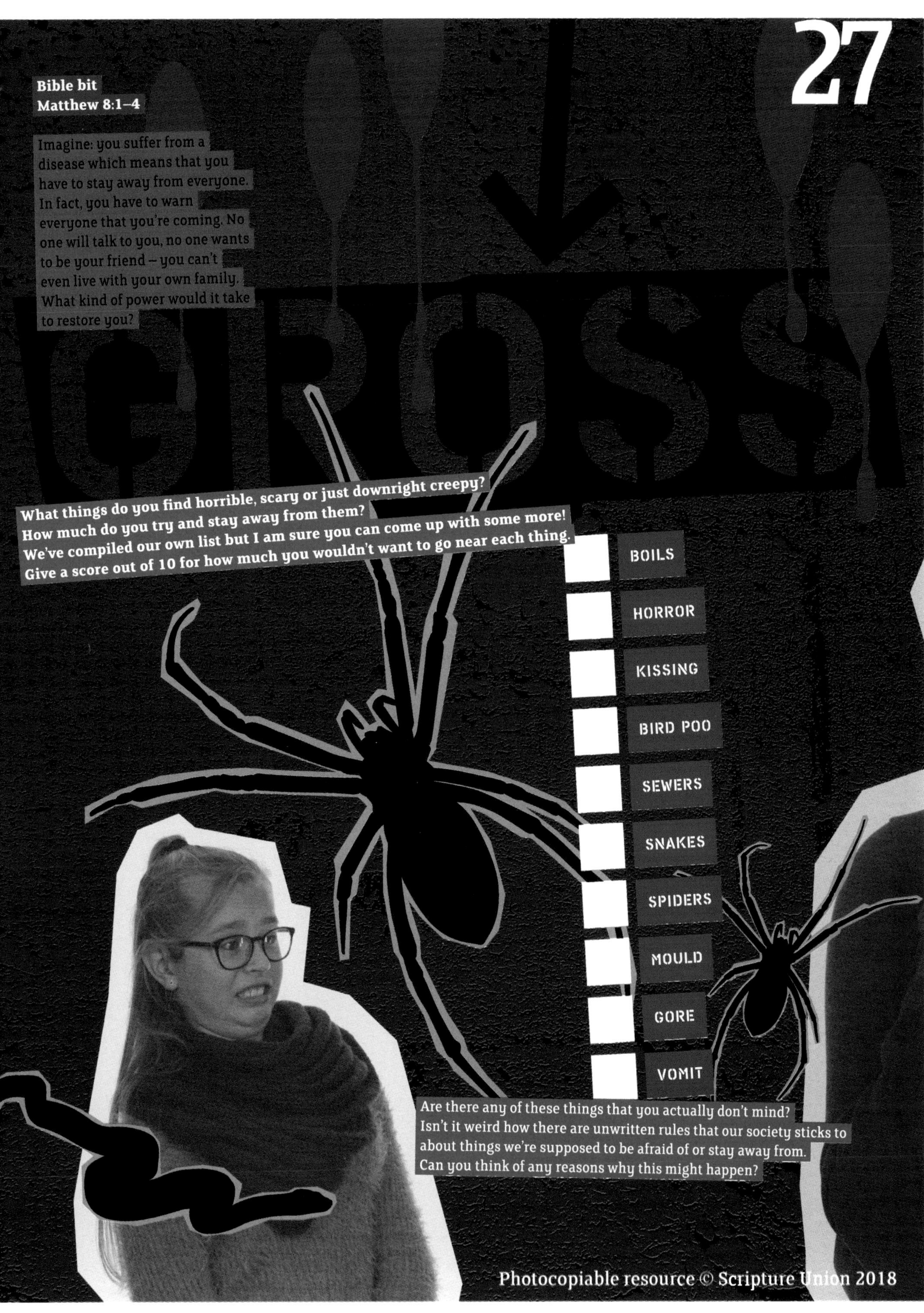
27
Bible bit
Matthew 8:1–4
Imagine: you suffer from a disease which means that you have to stay away from everyone. In fact, you have to warn everyone that you're coming. No one will talk to you, no one wants to be your friend – you can't even live with your own family. What kind of power would it take to restore you?
GROSS
What things do you find horrible, scary or just downright creepy?
How much do you try and stay away from them?
We've compiled our own list but I am sure you can come up with some more!
Give a score out of 10 for how much you wouldn't want to go near each thing.
BOILS
HORROR
KISSING
BIRD POO
SEWERS
SNAKES
SPIDERS
MOULD
GORE
VOMIT
Are there any of these things that you actually don't mind?
Isn't it weird how there are unwritten rules that our society sticks to about things we're supposed to be afraid of or stay away from.
Can you think of any reasons why this might happen?
Photocopiable resource © Scripture Union 2018

ALONE AND AFRAID

Read this story.
What do you think of Jesus because of it?

I am alone and afraid.
No one wants to know me.
I'm different, you see.
I sit on my own with nothing to do, just thinking about how unfair life is.
No one talks to me; I am avoided like the plague.
My life is not like the lives of others.
I don't get invited round to anyone's house.
I'm not part of any group of people – I am an outcast!
I have heard stories, well, caught snatches of conversations;
I don't get close enough to hear everything.
Stories about someone who could help me; someone who cares for others.
But they don't just care; they may really be able to help me.
But why would they come near me? Why would they do what no other person would do?
The person who could help is apparently nearby. He always is, helping others and...
well... doing the most amazing things really.
I could hear him if I listened carefully. If I looked for him... yes, he is there!
I can see others now and I can see him, the one who could help.
A crowd surrounds him, but I might be able to get through to him.
I pick myself up from the place where I waste away my days,
with nothing to do and no one to talk to. I walk towards him...
could he help? Will he even let me get near?
I walk up to the man I have heard about. I see no fear in his eyes, only compassion;
he... he... looks like he cares. If this man is who people are saying he might be,
and if the rumours of what he has done are true, then... just maybe...
'Lord, you can heal me if you will.'
He responds, but not like the rest. He doesn't pull away and reject me.
He reaches out, stretches his hand towards me...
He speaks to me and immediately I am whole, my needs are met –
and I am no longer alone.

USE WITH SESSION 27 BIBLE EXPERIENCE 'LEVEL 2 INTERFACE'

It's been a long day and you have been listening to the words of the teacher named Jesus. He's a pretty amazing guy and he's saying some pretty amazing things. There's something about the way he talks... it's like he really knows what he's talking about... like he really believes what he's saying! Anyway, he's leaving the hill where he was talking and is heading for the town. There's quite a crowd with you and you're not going to let this amazing guy go too far. Up ahead you can see a beggar... well, he looks like a beggar. He might just be one of the 'unclean' – someone with a skin disease. They look disgusting and their skin is all horribly disfigured. It's no wonder they're kept away from the rest of you. Of course, it isn't anything personal – they just give you the creeps; they're different.

You see the unclean man coming towards the crowd. You suppose he's after some money – after all, he can't work in his condition; in fact, he's not allowed to do much at all. You step away as you don't have much money yourself and, well, you'd have to touch him to give it to him properly.

You realise Jesus hasn't moved away. He's standing still, listening to the man. Then against all the odds, totally unbelievably, Jesus reaches out and touches the unclean, skin-diseased outcast. Jesus says something... you're so far away that you can't hear it properly. But before your eyes, the unclean is made clean. How do you feel?

28

Bible: Matthew 8:5–13

SICK!

THE AIM: To discover more about our powerful God and explore our response to him

The aim unpacked

The healing in this session's Bible passage shows Jesus overcoming social barriers between Jews and Gentiles and demonstrates his commitment to both groups. With a command, Jesus healed the servant of a Roman centurion, responding to the faith of the officer and showing more of his amazing power and authority.

WAY IN

theGRID MAGAZINE

WHAT: **discussion and starter**
WHY: **to discover our prejudices**
WITH: **magazine page 179**

1 Ask the group to define the word 'prejudice'. The Oxford English Dictionary definition says that it is 'a preconceived opinion that is not based on reason or actual experience'.

2 Give out copies of page 179 and ask the young people to do the 'Prejudice' activity.

3 Bring everyone together and chat about prejudice. Is it something we can't help because we are human? Can it be overcome? (Some sensitivity will be needed here, in case there are any such feelings among members of your group.)

SCENE SETTER

WHAT: **media search**
WHY: **to find out what human barriers there are in our society today**
WITH: **newspapers or video clips from TV news (collect and record these before the meeting), flip chart or whiteboard, marker pens**

1 Divide the young people into pairs or threes. Give each group some newspapers and ask them to find and cut out stories that show prejudice in some way. Give them the dictionary definition of prejudice: 'a preconceived opinion that is not based on reason or actual experience'.

2 Bring the group back together and invite the young people to read out any stories they have found. Alternatively, watch some pre-recorded video clips of such stories.

3 Ask the young people what prejudices or 'human barriers' they have found in their media search. Make a list on the flip chart or whiteboard.

THEMED GAME

WHAT: **active game**
WHY: **to see if we change our minds and opinions**
WITH: **page 181**

1 Designate areas of the room as 'yes', 'no' and 'maybe'.

2 Explain that you are going to read out a list of things that might change your mind about whether to be friends with someone or not. The young people must decide whether they will respond with 'yes – it would change my mind', 'no – it wouldn't', or 'maybe', and then run to the appropriate designated area of the room.

3 When the young people have run to the area of their answer, shout 'Runaround!' and give them the option to change their mind.

4 Use the list from page 181.

5 This game opens up many issues of following others, having prejudiced opinions and then changing your mind. Make sure there are plenty of leaders available to discuss and pray with any of the young people who would like to do this, and allow time at the end for this to happen.

6 Alternatively, if more appropriate for your group, you could make copies of page 181 and encourage the young people to score each item out of ten privately. Then total them up and compare scores.

BIBLE EXPERIENCE

LEVEL 1: CONNECT

WHAT: story to examine
WHY: to discover more about our powerful God and explore our response to him
WITH: magazine page 180

1 With the group together, ask the young people if they have ever felt pushed out, excluded or made to feel unworthy by what is happening around them. Ask them to suggest some words to describe how it felt.

2 Divide them into groups of three or four and give each group a copy of page 180 and a Bible.

3 Ask them to read the story 'Exclusion zone'. Then ask them to read Matthew 8:5–13 together in their groups.

4 Bring the group back together and ask what similarities there are between the Bible passage and the story. Zoe was excluded initially but was then given a chance by someone who saw her potential. The centurion, or soldier, was excluded because he was a Gentile, but Jesus, who was a Jew, saw his faith and helped him – overcoming human barriers.

5 Ask the young people to discuss the following questions in their small groups:

- Are there 'human barriers' today that hinder God's power from being seen?
- What can we do to break them down?

LEVEL 2: INTERFACE

WHAT: Bible history slot
WHY: to discover more about our powerful God and explore our response to him
WITH: magazine page 180

1 Read today's Bible passage with the young people: Matthew 8:5–13. You could ask a group member to read the passage or it could be read in parts from a dramatised Bible.

2 Make sure the information about Roman officers on page 180 is available, and invite the young people to read through it.

3 Ask the young people what was special about the officer in the Bible passage. You should try to draw out the following points:

- The officer was a Gentile and Jesus was a Jew.
- According to Jewish law, a Jew could not enter the house of a Gentile; it was considered 'unclean'.
- This was not a problem for Jesus – he was willing to go and heal the servant.
- The officer was used to giving and receiving commands, so he just asked Jesus to give the command for the servant to be healed, knowing it would happen!
- Jesus showed no prejudice towards either the officer or his servant.
- Jesus saw how much faith the officer had.
- Jesus is not the possession of any one race. He is the possession of every person in every race in whose heart there is faith in him! How cool is that?!

4 Ask the young people to consider these questions:

- How did Jesus respond to both the officer's faith and his need?
- What does this passage say about who Jesus is?

LEVEL 3: SWITCH ON

WHAT: in-depth Bible study
WHY: to discover more about our powerful God and explore our response to him
WITH: cards from page 182

1 Read out the following quote from the cards on page 182 to the whole group: 'Jesus is the passport of faith – to all people in every race in every time.' Invite the young people to read Matthew 8:5–13 individually.

2 Divide the group into pairs and give each pair a Bible and a card. Explain that there are two stories in today's passage that could be linked to prejudice. Ask the young people to identify the two stories and chat about what they think of them in the light of what's written on their cards.

3 The two stories are:

- Jesus was a Jew and the Roman officer was a Gentile – normally they would have nothing to do with each other. But Jesus saw that the officer had faith that Jesus could heal at a distance, and so the servant was healed. Jesus would have gone to the officer's house if necessary.
- The Jews believed that when the Messiah came there would be a great banquet for the Jews, and that Abraham, Isaac and Jacob would be there. The Jews never thought for a moment that Gentiles would be at this banquet. But Jesus says the kingdom of heaven will be a bit different!

4 Conclude by bringing the group together and discussing what the pairs have discovered. Focus on what they think the stories say about Jesus, God and prejudice, and also the importance of faith.

RESPOND

MUSICAL

WHAT: writing a song
WHY: to respond to Jesus' overcoming of human barriers
WITH: music books, instruments

1 Invite the young people to write some lyrics based on the theme of prejudice, showing how Jesus can overcome those barriers and demonstrate God's power.

2 If you have any budding musicians in your group, they could write music to accompany the lyrics. Alternatively, the young people could write new lyrics to a tune they already know. This could be worked on and be used as part of a church service on the theme of God's power.

3 Alternatively, some Christian songs that you could sing are:

- 'He Is the Lord and He Reigns on High' by Kevin Prosch
- 'Our God Is an Awesome God' by Rich Mullins
- 'There Is Power in the Name of Jesus' by Noel Richards

PRACTICAL

WHAT: prayer
WHY: to ask Jesus to overcome modern barriers and show God's power

1 With your group together, ask them to think back to the first activity when they looked at the sorts of things about which they are prejudiced.

2 Now invite the young people to give a quick summary of today's Bible passage.

3 We have seen that Jesus overcomes human barriers to show God's power. Ask the young people to think of five situations or issues, either at home or abroad, where Jesus could break through human barriers or prejudices and show God's power.

4 Encourage the young people each to choose one of these situations or issues and to commit to praying for it daily over the next week or until your next session.

5 Remember to feed back in your next session and look for God's answers to prayers.

CREATIVE

WHAT: prayerful and artistic response
WHY: to prayerfully and artistically respond to God's love
WITH: poem from page 183, art materials

1 Use the poem 'The international banquet' from page 183 as a prayerful response to today's teaching.

2 Give out copies of the poem and encourage the young people to read it on their own, in groups or all together.

3 Invite the young people to illustrate the prayer, using the art materials. The illustrations could show the overcoming of human barriers of prejudice.

MORE ON THIS THEME:

If you want to do a short series with your group, other sessions that work well with this one are:

27	*Unclean!*	*Matthew 8:1–4*
29	*In danger!*	*Matthew 8:23–27*
30	*Hungry!*	*Matthew 15:29–39*

28 PREJUDICE!

Think about whether the answers to these questions would give you an impression about someone. Tick the ones you think you would use to help you to decide what a person was like.

Be honest! What other things lead you to decide what a person is like?

- ■ WHAT DO THEY WEAR?
- ■ WHAT DO THEY BELIEVE?
- ■ HOW CLEVER ARE THEY?
- ■ WHAT DO THEY EAT?
- ■ HOW DO THEY SPEAK?
- ■ WHAT JOB DO THEY DO?
- ■ WHAT SCHOOL DO THEY GO TO?
- ■ WHAT MUSIC DO THEY LISTEN TO?
- ■ WHERE DO THEY COME FROM (COUNTRY, CITY, TOWN, VILLAGE)?

Bible bit
Matthew 8:5–13

Have you ever tried to control a remote-controlled car? It seems really easy when you watch someone else do it, but the first time you have a go, you realise how difficult it is to control the power of the car. But in this story, Jesus has power, not to control a small car, but to heal!

COULD YOU IMAGINE ANY OF THESE?

Draw a picture of one of these or come up with your own and write it in the space.

- a punk reading Shakespeare
- a country farmer being king
- a skater singing opera
- a ballerina boxing
- a pop star washing up

EXCLUSION ZONE

Zoe just needed a chance. Just because she dressed differently and talked 'posh', she didn't feel it was fair for her to be excluded. Now she knew what it was like when people talked about others 'being prejudiced' against them. All she wanted to do was help at the new club for teenagers that was being run on Saturdays in the old cinema. But some silly person had said she wouldn't 'relate' to the kids, just because of the way she looked and talked. Zoe knew her clothes and hair were a bit 'alternative', as she liked to call it, and she certainly couldn't help the way she talked, any more than anyone else could, but she loved working with teenagers!

Pete, one of the project leaders, gave her a chance. He had the deciding vote on the committee and he used his power to allow her to help. It was cool. Zoe got on really well, and the kids loved her. Zoe didn't mind at all that they teased her about her accent or arty clothes!

What similarities can you see between this story and the centurion in Matthew 8:5–13?

CENTURION FACT FILE

Who?
The centurion/army officer/Roman soldier (all the same – just called different things according to which Bible translation you're using!)

What?
Centurions were the backbone of the Roman army. In a Roman legion there were 6,000 men. The legion was divided into 60 centuries, each with 100 men. In command of each century was a centurion. These centurions were the long-service, regular soldiers of the Roman army – they disciplined the regiment.

Attire
What he wore! See below.

Interesting fact
Whenever centurions are mentioned in the Bible it is with honour! (For example, the one who recognised Jesus on the cross as the Son of God.)

The centurion in today's Bible passage had an unusual attitude for someone in his position. He cared about his servant, who was ill. The servant would have been a slave, and in the Roman Empire slaves did not count for anything! But this centurion cared enough to ask Jesus to intervene.

Both the centurion and the servant would have been expected to be 'out of range' for Jesus' healing, because Jesus was a Jew and the centurion was a Gentile – they did not mix! – but Jesus saw 'faith in action' from the centurion and honoured it.

Prejudices

Give each of the categories a score of between 1 (not bothered) and 10 (very bothered), according to how each thing affects what you think about a person.

The music they listen to ☐

The clothes they wear ☐

The colour of their hair ☐

What they look like ☐

The colour of their skin ☐

What political views they have ☐

What religion they are ☐

Their weight ☐

Where they live ☐

RESOURCE PAGE

USE WITH SESSION 28 BIBLE EXPERIENCE 'LEVEL 3 SWITCH ON'

'Jesus is the passport of faith – to all people in every race in every time.'	'Jesus is the passport of faith – to all people in every race in every time.'
'Jesus is the passport of faith – to all people in every race in every time.'	'Jesus is the passport of faith – to all people in every race in every time.'

The international banquet

Lord, on that great day we want to join with the angels, Abraham, Isaac and Jacob and all the company of heaven in praising you.

From all around the world we will meet and sing praises.

You are great; you are powerful; you are almighty.

Through the power given to your Son, Jesus, you overcome the barriers of prejudice, fear and hate.

You teach us to love, to reach out to those in need, and to reach out to those who feel excluded.

You are with us in our times of loneliness, rejection and when we feel 'left out'.

Thank you, Lord, for loving me, for being there... always and for ever.

Amen.

Bible: Matthew 8:23–27

IN DANGER!

THE AIM: To discover more about our powerful God and explore our response to him

The aim unpacked

The lives of our young people are bombarded with modern superheroes who regularly display amazing feats of supernatural ability. Every time these characters appear on the screen, young people are encouraged to marvel at their abilities. However, this passage shows us that the only person who has real supernatural abilities is Jesus, and those abilities help us to discover who Jesus is.

WAY IN

theGRID MAGAZINE

WHAT: survey
WHY: to think about how we react to stressful and potentially dangerous situations
WITH: magazine page 187

1 Invite the young people to look at a copy of page 187 and to fill in the 'Stress survival survey'.

2 Talk about the results together. Who's a chicken? Who's sensible? Who's a poser?

3 Extend the discussion, if it suits your group, by asking what scary real-life situations they've been in.

- How did it feel to be in that situation?
- How hard was it to know what to do?
- Was there anyone to help?
- How did it feel to be rescued?
- How come that person could save you when you couldn't save yourself?

SCENE SETTER

WHAT: discussion
WHY: to think about what it's like to be totally out of control
WITH: large sheets of paper (such as a length of lining paper), marker pens

1 Divide the young people into groups of three or four. Give each group a sheet of paper and marker pens. In the centre of the paper, ask them to write 'Out of control'.

2 Ask the group(s) to draw or write down as many people, situations or events as they can think of that they would call 'out of control'. They should think on a local scale, for example the state of their bedroom, and on a global scale, for example the situation in Syria.

3 Compare ideas from different groups and give lots of encouragement for imaginative and well-informed suggestions.

4 Ask the groups to underline, in a different colour, any of the situations where there seems to be no hope for the future. Then, in a third colour, ask them to circle any of those situations that make them personally feel scared, panicky or anxious.

5 Talk about the results, accepting the validity of the feelings expressed.

THEMED GAME

WHAT: game
WHY: to introduce the concept of the lack of control in a 'stormy' situation
WITH: large sheet or blanket, balls of screwed-up newspaper

1 Divide the young people into two teams. Team A should hold the sheet taut with players at the corners or edges. Team B must screw up newspaper and throw as many balls onto the sheet as possible, while team A try to shake them off. After a while, call out 'Stop!' Count the balls on the sheet and swap teams.

2 Explain that, like the team who were trying to throw the balls onto the sheet, anyone in a small boat in the middle of a fierce storm would have no control over what was going to happen.

BIBLE EXPERIENCE

LEVEL 1: CONNECT

WHAT: **reflection**
WHY: **to discover more about our powerful God and explore our response to him**
WITH: **Bibles**

1 Ask the young people each to imagine they are one of the disciples. They will need to focus on the feelings of the disciples and try to understand how afraid they were – remember that they were experienced fishermen.

2 Invite a good reader to read aloud Matthew 8:23–27.

3 Divide the young people into groups and invite them to discuss:

- What might be a modern equivalent of that scary, out-of-control situation where it seemed that all hope was lost?
- How would the people involved react?

4 Ask the groups to act out their situations. It's always fun to video the scenes, but check your church's child protection policy first and obtain parental permission if necessary.

5 Bring the groups together and invite them to share their situations.

- How are these new situations similar or different to the original story?
- What was the disciples' response to Jesus in both the original setting and in the modern improvisations?
- How would you have responded to what Jesus did?

LEVEL 2: INTERFACE

WHAT: **creative approach**
WHY: **to discover more about our powerful God and explore our response to him**
WITH: **art materials (optional)**

1 Read Matthew 8:23–27 aloud to the young people. Ask them to imagine how the disciples might have felt throughout the event.

2 Place a chair in front of the group. Invite anyone who feels confident to choose one of the characters from the passage (such as Jesus, a disciple or even the storm), to sit in the 'hot seat' and answer questions from that character's viewpoint. The rest of the group could ask some of the following questions:

- How did you feel when...?
- What were you thinking when...?
- Why did you...?
- What did you think of Jesus when...?

3 Ask the group to imagine the storm as a person or group of people. What would they look like? What would they be wearing? Carrying? Doing? (For instance, they might think of a crowd of football hooligans hurling broken bottles.) Invite the young people to draw those people on a large sheet of paper. The drawings don't all need to relate to the same situation – in fact, the more variety the better.

4 Ask:

- What would Jesus look like, standing up to this personification of the storm?
- What would he be wearing, carrying or doing? (For example, like a policeman quelling the riot.)

5 Display the results side by side and talk about them:

- Do you think of Jesus any differently now?
- How was he able to stop the storm like that?
- Do you think he still can stop terrifying phenomena like that storm?

6 Jesus stopped the storm because he had authority over the elements. In the modern situations the young people have created, in what ways could Jesus demonstrate his authority?

LEVEL 3: SWITCH ON

WHAT: **Bible study**
WHY: **to discover more about our powerful God and explore our response to him**
WITH: **magazine page 188**

1 Read Matthew 8:23–27 aloud together.

2 Use some or all of the following questions:

- What has Jesus been doing just before this episode?
- What does he do straight after it?
- Is there any significance in the order of these events?

3 Think about the sea – what does it make you think of? Jews, like Matthew and the disciples, believed that the sea was a symbol of the power that fought against God. Look at Genesis 1:1,2 – the waters were all over the earth, chaotic and untamed, before God brought order to the world.

- How does the creation story relate to this episode of the calming of the storm?
- What does this say about Jesus?
- If you'd been there, would you have been afraid?
- How did the disciples feel after Jesus had calmed the storm?
- How do you think you might have felt about him?

4 Think about the story of Jonah – how much of it can the group remember? Discuss the similarities and differences between today's story and the story of Jonah. Then use the table on page 188 to compare the two stories, including relevant Bible references.

5 Some further questions to discuss:

- What might Matthew be showing us about Jesus by including this episode?
- Are you going through a storm in your life?
- Do you feel as though Jesus is sleeping through it or standing up in authority over it? Does this story help?
- Does Jesus always save his followers from life's storms? Why? Why not?

RESPOND

MUSICAL

WHAT: **listening to music**
WHY: **to allow time to listen to God**
WITH: **CD or MP3 of 'Bridge over Troubled Water' by Simon and Garfunkel, playback equipment**

1 Give everyone a pencil and sheet of paper. (Try to use good quality pencils and paper, as you're all going to be giving God your best in worship.) Say that you are all going to listen out for God speaking to you and will be using some music as an aid to relate the storm and Jesus' awesome power to your lives. To begin, you might like to pray a short prayer along the following lines: 'Lord, we invite you to speak to us. Help us to keep our ears open for your voice while we listen to this music.'

2 Ask everyone to be open to God as they listen to the song, and invite them to sketch any pictures that come into their minds. It's not a drawing contest – it doesn't matter what it looks like – it's a way of representing what God is saying.

3 If appropriate, display the pictures and invite the young people to tell everyone what they've drawn and why. To show how much you value what the young people produce, you could mount the pictures in frames or on backing card, so that their pictures can look really professional.

PRACTICAL

WHAT: **an attitude change**
WHY: **to remember Jesus' power in our lives**
WITH: **small pieces of card**

1 Say that when Jesus calmed the storm he showed that he had authority over the elements. Elsewhere in the Bible we read, 'Don't be afraid, because I have saved you. I have called you by name, and you are mine. When you pass through the waters, I will be with you' (Isaiah 43:1,2). Knowing that Jesus has authority over storms (the storms we experience in our lives as well as external ones in the world around us) should alter the way we deal with issues in our lives. Jesus is Lord.

2 Give a piece of card to each young person. Invite them to write out the verses from Isaiah 43:1,2 and personalise them by including their name at the beginning.

3 Encourage them to keep the cards safe, perhaps in their wallets or purses, so that they have them at all times when they face problems or storms. The cards can remind them that Jesus is Lord and that his awesome power has authority over all storms.

4 Include the verse in any emails you send to your group during the week, or even text it to them.

CREATIVE

WHAT: **paper boats**
WHY: **to acknowledge Jesus' lordship over the storms we face**
WITH: **copies of page 189, water source or container (for example baby bath, stream, font, sink, bath)**

1 Give everyone a piece of paper and ask them to write down two or three 'storms' which are affecting them or someone they know, or an international situation.

2 Now invite them to make their sheets of paper into boats using the instructions on page 189.

3 Launch the boats onto the water and pray together, 'Jesus, we put our stormy situations into your hands and trust that you will carry each of us through them safely, because you are Lord.'

MORE ON THIS THEME:

If you want to do a short series with your group, other sessions that work well with this one are:

27	*Unclean!*	*Matthew 8:1–4*
28	*Sick!*	*Matthew 8:5–13*
30	*Hungry!*	*Matthew 15:29–39*

Bible bit
Matthew 8:23–27

Are you a sailor? Ever been on a boat? Maybe you know how rough the sea can get. If you don't, I'm sure you can imagine. All that raw power, all that danger, all that fear. But Jesus put a stop to it with just a few words. What do you think of that?

STRESS SURVIVAL SURVEY

Have you ever been in a real-life scary, stressful situation? Was there anyone there to help or rescue you? How did it feel?

You're trekking across the Rocky Mountains when suddenly an enormous, famished grizzly bear leaps out from behind a bush and starts lumbering towards you, growling hideously.

Do you...

a) collapse in a heap and cry?
b) climb a nearby tree and wait for Bruno to lumber away again?
c) raise your hand and say, 'Hellooo, I'm walking here!'?

You're deep-sea diving when a lobster snips your air tubes in half with its pincers.

Do you...

a) lie down in the sand and use your last mouthful of air to sing your own funeral aria?
b) take a deep breath and struggle upwards towards the boat?
c) find some sticking plaster in your first-aid pouch, casually stick your air tube back together again, then find the lobster and drag it back to the surface for lunch?

You're picnicking in a park when suddenly storm clouds gather and rain, thunder and lightning start right overhead.

Do you...

a) put earplugs in and have a nap under the rug?
b) run for the nearest safe shelter and wait out the storm?
c) rig up a DIY lightning conductor with the thermos flask and apply electrodes to your mate in the hope that he'll turn into a hideous monster or stop being a hideous monster?

You're orbiting Mars in Klutznik 4 when you're hit by a shower of meteorites.

Do you...

a) hide behind the pilot seat?
b) gallantly navigate your way through the storm?
c) collect the meteorites in a bag and use them for a game of interstellar marbles?

You're in a shopping centre when a crazed shop assistant runs amok with a plastic cricket bat.

Do you...

a) disguise yourself behind a pot plant till somebody arrests her?
b) alert a good-looking police officer?
c) rugby-tackle her, seize her cricket bat and knock her out in a sensitive and caring way?

Mostly As
Cluck cluck.

Mostly Bs
Blow me down with a bubble gun, you're soooo sensible.

Mostly Cs
You've been watching too many 'unsuitable' movies.

JONAH AND JESUS

Matthew's first readers would have known the story of Jonah back to front. Compare the stories of Jonah and of Jesus calming the storm. What's the same? What's different?

The story of Jonah: Jonah 1–4	Bible ref	The calming of the storm: Matthew 8:23–27	Bible ref
The storm blew up because Jonah disobeyed God.		The storm blew up because of the weather conditions.	
The storm stopped because Jonah was thrown overboard.		The storm stopped because	
Jonah spent three days inside a great fish, then was thrown up onto land.		Jesus spent three days in	
The foreign pagan city of Nineveh was saved because of Jonah's message.		was saved because of Jesus' message.	
Jonah was a great prophet.		Jesus was	

UNANSWERABLE QUESTIONS

Why does God let Christians go into storms in the first place? Wouldn't it be better if he didn't let storms happen?

What about times when God doesn't stop the storms and bad things happen to people?

What would have happened to the boat if the disciples hadn't woken Jesus up?

Take a few moments to think about what's rocking your boat at the moment – situations that scare you, where you can't see the way through, where it seems impossible that you're going to pull through OK, like the disciples felt in the boat. Write them in the storm clouds. Then quietly read the story in Matthew 8:23–27 again. What does God want to tell you about your stormy situations?

It's a stormy day at the boating lake.

'You'd better call in that last boat, Fred,' says George. So Fred calls through the loudspeaker: 'Boat number 99, come in please.'

'That's odd,' says George. 'We've only got 70 boats.'

Fred thinks for a minute, then lifts up the loudspeaker again and calls, 'Boat number 66, are you OK?'

RESOURCE PAGE

USE WITH SESSION 29 RESPOND 'CREATIVE'

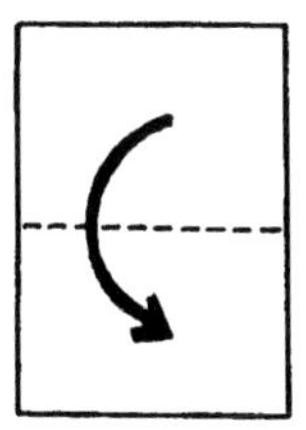

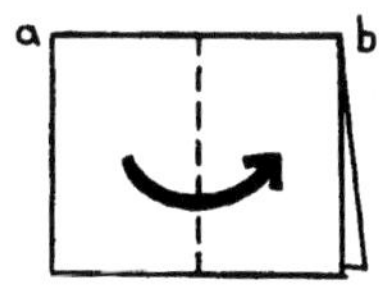

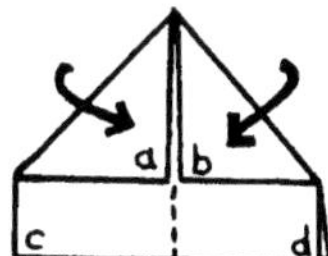

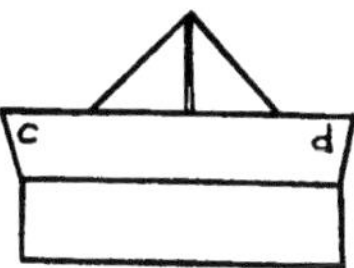

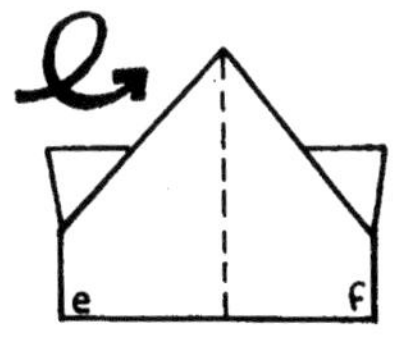

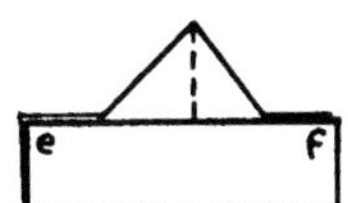

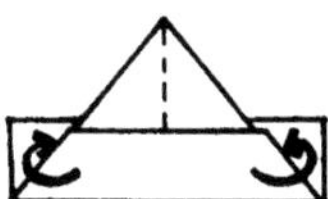

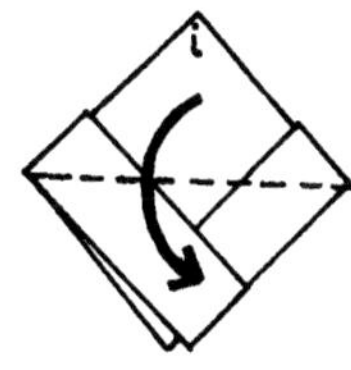

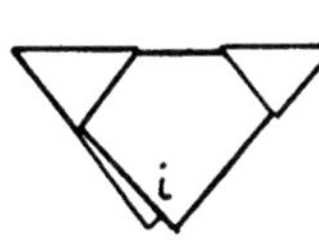

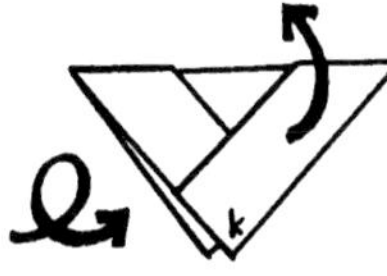

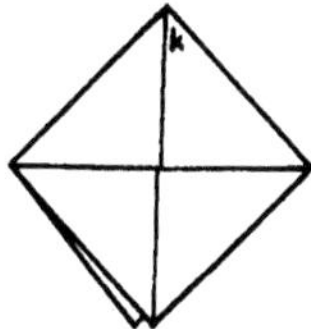

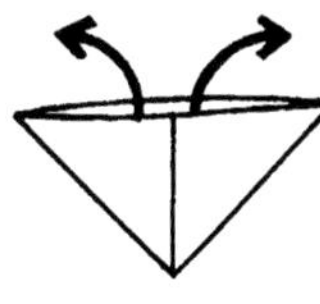

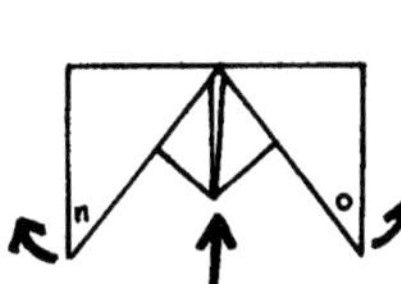

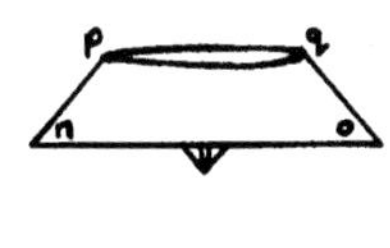

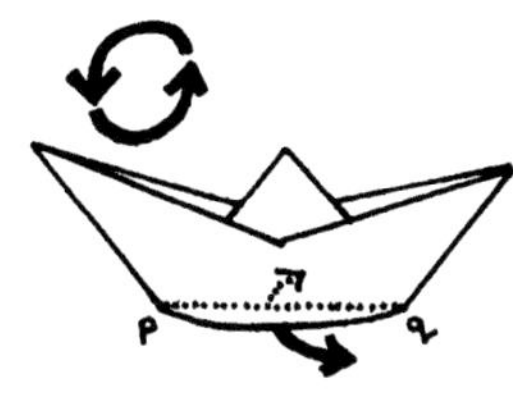

30

Bible: Matthew 15:29–39

HUNGRY!

THE AIM: To discover more about our powerful God and explore our response to him

The aim unpacked

Matthew points out that Jesus fed the people out of compassion for them. The power of God that was evident in Jesus' miracle was motivated by his compassion. As we grow more like Jesus, we should expect to show that compassion in our lives. Jesus had great power and he used it compassionately. We should praise him for that and pray that we will be motivated by God's compassion for those around us.

WAY IN

theGRID MAGAZINE

WHAT: questionnaire and discussion
WHY: to look at our response to hunger in the world
WITH: magazine page 193, play money (optional), seven boxes (optional)

1 Hand out copies of page 193. Invite the young people to complete the 'Hit hunger where it hurts' activity. For a group activity, you could all agree to start with the same amount of money. You could write the seven causes on boxes and provide each person with the same amount of play money to divide up.

2 Compare answers.

3 Chat about the activity and the answers, using the following questions:

- Was it hard to make choices?
- How did you make your choices?
- Do some issues seem too big for you to make a difference?
- If you really had that much money, how much might you give away?
- How else can we make a difference to hungry people, as well as by giving money? (For example, writing to politicians, praying, getting other people involved.)

SCENE SETTER

WHAT: simple drama activity
WHY: to explore responses to varying needs

1 In advance, prepare pieces of paper in sets of four with the words: 'I'm hungry!' (x 2), 'I can't help!', 'I can help!' (On others use the phrases, 'I'm scared', 'I'm lonely' or 'I'm depressed'.) Have enough for one each. Shuffle them together, making sure there is an 'I'm hungry!' piece on the top.

2 Clear a space, with half the group on each side of the room. Explain that this represents a street in your nearest town or city. You are going to create a freeze-frame showing some people who are hungry and others who either want to help them or feel that they cannot help. Ask a volunteer to take a piece of paper, to position themselves on the scene as a person who might say, for example, 'I'm hungry!', and freeze. Then the next person takes the next piece of paper and adds themselves to the scene, according to what is on their piece of paper. Repeat until everyone has a part.

3 Unfreeze and briefly ask the young people for their reactions to the activity.

THEMED GAME

WHAT: game
WHY: to imagine what it is like to be hungry
WITH: clean 'rubbish' (screwed-up newspaper, boxes, etc), food items – nice and nasty, dice, sheet to avoid mess

1 Put a large pile of assorted 'rubbish' in the middle of the room. Hide within it crumpled pieces of paper with numbers on them: perhaps eight of these, depending on how long you want the game to take. Have the same number of food items – ranging from very nice (for example, a chocolate bar) to disgusting (for example, old fruit) – labelled with the same numbers. Keep these hidden.

2 Take turns to roll a dice. When someone rolls a six, they must try to find a number in the 'rubbish tip'. When they find one, bring out the corresponding food item. They must then say whether they want it or not. If not, ask if they have ever been so hungry that they would have eaten it.

3 Explain how some young people of their age live on rubbish tips. They hunt for discarded food, or sell things they find to get money. Ask what they feel about situations like that. Does it make them want to do something to help these people?

BIBLE EXPERIENCE

LEVEL 1: CONNECT

WHAT: **Bible interaction**
WHY: **to discover more about our powerful God and explore our response to him**
WITH: **eight large speech bubbles with the text below**

1 Before the session, hang eight large speech bubbles made from card or paper around the room with the following words written on them: 'What's going on?'; 'Wow! Amazing!'; 'Thank God for Jesus!'; 'I'm hungry!'; 'It must be a trick!'; 'How did he do that?'; 'Why does he care so much?'; 'I want to know Jesus more!'

2 As a warm-up activity, call out the phrases in random order. The young people have to run, or point, to the appropriate speech bubbles.

3 Encourage the young people to imagine that they are living in the Middle East two thousand years ago. Say, 'Life would be very different. Many of you would be very poor. If you became ill, there would be little health care. If you heard amazing stories of people being healed by a healer who had arrived in the area, how might you react?'

4 Explain that you are going to read what happened next, when crowds went to see Jesus. Each time you pause, ask the young people how they might have felt at that point, as members of the crowd, and to go to or point to the appropriate speech bubble. Read Matthew 15:29–39, pausing after verses 31, 32, 35, 36, 38 and 39.

5 Lead a follow-up discussion:

- Which were the popular choices?
- How might their reactions to Jesus have changed as the events unfolded? Why?

6 Ask the group to think: if Jesus performed this miracle, as the Bible says, what does it say about who Jesus is?

7 Finally, ask each person to choose the speech bubble that most closely fits how they feel about Jesus after what they have heard. Encourage them to spend some time talking silently to Jesus about their reactions.

LEVEL 2: INTERFACE

WHAT: **dramatic dialogues**
WHY: **to discover more about our powerful God in Matthew 15:29–39 and explore our response to him**
WITH: **magazine page 194**

1 Split the group into two: 'crowd' and 'disciples'. Introduce the Bible reading and ask each group to listen out for how their group of people reacted to Jesus.

2 Read Matthew 15:29–39 together.

3 Divide the young people into pairs and invite each pair to look at one of the 'crowd' or 'disciple' dialogues on page 194. (You could allocate one to each pair to avoid duplication.) Ask them to look back at the Bible passage and decide whether these are likely reactions to Jesus. They should then practise performing the dialogues – extending or altering them if they wish. If you have a small group, work on all of the dialogues together.

4 Read the passage again, inserting the practised dialogues in the appropriate places.

5 Ask the young people what the implications of the events in the passage might have been to the disciples, to the crowd and to themselves. The events should lead everyone to wonder about who Jesus is. Challenge the young people to really consider who they think Jesus is and where his power comes from.

LEVEL 3: SWITCH ON

WHAT: **Bible study**
WHY: **to discover more about our powerful God in Matthew 15:29–39 and explore our response to him**
WITH: **sets of question cards from page 195, Bible atlas and commentaries (optional)**

1 Invite the young people to read Matthew 15:32–39.

2 Divide them into groups of between two and four. Give each group a set of the six question cards from page 195. Ask them to fill in the answers to the questions (Who? What? How? Why? When? Where?) using the Bible passage. For example, on the 'Who?' card they should write any information they can find about who was involved in those events. For 'Where?' they should write anything about where it happened. There are hints on some of the cards. You could provide further background help – for example, a Bible map indicating the Decapolis area.

3 Get together and quickly go round the groups and ask them to feed back their answers for 'Who?' Suggest anything they have missed, before covering the other five questions. Say that Jesus was showing God's love in this way in Decapolis – a non-Jewish area.

4 If there is time, in pairs, invite the young people to take a look at the following passages and discuss what links them together – the Jews being fed by God in the desert (Exodus 16), and Jesus' statement about being the 'bread that gives life' (John 6:30–40). Invite feedback on the young people's thoughts and comments from the Bible passages.

RESPOND

MUSICAL

WHAT: **planning a pop video storyboard**
WHY: **to express God's love for the hungry**
WITH: **copies of page 196 (optional), words and music for 'Beauty for Brokenness' by Graham Kendrick**

1 Ask the group to imagine they are making a video to help Christians respond to God's concern for people who are hungry. The backing track is the song 'Beauty for Brokenness' (or choose another song which expresses God's concern). Divide into smaller groups, if your group is large enough, and assign a verse of the song to each group. Not all the verses need to be covered. Ask each person to devise up to four visual images to use with these words. They should sketch what they would show like a filmmaker's storyboard using copies of page 196 or on blank sheets of paper. Encourage the young people to draw no matter what they feel about their ability, saying it's about ideas rather than artistic merit.

2 Invite the young people to show and describe the pictures they have drawn.

3 Put the pictures and song together. Either sing it as a group, listen to a musician or a recording, or ask group members to read the verses out loud.

PRACTICAL

WHAT: **promoting fair trade**
WHY: **to encourage people to buy fairly traded produce as a demonstration of Jesus' compassion**
WITH: **large sheets of paper, marker pens, paints, information about fair trade**

1 Say that the Bible events show us clearly that Jesus is God. This activity is one way of demonstrating his lordship in our lives.

2 Provide some information about fairly traded methods and products – or research these together. Fair trade gives food producers a fair price for their produce so they have enough money to live. The Fairtrade Foundation® has an excellent website, www.fairtrade.org.uk – follow the links on their site for international organisations. Or try Traidcraft, www.traidcraftshop.co.uk

3 Think about how you can encourage people in your church or area to buy more fairly traded goods – for example, you could make posters, or act out an advert in your church service. Consider what will really convince people of the importance of this. The young people could also write to local supermarkets to find out about their policy on fair trade and to encourage them to stock more products.

4 Alternatively, investigate another hunger relief project and take practical action to support that. For example, raise money by making food to sell.

CREATIVE

WHAT: **prayer**
WHY: **to pray for people who are hungry**
WITH: **bread roll or loaf, basket**

1 Tear a bread roll or loaf into as many pieces as there are people in your group (including leaders). Hand the pieces round, explaining that they are not to be eaten. As each person holds their bread, invite them to pray, either aloud or silently, thanking God for what they find most wonderful about food.

2 Ask them to tear their bread into smaller pieces. Invite them in silence to say sorry to God for the times and ways in which we ignore those who are hungry for food, and hungry to know him.

3 Ask them, in turn, to put the bread pieces into a basket in the centre. As they do so, they can pray aloud or silently for any of the people, projects or issues to do with hunger that have been raised in the session. Finish by thanking God for his love which never runs out and for Jesus' compassion in feeding those who are hungry.

4 After the session you might choose to invite the young people to take some of the bread and feed it to the birds. Whatever you decide to do with the bread, don't waste it!

MORE ON THIS THEME:

If you want to do a short series with your group, other sessions that work well with this one are:

27	*Unclean!*	*Matthew 8:1–4*
28	*Sick!*	*Matthew 8:5–13*
29	*In danger!*	*Matthew 8:23–27*

30

Bible bit
Matthew 15:32–39

Imagine you're miles from anywhere and you start feeling peckish. What do you do? There are no shops or kebab vans. No mobile phones to call for a takeaway. Nothing. There are thousands of people with you and they all want food too. But you're with Jesus. And suddenly he turns the small amount of food you have into a massive banquet. What you do think of that?

HIT HUNGER WHERE IT HURTS

So last week you earned a load of money doing that paper round for your mate. Write how much you got here (any amount – you choose):

£..........................

And being a nice, kind, generous person, you've decided to give it all away. You want it to go to help people who are hungry. Here are your choices. Decide how much of your cash you want to give to each one. It can all go on one if you want – or you can spread it round a few. It's your money, so it's up to you.

People in your nearest city are living on the streets. Some people take free hot soup and rolls for them every night. They need money to pay for more.

£..........................

A local church is setting up a lunch club for people who are lonely during the day. You can put your money towards some food for them.

£..........................

A family who visited your country are now back home. There's been no rain in their area this year. They and their neighbours have little food left.

£..........................

Support a campaign to persuade the governments of rich countries to change their unfair trade rules. That will give people in poor countries a chance to get what they need to live.

£..........................

Civil war in Ungalia has destroyed most of the crops. Thousands of people are starving.

£..........................

Your best mate is desperate for a burger and cola.

£..........................

Jose's parents died, so he lives on a rubbish dump in Guatemala City. He eats whatever he can find. There's a centre run by Christians which he can visit. They need money to provide healthy food.

£..........................

NOW THINK...

- How did you make your choices?
- How many causes of hunger and malnutrition can you spot in these examples?
- How else can we make a difference to hungry people as well as giving money?

THE MUCH-DRAMATISED VERSION OF THE FEEDING OF THE 4,000

CROWD

Read Matthew 15:29–31, then read the script below with some friends.

Crowd A: Why did I let you drag me out here?
Crowd B: But you've seen what he's done. Look around you. All these people made well!
Crowd A: A trickster. I still don't believe he's anything more. A foreign trickster.
Crowd B: But there's real power at work here. It must be his God – the Jewish God. It's breathtaking. Brilliant!
Crowd A: Except the food's run out and we're miles from anywhere. We should get away before things get any worse.
Crowd B: This is the best thing that's ever happened to me. I'd rather be here and starve.

Read Matthew 15:33–36, then read the script below with some friends.

Crowd A: This is incredible. Where did all this lot come from?
Crowd B: Don't touch it. It's probably drugged. It'll make us all go loopy so he can brainwash us into becoming his followers.
Crowd A: Look at it! Smell it! This is good.
Crowd B: It must be a trick. Don't be so stupid.
Crowd A: Ah! Just taste that! It's just got a hint of... of something. It is so...
Crowd B: Hmmmm! That bit's OK! I'll just try some of this...

DISCIPLES

Read Matthew 15:32, then read the script below with some friends.

Disciples A: I knew this was coming. He makes it look as if we should have brought food for them all.
Disciples B: I don't know. I think he's planning something.
Disciples A: It's all his idea – coming out here to the middle of nowhere. Getting a load of foreigners all hyped up. There are too many of them.
Disciples B: But it isn't just hype. He loves them. He makes them well. Look at that girl. She was carried here – now she's dancing.
Disciples A: And hungry. So what does he expect us to do? Well, I'm hungry too. I haven't eaten for two days.
Disciples B: But you know what he did before. With that crowd back home?

Read Matthew 15:37,38, then read the script below with some friends.

Disciples A: That was weird. He is something else.
Disciples B: Just hold the basket still, will you? We need to get on.
Disciples A: This power Jesus has – it's like something from the Bible – Moses or Elijah. What if he really is the Messiah?
Disciples B: I don't see the connection. When he comes, the Messiah will set us free. Us – God's people – the Jews. He won't go round feeding crowds of foreigners.
Disciples B: But this love Jesus has for people. Don't you think that's from God?
Disciples A: Of course it is. I just don't understand what he's up to. OK?

HOW WOULD YOU HAVE REACTED TO WHAT JESUS DID? WHAT DOES IT TELL YOU ABOUT WHO HE IS?

USE WITH SESSION 30 BIBLE EXPERIENCE 'LEVEL 3 SWITCH ON'

Who?	**What?**
• Who was involved?	• What was the problem? • What happened?
How? • How did it happen? • How did Jesus do that?	**Why?** • Why was the crowd hungry? • Why did Jesus do what he did?
When? • When did this happen? • What had happened before? (Look back at Matthew 15:29–31.)	**Where?** • Where did it happen? Check out Mark 7:31. Look at a map (in your Bible?) to find the area mentioned.

RESOURCE PAGE

USE WITH SESSION 30 RESPOND 'MUSICAL'

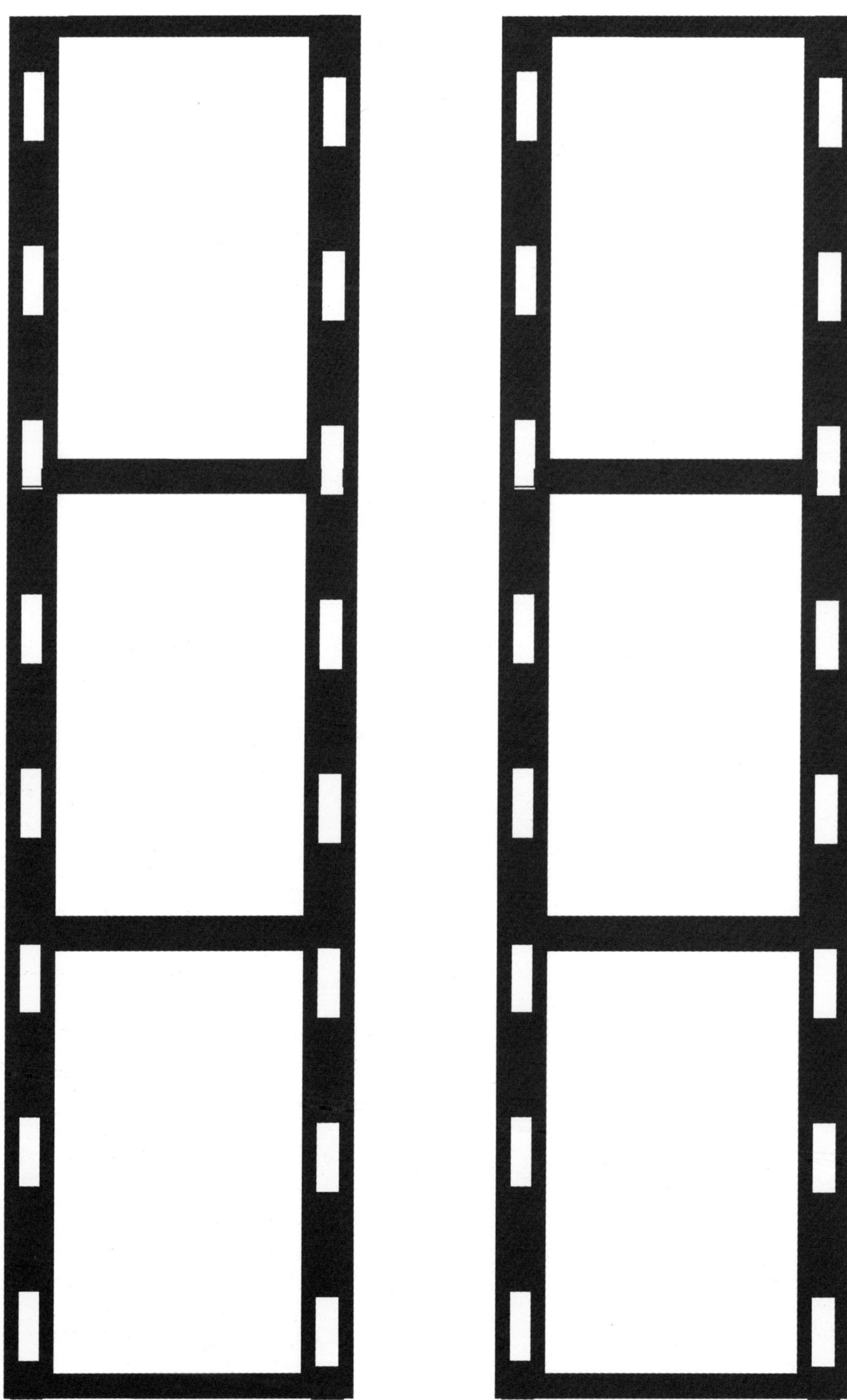

Bible: Mark 1:29–39

31

IN SICKNESS AND IN HEALTH

THE AIM: To celebrate that Jesus is Lord over demons and sickness

The aim unpacked

One of the key passages in Mark's Gospel is Mark 8:29, where Peter announces his belief in Jesus as the Christ or Messiah – God's anointed one. But what does this mean for our young people? With an increase in interest about things supernatural, it is of growing importance that we see Jesus as having power over demons and sickness. But this is something more than power; Jesus is Lord and his words are the commands of God.

WAY IN

theGRID MAGAZINE

WHAT: **questionnaire**
WHY: **to start thinking about sickness**
WITH: **magazine page 200**

1 Give out pens and copies of page 200 and invite the young people to complete the 'How likely is it?' questionnaire on their own.

2 Bring the group together and share together the categories each of the group members found themselves in at the end. You could pick out a few items on the list, ask the young people to show the scores they gave by holding up the number of fingers, and discuss any differences of opinion – for instance, where one group member has scored an item '1' and another has given it '5'.

3 Bring out the point that illness and injury are an everyday part of our world. It is very likely that most of the things mentioned in the quiz will happen, although faking illness is to be discouraged!

4 Be sensitive to any members of the group who may be facing issues of sickness, either directly or indirectly. You can do this effectively by simply listening to the young person. Depending on your group, they may be open to you and everyone else praying for them, but don't push this.

SCENE SETTER

WHAT: **game with a handicap**
WHY: **to show how debilitating sickness can be**
WITH: **plastic bottle of drink, plastic mugs, plastic tablecloth, blindfold, other handicaps (such as inflated balloons or mittens – optional)**

1 Produce the bottle of drink and a mug. You might like to put down a plastic tablecloth to protect against spills. Invite a volunteer to pour a drink.

2 Ask for a second volunteer to do the same. Blindfold them and then ask them to do the activity.

3 Ask for a third volunteer who must do the task blindfolded and one-handed.

4 If they are still enthusiastic, add further handicaps such as holding an inflated balloon or wearing mittens, having a personal stereo playing loud or annoying music or a jeering crowd trying to distract them (in a non-contact way).

5 Make the point that sickness or injury can be debilitating and can stop people carrying out normal activities, just like the handicaps in this game.

THEMED GAME

WHAT: **relay game**
WHY: **to introduce the idea of service**
WITH: **trays of objects for each team (similar objects on each tray)**

1 This is a team relay, so divide the group into teams of about six, although fewer is fine.

2 Give each team an empty tray. Explain that they are going to practise serving, like waiters and waitresses. At the far end of the room lay out the objects to be 'served'.

3 The first player in each team runs to the objects, places one on their tray and returns with it, balancing it, like a waiter. The next player then takes the tray with the first object and goes to collect the second object, and so on, so that by the end the tray is harder to balance. The winning team is the first to sit in a row with their tray filled with all the objects.

4 Explain that the purpose of the game was to introduce the idea of service. Jesus was the ultimate servant, bringing people exactly the kind of help they needed. We provide for the needs of others at a basic level – for example, parents or guardians give us dinner, or a drink when we are thirsty. Jesus can 'serve' us with what we need in a much deeper, more lasting way.

BIBLE EXPERIENCE

LEVEL 1: CONNECT

WHAT: **physical activity and discussion**
WHY: **to celebrate that Jesus is Lord over demons and sickness**
WITH: **page 202 (optional), Bibles**

1 In advance, think of some activities that are possible for your young people to do themselves, some that they might be able to do with lots of practice or hard work and some that are impossible for most people to do. For example, achieving 100 per cent in a maths test, flying a kite in a force ten gale, doing a bungee jump or lifting the lightest person in the group single-handed. Include 'touching someone to make them well' as one of the activities. (Obviously they won't need to prove they can do any of these!) Designate three areas of the room for 'definitely possible', 'may be possible' and 'definitely impossible'.

2 Explain that you are going to read out various situations and they need to respond by moving to the appropriate part of the room, depending on whether they think they could do each of the activities themselves. Don't spend too long on this activity and keep it moving.

3 When you've finished, gather the group together and read Mark 1:29–34 aloud, preferably from a modern paraphrased Bible such as the *Dramatised Bible* or *The Message*.

4 In smaller groups, ask them to discuss why they think it was possible for Jesus to heal the sick and drive out demons. Did it seem to be a difficult task for him?

5 If the young people ask what 'demons' were or are, use the background information on page 202.

6 Leave them with the thought that Christians believe that Jesus could heal people who had sicknesses and demons because he was God in human form. When you have power over something, it can be said that you are 'lord' over it. Jesus is Lord over sickness and demons because he has power over them.

LEVEL 2: INTERFACE

WHAT: **drama**
WHY: **to celebrate that Jesus is Lord over demons and sickness**
WITH: **magazine page 201, page 202 (optional)**

1 Give out a copy of page 201 to each young person. Either give everyone time to read the story 'What's for lunch?' to themselves or ask a volunteer to read it out while the young people follow.

2 Explain that this is based on a story from Mark's Gospel, but it's possible to lose the impact it would have had in those days. Ask them to imagine the different angles that a TV news team at the time might have taken on the story: a healing on the Sabbath; amazing miracles; the huge queues of people for healing; the 'secret' of who did it.

3 Split the group into pairs. Challenge each pair to develop a brief news item acting as a newsreader in a studio and a reporter on the scene. Invite them to use any of the 'news' angles given above or something else that has struck them from the Bible passage.

4 Allow a few minutes for preparation and then watch the presentations. Discuss any interesting angles they have used. Comment particularly on anything any pair spotted that is true but that you had missed.

5 If the young people ask what 'demons' were or are, use the background information on page 202.

6 If it hasn't come through in the discussions, explain that these verses show that Jesus has power over sickness and demons. Jesus displays both power (the ability to do or act) and authority (the power or right to enforce obedience). This is why we refer to Jesus as being Lord over sickness and demons.

LEVEL 3: SWITCH ON

WHAT: **Bible study**
WHY: **to celebrate that Jesus is Lord over demons and sickness**
WITH: **Bibles, page 202 (optional)**

1 Explain the context of the Bible passage: Jesus has just been to the synagogue (it is the Sabbath) where he spoke and drove out an evil spirit. People have been amazed at his authority. Now Jesus and his disciples are hungry.

2 Breaking into small groups or pairs, ask everyone to read Mark 1:29–34. Invite the young people to take one of the following sets of people and note on a sheet of paper any questions that these events might have raised for the characters:

- Peter, Andrew, James and John – Jesus' disciples who hadn't seen him perform many miracles yet
- Peter's mother-in-law – who was ill
- Jesus – who was at the starting point of his ministry
- The sick – who were healed from a variety of illnesses, not all from the same one
- The crowd – who witnessed each miracle

3 Listen to the questions and use them as the basis for a Bible study. One way to do this would be to pass questions from one group to another so that, for instance, the group that raised questions on behalf of the crowd have to try to answer the questions brought up by the disciples.

4 Listen to the answers from each group and then discuss any areas of disagreement. (If the young people ask what 'demons' or 'evil spirits' were or are, you could use the background information on page 202.)

5 Conclude by saying that Jesus was able to heal the sick because he had power and authority over sickness, in all its shapes and forms. Jesus is Lord over demons and sickness.

RESPOND

MUSICAL

WHAT: **songs**
WHY: **to celebrate that Jesus is Lord over demons and sickness**
WITH: **appropriate worship songs, instrumental music and playback equipment or musical accompaniment**

1 The song 'Jesus Is Lord' by David J Mansell has good lyrics, but it might be more relevant to play some instrumental music and read the words of the song over it. You could print out the words, or put them on PowerPoint.

2 Invite three willing young people to read a verse of the song each. Encourage the readers to be slower and more meditative than usual, pausing between each line.

3 If your group is musical, challenge them to create a new funky beat and tune for the words. How would it sound as a rap, heavy metal track or pop tune? The group may need to tweak the words a little to fit their new tune, but as long as it still conveys the same meaning, that's fine.

4 You could also use any of the following songs:

- 'At the Name of Jesus' by Caroline Maria Noel
- 'Jesus, at Your Name' by Chris Bowater
- 'You Are Lord of Our Hearts' by Trish Morgan

PRACTICAL

WHAT: **prayer promises**
WHY: **to celebrate that Jesus is Lord over demons and sickness**
WITH: **laminating equipment or sticky tape (optional)**

1 Explain to the young people that they have seen that Jesus is Lord over sickness and demons. Say that Jesus is still Lord over those things and we can ask for his help when we pray. Invite the young people to share some prayer needs (especially about sickness), either of their own or of their family or friends. (Remind them not to share anything that might be confidential.)

2 Give each group member a thin strip of paper and invite them to write a short reminder of one of the specific prayer needs on it.

3 Encourage everyone to bring this prayer need to the Lord every day this week, or every day until your next session.

4 The strip of paper could become a bookmark for their Bible or a wristband to wear. To make the wristbands stronger, strengthen them by laminating or covering them with sticky tape on both sides.

CREATIVE

WHAT: **display**
WHY: **to celebrate that Jesus is Lord over demons and sickness**
WITH: **coloured paper or card, quiet instrumental music, playback equipment**

1 Give out the sheets of coloured paper or card and invite everyone to tear out letters to make the word 'LORD' as artistically as possible.

2 Display all the works of art in the centre of the floor and gather around them. You could glue all the letters onto a large sheet of paper to create a permanent display for your wall.

3 Either allow time for quiet worship of Jesus as Lord (in silence) or play some quiet instrumental music in the background. Conclude by reading a passage that focuses on Jesus' lordship, such as Philippians 2:6–11, especially verse 11.

MORE ON THIS THEME:

If you want to do a short series with your group, other sessions that work well with this one are:

32	*I am the law*	*Mark 1:40–45*
33	*Rest in peace*	*Mark 3:1–6*
34	*Don't fear the reaper*	*Mark 5:21–43*

HOW LIKELY IS IT?

On a scale of '1' to '5', where '1' = very unlikely and '5' = almost certain to happen, rate the likelihood of the following things happening in the next few months:

	Someone in your family being ill
	One of your friends being ill
	A national political leader having to go into hospital
	A footballer missing the rest of the season through injury
	A major music artist cancelling a tour because of illness
	You having a day off school through illness
	You having a day off school by faking illness
	You having to take a painkiller
	Someone announcing a new health scare
	Health warnings being printed on junk food
	Total

Score 10–20: You are an optimist of the highest order. Are you a superhero in disguise?
Score 21–30: Slightly more realistic, but you probably forget to carry a handkerchief.
Score 31–40: More like it. You understand that illness and injuries are an everyday part of life.
Score 41–45: Do you know what 'hypochondriac' means?
Score 46–50: See me afterwards, you skiving, no-good waster!

Bible bit
Mark 1:29–34

What does it mean in Mark 8:29 when Peter announces his belief in Jesus as the Christ or Messiah, God's anointed one? Welcome to Mark's Messianic Mystery Tour, where we'll be looking at the key idea in Mark's Gospel that Jesus is Lord. With more and more people being interested in all things supernatural (just look at the number of TV programmes that deal with the issue), it's increasingly important that we see Jesus as having power over demons and sickness. But this is something more than power; Jesus is Lord and his words are the commands of God.

31

SICK(NESS) FACTS

Sickness is still very much part of our world today. Jesus showed that he was Lord over sickness and demons, and he still is. As we, his followers, continue to share the message that Jesus brought, how much can we do to help the sick of the world? There are many millions who die around the world due to sickness and disease who could be saved.

WHAT'S FOR LUNCH?

'Hey, Simon!' said Jesus. 'What's for lunch?' They'd just been at quite an eventful morning meeting and they were starving. Jesus hadn't told anyone he could make his own food... yet.

'Not sure,' said Simon. 'My mother-in-law is supposed to be doing the cooking but she didn't look too well this morning.' And indeed, when they arrived at Simon's house, his mother-in-law looked terrible, although frankly she always did. She was pretty poorly though, and her head felt like it was burning up.

'That's awful!' said James. 'What are we going to do about food now?'

'Hey, Mr Sensitive!' said Simon. 'Go and start peeling the potatoes before you get a slap.' James went off to the kitchen. He'd had one of Simon's slaps before and still had the scar.

Meanwhile, some people who had delayed Jesus on the way told him lunch wasn't looking too likely, so he did what every good Messiah should do in the circumstances – he went and healed the woman. She got up and her temperature went down. Jesus helped her stand, and as soon as her feet steadied she was ordering James out of the kitchen and getting on with the lunch herself.

Later that evening, after a cracking fine meal, Jesus found a queue of people at the door with a whole range of interesting sicknesses and problems. The people didn't want to come during daylight hours on the Sabbath, but after dark was OK. He healed them all, but he didn't let anyone say who he was, even if they thought they knew. There'd be plenty of time for that later.

(Based on Mark 1:29–34)

DID YOU KNOW?

In 2010, 660,000 people died of malaria. The majority of these deaths were in developing countries where health care is poor. 90 per cent of all malaria deaths occur in Africa, mostly among children under 5 years of age. Malaria can be treated and there are several medicines that can help, although many are expensive.

In 2012, 1.3 million people died of tuberculosis, a disease that is on the rise again. In the UK, most people are immunised against this disease with a simple injection – trust me, the scare stories about your BCG jab are untrue (mostly).

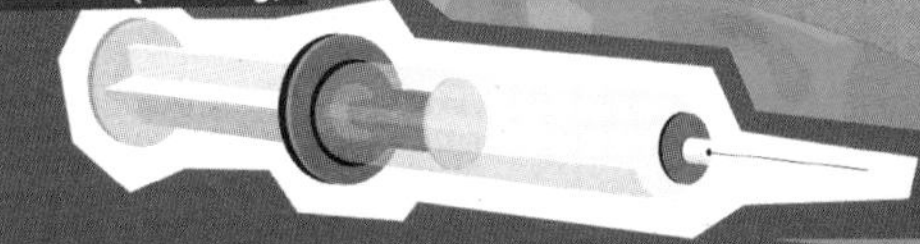

About five out of every 100 deaths each year could be prevented by improved health care around the world. So remember to pray for doctors, nurses and other support staff in medical centres around the world as they work to help those in need.

RESOURCE PAGE

USE WITH SESSION 31 BIBLE EXPERIENCE 'LEVEL 1 CONNECT', 'LEVEL 2 INTERFACE', 'LEVEL 3 SWITCH ON'

Demons and the New Testament

In the New Testament there are many references to demons. When they are mentioned they are always in opposition to God and humanity. In Mark 3:22 it says that Beelzebub is the ruler of the demons, so it could be said that demons are his agents.

There are references in the New Testament to people being possessed by demons, with a variety of effects – for example, not being able to speak (Luke 11:14), epilepsy (Mark 9:17–19) and strange behaviour (Luke 8:27). Many have said that the attribution to demons was the way in which the first-century people came to terms with different types of unexplainable sickness. What was then thought to be demonic activity could now be understood as mental and physical illness. However, the New Testament does distinguish between sickness and demonic possession (Matthew 4:24).

It becomes apparent that Jesus is in constant conflict with evil spirits. As Jesus brought the kingdom of God, he received a negative response from the demons. Overcoming the demons needed a greater-than-human power, and as Jesus demonstrated this, he demonstrated his lordship. Jesus is Lord over demons, and he is with us today as we continue to serve God's kingdom.

Bible: Mark 1:40–45

32

I AM THE LAW

THE AIM: To understand that Jesus is Lord of the Law

The aim unpacked

Here, in this encounter with the sick man, we can see Jesus' lordship over the Law. The man was 'unclean' and yet, after his encounter with Jesus, he was 'clean' – before, he was an outcast; after, he has become part of the community once again. Today's culture has many unwritten laws that, if broken, can make young people 'outcasts'. And yet, Jesus can overcome these barriers because he is Lord.

WAY IN

theGRID MAGAZINE

WHAT: **quiz**
WHY: **to think about uncleanness**
WITH: **magazine page 206**

1 Grab everyone's attention by explaining that you are going to look at some dirty words! Give out a copy of page 206 to each young person. Invite them to look at the 'Dirty words' feature.

2 Invite them to rank the words. They should give each of the words a number, putting them in order from '1' being the dirtiest to '20' being the least dirty.

3 Bring the group together and feed back the results. Discuss anything interesting that comes up, such as where the words suggesting 'inner' dirt come in the list, compared with those that are simply about surface 'dirt'. Think about what it would take to clean each of the conditions.

4 Finally, ask where they would put the word 'diseased'. Make the point that 'disease' literally means 'not at ease'. Illness tends to take away our ease or comfort. As we'll see later in this session, in Bible times in Israel, any 'disease' made people 'unclean'. When they were 'unclean', they weren't able to play a normal part in society; they had a life that was 'not at ease'.

SCENE SETTER

WHAT: **discussion**
WHY: **to think about contamination**

1 Invite everyone to sit in a circle. Ask the young people if they have ever had a contagious disease such as measles or chickenpox. If necessary, explain that contagious diseases are illnesses that can be passed on from one person to another.

2 Survey those who have had any such diseases to find out which is the most common in your group.

3 Ask individuals what happened to them when they became ill. Were they isolated? How did that feel? Be prepared to share this kind of information about yourself, especially if your group is quiet or unusually healthy!

4 Find out which contagious diseases the young people know they have been immunised against.

5 Explain that if you have a contagious disease, depending on the severity of it, your lifestyle can be completely altered. Encourage the young people to listen for what happened to one man long ago who was in exactly that predicament.

THEMED GAME

WHAT: **active game**
WHY: **to think about contagion**

1 Explain that you are going to ask the group to go round shaking hands with each other. However, someone has a contagious disease (one that can be passed on from person to person) and will pass it on to every fifth person they greet. The 'sick' person will do this by saying a codeword very quietly. If anyone hears the codeword from someone, they too must pass it on to every fifth person they greet from then onwards.

2 Secretly (if possible before the session) tell one person the codeword. Choose something memorable but unusual, such as 'pineapple'.

3 Now invite everyone to greet each other. See if any rumours begin about the 'carriers' and if they are to be avoided.

4 After a few minutes, bring the activity to a halt and see how many people have 'caught' the codeword. Discuss any avoidance tactics that were taking place.

5 Explain that isolation is still the only way to deal with certain infectious diseases, although modern medicines have changed the way we treat many of them. In the past, having a contagious disease often meant being excluded from the community and left as an outcast.

BIBLE EXPERIENCE

LEVEL 1: CONNECT

WHAT: **discussion**
WHY: **to understand that Jesus is Lord of the Law**
WITH: **drawing materials, large sheet of paper, Bibles**

1 Think together of different social groups the young people know, based perhaps on fashion, musical taste or interests.

2 On a large sheet of paper, encourage the artists in your group to draw cartoons that summarise each of these groups, and others to list the attributes of each one.

3 Ask, 'Which of these would be welcome at our group sessions?' Find out what about the people or groups might make them not be welcome. Is it something about them? Or about the group? Or both?

4 Now talk about rules. Ask for examples of genuine but petty rules. What is the daftest school rule?

5 Make the point that Jesus spent a lot of time during his early ministry with people who were usually excluded – tax collectors, people with skin diseases and other illnesses, women and children. He didn't break any of the important rules by which his community was run. In fact, he fulfilled the rules and showed people how they were meant to work, according to what God wanted.

6 Ask a volunteer to read aloud Mark 1:40–45. Explain that the sick man was excluded from his community because of what the Law said and because of his disease. What do the young people think about that – was it unfair or just sensible?

7 Explain that Jesus used his power to heal the man with the skin disease. This healing also brought him back into the community from which he had previously been cast out. The Law or rules of Israel meant that someone 'unclean' couldn't worship God like 'clean' people. But instead of staying away from him, Jesus healed the man and made him 'clean'. He fulfilled the Law in the most powerful of ways, because he is the Lord of it.

LEVEL 2: INTERFACE

WHAT: **discussion**
WHY: **to understand that Jesus is Lord of the Law**
WITH: **magazine page 207, Bibles, prompt card (optional)**

1 Practise a 'corporate gasp'. Using a hand gesture or prompt card as a cue, get everyone to turn to the person next to them and act shocked, gasping and muttering.

2 Encourage the young people to share some amazing things about themselves (don't force anyone to say something if they don't want to). Because each person is unique, everyone should have something to share, even if it's just that they are unique. After each person has spoken, gasp together on cue. Ask, 'What does that gasp mean?'

3 Give out copies of page 207 and look together at 'Rules, rules, rules'. Discuss where we might see these rules and score them out of ten for stupidity. Discuss how many are made for good reasons (albeit sometimes annoying ones) and how many are just petty.

4 Explain that in Jesus' day, anyone with a skin disease that was possibly contagious had to live outside the community. The rules also forbade anyone from touching such a person. These rules may sound extreme, but they weren't stupid. What do the young people think of them? What was the point of them?

5 Ask a volunteer to read Mark 1:40–45. Stop them abruptly after verse 41 and cue everyone to gasp. Ask, 'What does that gasp mean?' If it is not mentioned, suggest that those around Jesus would have been shocked that Jesus had touched the man. Ask the reader to carry on from verse 42.

6 Reiterate that Jesus healed the man and cue another gasp. Ask, 'What does that gasp mean?' Explain that, despite what the Law said, Jesus had an even better way of ensuring that no one else caught the disease! He fulfilled the reason for the Law in an amazing new way!

LEVEL 3: SWITCH ON

WHAT: **Bible study**
WHY: **to understand that Jesus is Lord of the Law**
WITH: **Bibles, the means to display the four words or phrases below, flip chart or whiteboard, Bible commentaries and dictionaries or internet access (optional)**

1 As a group, read Mark 1:40–45.

2 Display the following words or phrases, which all appear in the Bible passage: 'felt sorry'; 'skin disease'; 'gift'; 'healed'.

3 Invite the young people, working in small groups of about three, to come up with their own definitions of how each word or phrase is used in the Bible passage and to give a brief example to illustrate it. If possible, encourage them to use Bible commentaries or dictionaries to help them.

4 Bring the groups back together and invite them to share what they have come up with. It may be helpful to write the suggestions on a flip chart or whiteboard. Make sure that, by the end of the activity, the following points are covered clearly:

- felt sorry – literally 'had a gut reaction'; moved inside
- skin disease – one of a number of skin complaints or rashes; in those days they were all lumped together as 'leprosy'
- gift – an offering as demanded by the Law
- healed – cleansed (skin diseases were seen as 'dirty')

5 Discuss why Jesus broke the myth (and touched the man with the disease) but kept the Law (by sending him to the priest). What principle was at stake here?

6 End by making the point that, since Jesus' death and resurrection, the ceremonial law is no longer necessary as we can all approach God personally. Jesus fulfilled everything the Law required and so we no longer need to follow the ceremonial procedure: Jesus is Lord of the Law and we follow him.

RESPOND

32

MUSICAL

WHAT: **song**
WHY: **to make the connection between prayer and cleansing**
WITH: ***O Brother Where Art Thou?*** **DVD or words and music to 'Down to the River to Pray' by Alison Krauss (from the movie soundtrack), playback equipment**

1 Play the song 'Down to the River to Pray' from the movie soundtrack. Alternatively, if appropriate, show the scene from the film (it has a '12' age rating in the UK).

2 Explain that the main characters sing the song as they reach the river where a church is holding a baptismal service – people cleansing themselves of their uncleanliness and praying to God. Ask the young people to think about the man with the skin disease. In what way was he 'unclean'? (The Law said he was 'unclean'; through Jesus' healing, God made him 'clean' again.) We could say the same about ourselves: the wrong in our lives makes us 'unclean'; through Jesus, God can forgive us and make us 'clean' again.

3 Listen to the song again. If your group is happy to sing, either sing along with the whole track (providing lyrics or subtitles) or fade it out and allow the group to continue unaccompanied. As they sing, encourage them to pray silently from their hearts, asking Jesus to cleanse them. You could do this as you start the stone-washing activity in *Respond* 'Practical'.

3 Other songs that could be sung are:

- 'River, Wash Over Me' by Dougie Brown
- 'Spirit of the Living God' by Daniel Iverson

PRACTICAL

WHAT: **cleaning stones**
WHY: **to re-enact symbolically Jesus' cleansing power**
WITH: **bucket of muddy but smooth stones, bowl of water, cleaning brushes and cloths, permanent marker pens, background music, Bibles**

1 Play some gentle background music (this activity would work well with the songs from *Respond* 'Musical') and place the bucket of muddy stones at the front of your meeting area.

2 Explain that we are 'unclean', like the man with the skin disease, but we can be made 'clean' by God because of what Jesus has done, just like it happened for the man (see the explanation in 'Musical'). Reread the story of Jesus and the man with the skin disease from Mark 1:40–45.

3 As you read, encourage the group members to take a dirty stone, clean it with the brushes and water and take it back to their seat.

4 Invite everyone to use a permanent marker to write on their stone the name of someone they know who needs Jesus' healing power. Encourage them to take the stones home and use them to remind them to pray for that person during the week or until the next session.

CREATIVE

WHAT: **drawing**
WHY: **to illustrate the change that Jesus, as Lord, can make in our lives**

1 Give a sheet of paper and a pencil to each person and ask them to begin a simple line drawing of anything they like. Ask them to stop after three or four lines and write their name lightly on the reverse to identify their drawing.

2 Collect all the papers and shuffle them. Then give them out again.

3 Ask the new 'owner' of each picture to try and imagine what the drawing was meant to be and then to do something totally different with it.

4 Share the results by putting the pictures on display.

5 As the young people look at the drawings, encourage everyone to pray, if they want to, that Jesus will turn their life around, give them a fresh start and create something new and even better out of their old life.

MORE ON THIS THEME:

If you want to do a short series with your group, other sessions that work well with this one are:

31	*In sickness and in health*	*Mark 1:29–39*
33	*Rest in peace*	*Mark 3:1–6*
34	*Don't fear the reaper*	*Mark 5:21–43*

DIRTY WORDS

How dirty are these adjectives?
Give each word a number, putting them in order from '1' being the dirtiest to '20' being the least 'dirty' and all the numbers in between… being something in between.

IMPURE
ENCRUSTED
SMUTTY
FILTHY
GRIMY
STAINED
DIRTY
GRUBBY
MUDDY
SPOILED
INFECTED
CAKED
UNCLEAN
CONTAMINATED
TAINTED
MUCKY
POLLUTED
SMUDGED
RUINED
SOILED

How many of these conditions can be cleaned up with soap and water? Tick those that can.

Bible bit
Mark 1:40–45

Continuing Mark's Messianic Mystery Tour, here we can see Jesus being Lord over the Law. The man was 'unclean' and yet, after his encounter with Jesus, he was 'clean': before, he was an outcast; after, he became part of the community once again.

Today's culture has many unwritten laws that, if broken, can make people 'outcasts'. Some people 'choose' to become outcasts by following a certain fashion or lifestyle, and some people are treated like outcasts just because they are different from those around them. But Jesus overcomes all these barriers because he is Lord – no one is outside his power and he wants all people to be accepted into his community.

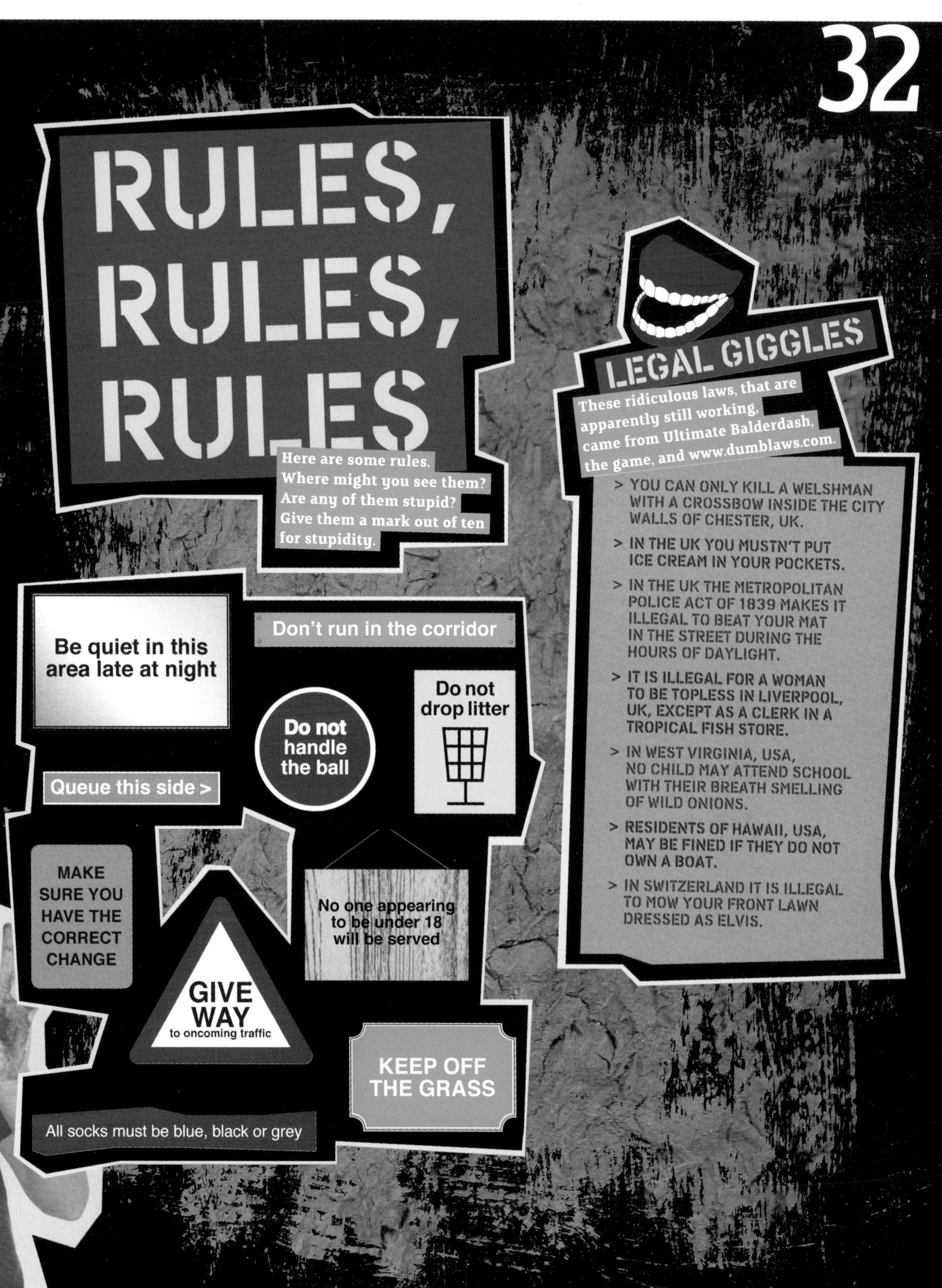

32
RULES, RULES, RULES
Here are some rules. Where might you see them? Are any of them stupid? Give them a mark out of ten for stupidity.
Be quiet in this area late at night
Don't run in the corridor
Do not drop litter
Do not handle the ball
Queue this side >
MAKE SURE YOU HAVE THE CORRECT CHANGE
No one appearing to be under 18 will be served
GIVE WAY to oncoming traffic
KEEP OFF THE GRASS
All socks must be blue, black or grey
LEGAL GIGGLES
These ridiculous laws, that are apparently still working, came from Ultimate Balderdash, the game, and www.dumblaws.com.
> YOU CAN ONLY KILL A WELSHMAN WITH A CROSSBOW INSIDE THE CITY WALLS OF CHESTER, UK.
> IN THE UK YOU MUSTN'T PUT ICE CREAM IN YOUR POCKETS.
> IN THE UK THE METROPOLITAN POLICE ACT OF 1839 MAKES IT ILLEGAL TO BEAT YOUR MAT IN THE STREET DURING THE HOURS OF DAYLIGHT.
> IT IS ILLEGAL FOR A WOMAN TO BE TOPLESS IN LIVERPOOL, UK, EXCEPT AS A CLERK IN A TROPICAL FISH STORE.
> IN WEST VIRGINIA, USA, NO CHILD MAY ATTEND SCHOOL WITH THEIR BREATH SMELLING OF WILD ONIONS.
> RESIDENTS OF HAWAII, USA, MAY BE FINED IF THEY DO NOT OWN A BOAT.
> IN SWITZERLAND IT IS ILLEGAL TO MOW YOUR FRONT LAWN DRESSED AS ELVIS.

33

Bible: Mark 3:1–6

REST IN PEACE

THE AIM: To recognise that Jesus is Lord of the Sabbath

The aim unpacked

After the healings of the previous sessions, Jesus is now confronted by questions about what is allowed on the Sabbath. We often equate the Sabbath with Sunday, and these days, Sundays are like any other day (especially in the UK). However, Jesus points out the true meaning of the Sabbath – that it was made for us (Mark 2:27). Therefore, what can or should we use the Sabbath for?

WAY IN

theGRID MAGAZINE

WHAT: **competition**
WHY: **to see that details can be important**
WITH: **magazine page 211**

1 Give a copy of page 211 to each young person and invite them to find the feature entitled 'Pay attention!'. Then ask them to look at the first sentence beginning 'Finished files...' and give them ten seconds to read it and count the number of 'f's in it. When they have finished they should close their magazines.

2 Ask for a show of hands against the number of 'f's they found: 3, 4, 5, 6 or 7.

3 Say that the correct answer is 6. Allow the young people to look again to check. Most people miss the 'f's in the word 'of' (three occurrences).

4 Read the other four sentences in the same way, giving the young people ten seconds to count the number of specific letters in each sentence. The answers can be found on page 333.

5 Ask the group why details can sometimes be important. Encourage the young people to look out for the details that were important to Jesus in this session.

SCENE SETTER

WHAT: **ice breaker**
WHY: **to think about who makes rules**
WITH: **cards from page 212**

1 Before the session, print and cut out the cards from page 212.

2 Divide the group into threes or fours (if necessary) and give each group one or two of the cards. Ask the groups to consider the following: if they could make one binding decision on behalf of the person on the card, what would they suggest? Some examples might be: 'Buy the best players for the team'; 'Invest only in technology companies'; 'Make sure they never wear horizontal stripes on TV'. Encourage everyone in the group to come up with their own ideas.

3 After a few minutes, encourage each small group to share their answers. Ask if the other groups agree with the 'binding decision'. Who would the binding decision affect? Who would benefit from the decision made? Who would not benefit?

4 If you have time, lead the group into a discussion about 'Who makes the rules?' and 'For whose benefit are they made?'

THEMED GAME

WHAT: **game**
WHY: **to think about rules and their arbitrary nature**
WITH: **straws, lots of coloured counters**

1 Give out a few coloured counters to everyone and then divide the group into small teams.

2 Draw straws to see which team 'makes the rules'. That team then gets to decide (secretly) which colour counter is 'bad' for the first round of play.

3 Invite everyone to mingle and swap counters – one for one, two for two, as they wish. Obviously, the team that made the rules will try to give away the counters they have nominated (although they may bluff). The other teams, by careful observation, must try to work out which is the bad colour.

4 Stop after two or three minutes and give each team a penalty point for each counter they hold of the 'bad' colour.

5 Draw straws to see who goes next (it could be the same team again) and play another round. If this provokes a discussion about fairness, introduce the theme of thinking about who makes rules.

BIBLE EXPERIENCE

LEVEL 1: CONNECT

WHAT: **discussion**
WHY: **to recognise that Jesus is Lord of the Sabbath**
WITH: **Bible, flip chart or whiteboard, marker pen**

1 Hand out paper and pens and divide the young people into small groups, if necessary. Ask, 'What should we do on Sundays?' Invite them to come up with a plan for a perfect Sunday. What will they do, with whom and where? Ask them to draw a timeline with lots of details – from waking up until bedtime. After a while, invite them to share their results with the other groups.

2 Now ask if there is anything they would never do, or try not to do, on a Sunday and why? On the flip chart, list the good and bad things (make two headings) people do on Sundays.

3 Read Exodus 20:8–10 to the group and explain that for Jewish people, Saturday is the Sabbath, though most Christians celebrate it on Sundays.

4 Ask a volunteer to read Mark 3:1–6 to the group from a modern Bible version. Ask the young people why they think the religious leaders seemed so upset by what Jesus did on the Sabbath.

5 In small groups again, invite everyone to think of examples of situations where someone's behaviour on a Sunday might upset other people. Do they think God would be upset by that behaviour as well?

6 Explain that Jesus upset the religious leaders of the day because his actions went against what they thought was acceptable behaviour for the Sabbath. Jesus was upset with the religious leaders because their rules were trying to stop something good happening. God created a day of rest for the people, but the religious leaders had turned it into a day when people were restricted. Jesus' actions showed that he is Lord of the Sabbath and he came to show people the real reason behind it.

LEVEL 2: INTERFACE

WHAT: **drama**
WHY: **to recognise that Jesus is Lord of the Sabbath**
WITH: **Bibles, page 213, clipboards**

1 Before your session, brief a couple of young people to burst in with clipboards (using a copy of page 213) and start making notes. Encourage them to be fairly puzzling in their behaviour – looking everyone up and down and writing down scores, but not showing their score sheets.

2 Talk about how it felt to be watched and assessed. Explain that this often happened to Jesus.

3 Give out Bibles and, in groups of four or five, ask someone in each group to read aloud Mark 3:1–6.

4 Ask each group to prepare a drama with the characters of Jesus, the man with the paralysed hand and some Pharisees. (The Pharisees could use a clipboard and score sheet.) Encourage the groups to think about what the Pharisees might have written on their score sheet. What is the final dramatic moment that shows clearly who's the 'boss' in this episode? The Pharisees should say at some point why they are going to plot against Jesus – what do they hold against him?

5 Invite the groups to perform their dramas.

6 Make the point that the authorities of the day were watching Jesus to see what he would do: in this case, what he would do on a Sabbath, about which there were rules. The authorities had made many of the rules, but Jesus overruled them, saying that the Sabbath was a day of rest, a gift from God for his people to enjoy. By redefining the rules, Jesus showed once again that he was Lord.

7 Look at the score sheets on the clipboards from step 1.

LEVEL 3: SWITCH ON

WHAT: **Bible study and interviews**
WHY: **to recognise that Jesus is Lord of the Sabbath**
WITH: **Bibles, flip chart or whiteboard, marker pens**

1 Give out Bibles and encourage everyone to turn to Mark 1. Explain that you will be looking at a passage in Mark 3, but it would be helpful for everyone to know what Jesus has done so far. Encourage everyone to skim read chapters 1 and 2 and call out everything that Jesus has done so far. List these on the flip chart or whiteboard, leaving space to write alongside.

2 Ask the young people which actions might have caused offence, to whom and why. Write their thoughts in the space that has been left. Examples: Jesus leaving town would have offended the people waiting in a queue for healing (1:36–38); Jesus forgiving sins would have offended the religious leaders, who believed only God could forgive sins and therefore that Jesus had blasphemed (2:5–7).

3 Now read Mark 3:1–6 together and ask the same question: 'Who is offended and why?'

4 Have some people prepare to play the parts of:

- the man with the bad hand
- the people watching closely (the Pharisees)

Interview these characters about how they feel about what Jesus has done. Ask the young people to think about why Jesus did what he did, even though he knew it would be controversial.

5 Lead into a discussion about how Sundays are spent today and what people do that is good or bad. Refer to Exodus 20:8–11 and Matthew 12:1–14.

RESPOND

MUSICAL

WHAT: **singing**
WHY: **to celebrate Jesus who is Lord of the Sabbath**
WITH: **worship songs, musical accompaniment or CD or MP3 player with speakers**

1 Explain that, because Jesus rose from the dead on a Sunday, Sunday is now a day of celebration and has become our Sabbath. Whether or not your group meets on a Sunday, emphasise the importance of taking some time out to celebrate Jesus.

2 Choose and prepare one or two songs so that after each verse is sung there is an instrumental verse. (Alternatively, you could simply play some background instrumental music.)

3 Encourage silence in some of the instrumental verses; in others, you could read parts of Psalm 138 or suggest that anyone who wishes to can say out loud prayers of thanksgiving for Jesus.

4 Possible songs that could be used are:

- 'Come, Now Is the Time to Worship' by Brian Doerkson
- 'The Lord's My Shepherd (I will trust in you alone)' by Stuart Townend
- 'This Is the Day That the Lord Has Made' by Les Garrett
- 'When I Was Lost' by Kate and Miles Simmonds

PRACTICAL

WHAT: **discussion**
WHY: **to remind everyone of how Sunday works**
WITH: **flip chart or whiteboard, marker pens**

1 Explain that, because Jesus rose from the dead on a Sunday, Sunday is now a day of celebration and has become our Sabbath.

2 Make a list of all the people you can think of who work on Sundays. Now highlight those occupations where Sunday work is essential. Talk about the consequences of some of those people not being willing to work on a Sunday: what would happen?

3 Encourage them to pray that the people in the 'essential' occupations they have talked about will find 'rest' at some point during the week. Also, as a group, make a commitment to pray for those people throughout the week, specifically that they will be at 'rest' when you are at 'work'.

CREATIVE

WHAT: **prayer**
WHY: **to respond to Jesus' example of healing by praying for the sick**
WITH: **copy of your church's prayer list, greetings cards**

1 Your church will probably have a list of sick people for whom it prays regularly. Obtain a copy and try to find out some background about the people on it so you can all pray more effectively. The Sabbath is a symbol of rest and so, as we pray for the sick, we can ask Jesus to bring 'rest' to them, through healing or comfort.

2 Read the list to the young people, adding any extra information you have that's relevant. Then split into groups and ask them to concentrate their prayers (aloud or silent) on one or two specific people.

3 Write a short greetings card to each person you prayed for, telling them what you did and wishing them well. You could include a short poem or a verse from the Bible for encouragement. If you have blank greetings cards, the group could decorate them and put images on the front of them.

4 Make sure the cards are delivered!

MORE ON THIS THEME:

If you want to do a short series with your group, other sessions that work well with this one are:

31	*In sickness and in health*	*Mark 1:29–39*
32	*I am the law*	*Mark 1:40–45*
34	*Don't fear the reaper*	*Mark 5:21–43*

33

Bible bit
Mark 3:1–6

Mark's Messianic Mystery Tour brings us to a place where Jesus is being confronted by questions about what is allowed on the Sabbath. Now if we view the Sabbath as being a Sunday, there aren't that many differences between it and any other day of the week these days (at least in the UK). Why do people care about what you can and can't do? Jesus points out the true meaning of the Sabbath, that it was made special for us (Mark 2:27).

So what can or should we use the Sabbath for? It seems that the old rules are out of the window, but that doesn't mean it isn't still important to God! Whatever we decide, we should recognise that Jesus is Lord of the Sabbath – it is his, and therefore we should look to him for guidance.

PAY ATTENTION!

1. Count the number of 'f's in this sentence:
Finished files are the result of years of scientific study with the experience of years.

2. Count the number of 'g's in this sentence:
I dig dunking doughnuts roughly as much as Doug does.

3. Count the number of 'o's in this sentence:
I owe you women nothing.

4. Count the number of 't's in this sentence:
Nation will rise up against nation, father against son.

5. Count the number of 'a's in this sentence:
Every opportunity we get to do good, we will strive to use in the best possible way.

RESOURCE PAGE

USE WITH SESSION 33 WAY IN 'SCENE SETTER'

Decisions, decisions

The manager of a major sports team	The chairman of a big retail chain
The head teacher of a large secondary school	The fashion adviser to the President or Prime Minister
The editor of a leading tabloid newspaper	The presenter of a popular breakfast radio show
The producer of the main evening TV news bulletin	A businessman with a huge amount of money to invest in a new business or idea

USE WITH SESSION 33 BIBLE EXPERIENCE 'LEVEL 2 INTERFACE'

My group

Answer with a mark out of 10 where 10 = good and 0 = terrible.

Leaders' dress sense ☐

Temperature of room ☐

Tidiness/cleanliness of room ☐

Behaviour of group members ☐

Music played ☐

Refreshments offered ☐

Length of meeting ☐

Hair styles ☐

Preparation put into the session ☐

Quality of relationships and care ☐

Total (out of 100) ☐

34

Bible: Mark 5:21–43

DON'T FEAR THE REAPER

THE AIM: To rejoice that Jesus is Lord over death

The aim unpacked

For many young people, the thought of death is totally alien. At their age, most will feel like they are going to live for ever (though be sensitive towards anyone who has experienced a bereavement recently). However, death is a fact of life. Yet for the Christian, it is not the end. In this passage, Jesus shows that he has power over death. Therefore, with faith in Jesus, we need never fear the reality of death.

WAY IN

theGRID MAGAZINE

WHAT: word check
WHY: to start thinking about death
WITH: page 219

1 Look together at the words and phrases from page 219. Ask the young people what all the words have in common. Point out that some of the words or phrases imply death and others don't. There are some that are ambiguous.

2 Distribute pens and paper. Working in smaller groups if necessary, invite the young people to write the words in two columns ('death' and 'not death'), and to leave the ambiguous words in the middle ('ambiguous').

3 Bring the group together. Invite them to share their results and see if there are any differences. Discuss briefly why we use so many phrases or expressions instead of the words 'death' or 'dead'.

SCENE SETTER

WHAT: improvisation
WHY: to think about comfort

1 Explain to the group that there are people who manage to say the worst thing in any event. Have they ever said anything like this?

2 Stand in a circle and list the following situations. Invite the group members individually to step forward and make suggestions as to the worst possible thing to say in the circumstances. Keep going on each one until the humorous potential is exhausted and then switch to a new situation:

- Your friend tells you her dog has died
- Someone tells you they are really scared about dying
- There is a serious outbreak of a contagious illness at school
- Your friend's parents are late home on a stormy winter's evening

Add other situations that may receive a good reaction in your group.

3 Finally, explain that finding the right words about death is often difficult but, when faced with death, we all need to find comfort somewhere.

THEMED GAME

WHAT: killer game
WHY: to play a game involving 'death'
WITH: small sticky labels, masking tape, bin liners (if you need to black out windows to make it dark)

1 Explain that in a moment you will turn out the lights briefly and hand some sticky labels to one person. They will hide them on their person. The lights will come on again and everyone will mingle around. The lights will then go out for a second time and the 'killer' will strike by placing a label on someone.

2 When the lights come on, everyone must stand still and notice each other's position. The person who has been labelled must 'die' – dramatically of course. Continue with one person being labelled at each 'lights out' until the 'murderer' is found or everyone is 'dead'.

3 While the lights are on, anyone who wishes to accuse someone of being the murderer may do so but if they are wrong, they too must die dramatically. If they are correct, they can appoint the murderer for the next round and sit it out as observer.

4 On the final round, draw round the bodies with masking tape as they do in all great murder mystery films. Leave the outlines as a visual aid for the rest of the session.

BIBLE EXPERIENCE 34

LEVEL 1: CONNECT

WHAT: **re-creation**
WHY: **to rejoice that Jesus is Lord over death**

1 Introduce this contemporary scenario. A young girl has died. Her body is still in the house. The undertakers have not yet arrived. A man you vaguely know arrives at the door. You ask him why he is here. He says, 'She's not dead, only sleeping.'

2 Breaking into smaller groups if necessary, encourage everyone to plan how the scene now develops as people react to this apparently tactless statement. Get them to think about the characters in the situation: How do the girl's parents react? What about close friends? Is there a doctor there?

3 Obtain feedback and then ask, 'What happened next?' You could encourage the group to act out the situation as a role play.

4 Now tell the story of Jesus raising the dead girl back to life in Mark 5:21–24,35–43. Omit the interruption from the woman with the haemorrhaging.

5 Comparing this Bible episode with their role play situation, ask whether the young people would have trusted Jesus if he had said that about the girl, or whether they would have thrown him out. Are there any differences between the contemporary situation and the story in the Bible? Point out that Jairus asked Jesus for help and he had faith that his daughter would be OK. And she was, because Jesus is Lord over death.

LEVEL 2: INTERFACE

WHAT: **quiz and challenge**
WHY: **to rejoice that Jesus is Lord over death**
WITH: **magazine page 217, Bible**

1 Give out a copy of page 217 to each young person and allow a little time for them to fill in the quiz 'Back from the dead'.

2 Give out the answers and discuss why they think so many fictional characters come back to life. Is it because we don't want death to be the end?

3 Read Mark 5:21–43 to the group or ask a confident volunteer to do it.

4 Talk together about how Jesus brought hope to Jairus, his daughter and the woman who had been bleeding for 12 years. Discuss the ways in which he changed each of their lives.

5 Finish by explaining that the Bible teaches us that Jesus is Lord over death. As with Jairus' daughter, it can also be true for those who trust him – death is not the end. During his earthly ministry, Jesus was able to change a lot of people's lives, including bringing people back to life; today he offers us the chance to change our life, to have hope and to experience eternal life.

6 You might want to use this opportunity to have some appropriate follow-up literature available for those who might now want to commit themselves to Jesus.

LEVEL 3: SWITCH ON

WHAT: **Bible study**
WHY: **to rejoice that Jesus is Lord over death**
WITH: **Bibles, prepared interruptions (see below)**

1 Brief a few leaders or older young people to interrupt you during your introduction to this item. Start to talk about things that are not as important as life or death, but that matter to the young people; react appropriately to the interruptions when they come:

- 'I've lost my mobile phone.'
- 'I need to borrow keys to a cupboard.'
- 'Whose turn is it to serve refreshments?'
- 'Would you like to come round for a meal next week?'

2 Explain that interruptions are frustrating. Even Jesus was interrupted. Read Mark 5:21–43 together.

3 Discuss how you think Jesus might have felt to be interrupted. Also think together how Jairus, the father of the dead girl, might have felt while all this was happening.

4 All together, or in small groups, look at some of the finer points and details in this story that give it its air of reality. Use the ideas below:

- ill for 12 years (v 25)
- touched his coat (v 27)
- shaking with fear (why?) (v 33)
- making lots of noise and crying loudly (v 38)
- laughed at him (v 40)
- 'Talitha, koum!' (v 41)
- 'Give her something to eat' (v 43)

5 Ask the young people for suggestions of the main, and unique, point that this passage teaches us. If no one comes up with it, suggest this: 'Jesus is Lord over everything, and nothing can interrupt or spoil that lordship.'

6 You might want to recap the previous three sessions to remind everyone that you have seen Jesus as Lord over demons and sickness, the Law, the Sabbath and now even over death itself.

RESPOND

MUSICAL

WHAT: **song**
WHY: **to rejoice that Jesus is Lord over death**
WITH: **'Hem of His Garment' by Faithless (from the album *Sunday 8pm*), playback equipment**

1 Invite the young people to make themselves comfortable and listen to the track. Encourage them to let their minds wander while it is playing.

2 Play the music.

3 Afterwards, invite the young people to share any thoughts and pictures that came into their minds as the music was playing.

4 Give thanks for the power of Jesus and his lordship over illness and death. The young people could do this by praying or simply saying out loud how they feel about Jesus as Lord. Why not encourage them to try shouting out their praise while listening to the track again?

5 You could also use some old hymns that have excellent words and that are often used at funerals, speaking them aloud over contemporary instrumental music:

- 'The day thou gavest' by John Ellerton
- 'Abide with me' by WH Monk
- 'Praise my soul, the King of heaven' by Henry Francis Lyte

PRACTICAL

WHAT: **party**
WHY: **to rejoice that Jesus is Lord over death**
WITH: **various pieces of party equipment, page 218**

1 Make a certificate for each young person using page 218.

2 Explain that we often find an excuse for celebrating fairly arbitrary things (becoming a year older, passing exams, winning sporting competitions), yet we forget to celebrate the best possible news – Jesus has conquered death.

3 Throw a party in honour of the resurrection of Jesus, not in a dull way, but celebrating as you would celebrate a human achievement – with party poppers, nice food, dressing up and dancing. This should all be done in a spirit of worship. Worship can be fun and doesn't have to be singing old hymns or songs. You could do this either as the last section of your session or as a separate event.

4 End the party by inviting everyone to fill in the details on their certificate of attendance and take it home.

CREATIVE

WHAT: **artwork**
WHY: **to rejoice that Jesus is Lord over death**
WITH: **mixed art materials, including magazines, glue, paints, card**

1 Invite the young people to produce a work of mixed media art that shows the Christian hope of victory over death. They could use a mixture of collage, painting or anything else they come up with, using the materials provided.

2 Explain that the subject might mean the picture they come up with could be a massive celebration or be gloomy or dark, with a small indication of hope. Death is still a reality and bereavement still hurts, but the Bible teaches us that while we will all still die, death has lost its sting (its ability to cause lasting damage).

3 After the art is finished, invite anyone who wishes to talk about their work to do so. (Don't make it compulsory – art can speak for itself.)

4 If possible, display the artwork somewhere prominent in the church for a few days, then let the young people take it home as a constant reminder that Jesus is Lord over death.

MORE ON THIS THEME:

If you want to do a short series with your group, other sessions that work well with this one are:

31	*In sickness and in health*	*Mark 1:29–39*
32	*I am the law*	*Mark 1:40–45*
33	*Rest in peace*	*Mark 3:1–6*

34

DEPARTED
INFECTED
SIX
FEET
UNDER

Bible bit
Mark 5:21–43

The final stop on Mark's Messianic Mystery Tour brings us to The End. You might sometimes feel like you're going to live for ever, but anyone who has been bereaved knows all too well that it is a fact of life, and possibly the only real certainty, that one day we will all die.

Yet for the Christian, that is not the end. Jesus shows that he has power over death – he is Lord over it. Therefore, with faith in Jesus, we need never fear the reality of death.

INACTIVE
EAD TIRED
MORTALLY
WOUNDED
DEAD
BEAT

BACK FROM THE DEAD

They say that death is the end, but not so in the wonderful world of TV, film, books and comics! Which of these fictional characters have come back from the dead? Tick the boxes and then check the answers on page 34.

- THE DOCTOR [DOCTOR WHO]
- OBI WAN KENOBI [STAR WARS]
- SUPERMAN [DC COMICS]
- ZOMBIES [LOTS OF THINGS!]
- ASLAN [THE CHRONICLES OF NARNIA]
- MUFASA [THE LION KING]
- SHERLOCK HOLMES [SHERLOCK]
- SIRIUS BLACK [HARRY POTTER]
- WICKED WITCH OF THE WEST [THE WIZARD OF OZ]
- GANDALF [THE LORD OF THE RINGS]

Everyone loves a good old resurrection – they bring hope that we'll see our favourite characters again and that the story goes on. But is it just a sci-fi thing? Jesus has proved (more than once) that death doesn't have to be the end, even in real life...

PASSED AWAY
TERMINAL
HE'S A
GONER
DONE IN
PUSHING
UP DAISIES
FELL
ASLEEP

USE WITH SESSION 34 RESPOND 'PRACTICAL'

I was there!

(Fill in your name in the first gap, the party venue in the second, and the date in the last.)

This is to certify that

....

was there at

....

on

....

to celebrate Jesus' once-and-for-all

conquest of death.

Thanks be to God!

RESOURCE PAGE

USE WITH SESSION 34 WAY IN 'THEGRID MAGAZINE'

poisoned

not much longer for this world

silenced

lifeless

buried alive

kicked the bucket

dead tired

mortally wounded

infected

expired

he's a goner

fell asleep

done in

inactive

departed

dead beat

terminal

six feet under

passed away

pushing up daisies

dead boring

35

Bible: Luke 14:15–24

ADMIT ONE

THE AIM: To recognise that the invitation from Jesus is for all people

The aim unpacked

It is very easy to restrict entry into God's kingdom, described in this particular parable in terms of a feast or party – either through prejudice towards others or towards ourselves. However, the invitation is to all people; it only needs to be accepted.

WAY IN

theGRID MAGAZINE

WHAT: **discussion**
WHY: **to think about excuses people make**
WITH: **magazine page 223**

1 Invite the young people to read the article called 'Excuses, excuses' on page 223.

2 Encourage the young people to discuss, in pairs, any bizarre or tenuous excuses they have heard or used.

3 Encourage them to think about why people might make excuses. How would they feel if someone gave a lame excuse not to go to a party they were throwing?

SCENE SETTER

WHAT: **game**
WHY: **to think about receiving an invitation from Jesus**
WITH: **two blank postcards for each young person, bucket, doorway to another room (or something to symbolise a doorway)**

1 Before the session, write forfeits on half of the postcards – eg, 'Jump up and down for 20 seconds', or 'Name ten famous footballers'.

2 On the other half of the postcards write 'An invitation from Jesus for…' and the name of each young person in the group. Put all the postcards in the bucket.

3 Divide the group into two teams and get them to line up at one end of the room. Place the bucket halfway down the room, or near the doorway. If you are not using a doorway, use two chairs instead.

4 The teams must take it in turns to run to the bucket and take a postcard. If they get an invitation for someone in their team, they take it back to their team. If they get a forfeit, they perform the forfeit and then return to the team. If they get an invitation for the other team, they give it to the other team and then return to their place. When everyone has their invitation, they join hands and run through the doorway!

THEMED GAME

WHAT: **party games**
WHY: **to play games associated with parties**
WITH: **music (optional), sewing thread (the thinner and weaker, the better), prizes**

1 If you have a lot of space, play musical chairs. Make it fun for the young people by choosing music they like. To encourage the young people to get into the spirit of it, offer a prize for the winner. Alternatively, you could play pass the parcel.

2 If you have limited space, play this simpler game. Before the session, tie several equal lengths of sewing thread to a small prize.

3 Ask for as many volunteers as you have pieces of thread. Invite the volunteers to hold a piece of thread and stand or sit in a circle around the prize. Say that the aim of the game is for each person to try to pull the prize towards them, without their thread breaking. Once everyone is ready, shout 'Pull!' The winner is the person whose thread does not break.

4 If you have a large group, you could have more parcels and thread to play the game in smaller groups so that everyone has a go.

BIBLE EXPERIENCE

LEVEL 1: CONNECT

WHAT: **discussion**
WHY: **to recognise that the invitation from Jesus is for all people**
WITH: **Bibles**

1 Read out the following list of people and ask the young people to discuss and decide, in pairs, who they would allow into heaven and why: bank robber, murderer, school teacher, church leader, nurse, drug dealer, pop star, TV celebrity (you could adapt or add to this list if you want to make it more topical).

2 Invite the young people to share as a whole group some of the things they have discussed. Ask:

- Who have you decided should be allowed into heaven?
- How did you make your decision?

3 Read or ask a confident volunteer to read Luke 14:15–24. Ask the group:

- Who was supposed to come to the banquet?
- Who actually came to the banquet?
- How many people were invited in the end?

4 Talk about what the banquet symbolises (heaven) and who the man, or master, in the passage represents (God). What does this Bible passage say about the group's earlier decisions about who gets into heaven and who doesn't? Do they want to change their minds? Point out that Jesus invites everyone into heaven and it's up to each person to accept the invitation. It's not about who we are or what we have done.

LEVEL 2: INTERFACE

WHAT: **photo story**
WHY: **to recognise that the invitation from Jesus is for all people**
WITH: **magazine page 224, flip chart or whiteboard, Bibles**

1 Invite the young people to read the photo story on page 224 and to talk about what is happening and why.

2 Encourage the young people to read Luke 14:15–24 and discuss the following questions, in pairs:

- What are the main differences in the two stories?
- Who do the people in the Bible story represent?

3 Invite the young people to suggest who they think the people in the story might represent. Write their suggestions on a flip chart or whiteboard. Then have a time of quiet and ask the young people to write down (or draw symbols to represent) the people who they think might be in each group – for example, who are today's poor, lame and crippled?

4 Invite everyone to look at the flip chart or whiteboard. Ask the young people to think about whether there is anyone they think might not have a chance of getting to heaven. Challenge them to work out why they might think that.

LEVEL 3: SWITCH ON

WHAT: **Bible study**
WHY: **to recognise that the invitation from Jesus is for all people**
WITH: **Bibles**

1 Invite the young people to read Luke 14:15–24 and discuss the following questions, in pairs:

- What excuses did the invited guests make for not going to the banquet?
- Do you think these excuses were reasonable?
- Who was invited after the first people refused to come?

2 Encourage each pair to feed back their thoughts to the rest of the group. Explain that the excuses used by the people in the passage are similar to excuses people make today. They put their lives, possessions and relationships before God. These are some of the things that stop them accepting Jesus' invitation.

3 Explain that a really good way of understanding the Bible is to use one passage to help us understand or expand on another. Say that we're going to do this by looking at Romans 3:9–31.

4 Encourage the young people to read Romans 3:9–31 and discuss the following questions in their pairs:

- What form does Jesus' invitation take (vs 22–25)?
- Who is the invitation for (vs 29,30)?
- What is the group's initial reaction to this passage? How does it affect them?
- What are they going to do about Jesus' invitation being for everyone?

RESPOND

MUSICAL

WHAT: **reflection with music**
WHY: **to think about what accepting Jesus' invitation means**
WITH: **instrumental music (preferably ambient or classical), playback equipment**

1 Invite the young people to find a comfortable place to be still and relax.

2 Explain that accepting Jesus' invitation means an eternal celebration with God. It is open to us all! We have all been invited to the feast.

3 Play some background music quietly as you read Revelation 21:1 – 22:5 slowly and clearly. Give the young people time to focus on the words and to imagine the scene as you read.

4 Either have a time of open prayer in response to the session or lead the young people in prayer, thanking God for the invitation to the ultimate party.

PRACTICAL

WHAT: **event planning**
WHY: **to prepare an event to tell others about Jesus' invitation**
WITH: **appropriate equipment**

1 Ask the young people to think of friends or relatives who haven't accepted Jesus' invitation. Together, come up with some ideas for an event that the group might be able to put on for these people. Challenge them to think about how they could use this event – perhaps a party – as an opportunity to invite their friends and tell them about Jesus.

2 Help the group choose an idea to work on, and plan it together. What kind of things will they need? Equipment? Food? Set a realistic date for the event and help the young people to plan how they might make sure everything is ready.

3 Spend some time thinking together about how you might tell people about Jesus' message for everyone. Will you have something on the invitation, or a short talk at the event? Pray about the event and that the people you are going to invite will come.

4 Make sure you have all the correct health and safety and child protection measures in place for the event. Then start inviting people!

CREATIVE

WHAT: **invitations**
WHY: **to pray for those who haven't yet accepted Jesus' invitation**
WITH: **page 225 copied onto card, envelopes, stamps**

1 Explain that the young people are going to create invitations that they can use to pray for people they know who have not yet accepted Jesus' invitation.

2 Encourage the young people to think of two or three people they would like to pray for. Give out the invitations from page 225 and ask them to write the name of each person on a separate invitation. Suggest that they personalise each invitation.

3 When they have finished, spread the invitations out and gather everyone round them. Lead everyone in prayer, asking God to work in the lives of the people named so that they might accept the invitation. Encourage the young people to pray, too, if they want to.

4 When you have finished, put the invitations into separate envelopes. Give each young person an invitation to take home and encourage them to pray for that person. Before your next session, send out another invitation to each group member, asking them to pray for that person too. Keep sending the invites out until there are none left.

MORE ON THIS THEME:

If you want to do a short series with your group, other sessions that work well with this one are:

36	*SOS*	*Luke 15:1–7*
37	*Whatever I've done?*	*Luke 15:11–32*

Bible bit
Luke 14:15–24

A great big party; many invites are sent. The day of the party arrives and... no one comes. They all make excuses. Jesus tells a story about such a party, but his meaning is not just about missing out on a great time. The party is a metaphor for God's kingdom, and everyone's invited!

EXCUSES EXCUSES

Read these excuses.
Which do you like best?
Which could you use?
What's the best excuse you've ever used?!

I can't walk the dog;
I'm superglued to the sofa.

I can't go to the party;
I haven't got anything to wear.

I haven't got my homework;
the dog ate it.

I can't tidy my room;
I'm blow-drying my poodle.

?!!

I can't come out to dinner
tonight as I'm fasting.

I can't dance with you;
your feet are too big.

No I can't do that, I have to
polish my One Direction CDs.

I can't wash the car;
I'm allergic to water.

I'm sorry, I can't come
out tonight because I'm
washing my eyebrows.

THE PARTY
Hey, I'm going to have a really great party; do you want to come?
Yeah, cool. I hope the bad people don't come, though.
The party is nearly set up. I've got the DJ, the food, the drink, and all the cool people are coming.
Great! But I think that some of the bad people have heard that you're having a party...
Oh dear!
Hey, I hear you're having a party. Can I come with all my bad mates?
Er... party? Er... no, you must have heard wrong. I'm not having a party; I'm having a parting. It is time to change my hairstyle.
No, you can't come to my party, because you have the wrong shape eyes.
Sorry, this party is for trendy people only, and your dress sense is soooo last week.
That's right, you can't come to the party because you have a letter 'q' in your name – vowels only.
Well, this is a success.
Yeah, and no one came who we didn't like!

USE WITH SESSION 35 RESPOND 'CREATIVE'

Invitation

This invitation is for

.... [name]

Jesus wants to invite you to know more about the freedom he offers, so that you can join him in heaven when the time comes.

RSVP!

This invitation is for

.... [name]

Jesus wants to invite you to know more about the freedom he offers, so that you can join him in heaven when the time comes.

RSVP!

This invitation is for

.... [name]

Jesus wants to invite you to know more about the freedom he offers, so that you can join him in heaven when the time comes.

RSVP!

This invitation is for

.... [name]

Jesus wants to invite you to know more about the freedom he offers, so that you can join him in heaven when the time comes.

RSVP!

36

Bible: Luke 15:1–7

SOS

THE AIM: To understand that Jesus' rescue mission is for each individual

The aim unpacked

In this session, we see that the shepherd is motivated by his concern for the one lost sheep. Likewise, God is motivated by his love for those individuals who have turned from him and found themselves wandering without his guidance. This message may be personal or you may want to focus on how it applies to other people in the world.

WAY IN

theGRID MAGAZINE

WHAT: **list-making and discussion**
WHY: **to introduce the theme of something going missing**

1 Hand out pens and paper and invite the group to write a list of the three things they would miss the most if they lost them.

2 Spend some time thinking together about what they would do if they lost any of these items. How might they manage without these things? Ask, 'Has your opinion of these objects changed, having realised how much they mean to you?'

3 Explain that today they're going to be looking at a story about something going missing.

SCENE SETTER

WHAT: **questionnaire**
WHY: **to think about being an individual**
WITH: **copy of page 231 for each person**

1 Give out the copies of page 231 and ask the young people to complete the 'Me, myself and I' questionnaire on their own.

2 Bring the group back together and collect in the answers. Pick one questionnaire at random and read out the answer to question 10. Challenge the young people to guess who that answer belongs to. If they get it wrong, read out the answer to question 9 and continue until the group has figured out whose questionnaire it is. If you have time, pick another one and do the same.

3 Read out the paragraph at the bottom of the questionnaire. Ask the young people if they think God, who sees everybody, cares about people as individuals.

THEMED GAME

WHAT: **decision-making game**
WHY: **to think about a rescue mission**

1 Ask the young people to get into groups of four or five. (If you have a small group, do this activity all together.)

2 Read out this scenario: 'The earth is doomed! Global warming has heated up the world so much that people won't be able to survive for much longer. Spaceships have been built that can take up to 1,000 people to search for another planet where the human race can carry on living. You are the selection committee. How will you choose 1,000 people to go on these spaceships? What criteria will you use? Who are the most worthy members of society who deserve to go on this mission?'

3 Remind the young people that this is just a fictional scenario. Ask them to discuss this in their groups and decide who will be saved on the spaceships.

4 Bring the young people back together. Encourage the groups to share their conclusions and explain how they made their decisions. If appropriate, talk about how Jesus' rescue mission is real and that he doesn't want anyone to be left behind!

BIBLE EXPERIENCE

LEVEL 1: CONNECT

WHAT: real-life story
WHY: to understand that Jesus' rescue mission is for each individual
WITH: magazine pages 229 and 230, Bible

1 Read or ask a confident volunteer to read Luke 15:1–7 to the group. Talk about who the shepherd and sheep represent in Jesus' parable. Ask, 'Do you think God cares about each person individually? Do you think there is anything that would stop God from reaching out to rescue lost people?'

2 Read the article about Peter Wynn on pages 229 and 230. Try to gauge the group's reactions to his story. Ask:

- Was he the kind of person you thought might be a lost sheep? Why?
- Have you changed your mind about the things that might stop God saving people?

3 Talk about the way God reaches out to the lost – through the death of his Son, Jesus Christ. Talk about how God used the Christian lady to tell Tony about Jesus and what he had done. Emphasise that Jesus died for everyone, not just the ones who are good!

LEVEL 2: INTERFACE

WHAT: writing a parable
WHY: to understand that Jesus' rescue mission is for each individual
WITH: copies of Luke 15:1–7

1 Distribute copies of Luke 15:1–7 to the group. Read it together and discuss what the parable means. Give some guidance if the young people are struggling, but try to allow them to tease out the message themselves.

2 Explain that Jesus used sheep in the story because of the culture and the audience he was talking to. Lost sheep would have been very relevant to a crowd of shepherds! Encourage the young people to get into pairs and have a go at writing a parable of their own, drawing on examples from today's culture.

3 Once they've had time to do this, invite each pair to read their parable out, followed by their explanation of its meaning.

4 Explain that the parable in Luke 15 means that Jesus' mission is for each individual, and that God is concerned about each individual who has turned from him and found themselves wandering without his guidance. Ask them to check whether their parable also has that message. Give them the opportunity to edit it if they want to.

LEVEL 3: SWITCH ON

WHAT: Bible study and discussion
WHY: to understand that Jesus' rescue mission is for each individual
WITH: Bibles

1 Ask a confident volunteer to read Luke 15:1–7 to the group.

2 Discuss together the following questions. If necessary, draw out the points listed, but try to let the young people come up with answers for themselves.

- Who is Jesus referring to as the 'lost sheep'? The Pharisees referred to the people Jesus spent time with as 'sinners', so this implies that the 'lost sheep' are non-Christians rather than Christians who have fallen away. However, God's heart is to have all his children safe and in his presence.
- Why did Jesus use the example of sheep? His audience would have been familiar with sheep and shepherds and what it meant to lose a sheep (a valuable object).
- What similarities are there between sheep and humans? Sheep all look the same from a distance; they can be stupid; they follow each other blindly; they are helpless without the shepherd.
- Does this parable mean that God doesn't care about the 99 sheep? God wants everyone to love him. He cares for each of us as if we were the one lost sheep.
- What does this parable tell us about Jesus' mission? Jesus came to save those who are lost.
- In what ways are we sometimes like the Pharisees in the story (v 2)? We can look down on those who aren't Christians or who have fallen away. We can sometimes take our salvation for granted and forget that we were once 'lost', or we can think that we are OK and don't need saving.

3 Give everyone a few minutes to reflect on their attitude towards 'lost-sheep'-type people or towards what God has done for us and ask him for forgiveness if necessary. Finish with a prayer.

RESPOND

MUSICAL

WHAT: **writing song verses**
WHY: **to think about the point of view of the lost sheep**
WITH: **CD or MP3 of 'Amazing Grace' and playback equipment, or sheet music and musical instruments, copies of 'Amazing Grace' lyrics**

1 Hand out copies of the lyrics of 'Amazing Grace'. Play a version of the song from a CD or MP3 or ask some musicians to play it to the group. If appropriate, encourage the young people to sing along.

2 Point out that the third line, 'I once was lost, but now I'm found', links with the lost sheep in the parable.

3 Challenge the young people to write some extra verses from the viewpoint of the 'lost sheep' or a person who has just been 'found'. They could do this on their own or in pairs.

4 If you have an instrumental version of the tune, or musicians, play this and invite the group to sing their own verses to God in their heads.

PRACTICAL

WHAT: **providing practical help**
WHY: **to demonstrate Jesus' love and desire to save each individual**
WITH: **appropriate equipment**

1 Ask the young people if they know anyone who is on the fringes of the church, or who doesn't go to church, who might appreciate some practical help.

2 Discuss the different kinds of things the young people could do for others – for example, gardening, cleaning, washing cars. Talk about the reasons why you might want to do this. Say that by showing Jesus' love to individual people, you open up opportunities to talk about Jesus and share with others what Jesus has done for you – how he rescued you.

3 Make sure the group understands that this does not mean they should preach to people for the whole time they are supposed to be helping them! If you prepare prayerfully, Jesus will give you the chance to share naturally his rescue mission with others.

4 Decide who you might approach and what you might be able to offer to do for them. Ensure that you keep to your church's child protection policy and bear in mind health and safety issues while you're helping people.

5 Plan and carry out this act of service.

CREATIVE

WHAT: **collage**
WHY: **to pray for people who are saved and who are lost**
WITH: **large sheet of paper, black marker pen, cotton wool balls, glue sticks, felt-tip pens or paint**

1 Before the session, ask someone to draw on a large sheet of paper the outline of 99 sheep in a field and one sheep separated from the flock.

2 Explain that you are going to use this as a time of thanksgiving for those who have already been saved by Jesus and to pray for those who still need to be rescued.

3 Work together to create a collage of the scene from the parable, using cotton wool balls for the sheep and filling in the background with paint or felt-tip pens. Young people of this age don't often have the chance to do something like this, so encourage them to enjoy it!

4 While you are working, chat together about people you all know who are 'saved' (including themselves). Encourage the young people to give thanks for those people and thank God that he has rescued them. Then suggest that everyone thinks about one or two people they know who are yet to be saved. Pray together for them, maybe mentioning them by name as you work on the picture.

5 When you have finished, hang the collage on the wall as a reminder of Jesus' rescue mission for everyone.

MORE ON THIS THEME:

If you want to do a short series with your group, other sessions that work well with this one are:

35 Admit one Luke 14:15–24

37 Whatever I've done? Luke 15:11–32

FROM MURDERER TO MENTOR

36

Peter Wynn got involved with crime for the first time aged just 10, committing a robbery with a gang in Toxteth, Liverpool. It was to be the start of more than two decades of criminal behaviour and gang violence.

'Gangs became a way of life for me. With no dad on the scene, the gangsters were who I looked up to and who I wanted to be like. I ended up mixing with some of the most notorious criminals in Liverpool – most are now either doing life sentences or are dead.'

Peter was involved in the Toxteth riots in 1981, and made a living running protection rackets and working as a bouncer on the south coast. Drugs, including cocaine, soon followed. He ended up standing trial for murder.

'I'd been charged with murder and on remand as a "Category A" prisoner. I was looking to serve at least 14 years behind bars. But then this woman started writing letters to me. She had seen me in the dock. Her letters said things like, "I believe that you are not the person that they say you are, but that you're a man of God."

Continued over the page >

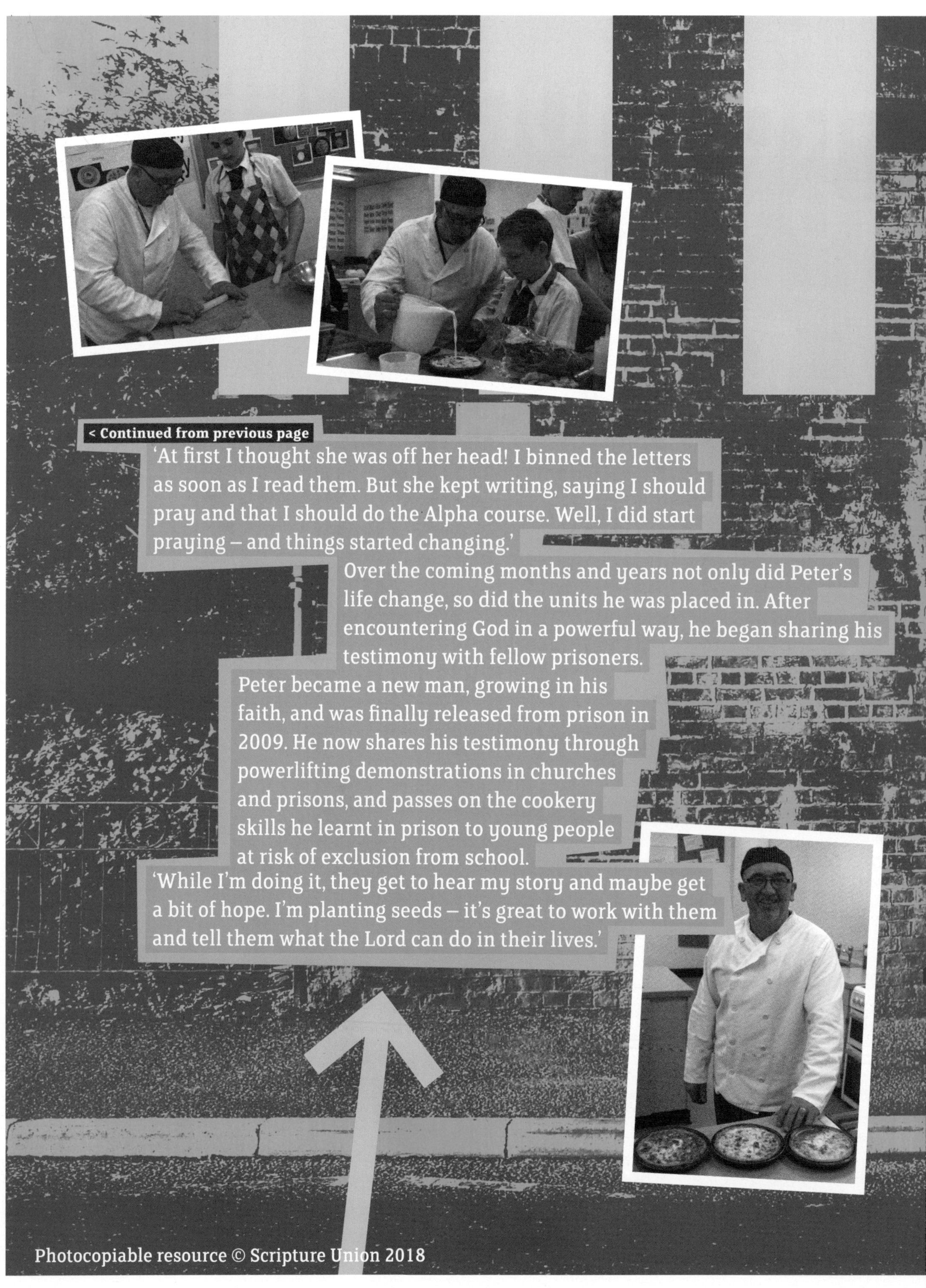

< Continued from previous page

'At first I thought she was off her head! I binned the letters as soon as I read them. But she kept writing, saying I should pray and that I should do the Alpha course. Well, I did start praying – and things started changing.'

Over the coming months and years not only did Peter's life change, so did the units he was placed in. After encountering God in a powerful way, he began sharing his testimony with fellow prisoners.

Peter became a new man, growing in his faith, and was finally released from prison in 2009. He now shares his testimony through powerlifting demonstrations in churches and prisons, and passes on the cookery skills he learnt in prison to young people at risk of exclusion from school.

'While I'm doing it, they get to hear my story and maybe get a bit of hope. I'm planting seeds – it's great to work with them and tell them what the Lord can do in their lives.'

USE WITH SESSION 36 WAY IN 'SCENE SETTER'

Me, myself and I

What is it that makes you an individual? Here's a chance to take some time to focus on yourself and discover just how individual you are.

1 What three words describe what you look like? (Be positive!)

2 What are you good at that most people around you aren't good at?

3 What's the first food that comes to mind right now?

4 What was the last thing that made you laugh?

5 What three words best describe your personality?

6 What is your least favourite subject at school?

7 What winds you up (annoys you) that wouldn't necessarily annoy others?

8 If you were given £100 million to make the world a better place what would you spend it on?

9 What was your weirdest dream?

10 What was the first piece of homework you can remember getting?

Whether you consider your answers to any of these questions good or bad, stupid or sensible, popular or unpopular, it doesn't matter. These are the types of things that make you who you are. There will never be another person in existence with the same looks, likes, personality, annoyances, ideas, dreams and memories as you.

That makes you an individual... That makes you special.

37

Bible: Luke 15:11–32

WHATEVER I'VE DONE?

THE AIM: To realise that we can all receive God's undeserved forgiveness

The aim unpacked

In this session, we explore the well-known story of the prodigal son. Although the focus is on the lost son returning to the father, it is vital that we take note of the reaction of the older son. He is shocked to see that his brother would be welcomed in such a way! Whatever we have done and whoever we are, we can all receive God's forgiveness.

WAY IN

theGRID MAGAZINE

WHAT: discussion
WHY: to consider who might be 'deserving'
WITH: magazine pages 235 and 236

1 Hand out copies of magazine pages 235 and 236 and invite the young people to read through the introduction to the 'Millionaire' activity.

2 Divide the young people into threes. Instruct them that they have to discuss and agree how they will distribute the money between the characters listed. They don't have to give all the money to one person or give something to everyone.

3 Get everyone back together and find out how the groups decided to share out the money. Were there any disagreements? How did they decide who was the most deserving? Did anyone think that the money would help someone change their ways?

4 Talk about how we all are undeserving of what God wants to give us, but God gives it anyway. Explain that the parable from the Bible that we're looking at today will help us explore this idea.

SCENE SETTER

WHAT: discussion
WHY: to see whether we can make ourselves 'deserving'
WITH: table, chairs

1 Hold a mock job interview or reality TV show audition (such as on *The X Factor*). Ask three leaders, or choose volunteers from the group, to be the judging panel who will decide which people deserve to get the job or opportunity of a lifetime. Set the scene by asking the 'judges' to sit on chairs behind a table.

2 Invite the rest of the young people to come up in turn, stand in front of the judging panel and explain why they think they deserve to get the job or to win the audition. You could either encourage them to be truthful and think about their own lives and characteristics, or you could allow them to come up with stories that they think would make them more deserving.

3 Ask the judges on the panel to decide quickly 'Yes' or 'No', but don't make too big a deal of this; the emphasis should be on the stories that the interviewees come up with.

4 Bring the group back together. Discuss what type of things make people deserve to win. If appropriate, ask, 'Can we make ourselves deserving of God's forgiveness?'

THEMED GAME

WHAT: game
WHY: to think about how we judge people
WITH: sticky notes

1 Write names of famous people on the sticky notes – for example, Adele, Hitler, Simon Cowell, The Queen, Jamie Oliver. (You could add names that are more relevant to your group, such as local celebrities or community figures, but choose names that will provoke a response in the young people.) Make enough for your group to have one each.

2 Stick a sticky note to each young person's forehead without them seeing what is on it. Invite them to go around the rest of the group, to ask questions to each of the other young people (one per person) and then to guess whose name is on their sticky note.

3 If appropriate, discuss which of the people you would least, and most, like to be stuck in a lift with and why.

BIBLE EXPERIENCE 37

LEVEL 1: CONNECT

WHAT: **role play**
WHY: **to realise that we can all receive God's undeserved forgiveness**

1 Read Luke 15:11–32 aloud to the young people, or ask a confident volunteer to read it.

2 In small groups, give the young people ten minutes to create their own modern-day drama or role play based on the passage. If they are struggling, you could suggest these:

- A boy gets heavily into gaming. He spends more and more time playing video games online and as a result his grades at school begin to slip. He pesters his parents for the latest games but when they won't give in, he steals the money to buy the latest console game, which turns out to be pants. Because he stole the money he can't go on a school trip to a theme park. Then he asks to be forgiven... How does this story turn out?
- A young person goes to a rock concert with their friends, despite being told not to. Meanwhile their sibling obeys the parents and stays at home. When the other child returns they say they are sorry and are taken out for a meal at Pizza Hut... How does this turn out? What are the feelings of the child who did what they were told?

3 Invite the groups to present their dramas or role plays to the rest of the young people.

4 After each one, chat through the following questions with the whole group:

- Why did the drama or role play end the way it did?
- Were there any differences between the drama and the Bible parable?
- Did the character deserve to be forgiven?
- What does this say about the way God forgives people?

LEVEL 2: INTERFACE

WHAT: **problem page and discussion**
WHY: **to realise that we can all receive God's undeserved forgiveness**
WITH: **Bibles, reflective music and playback equipment (optional)**

1 Ask the young people to read Luke 15:11–19 on their own.

2 Discuss together how bad the son had been. You may want to introduce these thoughts:

- Asking for his inheritance was as good as saying, 'Dad, I wish you were dead. Give me all my money!'
- The lifestyle he wanted to lead was totally against his father's wishes. Instead of working, he wasted his time and money.
- He ended up looking after pigs. This point would not have been lost on the original listeners of the story – Jews and pigs don't mix!
- Everything the son did would have hurt the father a great deal.

3 Ask the group to think about what advice they might give to the younger son if they were an agony aunt or uncle.

4 Give the young people a few minutes to write their letters. Invite some of them to read their advice to the rest of the group. Discuss together the advice given.

5 In pairs, encourage the young people to read the rest of the story in Luke 15:20–32 and discuss these questions:

- Why did the father react the way he did?
- Did the son deserve forgiveness?
- Do we act like the father or the other son towards our friends?

6 Bring the group together. Ask, 'If the father in the story represents God, what does this parable tell us about him?' Explain that God's love and acceptance of us is exactly like that of the father in the parable. Whatever we have done, he will accept us back with open arms if we return to him.

7 Play some quiet music and give the group some space to think about this.

LEVEL 3: SWITCH ON

WHAT: **Bible study**
WHY: **to realise that we can all receive God's undeserved forgiveness**
WITH: **Bibles (different versions), commentaries, Bible dictionaries**

1 Invite the young people to read Luke 15:11–32 on their own. If your group has heard the story before, it may be helpful to have several different versions of the Bible available, such as *The Word on the Street* by Rob Lacey.

2 Ask the young people to get into pairs and work through one of the following tasks:

- Look up the meaning of the word 'grace'. Discuss different ways to describe what grace is and what it means for us. How would you describe 'grace' to a non-Christian friend?
- Did the religious leaders and the older son have a point? Why should the son be welcomed back, having been so bad, while they had been very good and had done all that was asked of them? What Bible passages could you use to answer this question?
- Take a look at the book of Hosea. (Hosea 1:2,3; 3:1 – 4:3 are good places to start, but the whole book is full of imagery that paints a clear picture of what is going on.) What are the similarities between the story of Israel in Hosea and the son in the parable? How have the people of Israel rejected God? How does God get Hosea to illustrate Israel's rejection? What does God want Israel to do?

3 After a while, encourage each pair to join with another pair and share what they have found out. In particular, ask them if they have understood anything new about the parable today.

4 If you have time, discuss the following questions as a whole group:

- Why should we do what God says if we can simply ask for forgiveness afterwards?
- Is there a limit to God's grace?

RESPOND

MUSICAL

WHAT: **sung worship**
WHY: **to thank God for his undeserved forgiveness**
WITH: **worship songs, CD or MP3 player, playback equipment (optional)**

1 If your group enjoys worshipping through song, have a praise party celebrating Jesus' forgiveness! You could use either of the following songs, which have a thankful theme:

- 'Thank You for Saving Me' by Martin Smith
- 'I'm Accepted, I'm Forgiven' by Rob Hayward

2 Alternatively, explain that the father in the parable was overjoyed at the son's return, so much so that he organised a great big party. Think together about what sort of party the father might organise if this story happened today.

3 Get the young people to discuss in pairs what current 'secular' CDs or music he might play at the party. What words, if any, would they need to change to make the song fit this story?

4 Bring the group together to share their thoughts with one another. If there is time, you could encourage them to rewrite the lyrics of a song. Maybe you could all sing it together?

PRACTICAL

WHAT: **journal or diary**
WHY: **to think about how God's forgiveness impacts our daily lives**

1 Explain to the young people that this week you would like them to keep a journal (or diary) in which they can record their thoughts and struggles each day. Suggest that they start by recording some of these things:

- How has their day been?
- What prayers have they prayed?
- How has God helped them during the day?
- How have they been tempted and what did they do?

2 Remind everyone that, whatever situations they get into, God's grace and acceptance are there and their prayers asking for forgiveness will be heard. Encourage the young people to start filling in their journal for today.

3 Depending on the group, decide whether they will bring the journals back to the next session and share them or whether they will keep them private. Let the young people have a say in this!

CREATIVE

WHAT: **creative prayer**
WHY: **to respond to God's offer of forgiveness**
WITH: **party streamers (different-coloured lengths of paper strips or ribbons), marker pens**

1 Ask the young people to think about the Bible passage they have just been looking at. Which characters in the parable do they relate to? Do they feel like the son who left or the son who stayed? Do they feel more like the father, waiting for friends to see God's love in their lives?

2 Explain that you are all going to pray in response to your feelings in a creative and physical way by using streamers, which relate to the party theme.

3 Hand out at least one strip of paper or ribbon to each young person. Ask them to write on it their response to one of these questions:

- Do you need to ask for God's forgiveness?
- Do you need to ask for God's strength to do what he wants?
- Do you want to thank God for his acceptance?

4 When the streamers have been written on, you could hang them from the ceiling and wander through them, touching them as a physical representation of communicating with God. If you can't hang the streamers up, why not roll them up (not too tight!) and throw them up in the air as you would at a party?

MORE ON THIS THEME:

If you want to do a short series with your group, other sessions that work well with this one are:

35	*Admit one*	*Luke 14:15–24*
36	*SOS*	*Luke 15:1–7*

Bible bit
Luke 15:11–32

The good times can come to an end. Everything may be fine and life may be full of excitement and pleasure, but it could all end... just like that. It did for the son in this story. He had nothing; he had wasted his money and walked out on his family. He didn't deserve to have anything. Would his father ever take him back... whatever he'd done?

MILLIONAIRE

Imagine you are a millionaire. You have decided to give away £10,000 to deserving causes. After putting a small, innocent-looking advert in the local paper, you have received responses from the following people.

How much of the £10,000 will you give to each person?

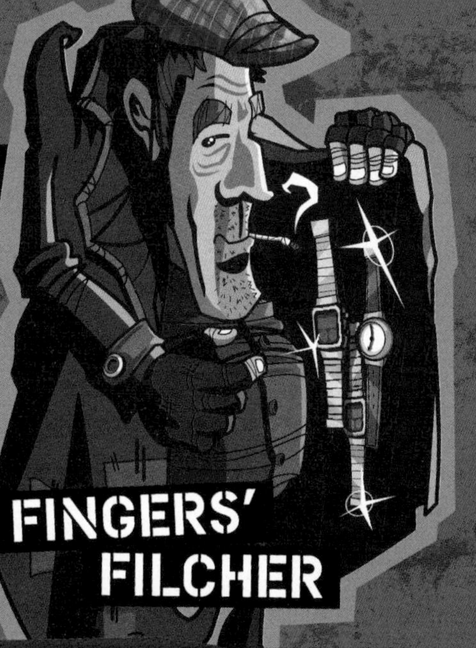

ADAM 'LIGHT FINGERS' FILCHER

Adam makes a living by 'ducking and diving' and 'wheeling and dealing'. He runs a stall on the local market, but his customers have often found that their new DVD player or plasma screen TV looks very much like one recently featured on *Crimewatch*.

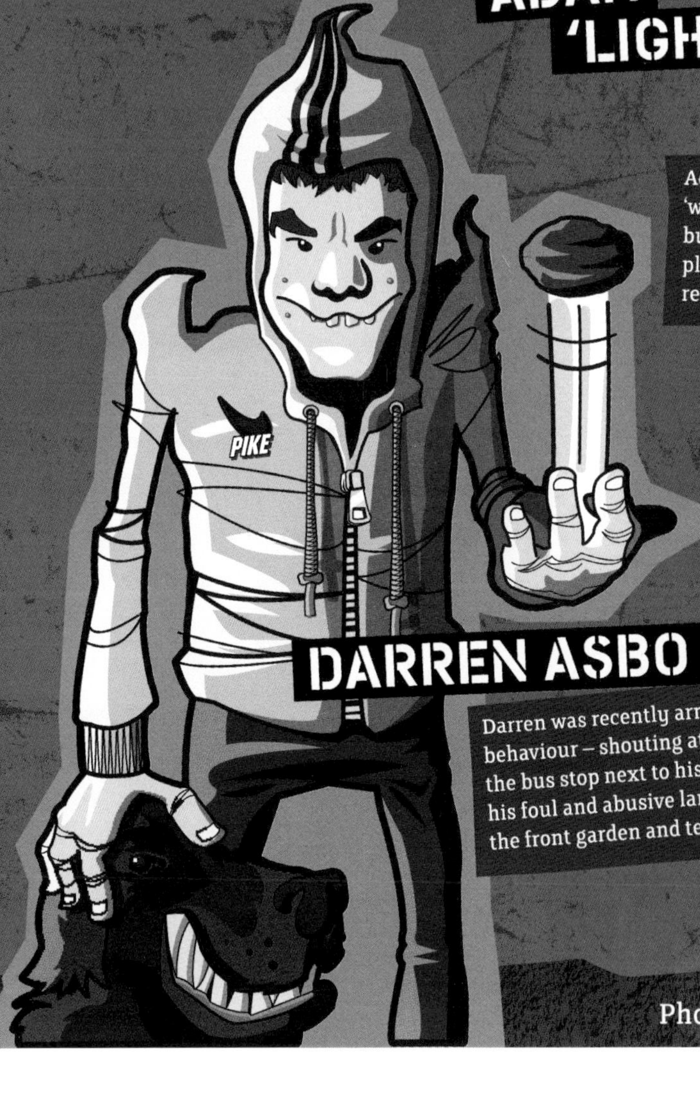

DARREN ASBO

Darren was recently arrested by the police for antisocial behaviour – shouting at the old ladies who were waiting at the bus stop next to his house. When they complained about his foul and abusive language, he let his Dobermann out into the front garden and terrified the poor senior citizens.

NATHAN GOODY

Elizabeth is 84 years old and lives on her own in an old terraced house. She doesn't go out much because she is scared of the young people who hang around at the end of her street. In the winter, she struggles to keep her house warm because she can't afford the gas bills.

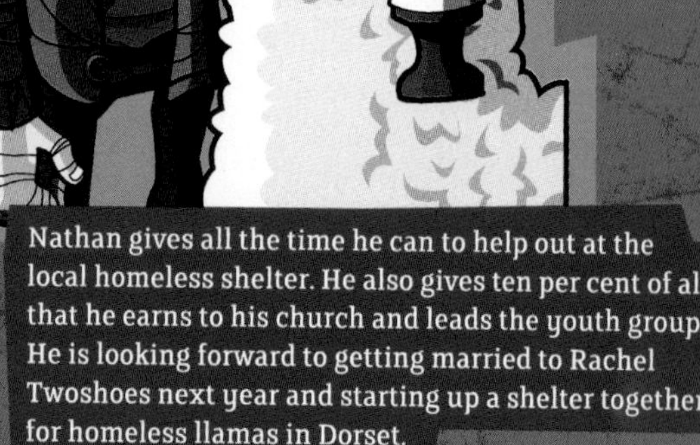

ELIZABETH SENIOR

Nathan gives all the time he can to help out at the local homeless shelter. He also gives ten per cent of all that he earns to his church and leads the youth group. He is looking forward to getting married to Rachel Twoshoes next year and starting up a shelter together for homeless llamas in Dorset.

CLARE BROKE

Clare is a single mum who struggles to make ends meet. She is bringing up two very 'lively' children on her own, and often doesn't have enough money at the end of the month to feed herself and her children. She works part-time in the local supermarket, but the pay isn't very good and she sometimes has to take time off unpaid if her children are ill.

What did you decide?
How did you make your decision?

DARREN: £ ______

ADAM: £ ______

ELIZABETH: £ ______

CLARE: £ ______

NATHAN: £ ______

Bible: John 6:1–15, 22–40

THE BREAD OF LIFE

THE AIM: To discover that Jesus offers us eternal life

The aim unpacked

In this session, the young people will be exploring Jesus' amazing offer of eternal life. They'll discover that after he took compassion on the thousands of people who had gathered to hear him teach by feeding them, he used this miraculous event as a powerful illustration. Bread might keep us alive physically, but only Jesus can keep us alive spiritually.

WAY IN

theGRID MAGAZINE

WHAT: **discussion**
WHY: **to discover what the young people consider is essential to life**
WITH: **magazine page 240**

1 Gather the group together and ask them all to think, without chatting, about what they consider to be essential to life. Ask them, 'What do you think you need in order to live?'

2 Make sure everyone has a copy of page 240 and invite them to look at Jed's and Lana's lists of what they consider to be essential for living.

3 Now encourage them each to write their own list of what they consider to be 'essential to life'.

4 Gather the young people together and discuss what they think about Jed's and Lana's lists. Encourage them also to share what they have written on their own lists.

5 At this point, a leader could share some of their own essentials for living – perhaps dropping in a few clues as to what today's teaching is going to be about.

SCENE SETTER

WHAT: **discussion**
WHY: **to think about what the word 'eternal' means**
WITH: **cut-up copies of page 242 (enough for one per pair)**

1 In small groups, ask the young people to come up with a definition of the word 'eternal'.

2 Gather the young people together and ask each group to share their definition with everyone else. Then, if necessary, read them this definition from the *Encarta World English Dictionary*:

- Eternal: existing through all time, lasting for all time without beginning or end, for example eternal life.

3 Divide the young people into twos and give each pair a cut-up copy of page 242. Ask them to put the ten words in order from the one that they think is likely to last the longest to the one that is most temporary.

4 Ask the young people if they believe in eternal life. If they do, encourage them to share what they think it will be like. Be prepared for some wacky answers here!

5 Explain that this is not an easy subject to grasp but hopefully, by the end of this session, they will have a clearer understanding of the complicated subject of eternal life.

THEMED GAME

WHAT: **Bread Olympics**
WHY: **to introduce the theme of bread**
WITH: **various types of stale bread, prizes**

1 If you can, get hold of some stale bread that would have otherwise gone to waste (perhaps from a local bakery at the end of the day).

2 Divide the young people into teams to represent a few different countries from around the world and explain that you are going to hold the Bread Olympics.

3 Play some of the following Bread Olympic sports. If the weather is good, do this activity outside; otherwise be prepared to have to spend time sweeping up lots of crumbs!

- Bread shot-put – use bread rolls instead of a shot-put and see who can throw the roll the furthest.
- Bread relay race – use baguettes as batons in a relay race.
- Naan discus – use naan or any flat bread instead of a discus and see who can throw it the furthest.
- French-stick javelin – throw French sticks instead of javelins.
- French-stick hurdles – place some French sticks between two chairs and use them as hurdles.

4 Have as much fun as possible and award prizes to the winners.

BIBLE EXPERIENCE

LEVEL 1: CONNECT

WHAT: **sketch and discussion**
WHY: **to discover that Jesus offers us eternal life**
WITH: **Bibles, copies of John 6:25–40, page 243**

1 Divide the young people into groups of about three. Invite them to read John 6:1–15 and to discuss why they think Jesus performed this miracle and what they can learn about him from it.

2 Gather everyone back together and encourage each group to feed back. Then explain to the young people that Jesus' miracles not only helped people, but they also revealed God's power, and he often used them as illustrations to make a spiritual point. (As an example, refer to an illustration you've used with the group recently and explain that Jesus' illustrations were somewhat more impressive than yours!) In this session, they'll discover that after Jesus had fed the people with 'physical' bread, he went on to talk about 'spiritual' bread.

3 Hand out copies of John 6:25–40 and ask a few volunteers to read it aloud. While the passage is being read, suggest that the young people underline any bits they find confusing or strange.

4 Now ask three young people to act out the 'See, come, believe' sketch from page 243.

5 Have a chat about the sketch. Encourage the young people to express their opinions about the different characters and what they were saying. Also discuss the parts of the passage that they underlined earlier.

6 Finish by concluding that Jesus had provided for the people's physical needs by feeding them (in the feeding of the 5,000). He was now saying that he could meet a greater need. See if the group can identify what that greater need was.

LEVEL 2: INTERFACE

WHAT: **quiz**
WHY: **to discover that Jesus offers us eternal life**
WITH: **Bibles, magazine page 241**

1 Give out pens and paper and ask a few volunteers to read John 6:1–15,22–48 to the group. If possible, ask them to read the passage from *The Dramatised Bible*. Encourage the young people to make notes about the passage while it's being read.

2 Now give out copies of page 241 and ask the young people to work in pairs to do the quiz. (They can use the Bible passage to help them.)

3 Gather everyone back together and go through the answers. They are: 1 life; 2 Jesus; 3 manna; 4 Moses; 5 hungry or thirsty; 6 the Jews; 7 Joseph's; 8 God; 9 eternal life.

Draw their attention to the question at the bottom of the quiz.

4 You may feel it is appropriate to talk about whether the young people will accept or reject Jesus at this point in their lives, or that it is appropriate to just give them some time to reflect and think. Finish by praying together.

LEVEL 3: SWITCH ON

WHAT: **Bible study**
WHY: **to discover that Jesus offers us eternal life**
WITH: **Bibles**

1 In small groups, ask the young people to make a list of things people can believe in. Be purposely vague when you pose the question!

2 Then ask them to discuss the following:

- If you believe in something, how does it affect your actions?

Use these examples to get them started:

- 'I believe the Earth revolves around the sun, therefore I...'
- 'I believe we should look after our environment, therefore I...'

3 Ask each group to read John 6:1–15,22–48 and chat about these questions:

- What did Jesus provide for the people?
- What does Jesus offer the people?
- What must we do to receive eternal life?

4 Chat all together about Jesus' offer of eternal life. Be available to help anyone who is grappling with the subject.

5 Encourage them to think (in silence) about this statement: 'I believe Jesus was sent from God to give me the bread of life, therefore I...' Say that this can be confusing and, as it was for the Jews, it can be hard to believe. But when we accept God's calling, we have the promise of eternal life.

6 Explain that a relationship with God isn't just for eternity – it starts now! We experience the life God has planned for his people in part now, and we'll experience it fully later. Jesus doesn't just provide us with what we need for eternal life; he provides for us in this life too. Christians often refer to this as the 'now and not yet'. Some things we have now; some things we have to wait for. Ask the group to chat about what they experience 'now' and what they are still waiting for.

7 Conclude by emphasising that we all have to decide whether or not to accept Jesus' invitation of eternal life.

RESPOND

MUSICAL

WHAT: **reflective worship**
WHY: **to respond to the fact that Jesus provides for us eternally**
WITH: **reflective music or words to worship song and accompaniment, playback equipment, large loaf of bread**

1 Place the loaf of bread in the centre of the room.

2 Play the reflective music and encourage the young people to think about today's teaching. Say that Jesus calls us to him, and if we respond we have the promise of eternal life – we will live with God today, tomorrow and for ever.

3 Encourage the young people to respond to what they have heard by breaking off a piece from the loaf of bread, eating it and saying thank you to Jesus for the gift of eternal life. (Be aware of allergies and provide a gluten-free alternative if necessary.)

4 Sing a worship song together that your group knows that fits in with today's theme. Alternatively, sit and listen to the reflective music while focusing on the bread in the centre of the room.

5 You could finish with the following prayer: 'Lord, you have given us the promise of eternal life. Help us to overcome our doubts and fears. May we see Jesus, and know that he is the Way, the Truth and the Life. Amen.'

6 You may like to listen to or sing one or more of the following songs:

- 'Eat This Bread' by Jacques Berthier
- 'I Am the Bread of Life' by Suzanne Toolan
- 'I Long for You, O Lord' by Steve and Vikki Cook
- 'Who Could Offer Us Abundant Life?' by Evan Rogers

PRACTICAL

WHAT: **saying grace**
WHY: **to thank Jesus for providing for our needs eternally**
WITH: **Bible**

1 Explain that saying grace before meals is something that has fallen out of practice in many homes, especially as more and more of us eat meals at different times to the rest of our families.

2 Recap what we have learned in this session about Jesus providing for all our needs eternally. It is therefore right that we should thank him as often as we can. One way is to remember to say thank you before every meal, such as by saying grace.

3 Give out pens and paper and encourage each young person to write a short prayer that they can say before meals, in which they thank Jesus for providing both the physical food that they are about to eat and the spiritual 'food' that he also provides. The prayer needs to be short and memorable.

4 Ask everyone to learn their prayer and to say it before every meal. Explain that this is one way to be focused on Jesus as often as possible. Remind the group that, when they say the prayer, they don't have to close their eyes and say it out loud, unless they want to.

CREATIVE

WHAT: **spiritual meal menus**
WHY: **to receive some of the spiritual food that Jesus offers**

1 Remind the young people that Jesus used a food analogy to tell his followers about how he can provide for them eternally. Say that they will similarly use a 'food' analogy in their creative worship.

2 Hand out paper and pens. Invite the young people, either on their own or in pairs, to devise their own 'spiritual meal'. For example, the starter could be a simple prayer, the main course could be some Bible reading, and dessert could be listening to a piece of Christian music. The object of the 'spiritual meal' is to promote belief and trust in Jesus, as shown in today's passage.

3 Ask them to be specific and write out any prayers and make a note of the Bible passages and the songs they would use. Give them the freedom to put what they like in the menus. It should provide a way to receive some of the 'spiritual food' that Jesus offers.

4 To close, invite some volunteers to share their menus. Encourage the others to participate in the activities on each menu, if there's time.

MORE ON THIS THEME:

If you want to do a short series with your group, other sessions that work well with this one are:

39 *The good shepherd* *John 10:1–15*

40 *The crying Saviour* *John 11:1–44*

ESSENTIAL TO LIFE

What do you think you need in order to live?

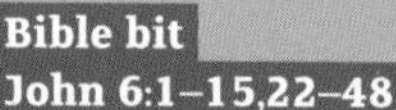

Bible bit
John 6:1–15,22–48

Jesus feeding thousands ofpeople because they were hungry was a very nice thing to do. And it was an amazing miracle. But he didn't stop there. He used it as an illustration to speak about something even more important than food! (I bet your youth leader has never done such an impressive illustration.)

Jesus goes on to refer to himself as the 'Bread of Life'. Food, of which bread is one of the most basic types, is essential for life. Jesus is essential if we want to have eternal life. Bread might keep us alive physically, but only Jesus can keep us alive spiritually.

Jesus offers us eternal life – are you going to accept his invitation?

JED'S LIST

1. OXYGEN
2. WATER
3. FOOD
4. SHELTER
5. PEOPLE TO LEARN FROM

LANA'S LIST

1. MUSIC
2. BOOKS
3. FRIENDS
4. FAMILY
5. CHOCOLATE!

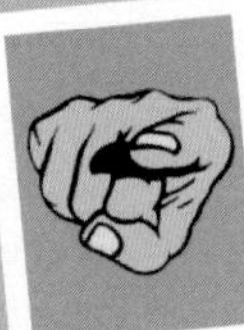

MY LIST

1.
2.
3.
4.
5.

BIBLE QUIZ

Read John 6:1–15, 25–48, and then fill in the blanks.

1 — Jesus is the bread of... ?

_ _ _ _

2 — Who gives eternal life?

_ _ _ _ _

3 — What did the ancestors of the Jews eat in the desert?

_ _ _ _ _

4 — Who led the people out of Egypt?

_ _ _ _ _

5 — If we believe in Jesus we will not be... ?

_ _ _ _ _ _ OR

_ _ _ _ _ _ _

6 — Who complained?

_ _ _   _ _ _ _

7 — Whose son did they say Jesus was?

_ _ _ _ _ _ ' _

8 — Who sent Jesus?

_ _ _

9 — What will you get if you believe in Jesus?

_ _ _ _ _ _ _ _   _ _ _ _

Will you accept Jesus' offer of the gift of eternal life?

RESOURCE PAGE

USE WITH SESSION 38 WAY IN 'SCENE SETTER'

The Pyramids	Flu
Microsoft Windows	*theGRID*
Rihanna	Wayne Rooney
Cheese	Radio One's Breakfast Show
Buckingham Palace	Bart Simpson

USE WITH SESSION 38 BIBLE EXPERIENCE 'LEVEL 1 CONNECT'

'See, come, believe'

Characters:
Mr Smart-Speak: intellectual-looking RE teacher
Jasmin: talkative, streetwise 13-year-old
Simon: questioning, shy 13-year-old (quite likes Jasmin!)
Scene: classroom

Mr Smart-Speak: So you see, class, in this passage Jesus says he is the bread that gives life. *(Jasmin sniggers.)*
Jasmin: *(mumbling under her breath)* Yeah, right, how can a man be bread that gives life? Stupid idea if ever I heard one. Even McDonald's don't claim that. And what if you have a wheat allergy? Bread's no good then.
Mr Smart-Speak: *(authoritatively)* No, he is using something called an 'analogy'. For example, you need bread to be able to live – *(almost irritated but not quite)* or other food if you have a gluten intolerance – so Jesus is saying that just as bread is essential for life, he is essential for eternal life.
(Simon puts his hand up to ask a question.)
Simon: Excuse me, Sir, but this is really complicated. Am I right in thinking that you're saying that this Jesus, who we can't actually see, says that if we come to him and believe in him, we'll have life for ever?
(Jasmin giggles and mimics Simon, who looks affronted.)
Mr Smart-Speak: Exactly, Simon, not easy to understand, I appreciate. In fact, down through history, just like the Jews in this story, people have had difficulty in getting their heads round it... *(gets ready to launch into a history lesson)*
Jasmin: *(interrupting)* So, Sir, you're saying that this Jesus bloke, who did loads of miracles and fed 5,000 people, can also help us have eternal life, just like he gave those people bread? Cool dude! That's what I say! I fancy having eternal life, with Coke and fries – in fact, supersize! *(starts singing 'I'm Gonna Live Forever' from* Fame*)*.
Simon: *(turning to Jasmin)* I can't believe it's that simple!
Jasmin: Well, that's what Sir read earlier, that if we come to this Jesus, say we're sorry, try to do better and believe in him, he's gonna be with us now and for ever.
(At this point, Jasmin and Simon strike up their own conversation on this subject while Mr Smart-Speak strives to get the class in order.)
Mr Smart-Speak: *(bell rings)* Right, class, gather up your books and we'll look at this some more tomorrow, unless of course you want to read it again to see for yourself? You'll find it all in John 6:25–40.

39

Bible: John 10:1–15

THE GOOD SHEPHERD

THE AIM: To realise that Jesus offers us the best

The aim unpacked

It's hard for us today to fully understand the metaphor of sheep and shepherds. For the original audience, this image would have had extra significance as it was a metaphor often used in the Old Testament to symbolise God and his people. What does come through strongly is the complete dedication of the shepherd (and so of Jesus), and his commitment to the welfare of the sheep.

WAY IN

theGRID MAGAZINE

WHAT: **discussion**
WHY: **to think about being safe**
WITH: **magazine page 247**

1 Divide the young people into twos or threes and make sure everyone has a copy of magazine page 247 and invite them to do the activity entitled, 'My precious'.

2 Gather the group together and find out how the young people would keep the various items safe.

3 Ask the young people to chat about any other precious or important items that people may have and how they might go about keeping them safe.

4 Then, ask them if any of the forms of protection truly guarantee the items' safety. Most will reduce the likelihood of damage or theft, but very few, if any, guarantee anything.

5 Explain that in this session, they'll be thinking about the safe-keeping of something far more important than material goods. They are going to consider how they can keep themselves safe.

SCENE SETTER

WHAT: **top ten**
WHY: **to think about being safe**

1 Say these two statements: 'Most accidents happen at home'; 'Flying is the safest form of travel'. Ask the group to remember these.

2 In pairs, ask the young people to create a list of the ten safest places in the world, and to come up with reasons for their choice.

3 Bring the group together and create a group top ten by collecting all the ideas and asking the young people to vote on them. Discuss why each of the places listed is safe and what makes it safe.

4 Ask, what makes you feel safe as an individual? What makes you feel unsafe?

5 Return to the two the statements you made at the beginning, and ask how many of the group feel safe at home. Then ask why so many people are afraid of flying, if flying is the safest form of travel. (Be sensitive here as there may be members who aren't feeling safe at the moment.)

6 Finish by saying that in today's session you'll be looking at feeling safe and secure.

THEMED GAME

WHAT: **game**
WHY: **to think about being kept safe**
WITH: **small sponge balls, targets (could be traditional bullseye targets or something like pictures of sheep)**

1 To play this game, you will need a large space that is free from breakable items.

2 Set up the targets. The targets can be any shape and made of any (safe) material. Make sure you have more targets than the number of defenders.

3 Divide the young people into two groups: defenders and attackers. There should be one defender for every five or six attackers. Explain that the attackers should try to hit the targets with soft balls. The defenders will be trying to stop the balls hitting the targets by knocking them off course with their hands.

4 Play the game. If you have time, swap the attackers and defenders around so that everyone has a go at both.

5 After a few minutes, gather the group together and chat about how hard or easy it was to stop the balls hitting the targets. Explain that today, they are going to be thinking about how and why Jesus keeps us safe.

BIBLE EXPERIENCE

LEVEL 1: CONNECT

WHAT: **drama and discussion**
WHY: **to realise that Jesus offers us the best**
WITH: **magazine page 248, Bibles**

1 Divide the young people into small groups and ask each group to prepare a short sketch based around John 10:1–6.

2 Once they've had time to prepare their sketches, gather the young people back together and invite each group to perform theirs.

3 Then, in pairs, ask the young people to read John 10:7–15 and chat about what they think it means. Encourage each pair to come up with a short summary that they can feed back to the group.

4 Once everyone has had an opportunity to share their summary, ask the young people to look at page 248. In pairs, get them to work through the article entitled 'Thief or shepherd?'

5 Bring the group together and encourage the young people to share any thoughts they may have, emphasising that Jesus is a shepherd, not a thief. Explain that although many people think following Jesus takes the fun out of life, that's just not true! Jesus didn't come to steal from us – he's not a thief. He came to give us life, to make life better, to love and to enable us to live more fulfilled lives, full of purpose and hope. Jesus is like a shepherd, not a thief. He wants what is best for us; he's not out to spoil our fun.

LEVEL 2: INTERFACE

WHAT: **drawing and discussion**
WHY: **to realise that Jesus offers us the best**
WITH: **flip chart or whiteboard, Bibles**

1 Give everyone a Bible, a sheet of paper and some felt-tip pens or coloured pencils. Encourage them to find some space on their own to read John 10:1–15. Then ask them to draw a picture that, to them, illustrates what Jesus is saying in the passage.

2 After about ten minutes, gather the group together and invite volunteers, in turn, to show and explain their picture to everyone.

3 Discuss together what they can learn from this passage. Then encourage the young people, all together, to make a list of words that describe a thief, and a list of words that describe a shepherd. Write them down on the flip chart or whiteboard.

4 Divide the young people into twos and ask each pair to write a sentence that starts, 'Jesus is like a shepherd because...'

5 Bring the young people together and ask them to read out their sentences. Then read verse 10 to your group and spend some time discussing how Jesus gives us life, and gives it to us in all its fullness.

LEVEL 3: SWITCH ON

WHAT: **Bible study**
WHY: **to realise that Jesus offers us the best**
WITH: **Bibles, concordances, study Bibles, access to the internet**

1 In pairs, ask the young people to read John 10:1–15 and chat about what they think it means. Ask them to imagine how they would explain it to an 8-year-old child.

2 Gather together and invite feedback. As the discussion draws to a close, point out the summary in John 10:27,28.

3 Jesus says that no one will be lost. Yet we know that many Christians have suffered for their beliefs, and some still do. So how do Jesus' promises measure up with the experiences of so many Christians?

4 Chat about this for a while, then, in pairs, invite the young people to use concordances or the internet to look up words about safety in the book of Psalms. Alternatively, suggest they look at Psalms 3, 18, 28, 38, 86, 91 and 116. Possible words include: fortress, protector, rock, shield and shepherd.

5 After a while, invite feedback. Emphasise that nearly all the psalms that express confidence in God who loves and cares for us so deeply remind us that he offers us the best – in terms of protection, safety and defence, as well as provision and love. The writer is or has been in serious danger – things have gone horribly wrong, enemies are threatening and death is only minutes away.

6 Explain that God does not offer freedom from pain or suffering. He simply promises to be with us throughout and assures us of his ultimate love. Ask the group if they can think of a reason why. One possible suggestion is that God wants us to love and follow him for who he is rather than for what he can do for us. If he promised a life without problems, probably more people would be Christians, but for the wrong reasons. God would be no more than an insurance policy.

RESPOND

MUSICAL

WHAT: meditation
WHY: to reflect on Jesus' love and care
WITH: meditation from page 249, reflective music, playback equipment

1 Before the session, read through the meditation on page 249 to familiarise yourself with it.

2 Explain to the young people that you want them to use their imagination as you read a meditation. Ask them either to sit comfortably or, if there is room, to lie on the floor with their eyes closed.

3 Play the music and start to read the meditation, pausing between each sentence.

4 Afterwards, say a simple prayer, such as, 'Thank you, Lord, that you are our good Shepherd. You know each of us and promise to watch over us if we come to you. As we go through this week, help us to rest in the knowledge of your love and protection. Amen.'

5 You may also like to sing or listen to one of these songs:

- 'The Lord's My Shepherd' by Iona
- 'Faithful One' by Brian Doerksen
- 'Never Been Unloved' by Michael W Smith
- 'I Got It', Mary Mary from *Thankful*
- 'One Thing', 'I Turn to You', Mel C from *Northern Star*

PRACTICAL

WHAT: personal psalms
WHY: to explore how 'the best' offered by Jesus impacts our lives
WITH: notebooks

1 Ask each young person to get into a pair with someone they feel comfortable talking to about the things that make them worry, fear or panic. Give them a few minutes to talk to their partner about these things.

2 Invite any groups to share what they have discussed if they want to, but don't force anyone. Perhaps you could suggest some general things, like school, health, exams.

3 Read a passage from a psalm that deals with trust in God's love and care but also mentions the threats and troubles that they are facing (use Psalm 91). Explain that the psalmists wrote down their worries as a prayer and also wrote of how God answered them.

4 Give out the notebooks and encourage the pairs to write down the concerns they talked about as a way of offering them to God. Explain that when God answers them they can write that down too, and how they feel.

5 Encourage them to write in the notebook whenever they have particular worries, so that in the end they will have their own book of psalms.

6 Try to follow this up in the weeks to come by reminding the group about their prayer/psalm books.

CREATIVE

WHAT: making a bookmark
WHY: to reflect on the power of God
WITH: Bibles, pieces of card (approximately 20 cm by 4 cm)

1 Ask a volunteer to read Psalm 23 to the group.

2 Encourage the young people to say short prayers thanking Jesus that he cares for and looks after us like a shepherd looks after his sheep. They can pray out loud or in silence.

3 Give everyone a piece of card. Ask them to draw a shepherd's crook on one side and to decorate it as they wish, using the available art materials. Also get them to write 'Jesus is the good Shepherd' somewhere on the same side.

4 Encourage them to write out the words of Psalm 23 on the other side and decorate it appropriately.

5 Suggest they put their bookmark in a book they read a lot and tell them that it will be a visual reminder that Jesus is their Shepherd, who loves them and is always with them.

MORE ON THIS THEME:

If you want to do a short series with your group, other sessions that work well with this one are:

38	*The bread of life*	*John 6:1–15,22–48*
40	*The crying Saviour*	*John 11:1–44*

MY PRECIOUS

39

This page contains images of items that our society thinks are precious. Can you link all the precious items to ways in which you might keep them safe? There may be more than one way to protect some of the items.

- HIDE IT
- IMMOBILISER
- BANK
- SOCK
- CASE
- GARAGE
- INSURANCE
- FILING CABINET
- KEEP IT WITH YOU AT ALL TIMES
- CUPBOARD
- ALARM
- BURY IT
- CARDBOARD BOX
- DAMP BASEMENT
- SAFE

Bible bit
John 10:1–15

Many people think that following Jesus takes the fun out of life. But that's not true! Jesus didn't come to steal from us – he is not a thief. He came to give us life, to make life better, to look after us and to enable us to live more fulfilled lives, full of purpose and hope. Jesus is like a shepherd, not a thief. He wants what is best for you; he's not out to spoil your fun!

THIEF OR SHEPHERD?

PSALM 23

The Lord is my shepherd;
I have everything I need.
He lets me rest in green pastures.
He leads me to calm water.
He gives me new strength.
He leads me on paths that are right
for the good of his name.
Even if I walk through a very dark valley,
I will not be afraid,
because you are with me.
Your rod and your staff comfort me.
You prepare a meal for me
in front of my enemies.
You pour oil on my head;
you fill my cup to overflowing.
Surely your goodness and love will be with me all my life,
and I will live in the house of the Lord for ever.

Now think of some of the things Jesus says to us. Do you think he's out to spoil our fun or do you think he wants what's best for us?

In a moment, we'll be thinking about whether Jesus is like a thief or a shepherd. But before we do that, let's think about our parents or guardians. For each statement, mark on the scale at the appropriate place.

Out to spoil my fun — 1 2 3 4 5 6 7 8 9 10 — Wanting what's best for me

If you eat that chocolate, you won't be able to eat your dinner.

Out to spoil my fun — 1 2 3 4 5 6 7 8 9 10 — Wanting what's best for me

Love your enemies. Pray for those who hurt you. (Matthew 5:44)

Out to spoil my fun — 1 2 3 4 5 6 7 8 9 10 — Wanting what's best for me

Make sure you're home by 9pm.

Out to spoil my fun — 1 2 3 4 5 6 7 8 9 10 — Wanting what's best for me

Don't take revenge. (Matthew 5:39)

Out to spoil my fun — 1 2 3 4 5 6 7 8 9 10 — Wanting what's best for me

I want you to finish your homework before you watch television.

Out to spoil my fun — 1 2 3 4 5 6 7 8 9 10 — Wanting what's best for me

Don't have lustful thoughts. (Matthew 5:28)

Out to spoil my fun — 1 2 3 4 5 6 7 8 9 10 — Wanting what's best for me

Do you really want to spend your money on that?

Out to spoil my fun — 1 2 3 4 5 6 7 8 9 10 — Wanting what's best for me

Focus on storing up treasures in heaven, not material possessions. (Matthew 6:19–21)

USE WITH SESSION 39 RESPOND 'MUSICAL'

Meditation

Close your eyes.

I want you to imagine that you're out in the open somewhere, perhaps on a hillside or a moor.

The wind is gently blowing across your face and a light drizzle is falling. It's quite lonely, and there is no sound other than the wind. You see someone approaching you. He calls you by your name. He knows you. As he gets closer, you see the smiling face of Jesus. What does he look like? He asks you to follow him. His voice is kind and reassuring, so you do as he asks.

You follow him along a well-worn path, and you start to feel anxious. Ahead of you, you can see the things that trouble you. Perhaps they are guilty feelings about something. They seem to be forming a barrier in front of you like a thorny hedge. Try to picture what they are. You hesitate, but Jesus turns to you.

'It's OK,' he says. 'I'm walking ahead of you. Follow me. I'll deal with them.'

You follow, and you see that these things are not blocking your way any more. They are still there, but they are no longer a threat to you. You continue to follow Jesus. He leads you to a house that has no door; just an opening.

'Come in,' he says. 'You'll be safe. I will be the door to your home. You can come in and go out as you please, but I will always be here with you if you want.'

Will you go in or not? It's up to you. Jesus won't force you. He smiles to you. What do you want to say to him? He wants to listen.

[Pause for about 30 seconds and then invite the group to open their eyes in their own time.]

40

Bible: John 11:1–44

THE CRYING SAVIOUR

THE AIM: To understand Jesus' power at work in his compassion for humanity

The aim unpacked

In this session, your group will see both Jesus' human side and his divine side. On the human side, they'll see him crying; on the divine side, they will see him bring his friend Lazarus back from the dead. They'll be thinking about how compassionate Jesus is. God is not distant; he shares in the suffering of his people. He is also a powerful God.

WAY IN

theGRID MAGAZINE

WHAT: **discussion**
WHY: **to think about friends being with us in good and bad times**
WITH: **magazine page 253**

1 Talk about best mates. Ask who in the group has had the same best mate for more than a week/a month/six months/a year/five years/all their life. What's so good about their best mate?

2 Give everyone a copy of the 'Top ten tips for best mates' on page 253. Ask whether anyone has ever experienced any of the 'don'ts'. What happened? What about the 'dos'? How did it make them feel?

3 Ask everyone to answer this question: If you had to choose just one 'top tip', which would it be? (It could be something from the list or a different one.)

4 Tell the group that Jesus had plenty of close friends while he was on earth, and that in this session, they're going to be looking at a story concerning some of them.

SCENE SETTER

WHAT: **shoe tower**
WHY: **to think about stepping into someone else's shoes**
WITH: **shoes, prize, sheets of card**

1 Divide the young people into teams and ask everyone to take their shoes off. Give them a couple of minutes to build the tallest shoe tower they can.

2 Award a small prize to the winning team, then chat about the meaning of 'stepping into someone else's shoes'.

3 Give everyone a sheet of card. Ask them to draw around their shoe and cut it out.

4 Divide them into pairs and get them to swap shoe shapes. Encourage them to talk about their lives so the other person gets an idea of what it's like to be them. They can talk about their families, daily routines, likes and dislikes. The person listening should make notes on the shoe shape.

5 Gather the group together. Ask if anyone has ever really stepped into someone else's shoes, perhaps as an understudy in a play or a substitute in a sports team. Has anyone ever tried to imagine what it's like to face someone else's difficult situation?

6 Explain that Jesus really cared about the people around him and knows what it's like to 'walk in our shoes'.

THEMED GAME

WHAT: **messy game**
WHY: **to get across the idea of friends being in bad times**
WITH: **page 255, custard pies (squirty cream on a paper plate) or buckets of gunge (cold, runny porridge dyed green), waterproofs, floor protection**

1 Say that you're going to do a quiz that the young people should all try really hard to win, because the loser faces a horrible punishment. (Don't explain what yet!)

2 Read the questions from page 255 and ask them to write down their answers. Then ask them to swap answer sheets to mark them as you read out the answers.

3 When the loser is revealed, bring them to the front and reveal the punishment – a pie in the face or to have gunge poured over them. (Don't forget the floor protection!)

4 Before you carry out the punishment, say that the victim is allowed to ask someone to go through it with them. Emphasise that they cannot force someone – the person has to be willing. Carry it out on both of them. (Give them something to protect their clothes first!)

5 Afterwards, find out how it felt for the first person to know someone else was going through the same thing as them. Did it help? How?

BIBLE EXPERIENCE

LEVEL 1: CONNECT

WHAT: story
WHY: to understand Jesus' power at work in his compassion for humanity
WITH: selection of pictures of Jesus, magazine page 254, large sheets of paper

1 In advance, gather together several pictures of Jesus. Also write the following on large sheets of paper:

- Why doesn't God do anything about the suffering in the world?
- Where is God when it hurts?
- Does God care about the little things that get me down when there are such terrible things going on elsewhere?
- If Jesus can make people come back to life, why doesn't he do it today?
- What makes Jesus weep now?

Stick the questions up around the room before the young people arrive.

2 Spread out the pictures of Jesus and ask everyone to choose the picture they think is most like their idea of Jesus. Encourage them to share with the rest of the group why they chose the picture they did.

3 Ask a few young people to read the story from page 254 to the group. Encourage them to take a close look at the picture of Jesus. What do they think of it? How does it compare to the one they chose earlier?

4 Say that some people struggle to think of Jesus as having human feelings, but here they see him feeling completely gutted. One of the reasons he chose to become a human was so that he could experience life as we do, even when it's painful.

5 Invite the group to go around and read the questions you stuck around the room earlier. Ask them to stand next to one they find difficult to answer. Then spend some time discussing the questions together.

6 Conclude this section in an appropriate way. How you do this will depend on what issues are raised as you chat about the questions. However you do it, make sure that you communicate that Jesus is involved in our pain, that he feels our pain and that he is always at work.

LEVEL 2: INTERFACE

WHAT: Bible study
WHY: to understand Jesus' power at work in his compassion for humanity
WITH: Bibles

1 Read John 11:1–44 as a dramatic reading with people taking the parts of the narrator, Jesus, the messenger, the followers, Thomas, Martha, Mary and Lazarus.

2 Divide the young people into small groups and challenge them to find (and make a note of) as many of the following in the passage as possible:

- sights (for example, seeing the mourners gathered around the house)
- sounds (for example, the stone being rolled back)
- smells (for example, the damp air coming from the grave)
- textures (for example, the feel of the grave clothes)
- emotions (for example, Martha's sadness)

3 Come back together as one group and ask the young people to feed back their ideas.

4 Discuss Jesus' emotions in this passage. In small groups, chat about these questions:

- Why do you think Jesus cried?
- Do you find it uncomfortable that the Son of God cried like this? Why (not)?
- What would make you cry in public?
- What do you think makes Jesus cry today?

5 Finish by reminding the group that here Jesus used his power because of his compassion. They'll be exploring this a little more during the *Respond* section.

LEVEL 3: SWITCH ON

WHAT: drama
WHY: to understand Jesus' power at work in his compassion for humanity
WITH: Bibles, teardrop-shaped pieces of paper, digital camera and laptop (optional)

1 Divide the young people into groups of between two and six. Give each group a part of John 11:1–44 to act out. Allocate the parts as follows: 1–16; 17–27; 28–34; 35; 36–44. (Give verse 35 to your most imaginative group!) Encourage them to perform their passage as imaginatively as possible, for example as a TV show, a mime, an acted narration, a rap, using only sound effects, or as a dance.

2 Invite the young people to perform their sketches to the whole group, in chronological order, so that everyone sees the whole story. During the performances, take photos of each scene to show and discuss later. Alternatively, you could ask the groups to take up 'freeze' positions of their scene to remind everyone what happened in that part of the story.

3 Then ask the following questions:

- Which part of the story makes you feel most uncomfortable?
- What do you learn about Jesus from each part of the story?
- What, if anything, surprises you?

4 Now focus on the scene of Jesus weeping. Ask, 'Why do you think Jesus was crying?' (You could explain that the Greek word for Jesus' feelings used earlier in verse 33 usually means 'very angry'.) Ask everyone to write on their teardrop-shaped piece of paper why they think Jesus might have cried. Ask everyone to share what they have written.

5 Conclude by summarising what we can learn about Jesus from this story before considering how all this should affect how we approach him.

RESPOND

MUSICAL

WHAT: **newspaper cuttings**
WHY: **to thank God for his involvement in our suffering**
WITH: **newspapers, sticky tack or sticky tape, flip chart (optional), appropriate piece of music, playback equipment**

1 Bring the group together and explain that Jesus used his power because he cared for Lazarus. He felt compassion for him, his family and his friends and then raised him from the dead. Say that together you are going to ask for God's help in the world.

2 Share the newspapers among the young people and ask them to find stories of people for whom they believe Jesus would have compassion, and cut them out.

3 Play the piece of music. While it plays, invite each of the young people in turn to take one of the newspaper cuttings and stick it to the wall or flip chart. The group should respond after each one by saying together, 'Jesus cries.'

4 Once all the cuttings are displayed, ask a leader or young person to lead the following prayer: 'Dear Lord, as you were moved with compassion to help your friend Lazarus, we ask that you will use your power in each of these situations. We thank you that you are with us and that you care for us. Amen.'

5 For this activity, you might like to use a piece of instrumental music, perhaps from a film soundtrack. Alternatively, you could sing or play 'Great is the Darkness' by Noel Richards and Gerald Coates.

PRACTICAL

WHAT: **prayer**
WHY: **to pray for those who are suffering**
WITH: **cards copied from page 256 (add some localised situations on the blank cards), candle**

1 Point out that Jesus chose to be involved in the suffering of those around him. He could have brought Lazarus back to life without going near the grave or the mourners. But he empathised with them and used his power to bring healing.

2 Show the cards to the group. Say that what is written on these cards is painful. There are suffering people and situations in the world. Like Jesus, we have a choice as to whether we involve ourselves in their suffering or not.

3 Ask the young people to sit in a circle. Light a candle in the middle of the circle. Put the cards down near it. Say that if anyone would like to commit themselves, firstly to finding out more about the people and situation, and secondly to praying during the week ahead, they should take that card.

4 Explain that because of Jesus' compassion for Lazarus, he brought him back to life. We can pray to Jesus and ask him to use his power to help humanity.

5 You may also like to mention members of your community, as well as people or situations featured recently in the national news, on some of the blank cards.

CREATIVE

WHAT: **praying with water**
WHY: **praying for those who are suffering**
WITH: **bottle filled with salt water with a small hole in the cap, glass bowl**

1 Shake a few drops of water into the bowl from the bottle and ask whether it reminds the group of anything – perhaps rain or tears. Invite someone to taste it so that the group knows that it's salt water – like tears.

2 Ask the young people to pass the bottle round. As they each hold the bottle, ask them to think of a situation in the world or in their own life that might be making Jesus weep. They can then bring that situation to God and shake a few drops of water into the bowl as a sign that they know God shares in the suffering.

3 Finish by reading one or more of these verses:

- 'You have recorded my troubles. You have kept a list of my tears.' (Psalm 56:8)
- '[The Lord said,] I have heard your prayer and seen your tears, so I will heal you.' (2 Kings 20:5)
- '[God] will wipe away every tear from their eyes.' (Revelation 21:4)

MORE ON THIS THEME:

If you want to do a short series with your group, other sessions that work well with this one are:

38	*The bread of life*	*John 6:1–15,22–48*
39	*The good shepherd*	*John 10:1–15*

TOP 10

TIPS FOR BEST MATES

1 **DO** shut up and listen to what they want to tell you.

2 **DON'T** bad mouth your best mate to someone else.

3 **DO** tell them when their fashion sense goes horribly wrong – but be tactful!

4 **DON'T** criticise their family, even if they do.

5 **DO** be there for them when they're going through a tough patch.

6 **DON'T** listen to gossip about them.

7 **DO** make time to hang out together and just 'be'.

8 **DON'T** think you have to agree with them about everything.

9 **DO** get in the habit of making up after you fall out.

10 **DON'T** be a friend only in the good times.

Bible bit
John 11:1–44

In this passage, we see both Jesus' human and divine sides. On the human side, we see him crying; on the divine side, we see him bring his friend Lazarus back from the dead. We're thinking about how compassionate Jesus is – our God is not distant; he shares in the suffering of his people. He is also a powerful God and can transform terrible situations.

This can be a great encouragement, but it can also be a hard truth to get our heads and hearts around. We all probably know people who have faced difficult situations, or we may have faced them ourselves, where God did not appear to transform the situation. It's at times like these that a great deal of questions can be asked. Never forget, though, that God feels our pain.

JESUS WEPT

'Oh here he comes at last. Late or what? Talks to Martha, talks to Mary. Looks at the grave where his best friend is. I want to shake him, this calm, cool preacher-man. You're too late, teacher! Lazarus is dead! Dead! And you could have saved him and you don't even... He's crying.'

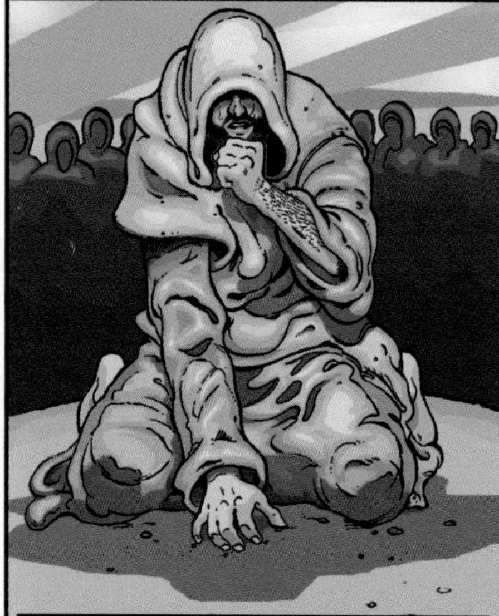

'He's down on his knees, sobbing his eyes out. He's beating the ground with his fists and choking. There's snot running down his face, all mixed up with the tears. He's so wild he's not even noticed. He's just crouching there, his brown tunic soaked in tears, rocking backwards and forwards, hugging himself, racked with great gasping sobs of sadness – and something else. Anger? Fury? He's so torn up it's hard to tell.

'And it's out of this whirlwind of emotion that he tells them to open up the grave, and calls, "Lazarus, come out!"'

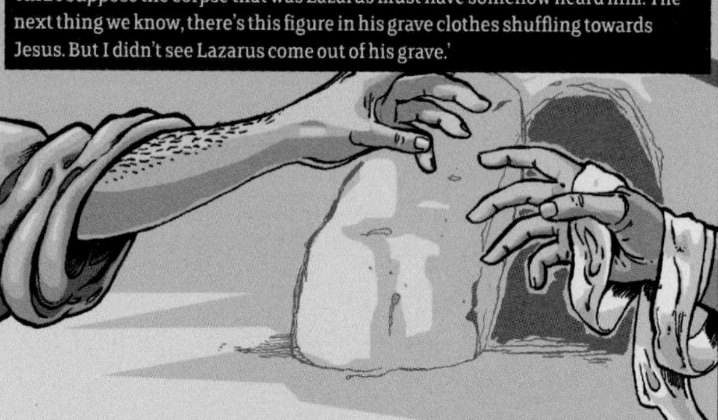

USE WITH SESSION 40 WAY IN 'THEMED GAME'

True or false quiz

1 The heaviest man to ever live was Jon Brower Minnoch and he weighed 100 stone.
(True.)

2 The longest ear hair ever recorded belonged to Mahatma Jaipur and was 7 cm long.
(False – it belonged to Radhakant Bajpai and it was 13.2 cm long.)

3 The tallest man in medical history for whom there is irrefutable evidence is Robert Pershing Wadlow. He was 2.72 metres tall.
(True.)

4 The longest recorded duration for balancing on one foot is 96 hours, by Chris Figgis.
(False – it was 76 hours by Arulanantham Suresh Joachim.)

5 Paul Lynch performed 124 consecutive one-finger push-ups at the Hippodrome, Leicester Square, London, UK on 21 April 1992.
(True.)

6 The world's deepest lake is Lake Baikal, in Siberia, Russia. The deepest point of the lake has a depth of 1,637 metres.
(True.)

7 The highest mountain in the world is Snowdon, in Wales, at 1,085 metres high.
(False – it is Mount Everest, in the Himalayas. It has been measured to have a height of 8,848 metres.)

8 The largest island in the world is the Isle of Wight.
(False – discounting Australia, which has an area of 7,682,300 sq km but is usually regarded as a continental landmass, the largest island in the world is Greenland, with an area of about 2,175,600 sq km.)

9 The most bricks balanced on one person's head was 202 by Lauri Ylonen of Finland.
(False – the record is only 101 bricks, which was achieved by John Evans for ten seconds in 1997.)

10 The longest river in the world is the Nile. Its main source is Lake Victoria, in east central Africa. From its farthest stream in Burundi, in eastern Africa, it extends 6,695 km in length.
(True.)

RESOURCE PAGE

USE WITH SESSION 40 RESPOND 'PRACTICAL'

Pray for Christians in Afghanistan, where openly belonging to Christ has often led to death.

Pray for Christians in Sudan, facing the horrors of prolonged civil war, rape, murder and slavery.

Pray for Christians in Iran, where they are spied on and discriminated against in education, employment and property ownership.

Pray for Christians in Syria, where churches and Christian-owned businesses are targets of IS bombings, and there have been many reports of Christians being abducted, physically harmed and killed.

Pray for Christians in Somalia, where if you are even suspected of being a Christian, you can be murdered on the spot.

Pray for Christians in Pakistan, where an estimated 700 Christian women and girls are abducted every year; many are raped and forced to marry Muslim men.

Pray for Christians in North Korea, where they have to worship in secret and in danger.

Bible: John 1:6–9

41

IN THE BEGINNING...

THE AIM: To see Jesus in all his glory!

The aim unpacked

This session has twin themes. Firstly, it's an opportunity for us to consider Jesus as the light of the world. Secondly, this passage introduces John the Baptist who, in many ways, was the first evangelist, telling people about Jesus. Therefore this session is not just about seeing Jesus in all his glory, but it's also about how we should be helping other people see Jesus in all his glory.

WAY IN

theGRID MAGAZINE

WHAT: **quiz**
WHY: **to introduce the theme of light**
WITH: **magazine page 260**

1 Hand out copies of page 260 and give everyone a pen. Ask them to have a go in pairs at the quiz, 'How much do you know about light?'

2 Gather the young people together and go through the answers from page 335.

3 Introduce the fact that, at Christmas, lights are a common part of the celebrations – candles, lights on Christmas trees, city centres decorated with lights, etc.

4 Give out some plain paper and encourage everyone to design some Christmas lights that could be used to decorate the local high street.

5 Encourage the young people to show their designs to the rest of the group. Then explain that it is appropriate that lights feature heavily at Christmas because Jesus, whose birth we are celebrating, is described as the 'light of the world'.

SCENE SETTER

WHAT: **drama or drawing**
WHY: **to introduce the idea of evangelism**

1 Ask your young people to imagine that they work for an advertising company. They have been approached to 'get the word out' about an exciting new product.

2 Divide them into groups of three or four and give them two minutes to 'design' a product. It could be a new toy being released in time for Christmas, a useful gadget or a new meal from a fast-food chain.

3 Once they've decided on a product, ask them to think about what the key components of their advertising campaign would be – for example, adverts in magazines, TV and radio commercials, billboards, website banner...

4 Then encourage them to set to work on one of these components. They could write a radio advert, prepare a drama sketch or a TV commercial, or design a billboard, magazine advert or a website banner.

5 Gather the young people together and ask them to present their creations to the other groups. Introduce the session by explaining that you're going to be thinking about how we need to 'get the word out' about Jesus.

THEMED GAME

WHAT: **building activity**
WHY: **to introduce the idea of light**
WITH: **newspapers, identical lightweight torches, small prize**

1 Divide the young people into groups of three. Give each group an identical torch, several newspapers and some sticky tape.

2 Tell them that they have ten minutes to construct a lighthouse with their supplies. Explain that their structure must be able to take the weight of the torch and must be free standing. They will be awarded points on two criteria: firstly, height (the taller the better), and secondly, how much it looks like a lighthouse. Warn them that if it doesn't stand up by itself they won't score any points.

3 Give the young people a time check every couple of minutes and after ten minutes instruct the groups to stop building. Judge their lighthouses and award a prize to the winning team.

4 Explain that in this session we're going to be thinking about the similarities between light and Jesus.

BIBLE EXPERIENCE

LEVEL 1: CONNECT

WHAT: **discussion**
WHY: **to see Jesus in all his glory**
WITH: **Bibles, large sheets of paper, marker pens**

1 Divide the young people into groups of approximately four. Then give each group a large sheet of paper and ask them to divide it into three sections. Invite them to discuss the question, 'What's good about light?' and to make a note of their thoughts in one of the sections on their sheet of paper. Next, ask them to discuss the question, 'What's bad about darkness?', again encouraging them to jot down their ideas in another section. Finally, ask them to discuss, 'What's good about Jesus?' and to scribble notes in the third section of their paper.

2 Gather the young people together and talk about their responses to the three questions.

3 Ask a volunteer to read John 1:6–9 to the group and explain that in this passage Jesus is described as 'the Light'. Now ask another volunteer to read John 8:12.

4 As a whole group, spend some time discussing the following two questions:

- In what ways is Jesus like a light?
- In what ways is living life without Jesus like being in darkness?

5 Conclude by asking another volunteer to read John 1:6–9 to the group once more. Point out that Jesus is not the only person mentioned in this passage. See if anyone can tell the group who the other person is and what his role was. Then spend a short while chatting about how John the Baptist helped people see Jesus in all his glory.

LEVEL 2: INTERFACE

WHAT: **thinking through some scenarios**
WHY: **to see Jesus in all his glory**
WITH: **magazine pages 261 and 262, Bible, small prize, candle, matches or lighter**

1 Ask the young people to get into pairs and to write down as many words associated with Christmas as they can think of. Give them three minutes to do this. Once the time is up, find out what words they have come up with. Award two points if a pair has thought of something no one else has, one point if another pair has the same word and zero points for words that you don't think have anything to do with Christmas. Award a prize to the winning pair.

2 Next, still in their pairs, ask them to write down as many reasons as possible why Jesus is great. After a few minutes, find out what they have written down.

3 Ask a volunteer to read John 1:6–9, then light a candle and ask the group why they think Jesus is described as 'Light'.

4 Ask everyone to look at 'Talking about Jesus' on pages 261 and 262. Introduce the idea that John came to tell people about Jesus; he pointed to Jesus and he helped people to see Jesus in all his glory. Invite them to read the scenarios in the magazine in pairs – they are all stories of people attempting to tell others about Jesus. Encourage the pairs to discuss what each person did well, what they did badly and how they might have communicated the greatness of Jesus more effectively!

5 Gather the young people together and ask each pair to feed back their thoughts on one of the scenarios. Then spend some time chatting about what opportunities they might have in the run-up to Christmas to tell other people about Jesus. How are they going to make the most of these opportunities in order to help people see Jesus in all his glory?

LEVEL 3: SWITCH ON

WHAT: **reflection and discussion**
WHY: **to see Jesus in all his glory**
WITH: **Bibles, selection of song lyrics, worship songs, playback equipment**

1 Before the session, find a selection of songs that speak about Jesus as the 'light of the world'. Having copies of the lyrics is essential; however, you may also like to find them on CD/ MP3 so the group can listen to them. Possible songs include:

- 'Endless Light' by Hillsong United
- 'Light of the World' by Tim Hughes
- 'Shine Jesus Shine' by Graham Kendrick
- 'Come See This Glorious Light' by Stuart Townend

2 Invite the young people to look at the words and listen to the songs and discuss, in small groups, why Jesus is often referred to as the 'light of the world'.

3 Ask a volunteer to read John 1:6–9. Pause and allow the young people to spend a few moments reflecting on how amazing it is that Jesus came into the world to live among us, as one of us. Then encourage the young people to say short, one-sentence prayers to thank Jesus for coming into the world as our light.

4 Explain that John came to point people to Jesus, to help people see Jesus in all his glory. Challenge the young people that we should all be like John.

5 Ask another volunteer to read Matthew 5:14–16. Chat to the young people about how Jesus doesn't just describe himself as a light; he also wants his followers to be lights. Ask the young people to discuss in small groups practical ways in which we might be able to follow Jesus' (and John's) example and be lights in a dark world. Conclude by bringing the young people back together to discuss their thoughts.

RESPOND

MUSICAL

WHAT: **singing**
WHY: **to worship Jesus in all his glory**
WITH: **words and music for worship songs, playback equipment or musical accompaniment, Bibles**

1 Conclude the session by singing some songs together.

2 If you used the 'Reflection and discussion' activity from the *Bible experience* section, you may like to sing those songs. Alternatively, choose songs that sing about Jesus in all his glory. For example:

- 'The Servant King' by Graham Kendrick
- 'In Christ Alone' by Stuart Townend and Keith Getty
- 'Greater Than' by Tom Field
- 'Crown Him with Many Crowns' by Matthew Bridges

3 If you have musicians in your group, ask them to accompany the singing. Alternatively, you could use pre-recorded music. Make sure everyone can easily see copies of the words.

4 Between songs, invite young people to read Bible passages that reveal Jesus in all his glory (for example, Colossians 1:15–20, Hebrews 12:1–3 and Philippians 2:5–11) and say short prayers of praise.

PRACTICAL

WHAT: **preparing to talk about Jesus**
WHY: **to encourage the young people to tell someone about Jesus this week**
WITH: **magazine pages 261 and 262 (optional)**

1 Remind the group that John told people about Jesus – and that's our job too!

2 Ask everyone to think of one friend or family member they would like to talk to about Jesus this week. Make the point that they don't have to tell them everything about Jesus all in one go. Remind them that when they chat to their friends about things that are important to them, like computer games, football or fashion, the conversation is natural – our conversations about Jesus shouldn't be forced but should come naturally too.

3 Next, encourage them to chat with a partner about:

- who the person is that they would like to talk to about Jesus
- what they would like to tell them
- how they think they should do that

4 If you haven't used the scenarios from pages 261 and 262, you might like to encourage the young people to read them as they discuss how they're going to approach chatting to a friend or family member about Jesus.

5 Encourage the young people to pray for one another in their pairs. Suggest they pray for boldness and an opportunity to talk about Jesus, and that God would be preparing the people they want to talk to for an encounter with Jesus.

CREATIVE

WHAT: **making candle holders**
WHY: **to remember, or share, that Jesus is the light of the world**
WITH: **candles, small glasses, sand, glass paints, small brushes**

1 In advance, purchase some cheap, small glasses (approximately 8 cm tall), some playpit sand (so it is safe for the young people to touch without wearing gloves), some candles (approximately 20 cm tall), some glass paints and small brushes.

2 Give everyone a glass and encourage them to decorate it using the glass paints. Explain that they can either keep the candle holder to remind them that Jesus is the light of the world or they can give it to someone as a Christmas present to tell them that Jesus is the light of the world. They may like to write a Bible verse on their candle holder.

3 Give them a candle to put in the glass, then they can half-fill the glass with sand to hold it in place.

MORE ON THIS THEME:

If you want to do a short series with your group, other sessions that work well with this one are:

42 Party time! Isaiah 9:2–7

HOW MUCH DO YOU KNOW ABOUT LIGHT?

TRUE OR FALSE?

Bible bit
John 1:6–9

Christmas is fast approaching and gives us an opportunity to reflect on Jesus' time on earth. However often we read about it, it's still staggering to think of God living among us, as one of us. Jesus is the light of the world – a light who came to pierce through the darkness (John 8:12).

This passage introduces us to John the Baptist, who in many ways was the first evangelist, telling people about Jesus. We shouldn't just spend time seeing Jesus in all his glory; we also need to help other people see Jesus' glory too. First look upwards; then look outwards.

1. The speed of light is 299,792,458 metres per second.
   TRUE FALSE

2. Thomas Edison invented the first ever light bulb.
   TRUE FALSE

3. One in 3,000 people in the US are struck by lightning in their lifetime.
   TRUE FALSE

4. The world's oldest lighthouse – that is still working today – was built in 1174.
   TRUE FALSE

5. There are approximately 2,000 different species of fireflies (glow-worms).
   TRUE FALSE

6. It takes about 8.5 minutes for the light from the sun to reach Earth.
   TRUE FALSE

7. When a candle is burning, only 10% of its energy output is light; the rest is heat.
   TRUE FALSE

8. In the song made famous by Michael Jackson, do the lyrics tell you to blame it on ...
   THE SUNSHINE
   THE MOONLIGHT
   OR THE BOOGIE?

41

TALKING ABOUT JESUS

ANNA CHATS TO SOPHIE...

Anna and Sophie have been best friends for years, but Anna has never really spoken to Sophie about Jesus. Recently, Sophie asked Anna why she goes to church. Anna responded by explaining to Sophie that she goes to church to worship Jesus who is the Son of God who came to earth in order to die for our sins, and because he rose again we can have a relationship with him, which means that when we die we can go to heaven. She went on to say that we need Jesus because we are all sinners and sinners can't have a relationship with God, therefore we need Jesus to bridge the gap between us and God. God doesn't force anyone to have a relationship with him, it's our choice; we have to ask to be forgiven and put our trust in Jesus. We have to say sorry for our sins and start following Jesus and make him King of our lives. Fifteen minutes later, Anna took a breath and let Sophie speak!

WHAT DID THIS PERSON DO WELL?

____

____

WHAT DID THIS PERSON DO BADLY?

____

____

WHAT COULD THEY HAVE DONE BETTER?

____

____

JOHN CHATS TO TOBY...

John is 50 and Toby is 15 years old. They have never met each other. On Saturday, Toby is in town when John walks up to him and tells him that he's heading straight to hell unless he turns away from his wicked lifestyle and puts his faith in Jesus. He explains that Jesus is the Lamb who redeemed us by shedding his blood for us on Calvary. John was about to say more when Toby politely said that he needed to catch the bus.

WHAT DID THIS PERSON DO WELL?

____

____

WHAT DID THIS PERSON DO BADLY?

____

____

WHAT COULD THEY HAVE DONE BETTER?

____

____

SIMON CHATS TO SARAH...

Simon has fancied Sarah for ages; only problem is she has never been to church, and he knows that his parents won't be happy if he goes out with a non-Christian. So he began to chat to his friends at school, including Sarah, about all the things he does with his friends from church and how his church is really interesting and relevant and not like so many other churches that are really boring. Last week, Sarah started talking to Simon about Jesus. She said she has often thought about Jesus, but considered he was irrelevant. She asked Simon why he thinks Jesus is so important. Simon began to explain how Jesus has changed his life and invited her to his church's youth group.

WHAT DID THIS PERSON DO WELL?

WHAT DID THIS PERSON DO BADLY?

WHAT COULD THEY HAVE DONE BETTER?

VICKY CHATS TO ADAM...

Vicky and Adam are cousins. Vicky has been going to church all her life; Adam only goes to church for weddings and funerals. Recently, Adam asked Vicky why Jesus means so much to her. She began to explain that her relationship with Jesus is the most important thing in her life. He asked more questions, and they ended up chatting about all kinds of things for an hour. Before he left, Vicky told him about an event his local church is running where he'll be able to find out a little more about Jesus.

WHAT DID THIS PERSON DO WELL?

WHAT DID THIS PERSON DO BADLY?

WHAT COULD THEY HAVE DONE BETTER?

Bible: Isaiah 9:2–7

PARTY TIME!

THE AIM: To celebrate that God has shown us his glory by giving us his Son

The aim unpacked

This Bible passage would have been a beacon of hope among some harsh (but not undeserved) words that God delivered through Isaiah to his people. Today, this passage speaks to us of Jesus and what he came to do, and still does. The hope of one to come has turned into the hope of one who came and saved and is still active.

WAY IN

theGRID MAGAZINE

WHAT: **TV clip discussion**
WHY: **to understand more about prophecy**
WITH: **cliffhanger video clip, playback equipment, magazine page 266**

1 Before the session, choose a video clip that ends with a cliffhanger. This could be a TV episode (the ends of soaps are often good examples), a film or a sports event. Play the clip and ask the young people, working in twos or threes, to try and predict what happens next. Obtain feedback as to what the groups think will happen, then play the rest of the clip to see who was closest. Alternatively, read a passage from a book and challenge the young people to write a short paragraph on how the story might continue.

2 Make the observation that a lot of people think prophecy is about predicting the future. But prophecy is passing on what God wants to say to his people. Sometimes this is about the future, but not always. Ask if the young people can name any prophets in the Bible.

3 Look at page 266 for more information about prophets.

SCENE SETTER

WHAT: **collage and chat**
WHY: **to think about why we celebrate**
WITH: **magazines and newspapers, large sheets of paper**

1 Split the young people into smaller groups and ask them to create a collage of things they like to celebrate (and maybe some of the ways they celebrate too), using the magazines and newspapers. Encourage them to discuss in their groups as they work how they celebrate these events. If they can't find a particular image they want, they can draw or write it on the collage.

2 When everyone has finished, compare the different collages. Are there any similarities? Any differences? What and how do the young people celebrate? Does anyone have any recent examples they'd like to share?

3 Talk about whether there is anything on the collages about God. Chat about why that is. What should we celebrate about God? Ask for suggestions and give the young people some time to add that to their collages if they would like to.

THEMED GAME

WHAT: **party games**
WHY: **to think more about celebration**
WITH: **equipment needed for your chosen games**

1 Play some party games together. For example:

- Who am I? Write the names of famous people on sticky notes and stick one to each person's forehead. Everyone guesses who they are by asking questions.
- Musical chairs, musical statues or musical bumps.
- The chocolate game. Sit in a circle with a chocolate bar on a plate and a knife, fork, gloves, scarf and hat nearby. Take turns to roll a dice. When somebody rolls a six, they put on the garments and begin to chop up the chocolate with the knife and fork. No hands! They can eat whatever they can cut with the knife and fork. Everyone else continues rolling the dice. If someone else rolls a six, the player in the middle takes off the garments and the new person puts them on. And so on! Stop when time is up, or when the chocolate is gone!

2 Ask if the young people remember the last time they played any of these games at a birthday or Christmas party. If appropriate, chat about what or how we celebrate and why.

BIBLE EXPERIENCE

LEVEL 1: CONNECT

WHAT: Bible discussion
WHY: to celebrate that God has shown us his glory by giving us his Son
WITH: large copies of Isaiah 9:2–7 and Luke 1:26–33 or Bibles, highlighters, flip chart or whiteboard, marker pens

1 If you didn't do the 'Party games' as your *Way in* activity, spend some time chatting about the different things the young people celebrate. Give out copies of Isaiah 9:2–7 and highlighter pens. With that air of celebration in mind, read the Bible passage together and ask the young people to highlight all the parts of the passage that they think are worth celebrating.

2 When everyone has finished, talk about what the young people have highlighted. Write anything that the whole group agrees about on the flip chart or whiteboard. Invite any comments about those things.

3 In a different colour, write the things that only a few people thought were worth celebrating. Ask people why they thought these things were worth celebrating and ask others why they didn't agree. Encourage some healthy discussion here, but if your group is reluctant to talk, don't try to force it.

4 Now give out and read Luke 1:26–33 in the same way, highlighting the things that are worth celebrating. This time, ask the group to look out for similarities between the two passages and underline them. When everyone is done, obtain feedback and look at the similarities together. Comment that the events prophesied by Isaiah came about here, with Mary and Jesus. What does that tell the group about God?

LEVEL 2: INTERFACE

WHAT: drama, discussion
WHY: to celebrate that God has shown us his glory by giving us his Son
WITH: Bibles, magazine page 267, costumes and props (optional), flip chart or whiteboard and marker pens (optional)

1 Gather the young people together and give out the Bibles. Recap what a prophet is, if you did *Way in* 'TV clip discussion', or briefly describe who Isaiah was. Read Isaiah 9:2–7 together and ask the group what they think the passage is about. If you wish, jot any ideas down on a flip chart or whiteboard.

2 Give out copies of page 267 and read together the drama, 'Isaiah on the box'. Are any of the ideas on the flip chart or whiteboard featured in the drama? Discuss what the words of Isaiah might mean for the people to whom Isaiah was giving the message (ie those who lived before the birth of Jesus), and what it might mean for us today.

3 Invite the group to perform the drama. Give them some time to put it together, using any props you have available.

4 After they have finished, gather any more feedback the group has about the passage, then ask:

- How has God shown his glory?
- Why should we celebrate?

LEVEL 3: SWITCH ON

WHAT: Bible study
WHY: to celebrate that God has shown us his glory by giving us his Son
WITH: Bibles, study Bibles, concordances, page 268, magazine page 266 (optional)

1 Chat about what the young people know about prophets (if you didn't do *Way in* 'TV clip discussion', you could look at page 266 together now).

2 Give out Bibles and read Isaiah 9:2–7 and ask the group to get into pairs and answer the questions:

- Who?
- What?
- How?
- Where?
- Why?

Some of the answers to these questions are more obvious than others, so give the young people some time to think about them. Obtain some feedback from the group, being sure to emphasise the need to understand what Isaiah's listeners would have thought at the time (before Jesus), as well as how we understand the passage today.

3 Explain that there are many prophecies that refer to Jesus' coming and God's plan. Give out copies of page 268 and challenge the group to discover some of the other prophecies about Jesus.

4 Discuss together what the other prophecies are about. What new things has the group learned about God? What is there to celebrate?

RESPOND

MUSICAL

WHAT: **singing and songwriting**
WHY: **to rejoice in and celebrate the fact that God sent Jesus**
WITH: **words and music to Christmas songs, playback equipment or musical accompaniment, Bibles**

1 Before the session, choose some Christmas songs that your group enjoys. Try to choose one or two songs that echo the words of the Isaiah passage, such as 'O come, O come Immanuel'. In addition, gather together the sheet music or backing tracks for a couple of well-known carols.

2 Sing some carols together in a lively fashion and enjoy praising God for what he has done in sending Jesus. If possible, invite the young people to use any instruments that they can play.

3 If you have time, encourage the young people to come up with new words to an old tune using some of the words from Isaiah 9. Pick a tune together and then split into small groups so they can come up with some of their own verses. Sing that song together and maybe use another song to express the mood of celebration for what God has done.

PRACTICAL

WHAT: **practical demonstration of God's love**
WHY: **to share some of the joy of Jesus' coming**
WITH: **flip chart or whiteboard, marker pens**

1 Before the session, think of some ideas as to how your group can share the joy of what God has done in sending Jesus. Maybe you could volunteer at an old people's home or a children's group.

2 During the session, encourage the group to come up with some ideas of what they could do to show God's love. Share your own ideas if the group has trouble coming up with suggestions of their own.

3 Select a suitable idea together and start to think about how you could put it into practice. Write down your plans on a flip chart or whiteboard and make sure everyone knows what they're responsible for.

4 Make sure you follow your church's policy for safeguarding children and that the group stays safe at all times.

CREATIVE

WHAT: **making a timeline**
WHY: **to follow God's plan for salvation and the part Christmas plays in that**
WITH: **Bibles, Bible timeline**

1 Show a Bible timeline to the group. Explain how it shows the whole sweep of the Bible and God's plan for salvation. Indicate where Isaiah is on the timeline and where Christmas is. Challenge the young people to produce their own timeline as a group, using the stories that are important to them.

2 Help the young people to think about the stories they want to depict and discuss how they link together in the big story of the Bible. Chat together as you work out what you have discovered about God today.

3 If you don't have time to finish this activity in your session, come back to it at a later date. Once finished, if possible, display the timeline where you meet so you can use it with future sessions.

MORE ON THIS THEME:

If you want to do a short series with your group, other sessions that work well with this one are:

41 In the beginning... John 1:6–9

TOP PROPHETS

KNOW ANYTHING ABOUT PROPHETS? CHECK THESE GUYS OUT!

ISAIAH

- Called by God to work for him in about 740 BC
- Saw a vision of God in the Temple, surrounded by smoke and four flying creatures
- Spoke to the people of Jerusalem about what God was saying to them
- Warned the people that they should turn back to God

JEREMIAH

- Started prophesying in 626 BC
- Was only a young man when God called him to be a prophet
- Spent most of his life in Jerusalem, telling the people there the word of God
- Most of his messages were to tell the people that they weren't following God's ways
- Was once put down a well because of what he said

EZEKIEL

- Worked for God for 22 years during the sixth century BC
- Lived in exile, mostly in Babylon
- God showed him visions of amazing things, such as a valley of bones being brought together and coming back to life
- Told the people in exile that God had not forgotten them

HOSEA

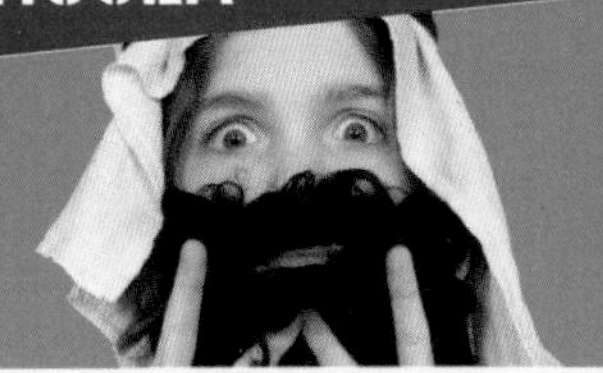

- God used Hosea's life to speak to the people. God told Hosea to marry a prostitute, Gomer, who was then unfaithful to him
- God said that his people were like Gomer and he was like Hosea
- God told Hosea to say to his people, 'I want faithful love ... I want people to follow me'

AMOS

- Amos prophesied during the same period as Isaiah and Hosea
- He was a farmer
- Was very concerned with justice and people being fair to the poor. He was angry with the rich who cheated people out of their money

MALACHI

- Possibly worked for the Lord around 420 BC
- Malachi might not have been his real name, as it means 'Messenger of the Lord'
- Spoke to the priests and people of Jerusalem about how their faith was empty. God didn't want meaningless sacrifices; he wanted people to follow him

ISAIAH ON THE BOX

Bible bit
Isaiah 9:2–7

42

Do you like Christmas? Do you look forward to it every year? Why/why not? Isaiah was a man with a message for God's people – God was going to do something great for his children, and it was worth looking forward to. But get this: you and Isaiah are looking forward to the same thing – celebrating God sending his Saviour.

Scene: TV jingle plays, the audience applauds as the Host arrives on the stage. There are two chairs placed for an interview, in front of which the Host stands to address the audience. Isaiah, the guest, waits off stage.

Host: Welcome, welcome to another edition of *Prophet's Profit*, where we get the lowdown on what God is saying to us, right here, right now. Today, we're excited to be talking with one of the biggies. Yes, it's the big 'I' himself, Isaiah!

(Audience applauds as Isaiah walks on stage and shakes hands with the Host.)

Host: Great to see you, Isaiah. Please take a seat.

(They both sit.)

Host: So, tell us more about this new word from God. It's nice to hear you saying something positive!

(Audience laughs; Isaiah looks slightly annoyed.)

Host: Who is this son God has given us?

Isaiah: Well, this is all part of God's ongoing message to his people. As you know, enemies like the Assyrians are all around us, and that is because the people of Judah are not following God's ways.

(Audience boos.)

Isaiah: I'm sorry, but that's a fact. As a country, we have ignored God, and God is not happy.

Host: Hang on, hang on, you told me your new message backstage, and it was much better than this 'It's all your fault' story you're telling now.

(Audience cheer their approval of the Host's question.)

Isaiah: Yes, yes, that's right, but you can't see this message as something separate from the rest of what God is saying. There is good news for us: relief is coming, but it doesn't change the fact that we have gone away from God and need to come back to him. But that's the good thing about God – there's always hope.

Audience member: *(Shouting.)* What's this hope you're going on about?

(Other Audience members shout, 'Yeah!', 'Tell us!' etc)

Isaiah: OK, I'm getting there! But it's important that you remember that we need to turn back to God. We have to say sorry to him and live his way again. Tough times are coming to Judah!

(Audience boos, but throughout the next section, they react with 'Oooh' and 'Aaah' as appropriate.)

Isaiah: But the people in darkness have seen a great light! Soldiers' uniforms will be thrown in the fire! A child has been born to us; God has given us a son. He will be called Wonderful Counsellor, Powerful God, Father who Lives For Ever, Prince of Peace. Power and peace will be in his kingdom. The Lord All-powerful will do all this because he loves his people!

(Audience cheers and claps; the Host joins in.)

Host: That's more like it – a message of hope. So, where is this son?

Isaiah: Well, he's not here yet, but the Lord will send his Saviour and we need to be ready. That means obeying God's laws: loving him and loving our neighbours.

Host: If God is giving us such a great Saviour, then I think I will definitely serve the Lord. What about you, Audience?

Audience: Yes, we'll follow the Lord!

(Everyone applauds, including Isaiah.)

Host: So that's it for this week on *Prophet's Profit*. Tune in next week for more!

(TV jingle plays again. The Host and Isaiah chat animatedly and silently. Lights fade.)

RESOURCE PAGE

USE WITH SESSION 42 BIBLE EXPERIENCE 'LEVEL 3 SWITCH ON'

Good news

There are many prophecies in the Old Testament that are fulfilled by Jesus. Check out some of these and write down what each one tells us about Jesus.

Jeremiah 23:5,6
Micah 5:2
Isaiah 7:14
Isaiah 11:1–5
Isaiah 61:1–3
Zechariah 9:9,10
Isaiah 53

What do these prophecies tell us about God?

Bible: Luke 1:26–56

43

ANGELS

THE AIM: To learn about angels as God's messengers

The aim unpacked

This series relates to the Christmas narrative and uses it as a starting point to explore a biblical theme. In this first session, we investigate angels. Our starting point is Gabriel and his visit to Mary, but we'll discover that, throughout the Bible, God uses messengers to interact with his creation.

WAY IN

theGRID MAGAZINE

WHAT: 'True or false' quiz
WHY: to find out what we know about angels
WITH: magazine page 272

1 Hand out copies of page 272 and ask the young people to look at the quiz. The quiz can be done on their own or in pairs. Tell the young people that they have three choices of answer: true, false and not sure.

2 When they have finished, go through the answers together and allow time for the young people to talk further about angels and ask questions.

SCENE SETTER

WHAT: discussion
WHY: to think about how angels are commonly portrayed
WITH: selection of Christmas cards depicting angels, other popular images of angels

1 Divide the young people into two groups. Give the first group the selection of Christmas cards and other images of angels. Ask them to talk about and then write down how angels are portrayed in the pictures.

2 Ask the second group to think about any films or TV programmes that have angels in them. After listing them, ask them to pick out two or three and to talk about the different ways that angels are portrayed in them.

3 Ask a spokesperson from each group to share some of their ideas. Use this as a starting point to talk about how angels are really described in the Bible.

THEMED GAME

WHAT: drama challenge
WHY: to recall what we know about angels
WITH: costumes and props (optional)

1 Divide the young people into groups and challenge them to re-enact a scene from the Christmas story that includes angels – either Gabriel's visit to Mary or the angels' visit to the shepherds. Most young people will have seen or taken part in nativity plays. Encourage them to identify how many details of the story they can remember.

2 When they have had time to prepare, invite the groups to present their scenes to the rest of the group.

3 If necessary, correct any serious deviations from the biblical account! Discuss together how we might remember things incorrectly. Where might we get any 'made up' bits of the story from?

BIBLE EXPERIENCE

LEVEL 1: CONNECT

WHAT: story and discussion
WHY: to learn about angels as God's messengers
WITH: magazine page 273, Bibles

1 Encourage the young people to read the story on page 273. Give them a few minutes to think about the story and discuss it among themselves.

2 Ask the young people to vote on whether they think the man was an angel or whether they think the incident was a lucky coincidence. Invite any volunteers to explain why they voted either way.

3 If anyone has heard any other stories of angel encounters, invite them to share them with the group.

4 Explain that 'angel' means 'messenger'. Ask:

- What message did the 'angel' in the story bring?
- Can you think of any angels in the Bible who brought messages?

5 Read Luke 1:26–38 to the group, then ask the following questions:

- Why do you think God uses angels to give people messages?
- How do you think Mary felt when she saw the angel?
- How do you think you would react if an angel appeared with a message for you?

LEVEL 2: INTERFACE

WHAT: story stations
WHY: to learn about angels as God's messengers
WITH: Bibles, copies of the chart from page 274, flip chart or whiteboard

1 Prepare four story stations around the room, each with Bibles and, if possible, a leader or another volunteer to read the story.

2 Read out Luke 1:26–38 and briefly chat through the details of the story. Then say that you are going to hear about more times in the Bible when angels appeared to people to give them a message from God.

3 Give each young person a copy of the chart from page 274 and a pen. If you have a large group, divide it into four smaller groups and send one group at a time to each story station. If you have a smaller group, the whole group could visit each station in turn.

4 When the young people arrive at a station, a volunteer should read them one of the following angel stories, as dramatically as possible:

- Balaam's donkey (Numbers 22:21–35)
- the birth of Samson (Judges 13)
- the resurrection (Matthew 28:1–7)
- Peter's escape from prison (Acts 12:1–11)

5 After each story, encourage the young people to answer the questions on their chart. Provide Bibles in case they want to look at the story again. When they have finished, they should move on to the next station, until they have completed all four.

6 Bring the whole group together and invite them to share some of their answers. Write them up on a flip chart or whiteboard and summarise what the group has discovered about angels from these stories.

LEVEL 3: SWITCH ON

WHAT: Bible exploration
WHY: to learn about angels as God's messengers
WITH: Bibles

1 Read Luke 1:26–38 to the young people. Ask, 'What were the first things the angel said to Mary?' (The angel told her that God was with her and that she shouldn't be afraid.) Challenge the young people to remember the message the angels brought to the shepherds (Luke 2:8–14). Can they remember the first words the angel spoke? (The angel told the shepherds not to be afraid.) Ask them what this suggests about angels. What was the purpose of both these visits by angels?

2 Explain that angels are powerful and that God does not use them just to bring good news, but also to bring warnings and punishment. Ask the young people, in pairs, to look up the following references in their Bibles:

- 2 Kings 6:8–23
- 1 Chronicles 21:15–17
- Psalm 35:1–6
- Matthew 28:1–7

Encourage them to discuss what these passages tell us about angels. Has their view of angels changed?

3 Read Psalm 34:7. Ask the young people if they think God still uses angels as his messengers today. Are angels present with them now? How does that make them feel?

RESPOND

43

MUSICAL

WHAT: **singing about angels**
WHY: **to remember the role of angels as messengers in the Christmas story**
WITH: **music and words for a variety of Christmas carols that mention angels, playback equipment (optional)**

1 Ask the young people to name as many Christmas carols or songs as they can that mention angels, for example 'Angels from the realms of glory'; 'Hark, the herald angels sing'; 'O come, all ye faithful'; 'While shepherds watched'. Read through some of the words, emphasising where angels are mentioned.

2 Invite the group to choose two or three carols they would like to sing. You could either have a time of traditional carol singing or, if you have a particularly creative group, encourage them to write their own Christmas carol or to sing the words of a traditional carol to a new tune.

PRACTICAL

WHAT: **making angels**
WHY: **to share the message of the Christmas angels**
WITH: **craft materials for making angels**

1 Ask the young people to think about the message the angels brought to Mary and the shepherds in the Christmas story – the amazing news that Jesus, God's Son, was coming into the world to be our Saviour. Encourage them to consider how they can pass this message on to others.

2 Invite the young people to make an angel each to remind them that they, too, can be messengers bringing good news. Provide a variety of craft materials for them to use, such as white card, doilies, pegs, glitter.

3 If your church is planning some special Christmas events, you could also encourage the young people to design invitations or posters with an angel theme as a practical way of sharing the message about Christmas.

CREATIVE

WHAT: **angel acrostic praise poems**
WHY: **to worship with the angels**
WITH: **quiet music**

1 Remind the young people that angels are part of God's creation and reflect his glory, but they themselves should never be worshipped. They are servants of God who direct us to worship him, as they do.

2 Invite the young people to write acrostic praise poems to God, using the letters from the word 'angel' as the first letter of each line.

3 Play some quiet worship music while they do this and then encourage them to read their praise poems aloud or to offer them silently as a prayer to God.

MORE ON THIS THEME:

If you want to do a short series with your group, other sessions that work well with this one are:

44 Look at the stars Matthew 2:1–15

45 Happy Christmas! Luke 2:1–20; Matthew 2:1–12

Bible bit
Luke 1:26–38

There is no description of what the angel looked like or how he appeared. In fact, the out-of-this-world visit by Gabriel is secondary to the message he brings. If God wants to pass something on to his creation, his messengers often get the job.

TRUE OR FALSE

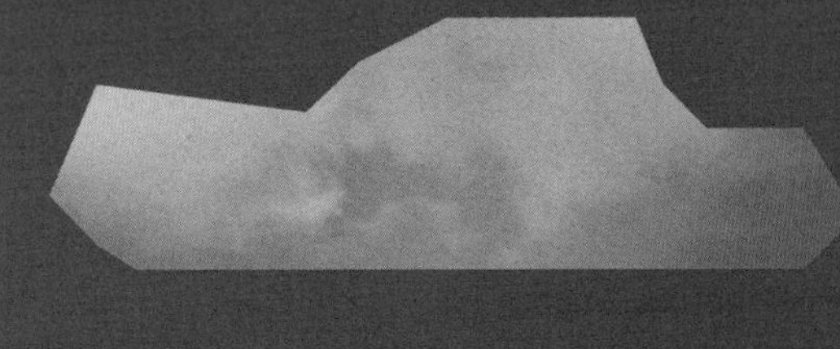

Q

1 Angels dress in white, have wings and a halo.
TRUE – FALSE

2 Angels are humans who have died and gone to heaven.
TRUE – FALSE

3 Angels deliver messages from God.
TRUE – FALSE

4 We can pray to angels for protection.
TRUE – FALSE

5 Angels are always male.
TRUE – FALSE

6 Everyone has their own guardian angel.
TRUE – FALSE

7 Angels are constantly worshipping God in heaven.
TRUE – FALSE

8 Angels sit on clouds, playing harps.
TRUE – FALSE

9 Angels are spiritual beings, created by God.
TRUE – FALSE

10 Only two angels are named in the Bible.
TRUE – FALSE

A

1. Not sure. We don't actually know what angels look like, although some are described as wearing white (John 20:12), and the Seraphim (who might be a type of angel) have wings (Isaiah 6:2). No halos are mentioned!

2. False. Angels and humans were both created by God, but they are very different. The Bible does not say that humans become angels after we die, although it does suggest that we may become like angels (Mark 12:25).

3. True (Luke 1:19).

4. Not sure. Some church traditions do pray to angels, and the Bible tells us that God does send angels to protect his people. But it is probably better to ask God himself when we need protection (Psalm 91:11,12).

5. Not sure. We don't know if angels are male or female. The angels mentioned by name in the Bible have male names, but it is likely that, like God, angels are neither male nor female.

6. Not sure. Some church traditions believe in guardian angels, but it is not clear from the Bible if we each have one who is with us at all times (Matthew 18:10).

7. True (Revelation 7:11,12).

8. False. This is a traditional view of angels, but when described in the Bible they are more likely to be holding a sword (Numbers 22:31) or blowing a trumpet!

9. True.

10. True. They are Gabriel and Michael.

While on holiday in LA, Kate and her family found themselves in serious danger when they wandered into the wrong part of town. But an unlikely stranger came to their rescue...

USE WITH SESSION 43 BIBLE EXPERIENCE 'LEVEL 2 INTERFACE'

Angel encounters

	Balaam's donkey (Numbers 22:21–35)	The birth of Samson (Judges 13)	The resurrection (Matthew 28:1–7)	Peter's escape from prison (Acts 12:1–11)
Who saw the angel(s)?				
What did the angel(s) do?				
How is (are) the angel(s) described?				

Bible: Matthew 2:1–15

LOOK AT THE STARS

THE AIM: To see that faith in God is the only way to face the future

The aim unpacked

In this session we start with the Magi, who were astrologers. Although there is little of direct comparison between astrology today and the 'science' it was during biblical times, there is still a link in that they both looked to the stars for guidance. People look to all sorts of things for guidance today. However, as we will be reminded, the only true way of facing the future is through faith in God.

WAY IN

theGRID MAGAZINE

WHAT: discussion and decision making
WHY: to explore ways of making decisions
WITH: magazine page 278

1 Give out copies of page 278. Ask the young people to look at the page and choose which they believe are the sensible and the silly ways of making decisions.

2 Together, talk about different ways of making decisions. Discuss how you make decisions yourself. If you want to, share a time when you were in a situation where it was hard to decide what to do and explain how you eventually made your mind up and what the outcome was. Relate to the group how you asked God to help you decide and how you listened to him.

SCENE SETTER

WHAT: discussion
WHY: to identify different people who can help with different problems
WITH: pictures of celebrities from magazines or newspapers (including some with specific expertise such as footballers and diet gurus), picture of your vicar or youth worker, picture of Jesus

1 Arrange all the pictures, except the picture of Jesus, where the group can see them. If you need to, add name labels and job descriptions.

2 Ask the group to suggest different types of problems they and their friends might face.

3 After each suggestion, ask which person, from the pictures displayed, they would ask to give them advice on that subject and why. For example, for advice on fashion, they might ask Gok Wan, as he presents TV shows on the subject. For advice on becoming fitter, they might ask a sportsperson!

4 Then put up the picture of Jesus and ask what he might be able to give advice on. What does he know?

THEMED GAME

WHAT: quiz game
WHY: to identify how we make decisions and what can help
WITH: board game or DVD game and TV (such as *Who Wants to Be a Millionaire?* or *Trivial Pursuit*), small prize

1 Split the group into pairs or threes to play the game. Remind the young people that their team has to agree before they give their answer.

2 Play the game and give a small prize to the winners.

3 Discuss what made them succeed and ask them to explain how they made their decisions when they were unsure of the answer. Ask how the young people make decisions generally on issues they are not sure about. Do they have people they ask?

BIBLE EXPERIENCE

LEVEL 1: CONNECT

WHAT: **discussion**
WHY: **to see that faith in God is the only way to face the future**
WITH: **Bibles, magazine page 279**

1 Ask the young people if they have ever read a horoscope and believed that it would come true. What do they think of horoscopes? Say that the wise men in the story were people who studied the stars. Read together the fact box on the Magi from page 279. Were they surprised by any of the facts there? Explain that the wise men were not astrologers like those in the newspapers today, trying to predict the future through movements of the planets and stars. They were simply wise men who followed God's directions to find Jesus.

2 Read Matthew 2:1–12 together. Give the young people copies of page 279. Encourage them to decide which of the methods of guidance are from God and which are not.

3 Explain that God guided the wise men so that they would see and worship his Son. What a fantastic thing! Other methods we might use to help us make decisions about our future are less reliable than God's guidance. What would have happened if the wise men had done what Herod advised them to do, rather than what God told them in the dream?

4 Together, think about different decisions the young people have to make and the ways they obtain advice on what to do. Are there any people or things the young people are turning to for advice which aren't the best sources of guidance?

LEVEL 2: INTERFACE

WHAT: **discussion**
WHY: **to see that faith in God is the only way to face the future**
WITH: **Bibles, flip chart or whiteboard, marker pens**

1 All together, come up with a few ideas on methods people use to try and help them make decisions about their future. Write them all down on the flip chart or whiteboard. Then go through the list and judge the effectiveness and reliability of each one.

2 Ask the group why they think people use things to help them make their decisions when those methods are not trustworthy or reliable. Make sure you cover the idea of using the stars to tell the future.

3 Read Matthew 2:1–12. The wise men were alerted to Jesus' birth through a star. Explain that the wise men were probably non-Jewish religious astrologers. Ask the young people why they think God used astrologers and stars to announce the birth of his Son. This isn't the first time God used a foreigner to help get his message across – can the group think of any others?

4 Give the young people the following Bible references and ask them to look them up. Record what they find out about stars:

- Genesis 1:14–19
- Deuteronomy 4:19
- Psalm 147:4
- Amos 5:8
- Amos 5:25–27

5 Some of these passages are about God making and naming each of the stars. He controls them. Other passages are about people worshipping the stars. What differences do the young people see between these two themes? Remind them that the star the wise men saw pointed them towards Jesus.

LEVEL 3: SWITCH ON

WHAT: **small-group Bible study**
WHY: **to see that faith in God is the only way to face the future**
WITH: **Bibles, page 280, flip chart or whiteboard, marker pens**

1 If you have a large group, split the young people into groups of four or five and nominate a leader in each group. Otherwise, do this activity all together. Give out copies of page 280. Ask the young people to look at the different methods people in the Bible used to try to find out what they should do in the future.

2 In the small groups, ask the young people to work out which of these people showed trust in God to lead and guide, and which showed distrust in God. Then decide whether any of these methods displeased God because they were counter to what he had revealed to his people.

3 Obtain feedback from the group(s). Write the ideas down on the flip chart or whiteboard.

4 Discuss where you agreed or disagreed. Talk about how the young people might change the way they live their lives – how will they face the future?

RESPOND

44

MUSICAL

WHAT: **personal meditation**
WHY: **to recognise that God will guide them if they ask**
WITH: **quiet background music, playback equipment, footprint-shaped stickers or sticky notes, page 281**

1 Start with background music. Get the young people to sit quietly in preparation for the meditation. Encourage them to think about the words and to pray as they hear them.

2 Read the meditation from page 281, allowing the guiding questions to aid reflection. Leave silence between each phrase to allow thoughts or prayers.

3 When you have finished, continue the atmosphere of stillness to allow the young people to think about the session and to reflect on how they are guided by God and how much they put their faith in him.

4 Round off the activity by saying a prayer, asking God to guide each of you in your future decisions. If any of the young people want to make a decision to follow God more closely, or to put their faith in God as they face the future, invite them to take a footprint sticker and put it in their Bible or wallet. Remind them that they should think about the decision they have made today whenever they see their sticker.

PRACTICAL

WHAT: **prayer**
WHY: **to pray for those in authority**
WITH: **newspaper headlines, sticky tack, sticky notes**

1 Before the session, collect lots of newspaper headlines about difficult world, national and local issues.

2 Spread out the headlines you have collected and ask each person to choose one that they would like to pray about.

3 Each person should stick the headline to the wall, then write or draw on a sticky note a specific request for the people involved. They should then stick this to the wall under the headline.

4 Encourage everyone to move around the different headlines and to add sticky-note prayers wherever they choose. If anyone is struggling to think of things to pray about, suggest that they pray for God to influence the people making the decisions – that they would look to him for guidance about the future.

CREATIVE

WHAT: **creative personal prayer**
WHY: **to commit to facing the future with faith in God**
WITH: **coloured paper, sticky tack**

1 Give out the coloured paper and ask the young people to draw around one of their feet (with or without a shoe!). Then ask them to cut the footprints out.

2 Invite the young people to think about a decision they have to make where they are unsure what to do or are tempted to choose what they know to be wrong.

3 Ask each person to write their name and their decision on their footprint. (If they don't want to be explicit about their decision, they could draw a picture or symbol to represent it.) Encourage them to talk to God about the decision, asking him to help them go the way he wants them to go.

4 When everyone has finished, ask the group to stick their footprints in a line on the wall. Finish with this prayer: 'Lord, give us the courage to choose wisely, despite opposition or ridicule. Give us a clear vision to see what you would like us to do. Give us confidence to trust that you'll be with us, even if we choose poorly. Amen.'

MORE ON THIS THEME:

If you want to do a short series with your group, other sessions that work well with this one are:

43	*Angels*	*Luke 1:26–56*
45	*Happy Christmas!*	*Luke 2:1–20; Matthew 2:1–12*

DECISIONS, DECISIONS!

Bible bit
Matthew 2:1–15

Dear stargazer, today you will see a giant star in the east. You will go on a long journey and meet some tall dark men. You'll then travel on and meet a mighty ruler, although he might seem a bit young for the job at this time. It might be helpful to take a few gifts along, though...

You are going to a party. Now, what do you wear? You don't know? Well, how do you make a decision?

Imagine you're staring at your wardrobe... You think, 'Wow! There's so much choice, I'm going to have a great outfit!'

YES

NO → 'No,' you think. 'Argh! There's too much choice, I don't know where to start!' How indecisive are you?! I bet you have trouble choosing which side of the bed to get out of in the morning...

You think, 'I've got great taste, I'm going to look fantastic!'

YES

NO → Well, let's hope you don't end up looking like someone who took a wrong turn into the 1970s.

You think, 'My friend's got good fashion sense and they know what the party's going to be like, I'll ask them for advice.'

YES

NO → Well, if you think it's a fancy dress party and you go dressed as Batman, what are you going to do when you find out it's not, and you're the only one who's dressed like a fool?!

They tell you not to dress too smart, as the party's just a laid-back chill-out time. Do you take their advice?

YES

NO → You've always suspected that they wanted to make you look stupid, so you don't believe them and dress to kill. When you get there, everyone is wearing jeans!

You arrive at the party to find you've picked the right stuff and you have a great time!

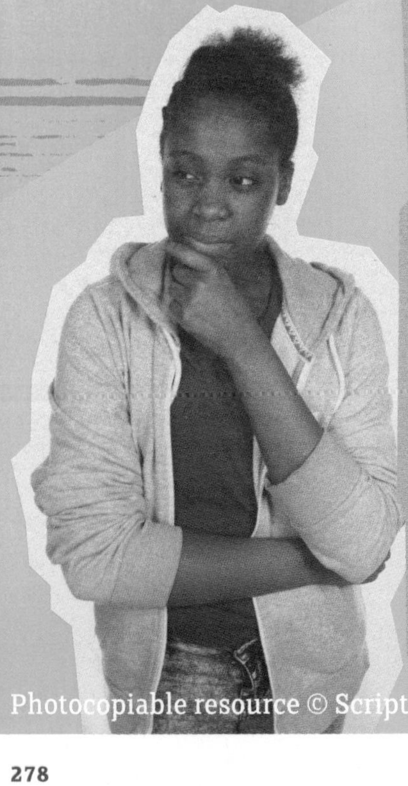

44

FACT BOX: THE MAGI

There are many traditions that have grown up around the Magi, but this is what the Bible says: 'When Jesus was born, some wise men from the east came to Jerusalem. They asked, "Where is the baby who was born to be the king of the Jews? We saw his star in the east and have come to worship him"' (Matthew 2:1b,2). The men are described as wise men, astrologers (star watchers), not kings! They came from the east, but we don't know where – Babylonia and Arabia are popular opinions. And we don't know how many there were – people assume there were three, because they brought three gifts (v11). But one person could have carried two gifts, couldn't he?!

GUIDING STAR

Draw a circle around the methods of guidance the wise men might have used to find Jesus. Then put a big tick next to the ones which were positive (from God) and cross out any ones which weren't!

Tossing a coin	The bright star in the east (Matthew 2:2)	The message of the prophet Micah (Micah 5:2)	Spinning a bottle	Their dreams (Matthew 2:12)
King Herod's advice (Matthew 2:8)	Their horoscopes	The *Daily Star's* agony aunt	The star moving towards Bethlehem (Matthew 2:9)	Google Maps

RESOURCE PAGE

USE WITH SESSION 44 BIBLE EXPERIENCE 'LEVEL 3 SWITCH ON'

Biblical guidance techniques

Which of these people showed trust in God to lead and guide them?

	Trust in God
Gideon tested his understanding of God's will by putting out fleeces (Judges 6:36–40).	
God wrote on the wall when the king ignored him (Daniel 5:1–9,12,23).	
God walked with his people and talked to them (Genesis 3:8–10).	
Saul went to see a medium (1 Samuel 28:6–14).	
A slave girl talked to her master to help him (2 Kings 5).	
Magi followed a star as a sign in the heavens that something wonderful was happening (Matthew 2:1–12).	
The leaders prayed and made a decision (Acts 15:22–29).	

What about these verses?

Deuteronomy 18:9–16; Acts 16:16–18; Jeremiah 33:3; Psalm 25:4–7; Isaiah 49:15; John 14:15–17; Proverbs 3:5,6

USE WITH SESSION 44 RESPOND 'MUSICAL'

What have I said this week that has been cruel... sarcastic... moaning... swearing?

Have I blessed people... encouraged them... spoken gently?

What about my thinking? Have I kept my thoughts pure or have I been distracted by things I should keep my eyes off? Have I been rude in my head, even if I kept my mouth shut?

Have my words and thoughts been a good reflection of who Jesus is?

Have my actions really been truthful... helpful... Christlike?

Does my life show Jesus to others, or do 'I' get in the way?

Am I glad to live a life of love – to give up ego, to serve others, to give of myself when it hurts?

Am I prepared to give all of me to Jesus – the dark bits, the hurt bits, the things I am ashamed of, as well as the good things, my gifts and my talents?

Am I really ready to surrender everything and follow Jesus, knowing that his path was lonely, misunderstood, painful, full of rejection and even led to death?

Lord, in all my doubts, in my insecurity, in my wavering faith, help me to make this song my prayer – in my head and in my heart.

Where have I looked to see Jesus this week – in my family, at school, with my friends? Have I asked for vision and confidence that can only come from God?

How have I tried to hear what God is saying so that I can be guided by him – through the Bible, at church, through circumstances, coincidences or in the words of others? Am I dreaming dreams from God?

Lord, help me to hold on to you as my hope, my light and the way. Help me to put down things that take me from you, that distract me, that undermine my hope and faith and love. Help me to walk in your light.

Lord, all too often I value the opinions of others, crave after fame, fortune and recognition. Help me to learn what is really valuable, to hear you whisper words of encouragement, of commendation, of love.

Oh Lord, as I make these words my prayer, be visible in me. Let my life reflect you in all your glory and love to my friends, family and neighbours, who are hungry for what you can give them. And Lord, help me to be wise in what I think, do and say, so that I can offer them all that you want to give.

45

Bible: Luke 2:1–20; Matthew 2:1–12

HAPPY CHRISTMAS!

THE AIM: To enjoy the season of Jesus' birthday

The aim unpacked
So what is it that we all celebrate at Christmas time? Being with family and friends? Giving and receiving presents? Underpinning it all, of course, is the birth of Christ, our Lord and Saviour, and its massive implications for all humankind. Without pouring cold water on all that the young people are enjoying during this time, here's our opportunity to remind them of that central truth.

WAY IN

theGRID MAGAZINE

WHAT: **quiz**
WHY: **to have fun checking our facts about the Christmas story**
WITH: **magazine page 286, bags of chocolate coins**

1 Divide the young people into teams of two or three and give each team a bag of chocolate coins and a copy of the 'chocolate coin drop' quiz from page 286.

2 Explain the game rules, making sure everyone has read and understood the instructions on the page.

3 Now run the quiz! Read the questions and give a minute or two for the teams to place their chocolate coins on the answer(s) they're most sure about. Reveal the answer from page 333 – any chocolate coins placed on a wrong answer are 'dropped' by the team and collected by you!

4 Let the teams eat any chocolate coins they have managed to keep by the end of question seven! And share out the ones you've collected along the way – it is Christmas after all!

5 Lead into the rest of the session by saying, 'So you know some facts about the first Christmas. But why are we still celebrating it over 2,000 years on?'

SCENE SETTER

WHAT: **cake decorating**
WHY: **to have fun celebrating the season of Jesus' birthday**
WITH: **paper plates, plain sponge cakes, cans of squirty cream, edible cake decorations, protection for clothes and carpets, candles (optional), prizes (optional)**

1 Get the young people into teams, each with a plain sponge cake on a plate, a can of squirty cream and plenty of cake decorations such as sweets, sprinkles, tubes of writing icing, etc. (Be aware of food hygiene and allergies.)

2 Remind everyone that we have been celebrating Jesus' birthday and say that you're going to make a cake to celebrate.

3 Give the teams five minutes to transform their plain sponge cakes into something spectacular with the cream, sweets, sprinkles, and so on.

4 Have fun looking at each other's cakes. Award a prize for the best one, if you wish.

5 Ask the young people whether they think there would have been cake like this at the first Christmas! How else might they have celebrated?

THEMED GAME

WHAT: **'guess the Christmas character' game**
WHY: **to recap the main characters in the Christmas story**
WITH: **sticky notes, prizes (optional)**

1 Before the session, write different characters from the Christmas story on separate sticky notes – one for each young person.

2 Invite the young people to sit in a circle and place one of the sticky-note characters on everyone's forehead without them seeing what's written on it. Explain that the aim of the game is for everyone to find out which character they are.

3 Choose someone to start the game: they ask a question which can only be answered 'yes' or 'no'. If they receive a 'yes' answer they can ask another question. They can keep asking questions until they receive a 'no' answer – then it's the turn of the next person round the circle.

4 Award prizes as the young people guess who they are, if you wish.

5 Say that, this session, you'll be looking at how these people spent the first Christmas.

BIBLE EXPERIENCE

LEVEL 1: CONNECT

WHAT: teen nativity
WHY: to reflect on why we celebrate Jesus' birthday
WITH: pens and paper, Bibles

1 Ask the young people to imagine that they are producing a new film aimed at teenagers about the Christmas story. The film has to be true to the meaning of the Bible text, but it can be creative with the details – for example, if the story were happening here and now, who would the Magi (wise men) or the shepherds be? And where would Mary and Joseph stay if there were no rooms left in the local hotel?

2 Read Luke 2:1–20 and Matthew 2:1–12 together, with young people reading the roles of the different characters.

3 Hand out pens and paper. Divide the young people into groups of three to six and give them time to plan their film, thinking about cast, location and scenes.

4 Now challenge them to write some of the script (with dialogue and stage directions). You could choose part of the story and work together as a whole group or assign different parts of the Bible text to smaller groups. Give this about 15 minutes, then hear and enjoy everyone's screenplay!

5 Move on by asking, 'What's special about this story? What do you think there is to celebrate in it?' Put the emphasis on Jesus: born to be our Saviour, God in human form, a gift for all humankind.

LEVEL 2: INTERFACE

WHAT: Bible study and discussion
WHY: to reflect on why we celebrate Jesus' birthday
WITH: magazine page 285, Bibles, flip chart or whiteboard (optional)

1 Chat with the young people about the following questions:

- Who did you spend Christmas Day with?
- What did you do together to celebrate?
- If you could have invited one other guest to your Christmas celebrations, who would it be? Why?

2 Explain that you're going to look together at who was there at the very first Christmas and what they did to mark the occasion.

3 Hand out copies of page 285, pens and Bibles and look together at the 'Christmas guest list'. Get them into twos or threes to fill in the details.

4 Come back together and obtain feedback as a whole group. Spend time chatting about the last question: 'What does that tell us about Jesus?' for each character. Possible points include:

- for the angels: Jesus is good news; he is Saviour; he is Lord; he is down to earth(!); he glorifies God and will bring peace.
- for the shepherds: Jesus was already really important – they left what they were doing to find out more and told other people about him.
- for the Magi: Jesus was also already very important – they journeyed a long way to find him; he is to be worshipped (you could discuss the meanings behind the three gifts).
- for Herod: Jesus has authority; he is King!

LEVEL 3: SWITCH ON

WHAT: DVD and discussion
WHY: to reflect on why we celebrate Jesus' birthday
WITH: *The Nativity Story* DVD, playback equipment, whiteboard or flip chart, marker pens, popcorn (optional)

1 Before the session, prepare a 'movie sound bites' board with quotes from *The Nativity Story* written in large text on a whiteboard, flip chart or large sheet of paper. You could include:

- 'He is for all mankind. We are each given a gift.' [Mary]
- 'God made into flesh.' [The Magi]
- 'Unto you is born this day a Saviour, who is Christ the Lord.' [The angel]
- 'Gold for the King of kings.' [The Magi]
- 'Frankincense for the Priest of all priests.' [The Magi]
- 'A gift of myrrh, to honour the sacrifice.' [The Magi]

Choose the ones which will most help the young people to focus on the message of Christmas from their level of interest and spiritual maturity.

2 Introduce the DVD by asking: 'Why are we celebrating a birthday more than 2,000 years on? What's the big deal about it? See what clues you can pick up as you watch the story.'

3 Play scenes 19 and 20 of *The Nativity Story*, which show Jesus' birth (you may want to skip the first 30 seconds!), the angel appearing to the shepherds, and the Magi presenting their gifts to Jesus. The whole clip lasts about ten minutes. Hand round the popcorn, if you wish (although make sure it's not a distraction!).

4 Kick off a discussion by asking: 'What was special about Jesus?' Show the 'movie sound bites' board and ask the group what they think about the quotes – what do they think they mean? End by emphasising Jesus as Saviour – 'God made into flesh', 'King of kings' and 'a gift for all humankind'.

RESPOND

MUSICAL

WHAT: **writing a Christmas hit!**
WHY: **to celebrate Jesus' birthday**
WITH: **flip chart or whiteboard, words and music for the current Christmas number one, playback equipment or musical accompaniment, recording equipment (optional)**

1 Chat briefly together about Christmas music. Do the young people like the Christmas number one this year? Does it have anything to do with Christmas?

2 Challenge the young people to write new words for the current Christmas number one (or another song of their choice) to celebrate Jesus' birthday!

3 Recap what you learned about Jesus in the *Bible experience* section. Write the key points on a flip chart or whiteboard for the young people to use in their new carol.

4 Then split into smaller groups to write some lyrics! Allow plenty of time for this.

5 With the whole group together again, enjoy listening to each group's carol. You may wish to record them so the young people can share them with their friends, perform them later to the rest of your church, or have the young people singing their song at the door as people leave the service!

PRACTICAL

WHAT: **reflection and prayer**
WHY: **to reflect on what we might offer Jesus on his birthday**
WITH: **flip chart or whiteboard, marker pens, wrapping paper, box**

1 Before the session, collect together offcuts of Christmas wrapping paper. Also find a box, wrap it and label it 'Jesus'.

2 Recap how the different characters responded to Jesus' birth from your *Bible experience* activity. Write the key points up on a flip chart or whiteboard – for example, the angels praised God; the shepherds found out more about Jesus and told other people about him; the Magi travelled a long way to worship Jesus, gave him gifts which cost them, and spent time with him.

3 Ask, 'What could we give Jesus as a gift for his birthday?' Help the young people with this, explaining that things like our time, interest and worship would be really precious to Jesus!

4 Give each person a small piece of wrapping paper and a pen, and ask them to write what they are offering to Jesus today. When they are ready, the young people can fold their paper and place it in the gift box.

5 End in prayer, committing these gifts to Jesus.

CREATIVE

WHAT: **'back of the bus' campaign**
WHY: **to focus our minds on what we celebrate at Christmas**
WITH: **large sheets of paper, paint (optional)**

1 Get the young people to think about the posters on the backs of buses. What different messages have they seen advertised there? (Has anyone ever seen the Alpha campaign?) Ask them to imagine their church wants to use that space to communicate something about the real meaning of Christmas. Can they come up with a really catchy slogan and an eye-catching image to go with it?

2 Split into small groups to gather ideas on some scrap paper. After about five minutes, hand out large sheets of paper, pens, felt-tip pens and paints for them to put together their best ideas.

3 Look together at each group's posters. You may wish to display them somewhere prominent – maybe on the noticeboard outside your church?

4 End with a time of prayer, thanking God for Christmas and asking that people in your area would know its real meaning.

MORE ON THIS THEME:

If you want to do a short series with your group, other sessions that work well with this one are:

43	*Angels*	*Luke 1:26–56*
44	*Look at the stars*	*Matthew 2:1–15*

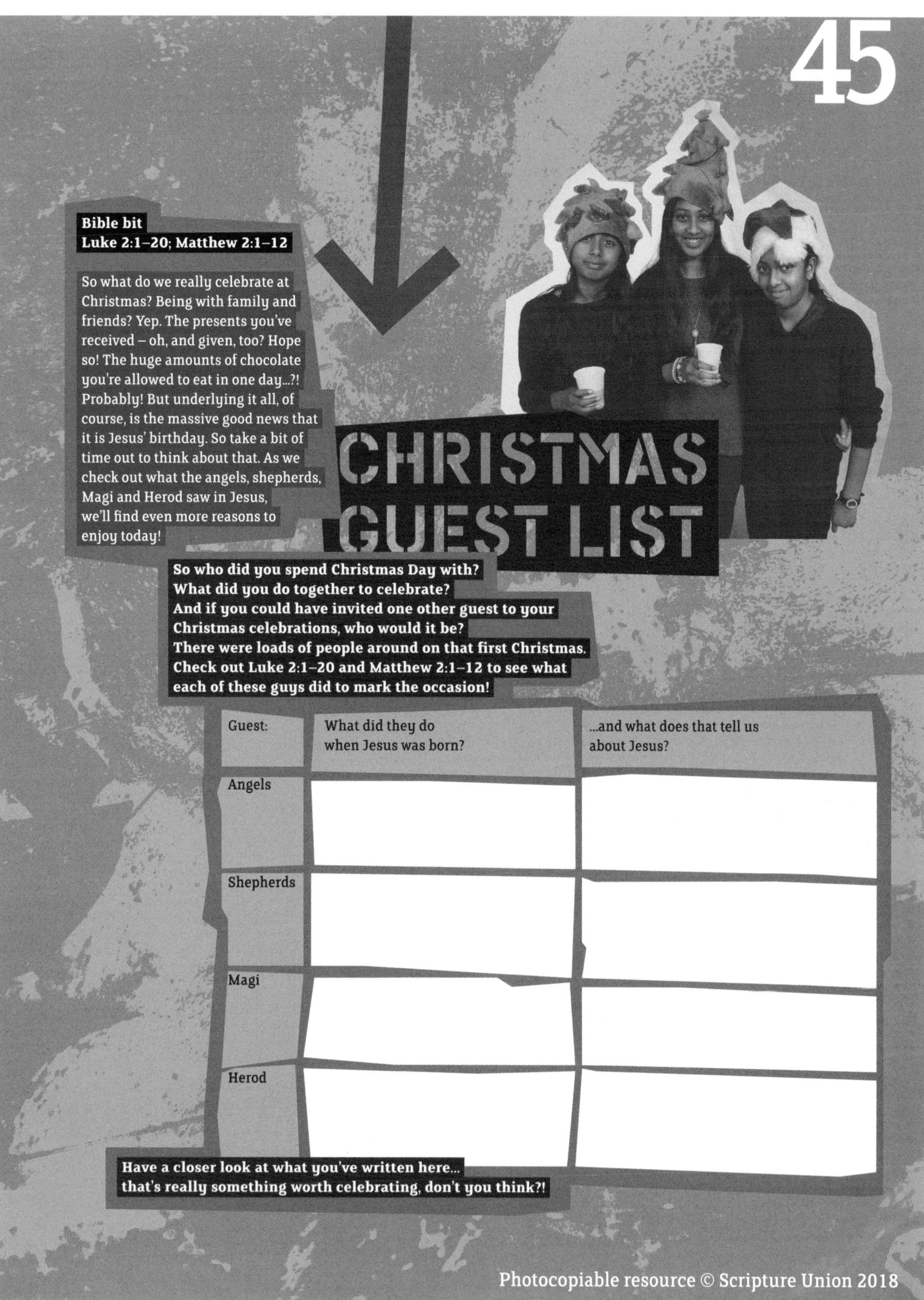

45

Bible bit
Luke 2:1–20; Matthew 2:1–12

So what do we really celebrate at Christmas? Being with family and friends? Yep. The presents you've received – oh, and given, too? Hope so! The huge amounts of chocolate you're allowed to eat in one day...?! Probably! But underlying it all, of course, is the massive good news that it is Jesus' birthday. So take a bit of time out to think about that. As we check out what the angels, shepherds, Magi and Herod saw in Jesus, we'll find even more reasons to enjoy today!

CHRISTMAS GUEST LIST

So who did you spend Christmas Day with?
What did you do together to celebrate?
And if you could have invited one other guest to your Christmas celebrations, who would it be?
There were loads of people around on that first Christmas. Check out Luke 2:1–20 and Matthew 2:1–12 to see what each of these guys did to mark the occasion!

Guest:	What did they do when Jesus was born?	...and what does that tell us about Jesus?
Angels		
Shepherds		
Magi		
Herod		

Have a closer look at what you've written here... that's really something worth celebrating, don't you think?!

THE CHOCOLATE COIN DROP
So you've probably heard the Christmas story squillions of times!
But how well do you really know it?
Get yourself a bag of chocolate coins and have a go at this fun quiz to find out!
Here's how it works:
• You start with all your chocolate coins – the aim is to keep as many as you can to eat at the end of the quiz!
• For each question, you will see four possible answers. Put your coins on the answers you're most sure are correct.
• You can put your coins on one, two or three of the answers, but you need to leave at least one blank each time.
• If you put any coins on a wrong answer, you will lose them.
• You need to use all the coins you have for each question – no holding any back!
READY TO PLAY? HERE GOES!
1
Which of these gifts did the Magi give to Jesus as a baby?
Gold
Silver
Myrrh
Frankincense
2
According to Luke's Gospel, which of these did the angels actually say?
'Do not be afraid.'
'Let there be peace among the people who please God.'
'You will find a baby lying in a feeding box.'
'Today your Saviour was born. He is Christ, the Lord!'
3
What does the Bible say the shepherds did that night?
They saw angels.
They went to Bethlehem.
They gave Jesus a baby lamb.
They told people Jesus had been born.
4
Who was the Roman emperor at the time of Jesus' birth?
Herod
Caesar Augustus
Julius Caesar
Tiberius Caesar
5
Why did Joseph and Mary travel to Bethlehem?
To take part in a census.
To be married.
Because Joseph was descended from King David.
To visit family.
6
How did the Magi (wise men) know that Jesus had been born?
Angels told them.
Shepherds told them.
They saw it in a dream.
They saw a star in the east.
7
Herod checked it out with the priests and teachers who'd read Micah's prophecy written 700 years earlier! But what did it say?
That Jesus would be born in Bethlehem.
That Jesus would be called Jesus!
That Jesus would be like a shepherd for his people.
That Jesus would be born in a stable.

Bible: Luke 24:1–12

LIFE RELOADED

THE AIM: To worship Jesus in response to the events of Easter

The aim unpacked

With everything that happens at Easter, it's easy to get caught up in the consumer hype of buying Easter eggs or having a quick holiday break. The resurrection of Jesus can be easily glossed over. However, the resurrection isn't only a 'death-changing' event for Jesus; it's a 'life-changing' event for us.

WAY IN

theGRID MAGAZINE

WHAT: visual memories
WHY: to recap on the story of Jesus' crucifixion
WITH: magazine page 290

1 Invite the group to split into pairs or threes and hand out copies of the Easter images from page 290. The images are visual reminders of episodes in the story of Jesus' death and resurrection.

2 Challenge the pairs or threes to work together to figure out which part of the story each image represents.

3 Obtain feedback from the young people to check that everyone knows what each image is a reminder of. Mention that the images are not in the right order, so...

4 Ask them to work together again in their small groups to number the images in the order in which they appear in the story. They can write a small number next to each image. Again, check this out all together.

5 If you think the young people need more reinforcement of the story, invite the small groups to retell it using the images as prompts. Invite two or three groups to present their own versions.

SCENE SETTER

WHAT: Easter egg hunt
WHY: to consider how we value things
WITH: eggs (hard-boiled and painted), chocolate egg prize

1 Before the session, paint lots of hard-boiled eggs in different colours, including one gold one. Allocate a score to each colour egg – for example, each blue egg is worth 10 points, each green egg is worth 15. You could include bonus points for sets. Make sure you give the gold egg a minus score!

2 Hide the eggs and then send the group out egg hunting. Explain that as they find the eggs, they can swap them with each other if they wish. Don't reveal your scoring system; rather invite them to guess the value of the eggs based on their colours and collect those they think are most valuable. They are likely to want to barter for the one golden egg!

3 Once all the eggs have been found, bring everyone together and count how many eggs of each colour they have.

4 Now explain the scoring system and invite everyone to calculate their scores. Give a chocolate egg to the person with the most points.

5 Explain that it's usually better to know the value of things before investing in them. Say that today you will be looking at the Easter story in the light of this.

THEMED GAME

WHAT: movie clips
WHY: to think about the powerful image of transformation
WITH: Disney's ***Beauty and the Beast*** DVD, ***The Lord of the Rings: The Return of the King*** DVD, playback equipment

1 Show the clip from *Beauty and the Beast* where the Beast turns back into a man (approximately 1 hour 13 minutes into the film). Ask the young people if they saw this film as small children. If so, can they remember their reaction when they first saw this scene?

2 Then show the scene in *The Lord of the Rings: The Return of the King* when Frodo wakes up after his ordeal on Mount Doom and is reunited with Gandalf and all his friends (approximately 2 hours 44 minutes into the film).

3 Say that in this session, we're going to focus on a transformation that is even more amazing than the Beast's and an even happier occasion than Frodo waking up. It is something that really happened (it's not fiction) and it's the transformation from being dead to being alive – there can't be a more mind-blowing event than that!

BIBLE EXPERIENCE

LEVEL 1: CONNECT

WHAT: **quotes, quiz and meditation**
WHY: **to worship Jesus in response to the events of Easter**
WITH: **magazine page 290**

1 Invite the group to get into pairs or threes. Together they should read the 'Believe it or not?' article from page 290 and decide which of the quotes were not generally believed at the time they were said but actually proved to be true, and which were generally believed but actually proved to be false.

2 Ask the pairs or groups of three to feed back and compare their answers with the rest of the group. You may need to give a few hints on the way through if they look blank! Of course, some quotes may be open to debate.

3 Ask the group to think of other big things in history that people have believed would happen and didn't, or things that people didn't believe which then did happen.

4 Without introduction, ask a few prepared readers to read out the following Bible passages in which Jesus predicts his death and resurrection: Mark 8:31; 9:9,10; 9:30–32; 10:32–34. Ask the young people to think silently about whether they think these quotes fall into the category of 'generally believed but didn't happen', or 'generally disbelieved but actually happened'. Why would these events have been so hard to believe?

5 Invite the young people to close their eyes and imagine they are with the women coming to Jesus' tomb: encourage them to picture the scene unfolding in their minds. As you read Luke 24:1–12 to the group, pause at the end of verses 3, 8 and 9 and ask, 'Do you believe it or not?'

6 Allow a short time of silence at the end of the reading, then ask if anyone would like to say anything about what they have heard.

LEVEL 2: INTERFACE

WHAT: **drama and discussion**
WHY: **to worship Jesus in response to the events of Easter**
WITH: **Bibles, props or craft materials (optional)**

1 Ask the young people to split into small groups and challenge them to create a short sketch where the hero is in danger of losing his or her life. They need to leave the drama at a cliffhanger, but work out how he or she is going to escape death. The young people could make props, costumes and scenery with art and craft materials.

2 Encourage each group to perform their sketch in turn.

3 After each sketch, invite the other groups to suggest how they think the hero would get out of the situation and then ask the original group to say whether or not they are right.

4 Give each group a Bible and ask them to read Luke 24:1–12 together, either by choosing one person to read it aloud or reading a verse each.

5 Ask the small groups to discuss the following questions:

- How is the story of Jesus' death and resurrection like the sketches they have just performed?
- How is it different?
- Is Jesus' resurrection more or less believable than their heroes' escape-from-death scenarios?
- How does this make you feel towards Jesus?

LEVEL 3: SWITCH ON

WHAT: **Bible research**
WHY: **to worship Jesus in response to the events of Easter**
WITH: **magazine page 291, page 292, Bibles**

1 Divide the young people into three small groups. It doesn't matter if there are only one or two young people in each 'group'. Each group will consider one of the following three questions about Jesus' resurrection:

- Who said what?
- Who saw what?
- Who changed how?

2 Give each group Bibles and a research card from page 292. If you have large groups, make several copies of each research card. Each group should appoint a leader to read out the card, someone to write down the answers and someone else to feed back to everyone later.

3 After the young people have had time to do the task, invite each group to feed back in turn.

4 Now give out copies of page 291 and ask everyone, individually, to do the quiz called 'What sort of believer are you?'

5 When they have worked out their results, ask them to think silently about the question, 'Does the result of the quiz actually match up with what you believe about Jesus rising from the dead?'

6 Finish by explaining to the young people the importance of Jesus' death and resurrection for Christians: these events are the focal point of the whole purpose of God with the human race. Jesus didn't stay a dead sacrifice for long: because he never sinned, death couldn't hold him. He's alive and his resurrection means that those who believe in him are saved from the punishment their sins deserve, and will be raised to life after death. What should our response be?

RESPOND

46

MUSICAL

WHAT: **DIY poetry praise**
WHY: **to worship Jesus for all he achieved through his death and resurrection**
WITH: **flip chart or whiteboard, ambient music, playback equipment, musical instruments (optional)**

1 Ask the young people to suggest key words or phrases that, in their view, sum up what Jesus achieved by dying on the cross and rising again. Write the words or phrases on the flip chart or whiteboard.

2 Now encourage everyone to turn the words or phrases into a poem of four-word lines that describe what Jesus has done. The kind of lines you're looking for are:

- People lover, sacrifice maker
- Enemy forgiver, soul searcher
- Death defeater, life provider
- Hope giver, heaven opener

3 Turn the poem into praise and thanksgiving. Play the ambient music quietly in the background and begin the praise with, 'Jesus, thank you for dying on the cross. We praise you...' and then either invite the young people to repeat the poem phrases or do so yourself.

4 If you have a musically gifted group, you could perhaps invite them to create their own percussion and instrumental accompaniment. Think how you might present it to the rest of the church, to help them worship the risen Jesus, if the opportunity arises.

PRACTICAL

WHAT: **hope messages**
WHY: **to help each other live daily with the truth and implications of Jesus' resurrection**

1 Discuss together what practical differences Jesus' resurrection might make to our daily lives.

2 Say that you will all send an encouraging message to another group member this week. The message should include a challenge about Jesus being alive. Ask everyone to sit in a circle – this will be the chain for sending the messages.

3 Ask everyone to swap details with the people either side of them so everyone knows who they will contact and who will contact them.

4 Invite them to decide how they will send their message – text, email, Facebook, phone call, hand-delivered letter or card... or something else – whatever best suits them and the person receiving the message.

5 Explain that during the week you will contact a group member, which should prompt him or her to contact the next person. The challenge is for messages to travel round the whole group before you next meet. Start it a couple of hours after your session ends. If your church's safeguarding policy makes it difficult for you to contact the young people individually, designate a reliable member to start the chain at a specific time.

6 Give out pens and paper and encourage the young people to write down what they will say based on the discussions in step 1. Encourage them to take the message home to put it into their chosen format.

CREATIVE

WHAT: **designer logo**
WHY: **to help focus our whole lives on Jesus, the Risen One**

1 Explain to the group that Jesus is the One who died and rose again so that we can live for ever with God, so he deserves to be 'Number One' in our life.

2 Using the phrase 'Number One' or something similar, encourage the young people to design a logo that represents the new life to which Jesus rose and which he now shares with us. They can sketch it roughly with paper and pencils. You could provide examples of existing designer labels to inspire them with styles of lettering, colour and design.

3 If together you come up with a really good logo, consider using it permanently by somehow incorporating it into your group name, as a T-shirt logo or renaming a regular service you help to organise. The key thing is that it should always be around to remind you of the One who died and rose again.

MORE ON THIS THEME:

If you want to do a short series with your group, other sessions that work well with this one are:

47	*What a difference a day makes!*	*Luke 24:13–35*
48	*We are witnesses*	*Luke 24:36–49*

Look at these images.
They relate to the Easter story in John 18,19 in the New Testament.
- What do they refer to?
- Can you tell the story from the images and put them into the right order?

Jesus - King of the Jews

Bible bit
Luke 24:1–12

The resurrection of Jesus can be easily glossed over: 'Christ has died; Christ has risen; Christ will come again.' However, the fact that Christ has risen should bring some response from us. We're not just talking about a 'Wow!' here – though too often we don't even let that take hold. If you think about it, Jesus rising from the dead means that we too will one day follow him in that resurrection – because he loved us, we are able to live again. The resurrection isn't only a 'death-changing' event for Jesus; it is a 'life-changing' event for us.

BELIEVE IT OR NOT?

Check out these quotes. These people all believed that what they said was true; some were believed by other people and others weren't. Time has proved some of these to be true and others false. Think about or talk with some friends about them.

'At midnight on 31 December 1999, when the clocks advance to 2000, all the computers will crash and the world will be thrown into chaos.'
Popular view of the Millennium bug, 1999

'Television won't matter in your lifetime or mine.'
Rex Lambert, editor of the *Radio Times*, 1936

'If excessive smoking actually plays a role in the production of lung cancer, it seems to be a minor one.'
WC Heuper, National Cancer Institute, 1954

'Airplanes are interesting toys but of no military value.'
Marshal Ferdinand Foch, who stopped the Germans at the Second Battle of Marne, 1918

'Louis Pasteur's theory of germs is ridiculous fiction.'
Pierre Pachet, Professor of Physiology, 1872

'The Son of Man must be handed over to sinful people, be crucified and rise from the dead on the third day.'
Jesus, Luke 24:7

'I think there is a world market for maybe five computers.'
Thomas Watson, chairman of IBM, 1943

'Production of excessive carbon dioxide will increase global warming and result in climate and weather changes.'
The majority of the scientific community, 2000 onwards

FRESHMAN
American Freshman

46

WHAT SORT OF BELIEVER ARE YOU?

Do you believe what you hear without questioning? Or are you the most hardened sceptic since 'No Way José' was born? Answer the questions to find out what sort of believer you are.

1 Your best friend says she has the home phone number of the latest pop sensation and she's been talking to him every night on the phone! Do you...

A – ask for the number so you can call him too?

B – wonder what the world record for saying, 'I really like your new single,' in one telephone conversation is?

C – say, 'Yes, dear, I'm sure you do. Did he mention the world tour that he's on – which is on the other side of the world at the moment?'

2 Your friend says a scout for Manchester United spotted him playing football in the park and offered to take him to meet the team! Unfortunately your friend had to go home for his tea so he couldn't go! Do you...

A – make sure your boots and kit are clean, ready to join in next time?

B – discuss with your friend which is better – a good defence or a good attack?

C – remind him that you were with him last night doing maths homework and the only football they played was kicking scrap paper into the bin?

3 You read a newspaper report on Hamish McMish, a lone crofter from the Highlands of Scotland who claims to have met aliens, had tea with them and discussed ways of safeguarding the future of the creature in Loch Ness! Do you...

A – bring out your Nessie and ET memorabilia and tell everyone you have always been a believer?

B – wonder whether there are any crofters left in the Highlands?

C – smile, smugly, at all the people out there who believe there is a conspiracy to hide the existence of aliens from the general public?

4 It is 1 April and the main news story is about the destruction of the 'Liquid' tree's environment. Apparently this is causing a national shortage of washing-up liquid. Do you...

A – tell your parents to rush out and buy as much washing-up liquid as possible?

B – think about what else you could grow on trees if the scientists creating genetically modified plants were permitted to do anything?

C – marvel at the inventiveness of the news team to come up with something the fiction department would be proud of?

5 Your friend tells you that the new kid in your class fancies you and wants to meet you at lunchtime to ask you out. Do you...

A – rush to the toilets, clean your teeth, comb your hair and make sure you look your best?

B – wonder what the school canteen is serving today and whether you have brought enough money to buy some chocolate?

C – remind your friend that there is no new kid in the class so you are quite worried about their state of mind; perhaps they have been working too hard recently?

Mostly As The fishhook is permanently in your mouth. You believe anything you are told – hook, line and sinker. Perhaps you need to question more, to get to the truth.

Mostly Bs Erm, you tend to pay little attention to anything you are told and are often distracted by the smallest detail. Not much hope for you, I'm afraid; however, there may be a job for you writing for *theGRID*.

Mostly Cs You are a sceptic and question everything. This scepticism could prevent you seeing the truth in front of your eyes if you automatically reject everything you're told.

RESOURCE PAGE

USE WITH SESSION 46 BIBLE EXPERIENCE 'LEVEL 3 SWITCH ON'

Group 1

Who said what?

Mark 8:30–33

John 12:23,24

Group 2

Who saw what?

Mark 16:12–16

Luke 24:1–12

Luke 24:13–16,30–33

John 21:1–13

1 Corinthians 15:3–8

Group 3

Who changed how?

Acts 5:29 32

Acts 13:32–39

1 John 2:1,2

1 John 4:7–15

Bible: Luke 24:13–35

WHAT A DIFFERENCE A DAY MAKES!

THE AIM: To review the evidence that Jesus is alive, discover the difference this can make, and help young people make up their minds about him

The aim unpacked

In this session, we'll focus on the two disciples walking to Emmaus. They were devastated by all that had happened to Jesus in Jerusalem and were confused by the first resurrection reports. Jesus met with them on the way and helped them to see how the recent events totally made sense in the light of Scripture. This gives us a fantastic opportunity to explore with the young people the evidence for Jesus' resurrection.

WAY IN

theGRID MAGAZINE

WHAT: **active opinion poll**
WHY: **to think about what we believe and why**
WITH: **magazine page 296**

1 Use the questions in the 'So what do you think?' section on page 296 to conduct a poll with your group.

2 Depending on how much space you have, you could ask everyone to move around the room: one end of the room represents 'No way!' and the other '100%'. Alternatively, make sure everyone has a pen and a magazine and ask them to complete it in pairs.

3 Throughout the poll, ask one or two young people for quick feedback, for example:

- Why do you/don't you believe this?
- How sure are you about it?
- What would help you make up your mind?

4 Using examples from the poll, comment that we tend to base our beliefs on evidence.

5 Lead in to the rest of the session by asking the final question: 'Do you believe Jesus rose from the dead?' Don't ask for any feedback this time, but say that you'll be looking at the evidence that he did!

SCENE SETTER

WHAT: **jigsaw hunt**
WHY: **to piece together evidence to make a picture**
WITH: **jigsaw puzzles, prizes (optional)**

1 Before the session, get hold of some easy jigsaw puzzles, or make some by pasting a magazine picture onto card and cutting it into about 15 pieces. You will need one puzzle for every four to five young people. Mark the back of each piece of the first jigsaw with a red blob, each piece of the second jigsaw with a blue blob, and so on. Mix up all the jigsaw pieces and spread them around your meeting room before the young people arrive.

2 Split the group into smaller teams of four or five: the red team, the blue team, and so on.

3 On the word 'Go', each team has to find all the jigsaw pieces marked with their colour. The first team to complete their jigsaw wins! Award prizes, if you wish. Make sure none of the young people takes another team's piece deliberately, to slow them down!

4 Lead into the rest of the session by saying something like, 'Today we're looking for bits of evidence to put together to get to the truth about Jesus' resurrection.'

THEMED GAME

WHAT: **truth game**
WHY: **to understand the need for evidence when we're deciding whether something is true or not**
WITH: **situation cards, sweets (optional)**

1 Before the session, think of about four fun, quirky and interesting things about yourself that the young people are unlikely to know. Ask your co-leaders to do the same. Write each one on the front of a separate sheet of folded card, with the word 'true' written in large letters inside the card.

2 Challenge the young people to find out whether you're telling the truth or not, and read out the first fact.

3 Invite them to ask you questions about it for a minute or so, then ask everyone to vote: true or false? Open your card to reveal that it's true. Give a sweet to everyone who guessed correctly. Repeat with the other cards.

4 Use these points from the game to link in with the rest of the session:

- The young people looked for evidence to help them decide whether each situation was true or not.
- The situations were difficult to believe... but they were all true!

BIBLE EXPERIENCE

LEVEL 1: CONNECT

WHAT: **interview**
WHY: **to review the evidence that Jesus is alive and make up our minds about him**
WITH: **page 297**

1 Before the session, copy the interview questions from page 295. Cut along the dotted lines and put each question in a separate envelope. Mark the envelopes with the question numbers. Use sticky tack to stick these under separate chairs before your young people arrive. Also before the session, ask two leaders or older young people to role play the disciples, making sure they prepare their story in advance by reading Luke 24:13–35.

2 With everyone together, introduce the 'disciples' and have the rest of the group interview them, using the questions tacked under their chairs.

3 Recap by asking, 'What evidence did we see that Jesus is alive?' (There were witnesses; it 'made sense' given what had been said about Jesus; people's lives were changed – develop this from step 5 of the 'Level 2 Interface' activity, as appropriate to your group.)

4 End by asking, 'What do you think of the evidence you've seen today? What difference does it make to you?'

LEVEL 2: INTERFACE

WHAT: **film documentary**
WHY: **to review the evidence that Jesus is alive and make up our minds about him**
WITH: **Bibles, evidence sources, pages 298 and 299, film camera (optional)**

1 Before the session, gather sources of evidence for Jesus' resurrection. For example:

- Bibles marked at Luke 24:36–43; John 21:1–23; Matthew 28:16–20; Acts 9:1–5; 1 Corinthians 15:5–7.
- A guest to talk about the difference Jesus has made to their lives.
- A short talk outlining resurrection evidence – eg 'The reliability of Christ's resurrection – Lee Strobel' on YouTube.
- Print the Wikipedia article on Albert Henry Ross (pseudonym: Frank Morison), who set out to disprove the resurrection and concluded that it happened! (*Who Moved the Stone?* Authentic Media, 2006.) Set up the evidence around your meeting room.

2 Split into groups of about four, each with a Bible, paper and pens. Challenge each group to make a film documentary about the evidence for Jesus' resurrection. Give out copies of pages 298 and 299 as an outline.

3 Begin with the incident on the Emmaus road (Luke 24:13–35) and consider:

- When and where this took place (v 13)
- What we know about the mood of the two disciples initially (v 17)
- What evidence Jesus showed them, even before they recognised him (vs 27,30)

4 Come together again and take feedback.

5 Ask the groups to move around the room and look at the evidence. Then invite them to script their documentary.

6 Either ask each group to perform its documentary for everyone else, or record each group and watch the films together.

7 End with a discussion: 'What do you think of the evidence you've seen today? What difference does it make to you?'

LEVEL 3: SWITCH ON

WHAT: **DVD and sticky note investigation**
WHY: **to review the evidence that Jesus is alive and make up our minds about him**
WITH: ***The Passion* DVD (BBC/ Acorn Media, 2008), playback equipment, evidence board**

1 In advance, make an evidence board: head a large sheet of paper with 'Evidence that Jesus is alive'. Add 'Clue 1: The change in the disciples' and 'Clue 2: Who is that man?! How do you know?'

2 Play the first four minutes of scene 4, episode 4 of *The Passion*, where Jesus appears to the disciples on the Emmaus road and then in the upper room (Luke 24:13–43. NB: the filmmakers used different actors to convey that Jesus was not recognised). Pause on Peter's face as Jesus asks, 'Why won't you listen?'

3 Split into twos or threes and give out sticky notes and pens.

4 Show the evidence board. Ask the groups to write on separate sticky notes any evidence they've seen that Jesus is alive, and stick them to the board.

5 Review the evidence board together. Add to it from these points:

- The witnesses: people saw Jesus after his death! Jesus also appeared to other disciples (eg John 21:1–23), a crowd of 500 (1 Corinthians 15:6) and Saul (Acts 9:1–5).
- The logic: Jesus argued the case for his resurrection from other parts of the Bible. It just makes sense! Lee Strobel, a legal journalist, set out to disprove the resurrection but ended up believing it's the only possible explanation for what happened! (*The Case for Christ*, Zondervan, 1998.)
- The change in people: the disciples were different after meeting Jesus. Those frightened, disappointed people started the church! Say that people's lives are still being changed through meeting Jesus.

6 Ask, 'What do you think of the evidence you've seen today? What difference does it make to you?'

RESPOND

47

MUSICAL

WHAT: **song**
WHY: **to respond in praise to the fact that Jesus is alive**
WITH: **music and lyrics for 'Happy Day' by Tim Hughes, playback equipment (optional)**

1 Watch or listen to a recording of the song 'Happy Day' by Tim Hughes.

2 If you have a 'Connect' level group, simply ask, 'What is this guy happy about?' and use the song to recap and reinforce what has emerged from this session for the young people. If you have an 'Interface' or 'Switch on' level group, encourage the young people to think a bit more about what Tim Hughes is singing. You might want to invite the young people to look at the song lyrics, which touch on lots of the benefits of Jesus' death and resurrection – forgiveness, eternal life, relationship with God through Jesus, death defeated.

3 If appropriate to your group, sing the song together. Use it as a springboard for your own prayers of praise and thanksgiving for all that Jesus' resurrection means!

PRACTICAL

WHAT: **testimony**
WHY: **to recognise the evidence that Jesus is alive through a person's changed life**
WITH: **guest**

1 In advance, invite a guest who can share in a teen-friendly way the difference Jesus has made to their life to share their testimony with the group, either as a short monologue or in the style of an interview, with you asking the questions.

2 Open it up to the young people to ask questions of their own and to share their own experiences, if appropriate.

3 Depending on the spiritual interest in your group, explain that the young people can test this out in their own lives. Offer an opportunity to talk further with individuals who would like to find out more.

4 End in prayer, either with space for everyone to dialogue with Jesus on their own or with you or another leader praying on everyone's behalf.

CREATIVE

WHAT: **thanksgiving prayer**
WHY: **to say 'Thank you' to God for our 'supporters'**
WITH: **long strips of paper, scissors, felt-tip pens, sticky tack, simple cross shape (could be cut out of paper or card) fixed to a wall or noticeboard**

1 Choose one or more of these ideas and gather suitable materials and equipment:

- Drama – nothing needed!
- Art – paper, pens, pencils or charcoal
- Photography – digital camera, PC and photo printer, board to mount the photos

2 The idea is for the young people to think about how the disciples on the Emmaus road responded to the risen Jesus – and about how they personally are responding to him now.

- Drama – seat the young people in a circle facing outwards. Ask them to picture how the disciples felt as they started their journey and to communicate that with their faces and bodies. Give them about 30 seconds' thinking time. Then ask everyone to turn around and freeze-frame with an appropriate facial expression. Do it again, asking them to imagine the disciples as Jesus broke the bread. Then a third time to show how they feel about it.
- Art – ask the young people to draw two faces: one of the disciples at any point in the story, and one of themselves, showing how they feel about all they've heard today.
- Photography – ask the young people to take photos of each other, showing how they feel about all they've heard today.

3 Enjoy the creations together! A puzzled or questioning response can be positive, so don't let anyone feel that their reactions are in any way wrong!

4 End in prayer, offering an opportunity to talk further with anyone who would like to.

MORE ON THIS THEME:

If you want to do a short series with your group, other sessions that work well with this one are:

46 *Life reloaded* *Luke 24:1–12*

48 *We are witnesses* *Luke 24:36–49*

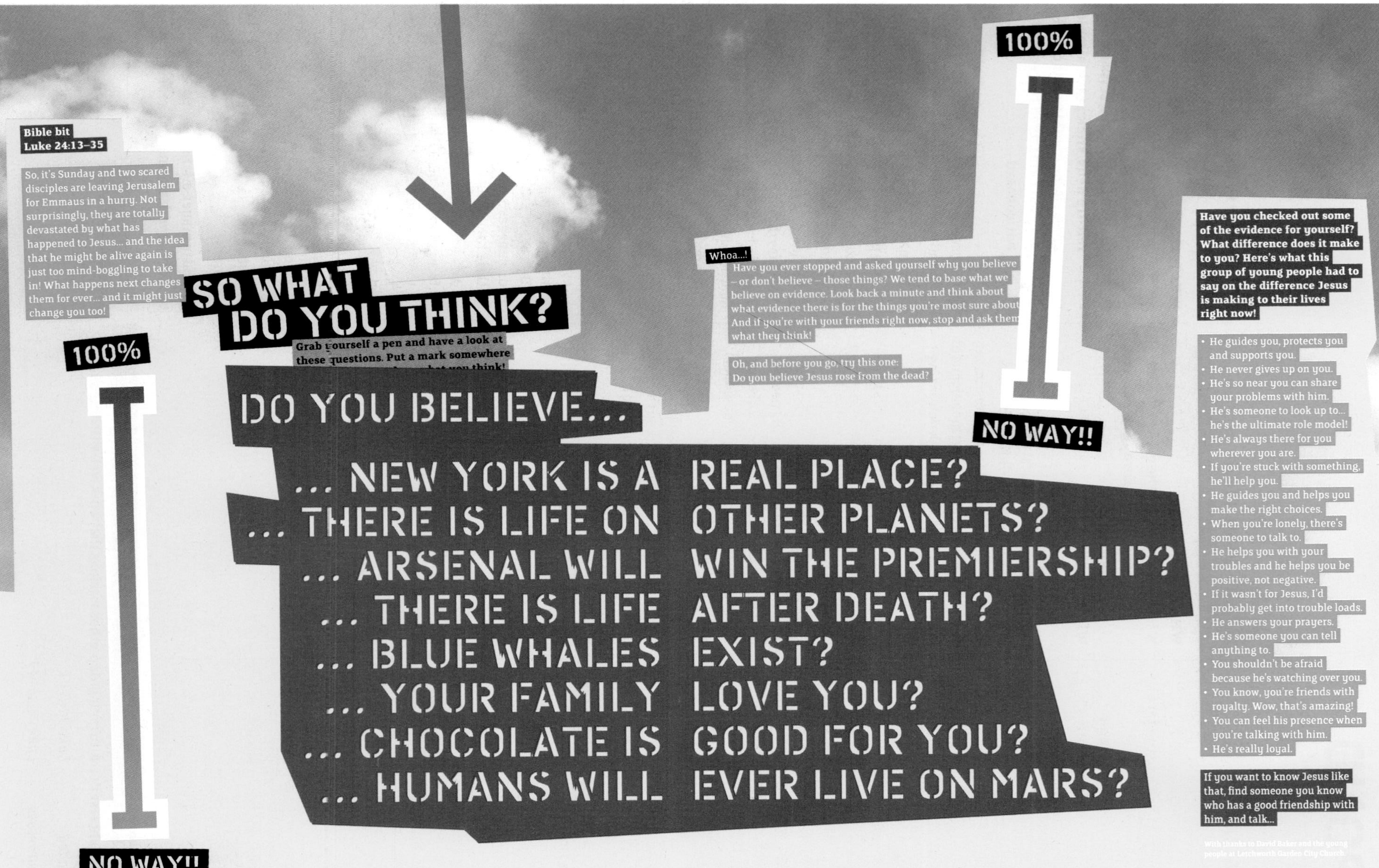
Bible bit
Luke 24:13–35
So, it's Sunday and two scared disciples are leaving Jerusalem for Emmaus in a hurry. Not surprisingly, they are totally devastated by what has happened to Jesus... and the idea that he might be alive again is just too mind-boggling to take in! What happens next changes them for ever... and it might just change you too!
SO WHAT DO YOU THINK?
Grab yourself a pen and have a look at these questions. Put a mark somewhere
100%
NO WAY!!
DO YOU BELIEVE...
... NEW YORK IS A REAL PLACE?
... THERE IS LIFE ON OTHER PLANETS?
... ARSENAL WILL WIN THE PREMIERSHIP?
... THERE IS LIFE AFTER DEATH?
... BLUE WHALES EXIST?
... YOUR FAMILY LOVE YOU?
... CHOCOLATE IS GOOD FOR YOU?
... HUMANS WILL EVER LIVE ON MARS?
Whoa...!
Have you ever stopped and asked yourself why you believe – or don't believe – those things? We tend to base what we believe on evidence. Look back a minute and think about what evidence there is for the things you're most sure about. And if you're with your friends right now, stop and ask them what they think!
Oh, and before you go, try this one: Do you believe Jesus rose from the dead?
100%
NO WAY!!
Have you checked out some of the evidence for yourself? What difference does it make to you? Here's what this group of young people had to say on the difference Jesus is making to their lives right now!
• He guides you, protects you and supports you.
• He never gives up on you.
• He's so near you can share your problems with him.
• He's someone to look up to... he's the ultimate role model!
• He's always there for you wherever you are.
• If you're stuck with something, he'll help you.
• He guides you and helps you make the right choices.
• When you're lonely, there's someone to talk to.
• He helps you with your troubles and he helps you be positive, not negative.
• If it wasn't for Jesus, I'd probably get into trouble loads.
• He answers your prayers.
• He's someone you can tell anything to.
• You shouldn't be afraid because he's watching over you.
• You know, you're friends with royalty. Wow, that's amazing!
• You can feel his presence when you're talking with him.
• He's really loyal.
If you want to know Jesus like that, find someone you know who has a good friendship with him, and talk...
With thanks to David Baker and the young people at Letchworth Garden City Church

USE WITH SESSION 47 BIBLE EXPERIENCE 'LEVEL 1 CONNECT'

Interview questions for the disciples on the Emmaus road

1 This incident you're going to tell us about – when did it happen?

2 Where did it happen?

3 How were you feeling as you set off on your journey? Why?

4 I understand someone joined you on the way. What did he talk about?

5 What happened when you got to the village?

6 What was unusual about the man?

7 How did that meeting affect you?

RESOURCE PAGE

USE WITH SESSION 47 BIBLE EXPERIENCE 'LEVEL 2 INTERFACE'

Jesus is alive! (But how do we know?)

When it comes to believing whether or not Jesus really did rise from the dead and really is alive today, we'll always need faith – BUT there is some hard evidence out there to help us make up our minds. So get yourself a drink, something yummy to snack on, a pen, your Bible, your laptop, tablet or mobile phone... and see what you discover.

Evidence source:	Check it out!
Eyewitness accounts: Luke 24:13–35 (Remember, the Bible is a historical document!)	When and where did the incident take place? What were the disciples thinking and feeling to start with (up to v 24)? What evidence did Jesus show them, even before they recognised him? How were the disciples changed (vs 33,34)?

RESOURCE PAGE

USE WITH SESSION 47 BIBLE EXPERIENCE 'LEVEL 2 INTERFACE'

Evidence source:	Check it out!
Changed minds	Find out about these guys online! Frank Morison Lee Strobel
Changed lives	Text or call a Christian you know and ask: How has Jesus changed your life? How do you meet with Jesus now?

So what do you think of all that evidence?

What difference does it make to you?

48

Bible: Luke 24:36–49

WE ARE WITNESSES

THE AIM: To realise that we must proclaim that Jesus is alive

The aim unpacked

Jesus appeared to his followers, but they thought he was a ghost! It seems they still weren't sure he had risen. Jesus explained the Scriptures to them and they finally understood what had happened. As well as convincing them that he was alive, Jesus entrusted the disciples with the task of telling all nations about him. And we are charged with that same task.

WAY IN

theGRID MAGAZINE

WHAT: **discussion**
WHY: **to think about things that are amazing but true**
WITH: **magazine page 303**

1 Split the young people into groups of three or four and give each group a copy of the 'Amazing facts' from page 303.

2 Invite the young people to read and chat about the facts. Which ones do they think are truly amazing? Encourage them to share any knowledge that they may have on any of these facts – including the last one about Jesus.

3 Chat briefly about how, when we find out something truly amazing, we usually tell other people about it. Challenge the young people: 'Does anyone do that with the amazing fact that Jesus died and came back to life again?'

SCENE SETTER

WHAT: **being alive**
WHY: **to see what 'being alive' means**
WITH: **prize (optional)**

1 Split the young people into two groups. Give each group pens and paper.

2 Give the young people three minutes to write down as many words and phrases as they can think of that express what it means to be alive. For example, 'I am breathing'; 'I can see, hear, talk, walk, think, run, jump, touch'; 'I can read, play music, play sport, dance'.

3 After three minutes come together and invite each group to share what they have written – they could use actions to illustrate what they have written if they want to. You could award a small prize to the most original thought.

4 Say that in today's Bible passage we will be seeing what it was like, and what it meant to the disciples, to know that Jesus was alive again.

THEMED GAME

WHAT: **Chinese whispers**
WHY: **to think about communicating a message**
WITH: **small pieces of card**

1 Before the session, put together a list of simple messages. Have a mix of ordinary and stupid messages. Write each message on a separate piece of card.

2 Split the group into two teams and ask them to sit in two lines (if you have a small number of people, stay as one group and play against the clock). Explain that you're going to play competitive Chinese whispers! Show the first person in each team the first message. They are to whisper it to the next person in their team. The message is passed down the line and the last person writes it down. The last person comes to you for the next message, which is then passed down the line. The first group to write all the messages down is the winner!

3 Chat about how difficult it was to communicate the correct message all the way down the line. If you had an important message, would you tell others by whispering it?!

BIBLE EXPERIENCE

48

LEVEL 1: CONNECT

WHAT: cartoon
WHY: to realise that we must proclaim that Jesus is alive
WITH: magazine page 304, Bibles

1 Give out copies of page 304. Ask the young people to read the comic strip 'He's alive!' which is based on the events in Luke 24:36–49. When everyone has finished, read Luke 24:36–49.

2 Explain that the disciples needed to be convinced by Jesus that it was really him and that he was indeed alive. Do the young people need any convincing? This is a good way of finding out where your young people are at with Jesus, but handle this discussion carefully – there may well be a diverse range of opinions within the group!

3 Explain that Jesus called the disciples to be 'witnesses' – that means they were to tell others about his message of love and forgiveness – and we, as Christians today, are called to do the same. Is this something the young people find easy? Or do they want to hide the message away?

LEVEL 2: INTERFACE

WHAT: interactive dramatisation
WHY: to realise that we must proclaim that Jesus is alive
WITH: page 305, available props, Bible

1 Ask for volunteers to read Luke 24:36–49 using the script on page 305. (Or you could read from *The Dramatised Bible*.)

2 Ask the young people what they think the 'core' message of this passage is (that Jesus is alive and that we have to tell others this good news just as the disciples were called to do).

3 The script on page 305 is deliberately brief. Ask the young people to create a new, more interesting drama that puts across the main message of the passage. Give out Bibles and encourage the group to work with the Bible text. If you have a large group, split into smaller groups to do this. When they have finished, perform the drama(s) (to other groups, if possible).

4 Conclude by saying that we, too, have that same exciting challenge set before us: to proclaim that Jesus is alive!

LEVEL 3: SWITCH ON

WHAT: in-depth Bible study
WHY: to realise that we must proclaim that Jesus is alive
WITH: Bibles

1 Divide the young people into two groups: a 'Jesus' group and a 'disciples' group. Give each group a Bible and ask them to read Luke 24:36–49.

2 Ask the 'Jesus' group to write a brief summary or some notes about what Jesus was doing in this passage, and ask the 'disciples' group to write about what the disciples were doing in the passage. Ask them to particularly look at some of the emotions that were expressed. For example, they might come up with fear, being troubled, doubt, amazement, happiness, belief, opening of minds.

3 Come back together after about five minutes and share what each group has discovered.

4 You could conclude by reading the passage again and asking the young people to listen and have their minds opened to understand, like the disciples did.

RESPOND

MUSICAL

WHAT: **listening, singing, composing**
WHY: **to discover how we can respond to the good news that Jesus is alive**
WITH: **worship songs on CD or MP3, playback equipment**

1 If your group likes to sing, sing some songs with the theme of proclaiming the message of what Jesus has done for us.

2 Alternatively, listen to songs on the theme of the cross. Here are some album suggestions:

- *Breathe* by Andy Smith (Survivor Records, 2007) – tracks 2 and 4
- *Take Me to the Cross* (Maranatha Music, 2006) – track 5 is particularly suitable
- *A Tree by the Water* by Chris Falson (Maranatha Music, 2006) – track 4

3 Alternatively, if your young people are musical, they could try to write lyrics and music for a new Easter song based on any aspect of the Easter message to sum up the last sessions, or a song of witness about sharing their faith. This song could be worked on and used as part of an outreach youth event or in a service at church.

PRACTICAL

WHAT: **prayer and reflection**
WHY: **to encourage the young people to respond to today's message**
WITH: **copies of page 305, reflective background music, playback equipment, candle**

1 Invite your group to sit in a circle. Place a lit candle in the centre. Play some reflective background music.

2 Give out copies of page 305 and encourage the young people to read the prayer 'That walk'. A leader or young person could read it first to the whole group.

3 When they have read it, ask the young people to reflect quietly on what the prayer is saying to them. They can look at the candle and listen to the music while they do this. Ask them to think about what response they should make to the fact that Jesus is alive and calls us to tell others. The young people can take their copies of the prayer home to use in their personal prayer times.

CREATIVE

WHAT: **dance, drama, art, clay, music, poetry**
WHY: **to interpret creatively all that the Easter story means to the young people**
WITH: **selection of resources, according to the options you can provide**

1 Before the session, decide what options you would like to offer to the young people, depending on the resources you have and the interests of the group.

2 Invite the young people to choose from a variety of creative activities. The idea is to create something, whether through dance, clay, music, drama, art or poetry, to interpret the Easter story that they have heard over the last few sessions. They could focus on a part of the story or on the idea that we are called to be witnesses and to share the good news with others.

3 Come together to share what the young people have produced. There may be things that could be used in church or as part of a youth outreach event.

MORE ON THIS THEME:

If you want to do a short series with your group, other sessions that work well with this one are:

46	*Life reloaded*	*Luke 24:1–12*
47	*What a difference a day makes!*	*Luke 24:13–35*

48

AMAZING FACTS

READ THESE AMAZING FACTS. WHICH ONE IMPRESSES YOU MOST?

Bible bit
Luke 24:36–49

Cleopas and his friend are halfway through telling their amazing story to the rest of the disciples when Jesus appears among them. Despite the story they are in the middle of hearing, they still think Jesus is a ghost! But, after Jesus has explained the story, they believe that he really is alive. Then Jesus gives them the task of telling the whole world!

Due to the natural momentum of the ocean, saltwater fish cannot swim backwards.

The Boeing 747 Jumbo Jet would be capable of flying upside down if it weren't for the fact that the wings would shear off when it tried to roll over.

King Henry VIII slept with a gigantic axe.

If you were to break wind continually for six years and nine months, enough gas would be produced to create the energy of an atomic bomb.

A giraffe can clean its ears with its tongue.

The human heart creates so much pressure as it pumps blood around the body that a wound can squirt blood up to 9 metres away.

A cockroach will live for nine days without its head before it starves to death.

Manatees (large mammals who live in swamps) possess vocal cords which give them the ability to speak like humans, but they don't do so because they have no ears with which to hear the sound.

On average, 100 people choke to death on ballpoint pens every year.

Human saliva has a boiling point three times that of regular water.

Coca-Cola would be green if colouring were not added to it.

Cat urine glows under ultraviolet light.

It's impossible to lick your elbow.

Honey is the only food that does not spoil. Honey found in the tombs of Egyptian pharaohs has been tasted by archaeologists and found to be edible.

The world's oldest piece of chewing gum is 9,000 years old.

In the weightlessness of space, a frozen pea will explode if it comes into contact with Pepsi.

Slugs have four noses.

Jesus Christ is the Son of God who lived, died and rose again for us!

theGRID cannot verify the accuracy of all of this information!

HE'S ALIVE!

Do you need convincing that Jesus is alive, like the disciples did?

And finally! This was to be the task of the disciples:

TO TELL OTHERS THE GOOD NEWS THAT JESUS IS ALIVE!

Is this something you find easy to do?

USE WITH SESSION 48 BIBLE EXPERIENCE 'LEVEL 2 INTERFACE'

Jesus appears to his followers

Cast: Jesus, the disciples and some women

Jesus: *(Standing in the midst of the assembled group.)* Peace be with you.
Disciple 1: He can't be real. It's a ghost!
(The other disciples look afraid.)
Jesus: What's the matter? I am real. Come and see my hands and feet. Touch me. I am not a ghost because I am a living body!
Disciple 2: *(Touching Jesus.)* Wow! That is amazing! He is real!
Jesus: Do you have any food I could have?
Disciple 3: We have some fish.
(He gives Jesus some fish. Jesus eats it.)
Jesus: Do you remember when I was with you before? I said that everything written about me must happen?
(Disciples all nod in agreement.)
Jesus: Well, it was written that I would suffer and then rise from the dead on the third day. It was also written that people's hearts and lives would be changed and that they would receive forgiveness in my name. This message is given to you, for all nations, starting in Jerusalem; you are to go and tell others, in my name, this good news, and I will send the Holy Spirit to help you.

USE WITH SESSION 48 RESPOND 'PRACTICAL'

That walk

Lord, you took that walk to the cross for me,
And as I stand with the disciples in your Resurrection glory,
May I truly know that you live,
That you live in the hearts of men and women today,
That you know me and have called me by name,
That like those first disciples I too am called,
That I am called to follow where you lead,
That I am called to tell all nations about the wonder of your love,
Your forgiving power, your sacrifice,
Made for me,
When you took that walk to the cross.

Bible: Mark 10:17–31

BARRIERS TO JESUS 1

THE AIM: To explore the choices that can keep us from following Jesus

The aim unpacked
Here we see the story of the rich man. Like this guy, we face tough decisions about issues, possessions and uses of our time that can keep us from following Jesus. The world's view is that what we have here on earth is of the utmost importance. But Jesus clearly points out that the only real 'safe' choice is to follow him!

WAY IN

theGRID MAGAZINE

WHAT: **questionnaire**
WHY: **to think about attitudes to wealth**
WITH: **magazine page 309**

1 Ask the group members to do the 'Got stuff? Want stuff?' questionnaire on page 309. Invite them to compare answers with those near them.

2 Chat together about their answers to one or two of the questions. Don't go through all of them; just pick some that have generated comments, or ask which they found hardest to answer. Keep the discussion fairly light – the aim is to get them thinking and talking.

3 Discuss their answers to the last question on the questionnaire. Do they think being a Christian makes a difference to people's attitude to money and wealth? Ask for examples to back up their views: what do Christians say or do that reveals their attitudes?

SCENE SETTER

WHAT: **persuasion**
WHY: **to think about choices concerning possessions**
WITH: **pairs of items representing choices (or pictures, according to what is available): branded trainers and tatty ones; holiday brochure and picture of local park; pictures from your country and mission information about another country**

1 Pick someone to be first in the 'hot seat'. Divide everyone else into two groups. Give one group the branded trainers and the other the tatty old ones (or other appropriate items). The person in the hot seat is going to buy some new footwear. Each group must persuade them to buy theirs.

2 The groups take turns to offer reasons for buying their item. Keep going until they run out of arguments. The person in the hot seat must then choose.

3 Change the person in the hot seat; maybe mix the teams and start again with a different item. If appropriate, finish with a choice between living in your country or working with a mission agency in a tougher situation abroad.

4 Comment that everyone with money and possessions has to make choices. Some choices might seem harder for people who don't have much. But is that always true?

THEMED GAME

WHAT: **game**
WHY: **to ask what kind of lifestyle we aim for**
WITH: **ring (30 cm card circle) or quoit large enough to land over objects, objects to represent different lifestyles – more objects than group members (see below)**

1 In advance, label the objects with the lifestyle they represent and 'wealth points' between 10 and 100. For example: 'cat food – keep animals 10 points'; 'tool – gardener 40 points'; 'travel bag – missionary 30 points'; 'tool – mechanic 50 points'; 'books – teacher 60 points'; 'ball – sportsperson 80 points'; 'photo – Prime Minister 90 points'; 'DVD – film star 100 points'.

2 Lay out the objects as targets. Give each person three throws to try to 'get a life'. If the ring goes over an object, they win that lifestyle. If they win a second, they return one. Once they have all had a go, explain that any further throws cost 30 wealth points. A 60-point lifestyle may be traded for two throws (with the object placed back as a target). A 50-point lifestyle is only tradeable for one throw. Those who haven't won a lifestyle are 'down and out'.

3 Ask: what sort of lifestyle are you aiming for? What will you give up to get there? Refer to these later as the questions the rich man faced in Mark 10.

BIBLE EXPERIENCE

49

LEVEL 1: CONNECT

WHAT: **script and dramatic reading**
WHY: **to explore the choices that can keep us from following Jesus**
WITH: **magazine page 310, copies of Mark 10:17–31**

1 Ask three leaders or group members to read or perform the script 'What's stopping you?' from page 310. Encourage everyone else to listen carefully because they will have to judge what the characters say.

2 Ask each person individually to decide a score out of ten for how much good sense each of the three characters speaks – they can write these in the space in the magazine. Ask everyone to share their scores for Rick, Chris and Petra. Add up the totals. Chat with the group about why they gave these scores. Pick up on any instances where people gave very different scores or any very high or low scores. Ask:

- How would that character have to change for you to give them a higher score?
- Would you have said the same thing in that situation?

3 Ask the same three readers to read Mark 10:17–31, speaking the words of the equivalent character(s) – the rich man (Rick), Jesus (Chris), the disciples and Peter (Petra). You will also need a narrator.

4 Invite comments on how the two stories link. Does it make a difference when the challenging words are spoken by Jesus himself? Encourage the young people to look back at the script in the magazine and circle any phrases they want to remember or think about further.

LEVEL 2: INTERFACE

WHAT: **hot-seating**
WHY: **to explore the choices that can keep us from following Jesus**
WITH: **chair, two signs: 'The man' and 'Follower', 'swingometer' (made from card with a pointer – label one end of the swing 'Follow' and the other end 'Not')**

1 Read aloud Mark 10:17–22. Ask the young people to imagine they are friends of the rich man. Divide them into two groups. One group must persuade the man that following Jesus is a good idea. The other group must persuade him that it is not.

2 Ask a volunteer to sit on the 'hot seat' (a chair labelled 'The man') holding the swingometer. Ask the groups to alternate in arguing for and against following Jesus. After each one, the 'man' should decide how good the argument is and move the swingometer towards 'Follow' or 'Not'. Continue until the arguments run out.

3 Read aloud Mark 10:23–31. Label the hot seat 'Follower'. Invite group members to take turns to sit in the chair and answer questions in that role. Use these questions as starters. Reuse the questions for each person, but vary them a little:

- What did you think of the man who talked to Jesus?
- Do you wish you were that rich?
- What do you think of Jesus? Why do you follow him?
- What do you think of the things Jesus said about rich people and God's kingdom?
- Did you have to leave anything behind to follow Jesus? Was it an easy decision?
- Jesus hinted at a new family and new work for people who follow him. What do you think of that?
- Jesus said his followers will have eternal life. How does that make you feel?
- Why do you think Jesus chose you to be one of his followers?

4 Invite the group to think silently about where they would be in this story. Are there things that they want to hold on to, or do they want to choose to follow Jesus?

LEVEL 3: SWITCH ON

WHAT: **Bible study**
WHY: **to explore the choices that can keep us from following Jesus**
WITH: **two large paper or card shoe shapes, card**

1 Read Mark 10:17–23 together. Explain that the first large shoe shape represents the rich man who approached Jesus. Invite everyone to write on it facts about the man from the verses, or any thoughts or questions they have about him. Ask:

- What did the man think of Jesus?
- What did Jesus think of him?
- What sort of life did he lead?
- How did he feel about his wealth?
- What did he think Jesus was worth?
- What effect did Jesus say his riches had on him?

2 Read Mark 10:23–31 together (the overlap is deliberate) and then write facts, thoughts and questions about Jesus' followers on the second shoe shape. Ask:

- What did the disciples think of Jesus?
- What did Jesus think of them?
- What sort of life did they lead?
- How did they feel about their possessions?
- What did they think Jesus was worth?
- What did Jesus promise them?

3 Place the two shoes together and invite comments. Say that both the man and the disciples had to 'choose their shoes' – how they would live their lives. The rich man thought Jesus was good – but not that good. The disciples discovered Jesus was worth giving up everything for, because he gave up everything for them.

4 Invite each group member to draw round one of their shoes on card and cut it out. Ask them to write on it one thing they want to remember or do concerning the things they own – to make sure they are not a barrier to following Jesus. They could turn the big shoes into a 'Choose your shoes' poster as a reminder to themselves and a challenge to others.

RESPOND

MUSICAL

WHAT: **song lyrics**
WHY: **to affirm that Jesus is better than anything**
WITH: **music and words for appropriate worship songs, playback equipment or musical accompaniment**

1 The songs listed below use different words and imagery to speak about Jesus as the greatest treasure in our lives. Print out or copy the words of these or similar songs, either from songbooks or from lyrics of recorded music. Invite the group to read through the words and to choose which they like best. Ask each person who chooses one to give a reason for their choice. Then sing that song, read out the words or play the recording.

2 Alternatively, you could ask one or two group members to choose from your list of songs beforehand (or find some that have the same message). Ask them in advance to prepare something to say to the rest of the group about how that song relates to their own life and experience.

- 'Jesus, You Alone' by Tim Hughes
- 'Cornerstone' by Hillsong Worship
- 'Be Thou My Vision' (verses 1 and 4)
- 'How Lovely Is Your Dwelling Place' by Matt Redman
- 'I Lift My Hands' by Andre Kempen
- 'Everlasting God' by Soul Survivor
- 'All I Once Held Dear' by Graham Kendrick

PRACTICAL

WHAT: **action projects**
WHY: **to use our wealth to please Jesus**
WITH: **information about a project working with people in need**

1 Explain that Jesus wasn't saying everyone has to give away all they have (although you can if you feel that is what God is calling you to do). The point was that the young man thought his wealth was more important than Jesus.

2 If your group is already involved with a project that helps people in need, this is a good session in which to provide updated information, pray and plan action – encouraged by Jesus' challenge to the rich man to use his wealth to benefit the poor as a first step in following him.

3 Alternatively, consider one of these examples: either can be linked to a 'shoes' theme. For a starter activity, get an old trainer and ask the young people to mark a line on it with a washable OHP pen, to guess what proportion of the price of a new sports shoe goes to the workers who made it. The correct answer is 1/200 – 35p for a £70 sports shoe (from Clean Clothes Campaign – www.cleanclothes.org). Toybox is a charity that supports work with street children in South America. See www.toybox.org.uk. Some street children clean shoes to survive. Group members could raise money by offering a shoe-shine service after a service or to family members. You could plan this together and give training on how to clean different shoes.

CREATIVE

WHAT: **making a game and praying**
WHY: **to accept that Jesus is of greater value than possessions**
WITH: **shopping catalogues or magazines, two large sheets of paper or card, words from Matthew 6:24 and Philippians 3:7, background music**

1 Divide the young people into two groups. Explain that each group is going to make a game in which the words of a Bible verse are hidden under pictures. The other team will have to guess which pictures to remove to reveal the verse. Give one team Matthew 6:24 and the other Philippians 3:7.

2 Each team must cut pictures out of a catalogue or magazine of 12 items they think are desirable. They should arrange them on a large sheet of paper and arrange the words (two or three per picture) under six of the items. The words don't have to be arranged in straight lines – to fool the other team – but the verse needs to be readable when it's revealed. They should stick the pictures over the words with sticky tack and add the other six pictures in the spaces left.

3 To play the game, the teams take turns to choose a picture to remove from the other team's sheet. The first team to reveal the complete verse underneath wins.

4 Arrange the torn-off pictures around the verses or on the floor in front. Put on some music and ask the young people to look at the pictures and the words. Invite them to talk to God silently about knowing Jesus and about their possessions.

MORE ON THIS THEME:

If you want to do a short series with your group, other sessions that work well with this one are:

50	*Barriers to Jesus 2*	*Matthew 8:18–22*
51	*The barrier to God*	*Mark 15:1 – 16:8*
52	*The barrier to life*	*Colossians 3:1–17*

49

GOT STUFF? WANT STUFF?

Check out your attitude to money, possessions and lovely, lovely piles of glorious, gleaming gold. Honest answers, please.

Bible bit
Mark 10:17–31

A good guy – a successful, well-respected guy – comes up to Jesus and wants to know how to get eternal life, to live for ever with God. But after some initial banter all about being good and doing what is right, Jesus drops the bombshell. The guy must sell everything he owns and give the money to the poor. Does this mean that anyone who is rich can't have eternal life? Well, the disciples wonder about this, and Jesus again gives them the answer – God!

*BARGAIN 5 FOR £1

1 Your home's on fire. You can save one thing from your bedroom as you run out. What would it be?

2 You know what you want for your birthday. But your parents say it's too expensive. How do you react?

a Go mad.
b Don't speak to them until they give in.
c Explain calmly why they're totally and utterly wrong.
d Say you'd prefer a surprise present.
e Other.

3 A friend is running a car boot sale for a charity you think is very important. What's the most valuable possession you'd give to help raise money?

4 'If I had more money, I'd be much happier.' What do you reckon?

a Dead right!
b Perhaps.
c Don't think so.
d No chance!

5 What thing, in all the world, do you most wish was yours?

6 How much would you be willing to give up to get it?

a Everything I'll ever own.
b My birthday and Christmas presents for the rest of my life.
c My allowance for the next year.
d The price of a Mars bar.

7 What's the most likely way that you'll become really, really rich?

8 If you did become hugely rich, what would you do first with those gleaming, glorious piles of lovely, delicious gold? Mmmmmm!

9 Rate yourself out of 5 as a...

☐ ...spender.
☐ ...saver.
☐ ...waster.
☐ ...giver.

10 Do you think Christians have a different attitude to money and stuff, compared to everyone else? Mark somewhere on the line.

same ——————— different

There's something dodgy about this sketch. I'm sure I've read something like it before. Bone idle writers, always pinching other people's ideas. Now, where was it...?*

WHAT'S STOPPING YOU?

RICK: Hey, Chris! I need to talk to you. You're a Christian, aren't you?
CHRIS: (Still jogging on the spot.) Yes. So what?
RICK: I've been wanting to ask you a question. It's about... you know... well... heaven and that.
CHRIS: Heaven? I'm just setting off on the biggest event of my life and you want to talk about heaven?
RICK: Yeah, I've been worrying about it a lot. I want to know how to make sure I'm in. I don't want to end up in the other place – if there is one. You're into all that Jesus thing, so what do you think?
CHRIS: Look, I'm a bit busy here.
RICK: I need to know.
CHRIS: Well, have you murdered anyone? Done any major armed robbery? Been rude to your mum recently?
RICK: Hold on. I don't do any of that stuff. So, er, do you think I'm in?
CHRIS: (Finally stopping jogging.) You're serious, aren't you? You really want to know? I think your problem is that it's always, 'Me, me, me!' You're desperate to have the best of everything for yourself. Start giving stuff away instead. Why don't you come running with us now? You need to make Jesus the top person in your life instead – do what he wants.
RICK: Straight up?
CHRIS: You did ask.
RICK: Blow that!
Rick leaves. Petra runs up to Chris.
CHRIS: It's tough for him. He's got a lot to give up.
PETRA: That was a bit heavy. Come on, we're supposed to be attracting people in to the group, aren't we? Not putting them off.
CHRIS: Well, it's pretty difficult for someone who's got as much as Rick has to become a Christian, that's all.
PETRA: Rubbish. If that were true there'd be no hope for anyone.
CHRIS: Except that God can do anything.
PETRA: Your answer to everything. Well, I feel I've given lots of things up. Look at what I've put in to this run of yours.
CHRIS: OK, OK! But we get much more out of following Jesus than we've given up, don't we? I mean, that's how you got to know me.
PETRA: Exactly.
CHRIS: And there's knowing it will get better – life with Jesus for ever.
PETRA: And Rick?
CHRIS: It's just that with Jesus, things are often back to front. The people everyone else thinks are top often get left behind when it comes to following Jesus.
PETRA: Well, we've certainly been left way behind now. Come on, I want to get there first. (They run off.)

So how do you rate the things that Rick, Chris and Petra said? Grab a pen and give each of them a good sense score out of 10:

- [ ] Rick
- [ ] Chris
- [ ] Petra

While you're at it, put a ring round anything in the sketch you think is worth remembering or thinking about some more.

* Mark 10:17–31, give it a read.

FOOTWEAR FACTS

When President Marcos fled the Philippines in 1986, his wife's collection of shoes was discovered. She had 1,220 pairs. She had travelled the world to buy them, though millions of people in her country were extremely poor.

The oldest existing footwear in the world is a sandal found in a cave in Missouri, USA, believed to have been made 8,000 years ago. (Information from Northampton Shoe Museum)

For his self-coronation on 4 December 1977, Emperor Bokassa of the Central African Empire (now Republic) commissioned pearl-studded shoes from Paris, costing a world record of US $85,000. (Guinness World Records)

Millions of people in the world have no shoes. Many children cannot go to school (or are ashamed to go) without shoes. This further traps them in poverty.

In the UK in 2003, about 240 million pairs of footwear were bought through shops and mail order. That's roughly four new pairs for each person. (British Footwear Association)

Bible: Matthew 8:18–22

BARRIERS TO JESUS 2

THE AIM: To recognise the radical demands of following Jesus

The aim unpacked

Families and friends are important to young people, whatever their home situation is. But at what point do these relationships start to come between our young people and God? Also, how do we balance an attitude of honouring our parents or guardians with Jesus' words in Matthew 8:22? There may not be ready answers for our young people, but what we do have to realise and hopefully accept is that following Jesus demands radical living.

WAY IN

theGRID MAGAZINE

WHAT: **award ceremony**
WHY: **to start talking about what makes a faithful fan**
WITH: **magazine page 314, sealed envelope, award for the winner, background music and tables (optional)**

1 Introduce the BUFFY 'Fan of the Year' awards by reading the paragraph on page 314. Ask the young people to read the four entries and to rate each one by colouring in the appropriate number of stars. Find out which character has the most stars.

2 Ask each person to complete their own fan profile in the magazine. Invite everyone to read theirs out. Give everyone a small piece of paper and ask them to vote for the group member they think should win the award. Add up the votes, open a fake sealed envelope (in the style of an awards ceremony) and announce the winner. Present the award. You could add to the occasion by dressing appropriately, sitting the group round tables and using appropriate music.

3 Chat about whether people who are devoted followers of something are to be admired or pitied. Does it make a difference what or whom they follow? Why? How far is too far? Are people who follow Jesus like fans?

SCENE SETTER

WHAT: **video clips**
WHY: **to introduce the idea of someone putting off followers**
WITH: **clips from appropriate films**

1 Show one or more clips from films that show a character putting off a would-be follower, such as *The Incredibles* – Mr Incredible throwing his young fan (who later becomes Syndrome) out of his car; *Shrek* – Donkey first trying to join Shrek; *The Fellowship of the Ring* – at the end, Frodo trying to escape without Sam.

2 Chat about what you have seen. Ask:

- Why did the followers want to go with the main characters?
- Why did the heroes try to put off their would-be followers?
- What would have happened next if things had gone the other way – if Mr Incredible had let the boy go with him; if Donkey hadn't joined Shrek; and if Sam hadn't bothered to follow Frodo?
- Do you think Jesus would ever try to put off people who wanted to follow him? Do not give away what's in the Bible passage here – just listen to their suggestions.

THEMED GAME

WHAT: **quick-thinking game**
WHY: **to introduce the idea of putting people off**
WITH: **page 316**

1 Place the situation cards from page 316 face down in a pile. Divide the young people into two teams. Explain that they must try to put off a friend from joining them in the activity explained on the card. The teams take turns to take a card and have 30 seconds to make as many excuses as they can as to why the friend should not join in – scoring a point for each. Give an example: if the card was 'A swimming trip' you might say, 'The water's freezing in that pool', 'We won't have long there', or 'There's slime on the bottom'. There are no points for just insulting the friend.

2 Make sure the last two cards are, 'A friend wants to come along to this group' and 'A friend wants to become a Christian'. After the game you could ask, 'Should we ever put people off following Jesus?' or 'Do you think Jesus would have ever put people off joining his followers?' You could either get some instant responses or leave it hanging as a link into your chosen *Bible experience* activity, depending on your group.

BIBLE EXPERIENCE

LEVEL 1: CONNECT

WHAT: drama scenes
WHY: to recognise the radical demands of following Jesus
WITH: page 317, dummy microphone (optional)

1 Divide the young people into groups of three or four. Give each group a set of three character briefings from page 317. Ask each group to think of a famous person to be their character A and to write that person's name in the blank space. Then invite them to write names for characters B and C in the blank spaces. Explain that they are to prepare a short drama scene based on the character briefings.

2 Give the groups time to plan and practise acting out their scenes. (One person could direct if you have a group of four.)

3 Watch the prepared scenes. After each one, take on the role of a reporter asking characters B and C, 'How do you feel about what happened? What do you think of (Character A) now?'

2 Ask four people to read out Matthew 8:18–22, each taking a different part from the passage (Jesus, the teacher of the law, the follower and a narrator). Ask the two would-be followers, in role:

- How do you feel about what happened?
- What do you think of Jesus now?

5 Ask everyone:

- Why do you think Jesus said those things?
- Was there anything similar in our acted scenes?
- Do you think Jesus had the right to make such demands of people? Draw out that Jesus expected to be more important to his followers than everything and everyone – even their own families. Ask, 'Do you think Christians today are that committed to Jesus? Should they be?'

LEVEL 2: INTERFACE

WHAT: photo story and storytelling
WHY: to recognise the radical demands of following Jesus
WITH: magazine page 315

1 Ask the group members to read the photo story on page 315.

2 Say that you would love to know what happened next with these characters:

- What will Andy or Kayleigh say when they next meet Chris or Petra?
- Will Andy or Kayleigh go to the group that night?

Take it in turns round the group to add a bit more to the story. The young people can add as much or as little as they like. Leaders should take turns too, helping to bring in new characters or moving the story on. Stop before the story runs out of steam.

3 Chat about the young people's reactions to Chris and what she said:

- Was she right?
- Should she have said those things?
- Why or why not?

4 Read aloud Matthew 8:18–22. Ask the young people what they think happened to these two men. Did they end up following Jesus? If so, how? Give them names. Ask the group to take turns at adding a bit more to the story, imagining what happened to them. Don't try to stretch this for too long.

5 Chat about the young people's reactions to Jesus and what he said. Point out the parallels with the things Chris said in the photo story. Was it different when Jesus said these, compared to the similar things Chris said? Make sure you talk about Jesus having the right to make these demands – this section of Matthew's Gospel emphasises his authority. Discuss:

- Do we expect following Jesus to be easy or an optional extra to other priorities in our lives?
- If Jesus is more important than homework, how can we follow him and not get into trouble at school?

LEVEL 3: SWITCH ON

WHAT: planning or creating a fanzine
WHY: to recognise the radical demands of following Jesus
WITH: flip chart or whiteboard, marker pens, fanzine (optional)

1 Read Matthew 8:18–22 to the young people twice. You could ask two group members to read aloud from different Bible versions.

2 Invite any initial comments or questions. Chat about the significance of the passage for people who want to follow Jesus today. You could discuss:

- How might Christians today take on a tough lifestyle because they are following Jesus?
- What other priorities might get in the way of us following Jesus?

3 Talk about fanzines and YouTube channels – magazines for fans written and created by fans – and show an example, if possible. Ask them to imagine a fanzine for people who follow Jesus and think of articles and items that might appear in it. Write these on a flip chart or whiteboard. Encourage them to think how it could reflect the whole life commitment Jesus says is needed from his followers. Make it fun, too. Some of these ideas might be helpful:

- quotes from people answering the question, 'Why do you follow Jesus?'
- profiles of one or more followers of Jesus in the Gospels and Acts
- profiles of followers of Jesus today
- interviews with the would-be followers from Matthew 8:18–22

4 Divide the young people into pairs or threes to work on the ideas. You could write and produce the fanzine over the next week or two. Print copies for the group – and to give to others in the church.

5 Alternatively, if your young people have the skills or facilities, you could make a fan website, or fan page on Facebook (be aware of age restrictions on social media, however). We would love to see any examples you come up with.

RESPOND

MUSICAL

WHAT: simple prayer song
WHY: to affirm that we will follow Jesus
WITH: music and words for 'O Lord Jesus' from page 317, sheets of paper each with one of these captions: 'I want...', 'I like...', 'I care for...', 'I'm a fan of...'

1 Try out the simple song, 'O Lord Jesus', from page 317. This is based on a short repeated line with the words, 'O Lord Jesus, O Lord Jesus, O Lord Jesus, I will follow you.' It can be sung without accompaniment. Teach it to the group.

2 Lay the sheets of paper where they can be seen. Ask the group members to think about how they would complete them. After you have sung the song once, invite anyone to say one of their sentences. The third person to do so should finish with 'but...' as the cue for everyone to sing the chorus again. Repeat with another three sentences. You could decide who will go first and then take turns round the group (with the option of 'passing'), or leave it free for anyone to speak each time.

3 You could also ask the group members to suggest different words to sing in place of 'I will follow you'. Or vary it by changing 'I' to 'we', or rewording 'O Lord Jesus' – improvising around the tune, adding claps or percussion or changing the key.

4 Other appropriate songs, expressing a commitment to put Jesus first and follow him, are:

- 'All I Once Held Dear'
- 'I Want to Walk With Jesus Christ'
- 'It Is the Cry of My Heart'
- 'Jesus, Be the Centre'
- 'O Jesus, I Have Promised'

PRACTICAL

WHAT: planning how to attract friends to Jesus
WHY: to let friends hear Jesus' challenge to follow him

1 Explain that from the beginning, following Jesus has meant helping other people to hear the challenge to follow him too. But how can we do that in a way that is true to what we have read in the Bible today – attracting people so they can hear about Jesus, but also being honest about the seriousness of following him?

2 Work together to think of ways to reach out to the young people's friends. You could use some of the following questions. If appropriate, this part of the session could be led by one or more group members, properly briefed beforehand:

- Do we already have friends we would like to invite to something?
- What would make our normal programme better to invite friends to?
- Would a special event help?
- For what or whom do we need to pray? (For example, friends who are not close enough to ask, those we're too embarrassed to mention, or those we know would say no.)
- How can we help each other to pray?
- Are there any practical steps we can take now?

3 If this leads to some clear direction and ideas, you could start work on some practical planning and prayer. Give the group members as much responsibility as possible, but make sure leaders support them properly.

CREATIVE

WHAT: graffiti and prayer
WHY: to express a desire to put Jesus first
WITH: three 2 m lengths of smooth wallpaper or lining paper, two poles (at least 1.5 m long), parcel tape, marker pens, protection for floor and clothes

1 Spread the lengths of wallpaper on the floor. Invite the group members to write or draw graffiti on them – words or pictures that symbolise anything that is important in life or in their lives in particular, but nothing specifically about God. Make sure they don't spend too long perfecting their creation so they won't be too upset about step 4!

2 Lay the poles on the ground and attach the lengths of wallpaper between them – one above the other – using parcel tape.

3 Talk about how, through Jesus, God broke down the barriers that stop us having life with him. But we can still let things in our lives get in the way, if they become more important to us than he is. Lift up the completed 'graffiti wall'. Pray, 'Lord God, thank you that you have broken down the barriers that stop us knowing you and your love for us. Help us not to let anything get in the way of following you.'

4 Ask two people to hold the poles firmly and let the rest of the group take turns at punching holes in the barrier, until there is a hole or tear big enough to walk through. Finish by reading Romans 8:38,39.

MORE ON THIS THEME:

If you want to do a short series with your group, other sessions that work well with this one are:

49	*Barriers to Jesus 1*	*Mark 10:17–31*
51	*The barrier to God*	*Mark 15:1 – 16:8*
52	*The barrier to life*	*Colossians 3:1–17*

FAN OF THE YEAR

Welcome to a glitzy night out as the great and gorgeous of the world of fandom gather to find out who will win this year's BUFFY (Biggest Utterly Faithful Fan of the Year) awards, sponsored by *theGRID*. And after the secret panel of judges was sacked for accepting bribes from the sponsors, this year it all depends on your vote.

So please welcome the four finalists and prepare to give them your star rating.

Bible bit
Matthew 8:18–22

If you thought following Jesus was all about being good, doing what the Bible says and going to church every so often, then this passage could be for you. Following Jesus is about radical living, and radical living will make tough demands on us. What this passage tells us is that nothing is more important than following Jesus.

CLARISSA CLEVERCLOGS

has spent the last five years reading every single word written by her hero, Professor Marietta Humdinger – the world's authority on Ancient Egyptian toenail clippers. 'I used to think toenails were just those hard bits on the ends of your feet. The professor has opened my eyes to a whole new world. The Ancient Egyptians really knew a thing or two when it came to keeping your cuticles cute.'

Clarissa's great ambition is to meet Professor Humdinger and spend time talking to her.

LENNY RELENTLESS

is the number one fan of round-the-world yachtsman Sir Francis Waveskimmer. 'I started out visiting his website every day to see where he was in the world and what he was having for breakfast, but it wasn't enough. So last year I built my own boat out of old wheelie bins and followed his course as closely as possible. I had to sleep standing up. He got a bit annoyed when I hooked my boat to his rudder.'

Lenny hopes to join Sir Francis' boat as a member of the crew on his next solo long distance voyage.

BRIAN BOUNCER

follows the fortunes of his local trampolining team, the Upley Downers, home and away. 'The lads have been really good to me. They always keep an eye out for me in the crowd, even though there can be as many as 20 people at a big competition. The only one I missed last season was when my dad had a bad cold and needed someone to look after him.'

Brian always wears orange, the Downers' team colours. His ambitions are to paint the world orange and to stop his dad getting any more colds.

JODIE SINGLEMIND

simply adores her favourite band GlitzGirlz. 'I am right at the front for every concert they do. I haven't missed any in the last year, though that did mean I didn't get to go to my boyfriend's funeral. Life must go on and the Glitzies are the best. They're so genuine. I love it when we get away from the crowds and I can find out more about their real lives.'

Jodie's ambition is to get off with a warning at her trial for stealing personal items from Gloria Glitz's dustbin.

And breaking news is that a late wild-card entry has been awarded to... you! Get your fan facts down fast and you may be in with a chance...

NAME: ____________________

____

FAN OF: ____________________

____

SHOWS SUPPORT BY: ____________________

____

QUOTE: ____________________

____

AMBITION: ____________________

____

THE BIG PUT OFF

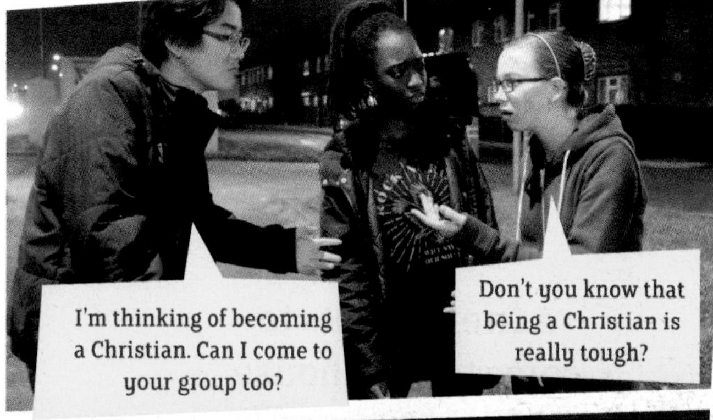

What do you think of what Chris said? A bit spikey? But take a look at Matthew 8:18–22 to see what Jesus had to say to some people who fancied being his followers.

RESOURCE PAGE

USE WITH SESSION 50 WAY IN 'THEMED GAME'

A friend wants to come to the cinema with you tonight.	A friend wants to sit next to you on the coach for a school trip.
A friend wants to buy the same clothes that you wear.	A friend wants to come skateboarding with you.
A friend wants to come to your house for a sleepover.	A friend wants to give you £100.
A friend wants to walk to school with you.	A friend wants to join in a trip to a concert.
A friend wants to come along to this group.	A friend wants to become a Christian.

USE WITH SESSION 50 BIBLE EXPERIENCE 'LEVEL 1 CONNECT'

Character briefings

A You are .... You are setting up a training scheme to pass on your skills. The people you choose for the scheme will follow you everywhere and learn from you. You need to decide if these two are up to the demanding programme you are planning.

B You have heard a lot about .... and really admire the things he/she says. You like the idea of joining the new training scheme and look forward to learning lots more. You think it will be pretty easy for a bright person like you.

C You have met .... before. You are very keen to join the training scheme. But you have some family problems to sort out first that may take a few weeks to deal with. You wouldn't be able to start the training scheme right away.

USE WITH SESSION 50 RESPOND 'MUSICAL'

O Lord Jesus

51

Bible: Mark 15:1 – 16:8

THE BARRIER TO GOD

THE AIM: To be encouraged that we can all approach God

The aim unpacked

In this session our focus is on the Temple curtain being torn in two. This session deals with the barrier that God broke down. Because of the events on the cross, we can boldly approach God. Whatever situation our young people are in, they can be encouraged that they can approach God and he will be there waiting for them.

WAY IN

theGRID MAGAZINE

WHAT: discussion
WHY: to look at the barriers we can have in relationships
WITH: magazine page 321

1 Give out copies of page 321. Ask the young people to look at the list of possible barriers in our human relationships. They can work on their own or in groups, and fill in additional ideas they might have.

2 Come together and invite the young people to share their thoughts and ideas.

3 In pairs, ask the young people to read through the 'Case history' of Polly and Susie and to discuss their thoughts. Invite feedback with the whole group.

4 Conclude by asking the young people whether they think the 'barriers' we have looked at are permanent or whether they can be broken down.

SCENE SETTER

WHAT: discussion about love
WHY: to think about what love really means
WITH: sticky notes (heart-shaped if possible), candy floss (optional)

1 Divide the young people into small groups and ask them to think about the meaning of love. Invite them to write individual words on their sticky notes that describe a particular element of what love is, eg care, compassion, trust, loyalty etc.

2 Come together and invite the groups to share their ideas.

3 Finish this activity by handing round some candy floss for the group share (if you have any) and by saying, if appropriate, that love is so much more than a warm fuzzy feeling. In today's activities they will be looking at the greatest act of love that broke down a barrier – Jesus dying on the cross that broke down the barrier between us and God, symbolised in the tearing of the Temple curtain.

THEMED GAME

WHAT: top ten
WHY: to think about barriers that keep us from others
WITH: sticky labels, whiteboard

1 Give each young person a sticky label and ask them to write the name of a famous person on it. They should write the name of a person who they admire and would like to meet one day. They should not show the name they have written down to anyone else in the group.

2 Divide the young people into pairs and invite them to stick their name labels onto their partner's forehead. Then each pair must ask one another questions (that can only be answered with 'yes' or no') until they are able to figure out which famous person is on their label.

3 Bring the group together and ask them how likely they think it is that they might one day meet these people. What would make meeting them difficult?

4 If appropriate, tell the group that today they'll be looking at why God was difficult to meet and how this was overcome.

BIBLE EXPERIENCE

51

LEVEL 1: CONNECT

WHAT: **drama**
WHY: **to be encouraged that we can all approach God**
WITH: **magazine page 322, *Doctor Who* theme tune (optional)**

1 Either prepare the drama 'Doctor Who and the Curtain of Hope' from page 322 before the session and perform it to the group, or hand out copies of the magazine and invite the young people to read it aloud in pairs. (You could make a performance more exciting by using the *Doctor Who* theme tune.)

2 After the drama, read Mark 16:1–8 to the group and explain that this was what the Doctor wanted to see on the Sunday.

3 Explain that among the first people to find out that Jesus was alive was Mary Magdalene. Jesus had healed her and forgiven her for all the things she had done wrong and so she was able to follow Jesus. Because of what Jesus did on the cross, shown by the tearing of the Temple curtain, this 'bad' woman was able to approach God.

4 Say that because Jesus took our punishment and died on the cross, everyone can approach God. What we do when we get there is up to us, but because of Jesus we can reach what was previously unreachable.

LEVEL 2: INTERFACE

WHAT: **letter writing**
WHY: **to be encouraged that we can all approach God**
WITH: **Bibles**

1 Read or ask a good reader to read Mark 15 to the group.

2 Hand out paper and pens, and make sure everyone has access to a Bible.

3 Encourage the young people to write a letter to God, expressing their thoughts and feelings about the passage they've just heard. Remind the group that asking questions to God, or expressing honest emotions when we speak to him, is a good thing.

4 If the young people are willing, invite some to share their letters with the group. For those who do share (or even if no one shares) invite everyone else to pray for each member of the group and their relationships with God.

5 Now read Mark 16:1–8 together. Explain that this is where we find out that Jesus did not stay dead in the tomb but was resurrected.

6 Explain that Jesus' death and resurrection broke the barrier to God once and for all. This was shown symbolically by the torn curtain in the Temple. Because of this, we can all approach God. Invite the group to add any final thoughts/reactions to their letters.

LEVEL 3: SWITCH ON

WHAT: **linking between the Old and New Testaments and now**
WHY: **to be encouraged that we can all approach God**
WITH: **Bibles, magazine page 322, big thick curtain (the bigger and stronger, the better)**

1 Invite the group to look at the 'Temple fact file' on page 322.

2 Show the curtain. Explain that the Temple curtain was much bigger and stronger than this one, and separated the Holy of Holies (the holiest bit of the Temple) from the rest. It was a symbol of the separation between God and humanity, caused by sin. The people could not approach God because of the wrong in their lives.

3 Ask someone to read aloud Mark 15:1–38.

4 Ask one or two young people to hold up the curtain and try to tear it in two. This should be impossible if the curtain is strong, but don't encourage them too much! The aim here is to try to imagine the event that took place in verse 38.

5 Ask the group to think about the curtain being torn in two. This was a symbol of God removing the barrier of sin between him and humanity, through the work of Jesus. However huge this barrier was, and however strong the curtain was, God is stronger! Emphasise that what Jesus achieved on the cross was truly amazing.

6 Now invite someone to read Mark 15:38 – 16:8.

7 In a relaxed atmosphere, ask the following questions, encouraging everyone to participate:

- Did anything new strike you as you listened to this well-known passage? Why?
- Had you understood the meaning of the curtain tearing before? Has it changed your understanding of the passage? Why?
- Is it significant that it is women who are first told that Jesus has risen from the dead?

8 Thank God in prayer for the events of that first Easter, which allow us to approach God.

RESPOND

MUSICAL

WHAT: **music and poetry response**
WHY: **to understand that there are no barriers between us and God**
WITH: **page 323, reflective music, playback equipment, candle, palm crosses or materials to make them from, instructions from page 324**

1 Play some quiet and reflective instrumental music and ask a volunteer to read the poem 'No barriers' from page 323. You could light a candle to focus on.

2 Give out the palm crosses (or make some using the instructions on page 324) and encourage the young people to think about their response to what God did for us when Jesus died on the cross (he broke down the barriers between us).

3 Invite them to place the crosses around the candle and to thank God as they do it for removing the barrier. If they want to, they could use this as a symbol to promise to follow Jesus in their lives this week and afterwards.

4 Remind the young people that what Jesus did for us on the cross is worthy of thanks all year round, not just at Easter time.

PRACTICAL

WHAT: **discussion and plan of action**
WHY: **to identify fully with what God has done**
WITH: **a map of your local community (optional)**

1 Lay out a map of your local community (if you have one) and ask the young people to gather around it.

2 Ask the young people to identify any areas on the map that in some way identify groups of people in your community who face barriers every day. For example, there may be a homeless shelter in your community – it is quite common for homeless people to face barriers of prejudice and insufficient support. It may be that there is a care home for the elderly in your community. How might the people who live there face barriers in their everyday lives?

3 Invite the young people to consider the unnecessary barriers that people in your community frequently encounter. Then challenge the group to think about how they might be able to address some of these barriers, and bring about change.

4 Remind the young people of how Jesus broke down barriers for them so that they can be close to God. How might the young people break down barriers in their community so that others may know God's love too?

5 If appropriate, make a practical plan of action that your group can engage in over the next few months.

CREATIVE

WHAT: **Jesus ribbons**
WHY: **to respond creatively to today's learning**
WITH: **lengths of red ribbon**

1 Give each young person a length of red ribbon.

2 Invite the group to take some time to be quiet and consider what Jesus did on the cross. Remind them that Jesus died for each one of them, and it was only because he did this that today we can easily access God. Encourage the young people to tie their ribbons around their wrists (make sure ribbons are not tied too tightly and offer help to any who may struggle with this task).

3 Say that as the tearing of the curtain showed that access to God was now available to all, we are showing our response to Jesus by wearing these ribbons on our wrists for all to see – remembering the sacrifice that Jesus made for us.

4 Encourage the young people to wear their ribbons until you next meet together (if appropriate) as a constant reminder of Jesus' sacrifice and God's nearness to them.

MORE ON THIS THEME:

If you want to do a short series with your group, other sessions that work well with this one are:

49	*Barriers to Jesus 1*	*Mark 10:17–31*
50	*Barriers to Jesus 2*	*Matthew 8:18–22*
52	*The barrier to life*	*Colossians 3:1–17*

51

Bible bit
Mark 15:1 – 16:8

In *The Lord of the Rings*, Frodo needs Gollum to lead him to Mount Doom in Mordor. In *Charlie and the Chocolate Factory*, young Master Bucket needs a golden ticket to gain access to Willy Wonka's fantastic factory. And we need Jesus to gain access to God. This was shown in a powerful way when the curtain in the Temple was ripped in two. The curtain had been a symbol of the barrier between God and humanity, but when Jesus died, the curtain was torn – access granted, the barrier overcome.

RELATIONSHIP BARRIERS

What keeps us from getting close to people?
Circle the things that would bother you. Add some of your own ideas too.

SHYNESS, SMELLY BREATH, AGGRESSION, TONGUE-TIED, ATTITUDES (CLASS AND CULTURE), LACK OF UNDERSTANDING, APPEARANCES (CLOTHES, HAIR), NOT HAVING THINGS IN COMMON, HOSTILITY, BEING TOO BUSY, NOT BEING 'COOL' ENOUGH

POLLY desperately wanted to get to know Susie, but whenever she tried to talk to her she got nowhere! Susie was 'cool'! She always had the latest gear and the trendiest mobile, and she was the most popular girl in the school. Polly was a bit plainer in her appearance and outlook on life; she didn't have the latest anything.

SUSIE secretly thought Polly was a nice person. She really wanted to be friendly but knew that her 'street cred' would take a serious downturn if she was even seen speaking to her!

POLLY

SUSIE

DOCTOR WHO AND THE CURTAIN OF HOPE

Scene: Rose and the Doctor emerge from the Tardis

The Doctor: See? I told you it could go further back in time.
Rose: So where are we?
The Doctor: We're in Israel... well, Judah, to be precise.
Rose: I thought Israel was warm and sunny?
The Doctor: Well, it is normally, but things are a little different today.
Rose: What do you mean?
The Doctor: You'll see. Come and have a look.

They walk to the top of a hill and look across to another hill.

Rose: Oh my... that's horrible, it's... I mean... isn't that...?
The Doctor: Yeah, crucifixion. There's no nice way to be put to death, and I've seen them all, from Dalek exterminators to Cybermen guns, but crucifixion is one of the most shocking. Did you know that basically the person would suffocate? All the muscles in the...
Rose: Please, Doctor, stop it! I don't want an autopsy.
The Doctor: Well, what do you expect from a doctor?
Rose: Actually, what I meant was, isn't that... you know...?
The Doctor: Yep, Jesus, son of Mary and Joseph – tried by the Roman authorities, on slightly dubious grounds, convicted and sentenced to be crucified, et voilà.
Rose: He's in pain; he's crying out.
The Doctor: (sadly) Yes, but there's something else I want you to see.

They go back inside the Tardis. The Tardis dematerialises and rematerialises inside a huge building. The Doctor and Rose come out.

Rose: So where are we now?
The Doctor: Same time but a different place. This is the Temple, or Herod's Temple to be precise. It's quite beautifully built.
Rose: But why are we here?
The Doctor: There, watch.
Rose: What's happening?

The ground trembles and the Doctor and Rose are slightly shaken.

The Doctor: There, you see that curtain? It separates the people in the Temple from God. Well, not literally, but symbolically.
Rose: Hey, what's happening? The curtain – it's tearing; it's being ripped apart.
The Doctor: Yeah. Now there's nothing to keep the people from God. Fantastic!
Rose: Well, I wouldn't say it's that fantastic. Some guy just died out there, and all for this curtain to be ripped apart?
The Doctor: Oh, Rose, you need to think a bit bigger than what you see. There's a lot more going on in the universe than you think. Yeah, it may look like some guy has just died and that a curtain has been ripped apart, but what just took place has cosmic consequences. Anyway that's not the end of the story. C'mon back to the Tardis – it's Friday now, but I want to take a quick look at Sunday morning. Something else happens that's quite significant... c'mon.

For the complete nerds among you (and if you're a *Doctor Who* fan, you're not alone!), this story takes place after the event of the episode 'The Unquiet Dead'. It therefore depicts the Doctor in his ninth incarnation as played by Christopher Ecclestone.

THE TEMPLE FACT FILE

The Temple: where the Jews worshipped, built on Mount Zion, in Jerusalem. There were three Temples (re)built by Solomon, Zerubbabel and Herod.

Who destroyed Solomon's Temple?
Nebuchadnezzar in 587 BC (Old Testament).

Who destroyed the rebuilt Zerubbabel Temple?
Antiochus IV Epiphanes (in between the Old and New Testaments).

When was Herod the Great's Temple destroyed?
AD 70 (New Testament – Jesus said this would happen!).

Was the Temple big?
Wow, yes!

Was it bigger than St Paul's Cathedral?
Yes.

Was it bigger than Westminster Abbey?
Yes!

Was it bigger than St Peter's in Rome?
YES!

The whole building was surrounded by a walled area probably the size of a huge sports stadium!

The curtain, or veil, separated the Holy Place from the Holy of Holies (see the plan). This curtain is what was torn in two when Jesus died on the cross.

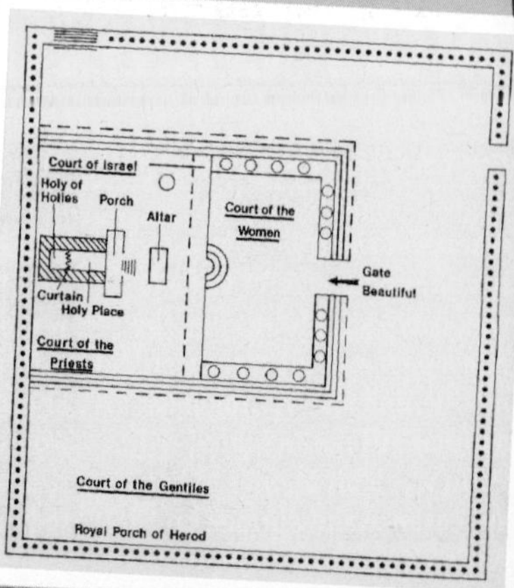

No barriers

There are no barriers,
When Jesus died
God broke them down.
Such is his love for us.
And now he waits,
We can approach him,
We can come to him,
With all our hurts and sorrows,
With all the complexities of our lives,
The way has been made clear,
There are no barriers.
God will love you,
He will guide you,
Put your trust in him,
He is waiting,
There are no barriers – such is his love for us.

USE WITH SESSION 51 RESPOND 'MUSICAL'

To make a Palm Cross

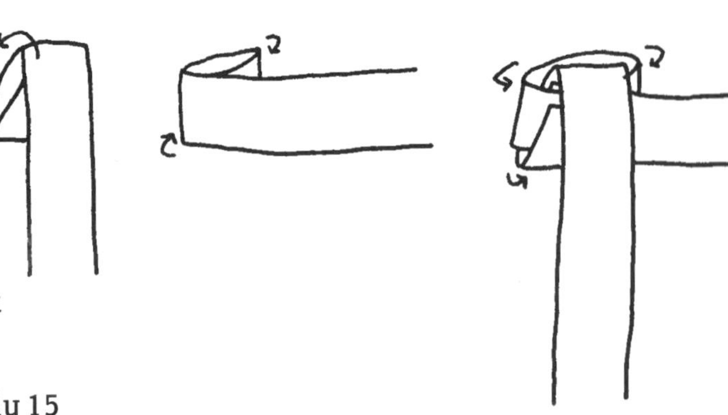

1 Cut off three strips from the long side of a sheet of A4 paper. Each strip should be approximately 15 mm wide. One strip will be used to form the crosspiece. Join together the other two strips with sticky tape and use this longer strip to form the upright of the cross.

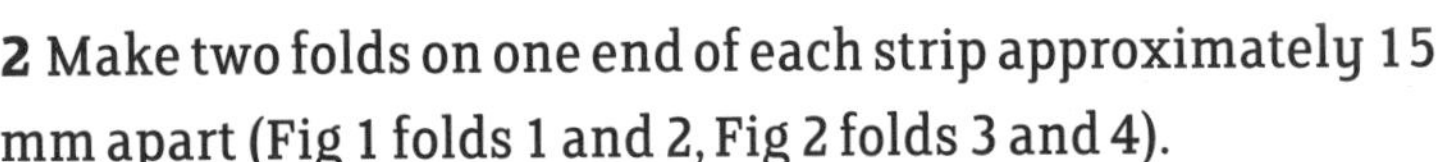

2 Make two folds on one end of each strip approximately 15 mm apart (Fig 1 folds 1 and 2, Fig 2 folds 3 and 4).

3 Join the two strips together by using the folds already made as a kind of 'hook' on the end of each strip (Fig 3 folds 5, 6 and 7). You will now have a firm join at this crossover point. Make sure the loose end of the crosspiece is to the right and the loose end of the longer strip hangs down over the front of the crossover point.

4 Take the loose end of the crosspiece and fold it forward, leaving a loop of paper of about 5 cm sticking out to one side (Fig 4, fold 8). Pass the loose end underneath the long strip hanging down at the front.

5 Form another loop sticking out 5 cm on the other side by folding the loose end of the crosspiece and tucking it into the back of the crossover point (Fig 4, fold 9, tuck 10). The crosspiece should now stick out evenly about 5 cm either side of the crossover point.

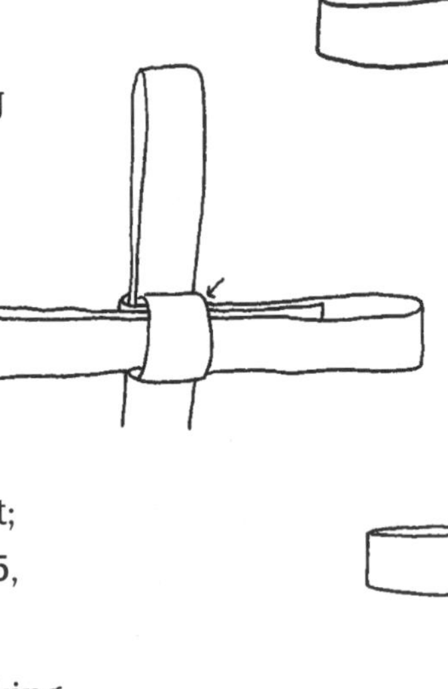

6 The long strip should still be hanging forward over the crossover point. Take the loose end and tuck it upward through the loop at the back of the crossover point; pull the strip right through and a firm knot is formed (Fig 5, tuck 11).

7 Fold the loose end backward leaving a loop of paper sticking up about 7 cm to form the top piece of the cross (Fig 6, fold 12). Take the loose end and tuck it down the back loop of the crossover point, pulling it through until the top loop forms neatly (Fig 6, tuck 13).

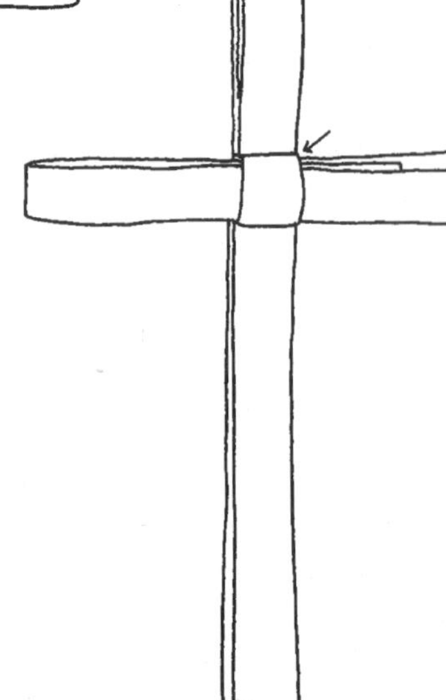

8 Finally, take the loose end of the strip and tuck it into the front of the crossover point, leaving a loop of paper hanging down about 14 cm to form the lower part of the cross. Press at the bottom to form a neat fold (Fig 7, fold 14, tuck 15).

Bible: Colossians 3:1–17

52

THE BARRIER TO LIFE

THE AIM: To develop the lifestyle of the saved and holy

The aim unpacked
In this session we focus on our ongoing development as followers of Jesus. Although being saved is ultimately the most important aspect of a relationship with God, we should also realise that we can live at an even better level as we grow in this relationship. This session looks at some guidance as to how we can live a life that's full-on for God.

WAY IN

theGRID MAGAZINE

WHAT: **getting motivated**
WHY: **to introduce the idea that motivation for behaviour can come from a relationship**
WITH: **magazine page 328**

1 Ask the young people whether anyone has ever changed their behaviour in a positive way because of someone else's influence. Perhaps they have behaved better for a teacher they respect? Or made an extra effort in athletics to impress the coach? Or tidied their room without moaning (ha ha!), to give their mum a break?

2 Allow them to respond in a light-hearted way. Encourage all the group members to respond.

3 Hand out copies of page 328 and invite them to read 'Shula's story' on their own.

4 In pairs, invite them to discuss why she changed her behaviour.

5 Ask for a volunteer to pretend to be Shula. Invite the young people to ask questions to try to find out what made her change.

SCENE SETTER

WHAT: **habits**
WHY: **to see that an action can become a habit**
WITH: **copies of page 330 (one for each young person), flip chart or whiteboard (optional)**

1 Divide the young people into pairs and give out copies of the two surveys from page 330. Each person should have a different survey from their partner. Ask them to interview each other and then, if there is time, to interview someone else. You will need to introduce this carefully and in a light-hearted way; we don't want them to reveal anything too personal.

2 Bring the group together and compile the results on a flip chart or whiteboard or in a discussion, and see what the results show. Any similarities or differences?

3 Say that the author Thomas Hardy said that an action makes a habit and a habit makes a character. Ask the young people if they agree with this. They could discuss it with their partner and then feed back their thoughts to the group.

THEMED GAME

WHAT: **to introduce the idea of new clothes**
WITH: **bin bags and carrier bags, lining paper or newspaper, staplers**

1 Divide the young people into groups of four and give them bin bags, carrier bags, lining paper or newspaper, sticky tape or a stapler and challenge them to make a makeshift outfit. Explain that they have ten minutes to design the coolest, funkiest set of clothes possible for a member of their group. They'll need a hat, shoes and jewellery as well as something more substantial to preserve their modesty.

2 Hold a fashion show with members of the group commenting on the clothes as the model parades down a catwalk.

3 Say that today we're thinking about getting rid of old stuff and putting on new kit. But we're not necessarily talking about clothes.

BIBLE EXPERIENCE

LEVEL 1: CONNECT

WHAT: makeover
WHY: to develop the lifestyle of the saved and holy
WITH: two sets of clothes (or pictures) – one old and untrendy, the other new and fashionable, large hoodie, labels, bin or bin bag, air horn or squeaker sound effect

1 Before the session, pin labels on the clothes. The old, untrendy clothes have these labels: 'sexual sinning'; 'wanting things that are evil'; 'being greedy'; 'being angry'; 'being moody'; 'hurting others'; 'swearing'; 'lying'. The new, fashionable garments have these labels: 'being kind'; 'being humble'; 'being gentle'; 'being patient'; 'getting along with others'; 'forgiving others'. Pin the word 'Love' on the hoodie.

2 Ask the young people to pick at random an item from the clothes with the negative attributes and put it on. (With a large group, ask for volunteers.) Say that these people now represent people with these habits. Ask them to suggest some things that a person with each habit might think, do or say. Encourage them to use an air horn or other sound effect instead of saying swear words. Make sure no one feels uncomfortable by what they are asked to say.

3 Ask the group to imagine what the world would be like if everyone acted like that, all the time. Say that when people become Christians, it's like taking off all those horrible habits. Invite the young people to take them off and put them in the bin.

4 Say that God gives them new clothes that are a billion times better than the old ones. Give out the garments with the positive labels. As Christians we choose whether to stick with our old horrible habits or ask God to give us new habits like these so we can behave more like Jesus.

5 Explain that God also gives us a fantastic item to put on over the top of everything: bring out the 'Love' hoodie. When people see Christians, they should see the way they love others, more than anything else. Ask, 'How could it change your school (or community) if you deliberately "put on" these habits every day?'

LEVEL 2: INTERFACE

WHAT: choices
WHY: to develop the lifestyle of the saved and holy
WITH: page 331, Bibles, sticky tack (optional)

1 Designate one end of the room 'God's the boss' and the other end 'The world's the boss'.

2 The Bible says that something is in charge of our lives. Christians ask God to be the 'boss' of their lives. But everyone has a 'boss' of some sort. 'The world' can be the shorthand for the 'boss' of wrong choices, of bad ways of living.

3 Call out the statements on page 331 and invite the young people to choose which 'boss' the speaker belongs to by running to that end of the room.

4 Check out Colossians 3:1–17 together. Challenge the group to find examples of what Paul is writing about in the statements from the resource page – an example of verse 5 could be: 'I really want that top she's wearing.'

5 Explain that Paul is desperate to show the Christians in Colossae what makes God happy or angry, so they can avoid the things that anger him and do more of what pleases him. Point out that the things that make God happy also make the people around us happy.

6 Ask the following questions one at a time and invite answers. Encourage everyone to say something, but don't pressurise them:

- Is there anything in this passage that puzzles you?
- Is there anything you disagree with?
- Which of these things would you find hardest to do?
- Which would you find hardest not to do?
- Which part feels as if God's speaking to you directly?

LEVEL 3: SWITCH ON

WHAT: Bible discovery
WHY: to develop the lifestyle of the saved and holy
WITH: magazine page 329, Bibles or copies of Colossians 3:1–17, plain T-shirts, fabric paints (optional)

1 In pairs, ask the young people to read 'Fit kit?' from page 329. Discuss Katie's problems and how she and Alex were different.

2 Explain that Paul describes habits of Christian living like clothes. With Jesus' help we can choose which bad habits we throw out of our 'wardrobes' and which good habits we put on. Say that some bad habits are deeply rooted, but God wants us to keep 'becoming like the One who made you' (v 10). What an amazing thought!

3 Read Colossians 3:1–17 together by reading one verse each. Back in pairs, invite the young people to find:

- the bad habits Paul thinks we should bin (vs 5–9)
- the good habits we should keep putting on (vs 12–17)

Then discuss which of these habits are hardest and easiest to take off or put on.

4 Bring the group back together. Remind them that although it seems very hard, Jesus wants us to succeed and will help us if we ask him. It is also true that we 'are becoming like' Jesus – it can be a very gradual process, but one way we can live life to the full is by making a decision every day to become more like him.

5 Challenge the young people to think of a slogan that tells why we should bother to do what we have been reading (vs 1–4,6,10 might help).

6 Invite them to decorate a plain T-shirt with their slogans, using the fabric paints. They could take the message to the world by wearing their T-shirts!

RESPOND

MUSICAL

WHAT: **songs of praise**
WHY: **to link real life with real worship**
WITH: **words and music for appropriate songs from songbooks or worship CDs, playback equipment or musical accompaniment**

1 Read Colossians 3:16 again. Say that you're going to do what Paul suggests – praise God – in a *Songs of Praise* style. Give out the songbooks or worship CDs and ask each person, pair or group to choose a song that means a lot to them for some reason. It might be because it says something about God that they think is really important, or perhaps they associate a particular song with a time in their life when they felt close to God.

2 Introduce the songs (you may want to play excerpts rather than the whole songs) and ask the person who chose it to say why it is special to them. In this way, you'll be learning about each other and about God through music, just as Paul advises in verse 16. Think about going into church for this activity, or filming the testimonies on video.

3 Songs that fit well with this theme include:

- 'Change My Heart, O God'
- 'O Lord, Your Tenderness'
- 'From the Inside Out'
- 'Spirit of the Living God'

PRACTICAL

WHAT: **making habits**
WHY: **to reinforce the fact that worship is for every day, not just Sundays**
WITH: **copies of page 332 (one for each young person), Bibles**

1 Remind the young people that true worship is about living a life that makes God happy, not just singing or praying in church. So, true holiness is in what we do every day. To help them put on God's habits and to bin those old habits, give each young person a copy of the challenge chart from page 332. Explain that each day over the week ahead has space to write in one godly habit to do actively and space for an old, bad habit to avoid.

2 Ask each person to use Colossians 3:1–17 to prayerfully fill in the good or bad habits they think are most relevant to their own life. Suggest that they keep an eye on each other over the following week in pairs or threes, pledge to ask each other each day how it's going and support each other in prayer.

3 Conclude by praying that Jesus will help everyone in the group this week to become a little more like the person God made them to be.

CREATIVE

WHAT: **worship with visuals**
WHY: **to confess to God and celebrate our forgiveness**
WITH: **Bibles, cardboard or wooden cross, mannequin or life-size cardboard cut-out of a person, assortment of dirty rags and brightly coloured strips of material, fabric pens, glue or pins, atmospheric background music, appropriate worship songs**

1 With some atmospheric music playing, encourage the young people to use the fabric pens to write bad habits on the rags and good habits on the bright strips of cloth. Use Colossians 3:1–17 for inspiration.

2 Invite the group to pin the rags onto the mannequin or cut-out person. Say that, of course, this isn't what God wants for his people, but as we go through life, we tend to pick up bad habits that stop us from being the person God wants us to be. Remind the group, if necessary, of the story of the lost son (read Luke 15:17– 19). Sing or listen to a song of repentance, such as 'Create in Me a Clean Heart, O God'. As you do so, remove all the bad habits from the figure and attach them to the cross instead.

3 Read Luke 15:20–22. Thank God that he welcomes us back with open arms and gives us new habits to put on. As a sign that they want to become more like Jesus, invite each person to pick up a 'good habit' piece of cloth and glue or carefully pin it to the figure. As you do this, you could sing or listen to 'I Am a New Creation'.

MORE ON THIS THEME:

If you want to do a short series with your group, other sessions that work well with this one are:

49	*Barriers to Jesus 1*	*Mark 10:17–31*
50	*Barriers to Jesus 2*	*Matthew 8:18–22*
51	*The barrier to God*	*Mark 15:1 – 16:8*

Bible bit
Colossians 3:1–17

Old clothes, new clothes? At first glance you may think that Paul has gone a bit 'Gok Wan' and is concerned that you are wearing the right clothes for the right situation. However, Paul is talking about something much deeper: he's talking about a complete life makeover here. He uses the clothes image because it's easy to understand, but the change he's suggesting goes much deeper. Paul wants us to be the people God wants us to be, and so in the style of all great makeover shows, he gets rid of the bad and brings in the good.

SHULA'S STORY

Shula got a Saturday job in a big fashion chain store in town. She didn't like it much, but it made her some extra money. After a while, she started learning how to do as little work as possible. She'd take an extra few minutes' break. She'd hide among the clothes rails and gossip with one of the other girls instead of sorting the stock. She'd sneak the odd T-shirt into her bag when no one was looking. She'd be rude to customers at the till when the supervisor couldn't hear her.

But then one day, the store manager had all the Saturday staff in for a chat. Shula met him for the first time, and she found to her surprise that he knew her name and where she went to school; she'd always thought she was completely insignificant. He told them all about the store and how much it meant to him to have it running smoothly. Shula realised it really mattered to him that customers were happy. He told them what a good job they did, and for the first time Shula felt a glow of pride in her work. He showed them sales figures going up and down, and Shula decided she actually wanted the figures to go up for his sake. 'You're really important to this store,' he said to them, looking at them all with a big, friendly smile.

The job hadn't changed. The store hadn't changed. But Shula never worked in quite the same way again.

Alastair Wallace / Shutterstock.com

FIT KIT?

KATIE bought cheap clothes. Clothes that would fit in with what everyone else was wearing. Clothes that meant she wouldn't stand out in the crowd. Except that, of course, she wanted to look incredibly fit. However, what suited her mates looked a bit trashy on her.

And Katie would wear the same stuff day after day. She couldn't be bothered to change from one day to the next. She would just pick up whatever was on the floor and put it on again without really thinking. So quite frankly, Katie was a walking stink bomb. Her mates told her she should change, but Katie just couldn't be bothered.

Ever since that visit to London Fashion Week, **ALEX** knew what he wanted to look like. He dressed to look good. He didn't care about what everyone else was wearing. He put on exactly what he knew suited him best. Every day he would open his cupboard and carefully choose just what he would wear. He didn't just throw on any old thing: every bit of kit was a deliberate choice. Sometimes he felt like putting on yesterday's grubby togs, or last year's outgrown stuff, but then he would remind himself of what he could look like. Then he would go for the clothes he knew were right for him that day.

Of course, as he got older, he didn't have to think quite so hard each time. Picking the right clothes had become a habit.

CHANGING TIMES

WHEN GOD MADE ME, HE MADE ME GOOD.
HE MADE ME JUST LIKE HIM.
BUT FROM THE DAY THAT I WAS BORN
HIS LIGHT IN ME GREW DIM.
I PICKED UP STUFF I SHOULDN'T HAVE
AND MADE UNHELPFUL CHOICES
AND WHEN HE TRIED TO CALL ME BACK,
I TURNED TO OTHER VOICES.
BUT EVERYTHING IS CHANGING NOW;
I'M NOT WHAT I COULD BE.
I WANT TO FIND OUT WHO I AM
AND BE THE REAL ME.

RESOURCE PAGE

USE WITH SESSION 52 WAY IN 'SCENE SETTER'

Survey 1

1 Name three of your bad habits.

-
-
-

2 What's your worst habit?

3 How did you start this habit?

4 When did you start this habit?

5 What makes you carry on this habit?

6 What might make you stop this habit?

7 How does it affect your life?

Survey 2

1 Name three of your good habits.

-
-
-

2 Which habit are you most proud of?

3 How did you start this habit?

4 When did you start this habit?

5 What makes you carry on this habit?

6 What might make you stop this habit?

7 How does it affect your life?

USE WITH SESSION 52 BIBLE EXPERIENCE 'LEVEL 2 INTERFACE'

I really want that top she's wearing.

What does it matter what he looks like? It's what he's like inside that counts.

Yeah, you owe me 50p, but I'll let you off as you can't pay me.

Did you know Simon's got BO?

Phwoar, her skirt's like a belt!

He is one fit lad – let me at him!

Don't cry. Look, you can borrow mine.

Just one more doughnut – I've only had 16.

I hate your guts!

Yes, I might have got into the first eleven, but Dave's much better at tennis than I am.

Look, it's only a spider. I'll just pick it up and pop it outside without hurting it.

I could slap 'em.

Would you like me to help you with your geography again?

She really, really winds me up.

You do know everyone thinks your trainers are *soooo* last year?

You can come in our team!

I was walking down the [censored] road when this [censored] girl walks past with a [censored] poodle.

I forgive you.

Oh yes, I have done my homework, Miss, honest, I just accidentally left it at home...

You're a wonderful person and God thinks you're fantastic.

RESOURCE PAGE

USE WITH SESSION 52 RESPOND 'PRACTICAL'

Day	Habit to put on	Habit to ditch
Monday		
Tuesday	Forgiving someone who does something wrong to me	
Wednesday		
Thursday		
Friday		Daydreaming about wrong things
Saturday		
Sunday	Being peaceful	

Session 4 Amazing animals

1) True

2) False (they have black skin)

3) False (they can jump up to six feet in the air)

4) True

5) True

6) False (it can turn its head 360 degrees)

7) False (it's white with black stripes)

8) True

9) False (gorillas don't have fingerprints)

10) True

Session 25 Match up

Hiker – Map

Miner – Lamp

Footballer – Boots

Fisherman – Rod

Construction worker – Hard hat

Cowboy – Horse

Christian – Bible

Designer – Computer

Soldier – Gun

Plumber – Wrench

Dancer – Ballet shoes

Artist – Easel

Decorator – Pot of paint and rollers

Chef – Chef's hat

Police Officer – Handcuffs

Queen – Crown

Session 41 How much do you know about light?

1) True

2) False – he didn't invent the first light bulb but he was responsible for the first commercially practical lighting system and light bulbs being mass-produced

3) True

4) False – it was built by the Romans in the second century AD and called the Tower of Hercules

5) True

6) True

7) False – in fact, only 0.05% of a candle's output is light

8) The boogie

BIBLE INDEX

WHAT'S YOUR STORY?

TRUE STORY is a short evangelistic booklet that helps your church introduce teenagers to the message of Christianity.

Written by youth pastor and evangelist Pete Brown, **TRUE STORY** invites teenagers to reflect upon six key interactions Jesus has with characters from the Gospels.

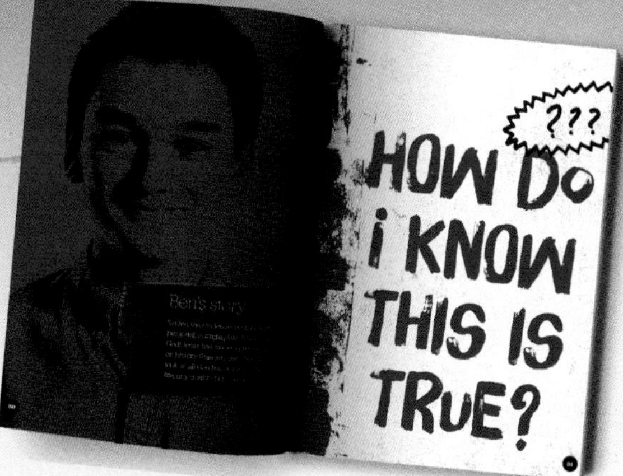

FEATURES INCLUDE:

- Rich and contemporary visual language.
- Interactive components, including questions for reflection and space to write notes.
- Accessible format where the Bible text is presented in manageable sections within a specially designed internal booklet.

PERFECT FOR:

- Giving away to youth with minimal Bible knowledge.
- Holiday clubs and mission.
- Small group sessions.

ISBN 9781785065194
True Story (10 pack) £20

ISBN 9781785065200
True Story single £3.50

Order from your local Christian bookshop | Order from Scripture Union: 01908 856006 | Order online www.scriptureunion.org.uk